W9-BIT-181

The Mild Reservationists
and the League of Nations Controversy
in the Senate

The Mild Reservationists and the League of Nations Controversy in the Senate

HERBERT F. MARGULIES

UNIVERSITY OF MISSOURI PRESS
COLUMBIA AND LONDON

Copyright © 1989 by
The Curators of the University of Missouri
University of Missouri Press, Columbia, Missouri 65211
Printed and bound in the United States of America

Library of Congress Cataloging-in-Publication Data

Margulies, Herbert F.
 The mild reservationists and the League of Nations
controversy in the Senate / Herbert F. Margulies

 p.   cm.
 Bibliography: p.
 Includes index.
 ISBN 0-8262-0693-X (alk. paper)
 1. League of Nations—United States—History. 2. United
States—Foreign relations—1913-1921. 3. United States.
Congress. Senate—History. 4. Treaty of Versailles (1919)—
History. I. Title.
JX1975.5.U5M27   1989
341.22'73—dc19   89-4702
                                                          CIP

⊛™ This paper meets the requirements of the American
National Standard for Permanence of Paper for Printed
Library Materials, Z39.48, 1984.

5   4   3   2   1   93   92   91   90   89

TO FRAN

CONTENTS

PREFACE

A "what if" question is unanswerable, but when it is about something that is very important, it persists. So it is with the following questions: "What if the United States Senate had approved the Versailles Treaty and permitted the country to join the League of Nations that was being formed after the First World War? Would the course of history have been so altered that the Second World War would not have occurred?" Presuming at least the possibility that the outcome was important, historians are often asked how and why the United States failed to join the League. The inquiry has been so enduring that the story of the League's rejection has entered folklore and become almost mythological, with President Woodrow Wilson and Senator Henry Cabot Lodge the larger-than-life protagonists. Thus, whenever a controversial treaty goes before the Senate, wary proponents look for lessons in the history of the conflict over the League. These things being so—that the subject is important and that it is in continuing use—historians are obliged to give a full and accurate account and evaluation of the Senate battle of 1919 and 1920, and of the circumstances surrounding it. The enterprise is ongoing and unending, and this book is a part of it.[1]

The story is familiar in its main outlines. Increasingly during the First World War, President Wilson became determined to create a League of Nations and to see the United States join it. After the defeat of Germany and her allies in 1918, Wilson succeeded in having a charter for a League of Nations incorporated in the Treaty of Versailles, the peace treaty with Germany. But in the Republican-controlled Senate, headed by Lodge, strong but diverse opposition arose. The most extreme Republican opponents, joined by two Democrats, opposed the League in

1. Treaty ratification is completed by the president, after he has obtained the advice and consent of the Senate. Since the Senate plays a substantial, usually decisive, part in the process, I shall refer occasionally to "ratification" by the Senate.

any form. These were the *irreconcilables*. They, however, were not numerous enough to defeat the treaty. Most Republicans proposed ratification conditional on the adoption of reservations that would in effect define and limit American commitment. Some of these Republicans followed Lodge's leadership and came to be called *strong reservationists*. The members of a smaller group were labeled *mild reservationists*.

In September 1919, while the lines of battle were still being drawn, Wilson took his case to the country, urging an unqualified ratification. During the tour he fell victim to a physical breakdown and was rushed to Washington. There, on 2 October, he suffered a severe stroke, and was seriously ill for months thereafter. From his sickbed Wilson periodically urged Senate Democrats to stand firm against the kind of reservations that Republicans had offered. For their part, Republicans of all factions coalesced in favor of a reservationist program, though the irreconcilables reserved the right later to vote against approval even with the reservations appended. In November the reservations were adopted but the treaty with the reservations attached failed of approval, as administration Democrats and irreconcilables united in opposition. In March 1920 the Senate tried again, and a number of Democrats broke from Wilson's lead, but the treaty with reservations attached fell seven votes shy of the necessary two-thirds. Anticipating and welcoming this result, Wilson had called for a "solemn referendum" on the League of Nations in the presidential election of 1920, but no such single-issue election occurred, and the new president, Warren Harding, made no effort to bring the United States into the League.

Another fact is salient. Had the Senate approved the treaty with the so-called Lodge reservations, Wilson might have refused to complete the process of ratification, as he had threatened. Why then, one might ask, give further attention to the battle in the Senate? Several answers suggest themselves. First, it is far from certain that Wilson would have carried through on his threats; he would have felt strong pressure from party leaders and the European Allies to complete the ratification. Second, in theory the Senate could have approved the treaty with a resolution less offensive to Wilson than those of November and March, a possibility that warrants exploration. Third, had the treaty won approval through the votes of Republicans, that party might itself have revived it after taking power in 1920. Finally, if we accept the possibility that the obstacles to ratification were simply too great, it remains to be determined why this was so.

The irreconcilables and the Democrats have been closely studied by historians; the reservationists have not.[2] In this book, I shall try to remedy this situation in part, focusing on the mild reservationists.[3] What were their motives and beliefs? How important were they? Above all, what did they do, and how well did they do it?

On 27 October 1919 nine Republican senators broke party ranks and helped defeat the hotly controversial Johnson amendment. Hiram Johnson's popular proposal was, in part, to alter the League Covenant to give the United States as many votes in the League Assembly as the British Empire had, six. Soon after the vote, the senators issued a statement indicating that so long as proper reservations were adopted, they would oppose all other direct amendments to the treaty. Reservations, they understood, would serve as expressions of their nation's understanding of certain treaty provisions. Unlike treaty amendments, reservations would not require a full renegotiation of the treaty. Their joint statement effectively doomed all other amendment proposals and, as they saw it, made possible a speedy approval in the Senate for the League and the treaty.

The nine senators, with one other, were the mild reservationists. They differed among themselves on many things relating to the League and the treaty, but their statement reflected a common denominator of agreement: they would oppose amendments "in the interests of expediting action, and to bring about a final ratification of the treaty."[4] With varying degrees of emphasis, they felt that the restoration of peace on a legal basis would deal a blow to the chaos in Europe, would check communism, and would facilitate the resumption of normal trade relations between the United States and Germany.

For some of the mild reservationists, these purposes were foremost, whereas entry into the League of Nations was incidental. Others were truer friends of the League. The latter saw reservations mainly from the standpoint of expediency, as necessary to advance ratification. These friends of the League wanted truly mild reservations. Some of their col-

---

2. On the irreconcilables and the Democrats, see Ralph Stone, *The Irreconcilables: The Fight Against the League of Nations*; Dewey W. Grantham, Jr., "The Southern Senators and the League of Nations, 1918–1920"; and Thomas N. Guinsburg, *The Pursuit of Isolationism in the United States Senate from Versailles to Pearl Harbor*. The reservationists, positioned in the middle, were not spectacular. And, in the case of the leading mild reservationists, manuscript collections are absent altogether, or sparse for the period of the League fight.

3. Chapter 8 of my *Senator Lenroot of Wisconsin: A Political Biography, 1900–1920* discusses the mild reservationists, but in less detail and with attention focused principally on one of the reservationists, Lenroot.

4. *Minneapolis Tribune*, 28 October 1919.

leagues favored reservations for their own sake and were not displeased when, in the course of the prolonged contest, proposed reservations became stronger. Even so, either out of regard for the League or concern for compromise with the Democrats, or both, at any given time the mild reservationists were more moderate than most of their Republican colleagues. But it is not only this that distinguishes them from the rest. They stood apart also in their consistency and their persistence and especially their willingness at critical points to act together.

A pioneering leadership group was formed early in September 1919 as the Committee on Foreign Relations prepared to report the treaty to the Senate. It consisted of LeBaron B. Colt of Rhode Island, Frank B. Kellogg and Knute Nelson of Minnesota, Porter J. McCumber of North Dakota, Charles L. McNary of Oregon, and Irvine L. Lenroot of Wisconsin. Lenroot, with Kellogg, was soon the most active of the group in drafting and promoting reservations that might serve as alternatives to amendments, but for reasons to be explained later, he did not vote against the Johnson amendment and therefore could not join the others in their antiamendment statement. The other mild reservationists were Walter E. Edge of New Jersey, Frederick Hale of Maine, Henry W. Keyes of New Hampshire, and Thomas Sterling of South Dakota.

As matters developed, senators and observers calculated that twenty Republicans would have to join forty-four Democrats to make up the two-thirds needed for treaty approval. The mild reservationists could contribute just half of the votes needed. Even so, they had influence. Inevitably, the distinction between mild and strong reservationists is an oversimplification. In fact, between the mild reservationists and the strong reservationists was a group of eight senators, all of whom at one time or another were considered part of the mild reservationist faction. These senators, who warrant our attention limited only by considerations of space, I shall refer to as *moderates.* They were Arthur Capper of Kansas, Albert B. Cummins and William S. Kenyon of Iowa, Wesley L. Jones of Washington, George B. McLean of Connecticut, Reed Smoot of Utah, Selden P. Spencer of Missouri, and Charles E. Townsend of Michigan. When, in August 1919, the mild reservationists and the moderates united, politicians understood that other Republicans, and indeed Lodge himself, would join them rather than see the Republican party take the blame for the defeat of the treaty. Only Wilson's caution prevented the matter from being put to the test. Even without the moderates, the mild reservationists had bargaining power within their party. The Republican margin in the Senate was slim, forty-nine to forty-seven. The mild reservationists, or even some segment of them, could always threaten to join the Democrats in framing a compromise resolution of ratification, which, if done, would again put the Republicans in a negative and politically unfavorable position.

Though influential, the mild reservationists were not in a commanding position. The Democrats, following the lead of President Wilson, were usually uncompromising, until the last stages of the battle. In the main, then, the mild reservationists had to work with Lodge and within their own party. But the Massachusetts senator, though amenable to compromise with them, would not and from a political standpoint could not yield to them entirely. Thus, although the fourteen reservations named for Lodge were in fact primarily the work of mild reservationists, they were produced with an eye toward satisfying all of Lodge's diverse flock.

Ultimately, the mild reservationists did not accomplish their ends. Some historians have held them partially to blame for the outcome. "Republican moderates," one historian has written, "lacking real leadership or direction, muddled about, wavering between devotion to ideals and loyalty to party; in the end they counted for little. The outcome might have been different had the mild reservationists exerted anywhere near the grit and cohesiveness exhibited by the irreconcilables."[5] Is this judgment fair? I shall try to show that, to the contrary, the mild reservationists, especially their leaders, were high-minded in their purposes and that, though not faultless, the group played reasonably well the hand that was dealt them. Indeed, they did more to accomplish ratification than did President Wilson, the League's principal sponsor, and more than the Senate Democratic leadership, headed by Gilbert Hitchcock of Nebraska.

To be sure, the mild reservationists asked Wilson to concede a great deal on American commitment to collective security under Article 10 of the League Covenant. But what they asked was no more than what was required as the price for American entry into the League. Paradoxically, the mild reservationists attributed more value than did Wilson to other features of the Covenant unaffected by reservations.

Although the focus of my attention is the mild reservationists, I hope to shed light on the treaty battle as a whole. Excellent work on that struggle, or on aspects of it, has been done by Thomas A. Bailey, W. Stull Holt, Denna Frank Fleming, Jack E. Kendrick, John Chalmers Vinson, Warren F. Kuehl, Dewey W. Grantham, Jr., Ralph Stone, Robert H. Fer-

---

5. Robert James Maddox, *William E. Borah and American Foreign Policy*, 70. After calling Wesley Jones a mild reservationist, his biographer adds that this was "a position which would appeal to his essentially irenic and compromising manner of doing things" (Willam Stuart Forth, "Wesley L. Jones: A Political Biography," 429).

rell, William C. Widenor, Lloyd E. Ambrosius, and others.[6] I shall try to build on this foundation, to elaborate and refine, and, in turn, to contribute something to the studies that will follow this one.

A further word on terminology must be added. As noted, the distinction between the mild reservationists and the moderates was not always clear-cut. The more conservative mild reservationists were close to the moderates in their thinking; and in the formative period especially, some moderates were less conservative than they would later become. In addition to the fuzziness of the distinction, reporters often lumped the two groups together when referring to both. In such instances, they sometimes used the term *middle grounders.* When convenient, I shall use the same term in the same way.

I wish to thank two colleagues for their close reading and helpful criticisms of portions of this book: Cedric B. Cowing and I. A. Newby of the University of Hawaii at Manoa. My son Natan has been most helpful in the same way. I also thank Professor Gary Dean Best of the University of Hawaii at Hilo for bringing certain letters to my attention. I owe the deepest debt of gratitude to Professor Lewis L. Gould of the University of Texas at Austin for twice reviewing the full manuscript and offering many astute observations and detailed editorial suggestions.

6. Thomas A. Bailey, *Woodrow Wilson and the Great Betrayal;* W. Stull Holt, *Treaties Defeated by the Senate: A Study of the Struggle Between President and Senate Over the Conduct of Foreign Relations;* Denna Frank Fleming, *The United States and the League of Nations, 1918-1920;* Jack E. Kendrick, "The League of Nations and the Republican Senate, 1918-1921"; John Chalmers Vinson, *Referendum for Isolation: Defeat of Article Ten of the League of Nations Covenant;* Warren F. Kuehl, *Seeking World Order: The United States and International Organization to 1920;* Grantham, "Southern Senators and the League of Nations"; Stone, *The Irreconcilables;* Robert H. Ferrell, *Woodrow Wilson and World War I;* William C. Widenor, *Henry Cabot Lodge and the Search for an American Foreign Policy;* Lloyd E. Ambrosius, *Woodrow Wilson and the American Diplomatic Tradition: The Treaty Fight in Perspective.*

*The Mild Reservationists
and the League of Nations Controversy
in the Senate*

1 THE ADVENT OF RESERVATIONISM, 14 February–10 July 1919

For President Woodrow Wilson, 14 February 1919 was a momentous day. In measured, impressive tones, he presented to the Paris Peace Conference a plan for a League of Nations, declaring it "a definite guarantee of peace . . . a definite guarantee by word against aggression." The plan would be revised, he understood, but not in very serious ways; thus the occasion marked the completion and fulfillment when "a living thing is born."[1]

Though an armistice had commenced on 11 November 1918, the peace conference, ostensibly a preliminary conference of the victors, had not begun until 18 January 1919. Quickly, the five principal powers—Great Britain, France, the United States, Italy, and Japan, each represented by two men—constituted themselves the Council of Ten. Anxious to counter the spread of hunger, disorder, and bolshevism, the Allies sought a speedy peace settlement and so favored either deferring consideration of the League altogether or dealing with it initially in only general terms.[2] But Wilson, distrustful of his counterparts in Paris and still more so of the Senate, insisted on early and favorable action on the League and its incorporation in the treaty. The Council of Ten acceded on 22 January, and three days later a plenary session agreed. Wilson then became chairman of the League of Nations Commission.

The British had done more detailed advance work than had the Americans and thus substantially contributed to the working draft the commission would use.[3] But Wilson had exercised veto power in

1. Warren F. Kuehl, *Seeking World Order: The United States and International Organization to 1920*, 271; Thomas A. Bailey, *Woodrow Wilson and the Lost Peace*, 193.
2. Bailey, *Lost Peace*, 179.
3. See George W. Egerton's excellent discussion in *Great Britain and the Creation of the League of Nations: Strategy, Politics, and International Organization, 1914–1919*.

favor of his own ideas from August 1918—when he revised a draft that Colonel Edward House had prepared—until almost the eve of the commission's first meeting.[4] At the commission's eleven sessions, starting 3 February, Wilson dominated, abetted by Lord Robert Cecil, with whom Wilson had collaborated in advance.[5] The "living thing" that had been born was very much Wilson's own. And he would nurture it with his every power.

Article 10 was the heart of the Covenant of the League of Nations, in Wilson's view. Detractors came to see it as the most dangerous feature. It read: "The Members of the League undertake to respect and preserve as against external aggression the territorial integrity and existing political independence of all Members of the League. In case of any such aggression or in case of any threat or danger of such aggression the Council shall advise upon the means by which this obligation shall be fulfilled."[6] Though Wilson never seemed to realize it, the use of the words *undertake to* in place of *guarantee* (as worded in an earlier draft), the inclusion of the second sentence, and most especially the use of the words *advise upon* left the meaning of this critically important article subject to debate in the United States and abroad.[7]

Initially the members would be the victor powers, some invited neutrals, and on vote of two-thirds of the Assembly, any self-governing state, dominion, or colony. The Assembly would be composed of each member state, equally represented. The more powerful body was the Council, a group of nine states; five of these would be the major powers, permanently represented, and the other four would be chosen periodically by the Assembly. A permanent Secretariat would perform executive functions. Wilson had favored a strong disarmament provision, but he yielded to objections from France, Italy, and Japan.[8] The resultant articles were weak.

4. George Curry, "Woodrow Wilson, Jan Smuts, and the Versailles Settlement," 982.

5. David Hunter Miller, *The Drafting of the Covenant*, 1:126; Alfred Zimmern, *The League of Nations and the Rule of Law, 1918-1935*, 339. Cecil, taking advantage of Prime Minister David Lloyd George's loose system of controls, ignored the prime minister's objections to the Wilson plans. Later, the British government tolerated the results, giving higher priority to other issues before the conference (George W. Egerton, "The Lloyd George Government and the Creation of the League of Nations," 439-42).

6. The text of the 14 February Covenant may be found in Ray Stannard Baker, *Woodrow Wilson and World Settlement*, 3:163-73. See also Thomas A. Bailey, *Woodrow Wilson and the Great Betrayal*, 384-87.

7. Zimmern, *League of Nations*, 240-44.

8. Denna Frank Fleming, *The United States and the League of Nations, 1918-*

Article 11 was Colonel House's main contribution, though it was not original with him.[9] This article stated that war or the threat of war concerned the League and that, on petition of any member, the Council should meet and the League should take such action as it deemed fitting. Further, any member might bring to the attention of the Council or the Assembly "any circumstance whatever affecting international relations which threatens to disturb international peace or good understanding between nations upon which peace depends." This article, though broader in scope than Article 10, committed no one to forceful action.

Articles 12 through 17 were seen by many supporters of the League as the most important in the Covenant. These were the so-called pacific settlement provisions. Articles 12 through 15 provided for the settlement of international disputes, either through arbitration or through the good offices of the Council, and authorized the establishment of a Permanent Court of International Justice for arbitral functions. Under these provisions, states were urged, but not forced, to eschew war. In any case, the provisions called for a delay of three months before war. Article 16 strengthened the pacific settlement procedures. Should a member resort to war in contravention of the preceding articles, the other members guaranteed to apply sanctions, ranging from boycott to use of military force, on recommendation of the Council. Article 17 in essence extended the provisions of Articles 12 through 16 to cover nonmembers. Nonmembers would be invited to use the pacific settlement services of the League but, failing to do so, would be subject to sanctions.

Historians are not in complete agreement on Wilson's attitude toward the pacific settlement provisions.[10] Clearly, however, these articles were most fully developed before the conference by the British, and the French wanted still stronger provisions.[11] Whatever Wilson may have thought about the rest, he was cool to the World Court idea, and the provision for the court was rather vague and weak.[12]

1920, 112–14; William E. Rappard, *The Quest for Peace*, 132.

9. Rappard, *Quest for Peace*, 113.

10. Edgar William Schmickle, "For the Proper Use of Victory: Diplomacy and the Imperatives of Vision in the Foreign Policy of Woodrow Wilson, 1916–1919," pp. 90, 125, 126, 198–99.

11. Miller, *Drafting of the Covenant*, 1:9; Rappard, *Quest for Peace*, 108–10; Egerton, *Creation of the League*, 65–69.

12. Robert Lansing, *The Peace Negotiations: A Personal Narrative*, 68–69; Kuehl, *World Order*, 280. The provision was strengthened somewhat in the final version of the Covenant, and the Court, when constituted, construed its powers broadly.

Three other articles are noteworthy. One of these established a system of mandates for the colonies and territories of the defeated powers. Another set out to maintain fair, humane conditions of labor under a League-sponsored organization. A third concerned the very important matter of future territorial changes. Wilson had favored something strong on the subject and had dealt with it as part of the Article 10 proposal. He did not want the guarantee of territorial integrity to be a commitment to an unreasonable and unchanging status quo. Chiefly because of French fears, the result was an innocuous provision permitting the Assembly to advise the reconsideration of treaties "and the consideration of international conditions whose continuance might endanger the peace of the world."[13]

Neither British nor French leaders were ecstatic about the Covenant, but they saw enough virtue in it to accede without protest. The British did not care for the potential encroachment on their sovereignty implied in Article 10.[14] The French, by contrast, thought Article 10 did not go nearly far enough toward giving them security against Germany. The article's meaning was uncertain and its implementation might be slow. They would have preferred an international general staff. But the article was better than nothing, and when in March the British and the Americans offered treaties of security, activated through the League Council, the French had further reason to support the League.[15] The British were consoled by the creation of the Council, in particular, and to a much lesser extent by the creation of the Assembly. These agencies might perform the conference function that Sir Edward Grey thought could have prevented the Great War and that had seemed to other British leaders to have worked well during the war, as the Imperial War Cabinet and the Supreme War Council.[16] British leaders knew also that

13. Wilson's thought and actions respecting boundary changes are discussed in Edward H. Buehrig, "Woodrow Wilson and Collective Security," in Buehrig, ed., *Wilson's Foreign Policy in Perspective* (Bloomington: Indiana University Press, 1957), 57–59; Quincy Wright, "Woodrow Wilson and the League of Nations," 73; Sondra R. Herman, *Eleven Against War: Studies in American Internationalist Thought, 1898–1921,* 209; and Lansing, *Peace Negotiations,* 55, 94–95. The weakness of the article is noted in Seth P. Tillman, *Anglo-American Relations at the Paris Peace Conference of 1919,* 126, and in Zimmern, *League of Nations,* 241.

14. Egerton, *Creation of the League,* 121–27, 143–45; John Chalmers Vinson, *Referendum for Isolation: Defeat of Article Ten of the League of Nations Covenant,* 22.

15. Egerton, *Creation of the League,* 134–45, 169; Zimmern, *League of Nations,* 247; Louis A. R. Yates, *United States and French Security, 1917–1921,* 71, 80, 84, 99, 102, 218.

16. Egerton, *Creation of the League,* 89, 99–100, 104–5, 115–16, 140, 202; Keith

the creation of the League would appease influential elements at home.[17] For these nations bled white by war and fearful of a resurgent Germany, of the bolshevik incubus already spreading from Russia into Germany, and of the "backward" peoples of Asia and Africa, it was essential that the mighty United States be drawn into a large and cooperative world role. Wilson's treasured League seemed the surest way to accomplish that.[18] Since the treaty was only in its initial stages of preparation, moreover, the League might still be held hostage against Wilson as a bargaining tool.[19] For these reasons, Wilson had no trouble when he presented the Covenant to the plenary session on 14 February.

Prospects for Senate approval of the League seemed favorable as Wilson hurried to Brest, where the *George Washington* waited to take him home to attend to duties relating to the end of the Sixty-fifth Congress. Certainly, the American public appeared to be a strong ally. The idea of a world organization for preserving peace, to be created after the horrors of the Great War had ended, had spread rapidly since 1916. Wilson gave the idea its biggest push, starting with his speech before the League to Enforce Peace (LEP) on 27 May 1916.[20] Following America's entry into the war, patriotic ardor focused on the commander in chief. Giving lofty purpose to the war and advancing his own hope for a permanent peace, Wilson made the creation of a League of Nations one of his country's principal war aims, most notably as the last of the Fourteen Points.[21] A survey conducted in December 1918 showed that of 833 editorials, only 20 were hostile to the League idea. It had long since won the support of journals of opinion, learned societies, and public-spirited individuals. Protestant churchmen, especially those touched by the "social gospel," had given the League idea strong support since 1917.[22]

Robbins, *Sir Edward Grey: A Biography of Lord Grey of Fallodon*, 299; Tillman, *Anglo-American Relations*, 102, 113–14, 127; Zimmern, *League of Nations*, 247.

17. Egerton, *Creation of the League*, 94, 175.

18. Arno J. Mayer, *Politics and Diplomacy of Peacemaking: Containment and Counter-Revolution at Versailles, 1918–1919*, 110–12, 116, 258–59, 493, 753; Egerton, *Creation of the League*, 83–84, 108–9, 180; Inis L. Claude, Jr., *Power and International Relations*, 138–39; Mayer, *Diplomacy of Peacemaking*, 692.

19. Inga Floto, *Colonel House in Paris: A Study of American Policy at the Paris Peace Conference, 1919*, 163, 191, 205, 207; Egerton, *Creation of the League*, 160.

20. The public commitment was part of an unsuccessful effort to bring about American mediation of the World War. See Arthur S. Link, *Woodrow Wilson: Revolution, War, and Peace*, 75.

21. Edward H. Buehrig, *Woodrow Wilson and the Balance of Power*, 266; Robert E. Osgood, *Ideals and Self-Interest in America's Foreign Relations*, 194.

22. Kuehl, *World Order*, 291; Osgood, *Ideals and Self-Interest*, 247; James L. Lan-

Whereas anti-League forces remained unorganized, Wilson had a powerful, efficient, and popular ally in the LEP, which had been propagandizing for world organization since 1915. Support for preparedness and then for the American war effort had helped the LEP gain public esteem for itself and its postwar program. Initially, that program differed from Wilson's, but sensing the drift of his thought, the LEP accommodated to it in 1918 and early 1919. At its height in 1919 the LEP employed 110 people and had about 300,000 members.[23]

In the next Congress the Senate, which would have to approve the treaty by a two-thirds vote, would be controlled not by Wilson's Democrats but by the Republicans. Yet an LEP poll taken in November 1918 showed most senators favorable. And the Republican party had a strong internationalist tradition. Republican Secretaries of State John Hay, Elihu Root, and Philander C. Knox had promoted arbitration, and Root had worked for a world court. Charles Evans Hughes, the GOP presidential candidate in 1916, had flirted with the principles of the LEP during the campaign. Most of the founders of the LEP were Republicans. Former President William Howard Taft was the LEP president, and another Republican, A. Lawrence Lowell, president of Harvard, headed the executive committee. At the very time Wilson was laboring in Paris, Taft, with other prestigious speakers, was on a coast-to-coast tour for the League. In the Senate in December 1918, some had spoken against the immediate formation of a League, but on 9 January Porter J. McCumber of North Dakota responded. McCumber, who would be the second-ranking Republican on the Foreign Relations Committee in the new Congress, emotionally appealed for a world organization that would prevent another horrible and evil war like the one just ended. Furthermore, the Republican majority in the Senate would be narrow, forty-nine to forty-seven. If most Democrats followed the president, only about twenty Republicans would be needed for treaty approval.[24]

There were, however, significant obstacles. Failing to appreciate

caster, "The Protestant Churches and the Fight for Ratification of the Versailles Treaty," 597–616.

23. The standard work on the League to Enforce Peace is Ruhl J. Bartlett, *The League to Enforce Peace*. Kuehl, *World Order*, 240, 289–90; H. A. Yeomans, *Abbott Lawrence Lowell, 1856–1943*, 435.

24. Kuehl, *World Order*, 293; Fleming, *League of Nations*, 82–83; Martin David Dubin, "The Development of the Concept of Collective Security in the American Peace Movement, 1899–1917," 246–47; Yeomans, *Lowell*, 436; Bartlett, *League to Enforce Peace*, 114–15; Fleming, *League of Nations*, 84–85; *Congressional Record*, 65th Congress, 3d session (hereafter *CR* 65:3), 1087–88 (7 January 1919).

their magnitude throughout what would prove to be a prolonged contest, the president never established a cooperative relationship with the Republican senators who were friendliest to his cause, those who would later be called "mild reservationists."[25] Critical of Article 10, among other things, most of these senators joined others in their party in seeking changes in the Covenant while it remained in the negotiating stage. Dissatisfied with the changes Wilson effected, these senators embraced reservationism when it emerged to clarify America's understanding of the Covenant and the conditions of the country's commitment. A few mild reservationists did not share the qualms of the rest, but by the time Wilson was ready to present the full treaty to the Senate in July, they too supported reservations, to achieve ratification.

Though disappointing to Wilson, the mild reservationists were not enemies of the League. They sought to improve it according to their own lights, to ward off outright rejection, and to forestall long delay through renegotiation. In finally uniting behind reservations, they took the position most likely to bring Senate approval, in a form as close to Wilson's own as was politically practical. Even when joined by Republican moderates, the mild reservationists were but one of several blocs within their party and were not in a position to dictate terms. But they were potent. Though they had no immediate occasion to break from their party's leadership and ally with the Democrats on the League, this implicit threat contributed to the establishment within the GOP of a reservationist position. Though this position was not yet fully clear when the treaty came before the Senate, it nevertheless gave a basis for a swift and, to the mild reservationists, satisfactory ratification. In June and July Wilson declined to seriously explore ratification possibilities on their terms, but the reservationism that these men stood for remained as a basis for possible compromise in the months that followed.

Republican senators of all stripes were eager to learn more about the Covenant that Wilson brought home in February but were also suspicious of the president. During his first administration, starting in 1913, Wilson had alienated progressive Republicans in particular by his exclusive reliance on Democrats for the enactment of legislation. During the war years he had acted as a virtual dictator, and though Republicans felt compelled to acquiesce at least on the sur-

25. For the sake of simplicity, I shall refer to these men as "mild reservationists" even when discussing the period before the term came into common use.

face, they did not like it. Near the war's end, Wilson infuriated Republicans by appealing to the people for a Democratic Congress, in seeming defiance of his May 1918 statement that "politics is adjourned." Wilson called the GOP "anti-administration" and implied that Republicans had been unreliable supporters of war measures.[26]

Wilson's early handling of the treaty situation further antagonized Republican senators. Choosing a Republican for membership on the peace delegation, he passed over all Republican senators and such luminaries as Elihu Root, William Howard Taft, and Charles Evans Hughes, naming instead Henry White, who was retired, resided abroad, and was only nominally partisan. Wilson named himself head of the delegation, controlled its activities, and, by absenting himself from the country for months, raised doubts about whether he was performing his constitutional duties. In December he promised to keep the Senate informed, but he failed to do so. Acting behind closed doors, contrary to the promise of "open covenants, openly arrived at," Wilson lessened the usefulness of press reports. Ignored for advice on the treaty and intensely protective of the Senate's constitutional responsibilities, Republican senators would give more than ordinary attention to their consent function.[27]

It was Wilson's misfortune that the Republican senator who most disliked and despised him was also the man who in the next Congress would be the majority leader and chairman of the Committee on Foreign Relations, Henry Cabot Lodge of Massachusetts. As early as January 1915, Lodge wrote of his feelings to Theodore Roosevelt and said, "I live in hopes that he will be found out by the people for what he really is." During the 1916 campaign, Lodge accused Wilson of lying. The president, cultivating a strong antipathy toward Lodge, refused to speak on the same platform with him or to permit any member of his administration to do so.[28]

26. Seward W. Livermore, *Politics Is Adjourned: Woodrow Wilson and the War Congress, 1916–1918.*

27. Although partisanship was a factor, Republican senators were sincere about defending the Senate's prerogatives concerning foreign relations. Over the preceding two decades, the Senate had emasculated or rejected every general arbitration treaty presented to it, charging that the executive was seeking to gain independence from other branches through those treaties. In these instances McKinley, Roosevelt, and Taft had seen their plans frustrated by Republican-controlled Senates. See Vinson, *Referendum for Isolation,* 9–10.

28. Lodge to Theodore Roosevelt, 15 January 1915, Henry Cabot Lodge Papers, Massachusetts Historical Society, cited in William C. Widenor, *Henry Cabot Lodge and the Search for an American Foreign Policy,* 198; Wilson to Dr. Roland Cotton Smith, 29 December 1916 and 5 January 1917, Woodrow Wilson Papers, Library of Congress.

Relations between Wilson and Senate Republicans did not improve during Wilson's brief return to the United States. Before the trip he rejected Colonel House's advice to compromise, saying he would fight.[29] Having asked senators to refrain from comment on the League until he could meet with the foreign relations committees of each house, Wilson landed in Boston and himself commented, exhorting Lodge's constituents to support the League. After he arrived in Washington, he declared that he would not call a special session of Congress until he had returned finally from Paris. Senators would have no forum for early criticism. At the White House dinner with foreign relations committee members, Wilson responded vaguely to questions. Afterwards, he announced that he would resist all but verbal changes in the Covenant, which already reflected compromise.[30]

Frustrated in various ways by Republicans in the Senate, and warned that he must separate the League from the rest of the treaty, Wilson defied his critics in a speech in New York on the eve of his return to Europe. "When that treaty comes back," he announced, "gentlemen on this side will find the covenant not only in it, but so many threads of the treaty tied to the covenant that you cannot dissect the covenant from the treaty without destroying the whole vital structure."[31]

Thomas J. Walsh of Montana, a very able and loyal Democrat, concluded, "The President has handled the thing most maladroitly and has evidenced a disposition to exclude the Senate from any real, active participation in the making of the treaty." Elihu Root, a former senator, found his old colleagues enraged at "Wilson's refusal to consult them and his practical denial of their right to discuss the subject at all." That Republicans suspected Wilson of campaigning for a third term worsened matters. Their hostility toward the president, particularly with respect to his handling of the Covenant, provided a suitable backdrop for the activities of key Republican leaders, notably Lodge, Philander Knox, and Will Hays.[32]

29. Stephen Bonsal, *Unfinished Business*, 60.

30. Henry Cabot Lodge, *The Senate and the League of Nations*, 100; *New York Tribune*, 1 March 1919; Arthur Walworth, *Woodrow Wilson*, 2:273; Jack E. Kendrick, "The League of Nations and the Republican Senate, 1918–1921," 81. Wilson was provoked not only by the outcome of the dinner but also by disparaging accounts of it in the *New York Sun* and by caustic criticism in the Senate.

31. Ray S. Baker and William E. Dodd, eds., *The Public Papers of Woodrow Wilson, War and Peace, Presidential Messages, Addresses and Public Papers (1917–1924)*, 5:444–55.

32. Walsh to James Donovan, 2 April 1919, Thomas J. Walsh Papers, Library of

Through the entire conflict over the League, the chairman of the Republican national committee, Will Hays, played an active role. A suave, personable young man, "albeit adroit, diplomatic and tactful," Hays had pacified the warring party factions in Indiana and had been brought to the national level to do the same thing in advance of the 1920 elections.[33] He proposed to minimize internal division over the League. In this, Hays always had the sympathy and help of Lodge.

Hays later credited Henry L. Stimson with being the first to make him "stop, look and listen" to the need for the Republican party to take a proper position. Perhaps he flattered Stimson. In any case, when Stimson, the former secretary of war under Taft and a law partner and friend of Root's, gave his views on the morning of 18 February, Hays saw their value and asked Stimson to commit his ideas to writing. Stimson quickly dispatched to Hays a nine-page letter, and Hays sent copies to every Republican senator and most Republican representatives. Stimson warned that the Republican party should not take a position of opposition to any League, on grounds of right and of expediency; he urged that objections be made in time for action in Paris; and he detailed his own principal objection, that Article 10 would work against the Monroe Doctrine, which he saw as the bedrock of American foreign policy.[34]

The letter served the purposes not only of Hays but of Lodge and Knox as well. Though the latter were more dubious of the League than was Stimson, neither was then prepared to reject the idea outright. They preferred to solidify party objections to specific features of the Covenant. For the moment, the prime task was to prevent Republicans from being swept into a blanket endorsement. Ideally, the senators would make peace with Germany before even considering the League, in accordance with a resolution Knox had offered in December.

Lodge and Knox substantially advanced their ends with speeches in the Senate on 28 February and 1 March. They were but two of ten senators who spoke on the League between 14 February and 3 March, and it would not do to discount the influence of the others,

---

Congress; Root to Lowell, 29 April 1919, Elihu Root Papers, Library of Congress; Floto, *Colonel House in Paris*, 146–49.

33. David Lawrence, quoted in *St. Louis Post-Dispatch*, 21 June 1919.

34. Stimson to George Wharton Pepper, 14 January 1920, to Hays, 18 February 1919, and to Felix Frankfurter, 23 September 1919, Henry L. Stimson Papers, Sterling Library, Yale University. For Stimson's views as they developed, see Kent G. Redmond, "Henry L. Stimson and the Question of League Membership," 200–212.

such as the vociferously isolationist William Borah and James Reed, yet it was probably Lodge and Knox, both learned and experienced, who received the greatest attention in the Senate.

In his sixty-ninth year, Lodge was a tall, thin man "with immaculate silvered hair and beard." With his thumbs adjusted in his armpits and with a copy of Shakespeare in his pocket, he spoke, in rasping tones, words that were brilliant but often bitter. There was "pepper" in his makeup, but much caution and resourcefulness too.[35]

As events unfolded, it seemed to many that Lodge was indifferent to the League question and was simply using it as a political instrument. There was some truth in that view. But the fuller truth is that Lodge wanted to oust the Democrats and Wilson not only because of partisan ends but mostly because he thought them incapable of properly conducting American foreign relations. A staunch defender of national honor, Lodge feared commitments that the country would not later carry out.[36] He appreciated the nation's interest and duties in world affairs. In the postwar world, he hoped to continue close association with Great Britain and France to prevent Germany from again menacing the peace. He thought an alliance impossible but would welcome cooperation through periodic conferences. Beyond that he would not go, feeling that in the long run the people would not sustain fuller involvements and obligations and that universal obligations were not in the national interest.

Even before he knew the details of Wilson's League, with its Article 10, Lodge saw that the chief problem related to force: a League able to command the use of force was inadmissible, but one without that power was of little use. Yet Lodge was willing to back the establishment of some sort of league, suitably limited. Everything depended on the exact details. Prior to 14 February, he moved cautiously. Presuming that Wilson's proposal would be unacceptable yet initially popular as a league for peace, he awaited the details as a general might await a shipment of arms. Once supplied, he would lead his party in a counterattack that would bring either an acceptable league or, if Wilson blocked that, no league at all. Armed now with the details, he began his counterattack before an almost full chamber.

After criticizing Article 10 and other features of the Covenant,

---

35. Margaret L. Coit, *Mr. Baruch*, 286; *Portland Oregonian*, 7 November 1919; George Wharton Pepper, *Philadelphia Lawyer: An Autobiography*, 124.

36. *CR* 64:2, p. 2367 (1 February 1917), in Robert James Fischer, "Henry Cabot Lodge's Concept of Foreign Policy and the League of Nations," 160.

Lodge offered what he called "constructive suggestions." He proposed protecting the Monroe Doctrine, excluding domestic questions (such as control over immigration) from League consideration, adding a withdrawal provision, and making a definite statement about whether the League would have a force of its own and, if not, whether its recommendations would be binding, "technically or morally." Lodge advised ending the war before wrestling with the complicated issues relating to the League. "What is it that delays peace with Germany? Discussions over the league of nations; nothing else."[37]

Knox mainly reinforced Lodge's points. He stressed, in particular, Article 10 and dangers to the Monroe Doctrine. He thought that for the moment the best course was to end the war and bring the boys home, postponing consideration of a world organization until all nations might participate.[38]

Less influential than Lodge and Knox and less eloquent than Borah and Reed, the two mild reservationists who delivered set speeches in this period, Irvine L. Lenroot of Wisconsin and Porter J. McCumber of North Dakota, made important contributions. They let Lodge know their views and what would be needed to get their support; in greatly varying degrees they showed the flag for Republican internationalism; and they began the process of compromise with Wilson, putting proposals for change in the context of overall approval for the League. Both would emerge as leaders among the mild reservationists; thus they warrant introduction.

Born in the frontier of northern Wisconsin in 1869, the son of upstanding Swedish immigrants, Lenroot began his upward climb as a protégé of Robert M. La Follette and served as Speaker of the Wisconsin Assembly while La Follette was governor. In 1909 he advanced to the House of Representatives as an ardent insurgent and took a leading role in the fight against Speaker Joseph Cannon and the undemocratic House rules. After the Democrats won control of the House, Lenroot found ample grounds for ire in gag rule, government by caucus, and, after Wilson's election, subservience to presi-

---

37. *Providence Evening Tribune*, 28 February 1919. These paragraphs on Lodge are based principally on Widenor, *Henry Cabot Lodge*. Widenor's interpretation is consonant with that of James E. Hewes, Jr., "Henry Cabot Lodge and the League of Nations," and of Fischer, "Lodge's Concept of Foreign Policy." See also John A. Garraty, *Henry Cabot Lodge: A Biography*, for an interpretation somewhat less friendly to Lodge, and David Mervin, "Henry Cabot Lodge and the League of Nations," for one that is very hostile to Lodge. Lodge's speech is in the *CR* 65:3, pp. 4520–28 (28 February 1919).

38. *CR* 65:3, pp. 4687–94 (1 March 1919).

dential dictation. The Republican leader, James R. Mann, encouraged him and usually supported him in his conservationist interests as well, and Lenroot gladly cooperated with Mann when he could.[39]

Lenroot gradually drew away from La Follette, and the estrangement became complete in 1917. Lenroot, differing with La Follette and most of the Wisconsin delegation in the House, stood for a strong policy against Germany in the face of renewed submarine warfare, and when that failed, he voted for war. In 1918 the death of Paul Husting created a vacancy in the Senate. Lenroot ran and won in the Republican primaries against a La Follette–backed candidate, demonstrating that Wisconsin was loyal despite its large Germanic population, its strong anti-war Social Democratic party, and the anti-war stand of La Follette. Even though President Wilson intervened, Lenroot won in the special election.[40]

A man of middling height, strong and regular features, and deep-set, piercing eyes, Lenroot was a clear thinker, a hard worker, a fine speaker and debater, an astute legislative draftsman and negotiator, and an informed parliamentarian. California's reformist Congressman William Kent called him "the strongest, cleanest man in either house of congress." Conservationist Gifford Pinchot agreed. Years earlier, the more conservative Augustus Peabody Gardner had commended Lenroot to his father-in-law, Henry Cabot Lodge, as the ablest man to come into the House in his time. In 1917, Gardner was one of those who advanced Lenroot for Speaker or majority leader should the Republicans organize the House.[41]

Lenroot came to the Senate in May 1918 prepared to cooperate with Lodge and the party leadership as fully as conscience would permit. He had fought some notable battles on the side of progressivism and insurgency, but he was happiest as a legislative draftsman and parliamentarian. He saw uses for open conflict, but his concern was usually accomplishment, not political advantage. Quiet and fair-minded, though intense, he usually attributed worthy motives to others and looked for common ground before starting a fight. He would not be a rubber stamp, but he understood the uses of party and the desire of Lodge and Will Hays to conciliate progressives and reunite the GOP.

Supporters of the war, more than its opponents, looked toward

39. Herbert F. Margulies, *Senator Lenroot of Wisconsin: A Political Biography, 1900–1929*, 1–185.
40. Ibid., 109–228.
41. *Milwaukee Sentinel*, 27 March 1918, 18, 26 October 1920; Lodge to Lenroot, 3 September 1920, Irvine L. Lenroot Papers, Library of Congress.

an active postwar American role in maintaining the peace. This seemed a logical extension of the war itself and was a justification for wartime sacrifice. "Clinch the Victory—Keep the World Safe by a League of Nations" was the slogan atop LEP stationery. And Wisconsin's wartime loyalty forces were more than ordinarily strident. Some were conservatives who welcomed the opportunity to excoriate La Follette and the Social Democrats. But even these—and they were not alone in what was a broadly based pro-war coalition—felt genuine alarm both for the cause of America in the war and for the reputation of Wisconsin.

It was elements of the "loyalty" group, looking toward fulfillment of wartime purposes in the postwar world, who helped form one of the first state branches of the LEP. Though not himself a member, Lenroot, during his 1918 loyalty campaign for the Senate, declared himself for a congress of nations armed with the power, by economic and military pressure, to enforce its decisions. On the other side, La Follette and his supporters increasingly opposed the Versailles treaty and the League Covenant.[42]

The point should not be overstated. In Wisconsin as elsewhere, the League's natural constituents were the preachers and teachers and women's clubs that had traditionally backed the cause of peace. Further, in time the wartime patriots divided, some allowing their nationalism and Republicanism to move them to the trail blazed by Lodge or Knox or Borah. Nevertheless, in Wisconsin there was a strong link between support of the war and support of the League, influencing a part of Lenroot's constituency and working directly on the senator's own thinking.

Porter J. McCumber was senior to Lenroot in years—he was sixty-one—and in service in the Senate, which he had entered in 1899. His photograph in 1919 newspapers showed a serious, younger-seeming man—clean-shaven with regular features, somewhat feline eyes, and hair parted in the center, plastered to either side. Though a party man, McCumber was not part of the Republican leadership clique. But his seniority earned him second place to Lodge among Republicans on the Foreign Relations Committee, and in 1919 he also headed his party's steering committee. Although he was not a great orator—he spoke in a meticulous, precise manner, enunciating every syllable as though speaking to an audience unskilled in En-

---

42. "Report of the Field Committee, Nov. 15, 1917," League to Enforce Peace (LEP) Papers, Houghton Library, Harvard University; *Milwaukee Sentinel*, 10 March 1918.

glish—McCumber was able, studious, very conscientious, and strong in his convictions. He was a man to reckon with.[43]

He had grown up on a farm in Minnesota, had taken a law degree at the University of Michigan in 1880, and had then begun his steady rise in North Dakota law and politics. Though conservative, he got some support in his 1916 reelection campaign from the Nonpartisan League, a radical farm organization, since he had attended to the needs of his constituents and was seen as standing above faction.[44]

McCumber was not belligerent before America entered the war, but once the United States was in the conflict he became ardent for the war effort. He was strongly determined that Germany should be crushed and made to accept a lasting peace. His background was Scotch and English, and as the League fight began Hiram Johnson privately named him one of four "Senators from England."[45]

McCumber was a strong internationalist of long standing. Initially a staunch imperialist, he had also backed the Hague Conferences of 1899 and 1907 and the American intervention in the Moroccan crisis in 1905. Legalism informed his internationalism, and McCumber, one of the few in the Senate not concerned about senatorial prerogatives as opposed to the executive, voted for every arbitration treaty submitted during his twenty-four years in the Senate.[46]

McCumber's interest in foreign relations increased after 1911 when he became a member of the Foreign Relations Committee. Even before Wilson, he had supported the idea of a League of Nations. During the war, he continued to espouse peace through law, yet he saw a need also for enforcement. On 3 December 1918, as Wilson embarked for Europe, McCumber wrote to pledge support for "a treaty which shall bind the nations together to maintain justice and peace."[47]

---

43. *Boston Herald*, 25 August 1919; Allen Johnson and Dumas Malone, eds., *Dictionary of American Biography*, vol. 11, supplement 1, pp. 525–26; Charles Michelson in *New York World*, 14 September 1919.

44. Johnson and Malone, *American Biography*, vol. 11, supplement 1, pp. 525–26; Paul Willard Morrison, "The Position of the Senators from North Dakota on Isolation, 1889–1920," 217.

45. Morrison, "Senators from North Dakota," 244–45; Johnson to Hiram Johnson, Jr., 16 February 1919, Hiram Johnson Papers, Bancroft Library, University of California, Berkeley. Support for the League was evidently not the whole basis for the judgment, since the irreconcilable Miles Poindexter was also named.

46. Morrison, "Senators from North Dakota," 330.

47. Ibid., 161, 222–25, 251–58; McCumber to Wilson, 3 December 1918, Wilson Papers, in Leonard Schlup, "Wilsonian Republican: Porter James McCumber and the League of Nations," 18.

McCumber and Lenroot withheld public comment on the League until after Wilson met with the foreign relations committees, as the president had requested. Two days after that meeting, on 28 February, Lenroot addressed the Senate. Earlier in the month the Wisconsin legislature had passed a pro-League resolution.[48] On the other hand, the state's leading Republican paper was beginning to hedge, following the line of national party leaders critical of the Covenant.[49] Lenroot was surely influenced by these factors. Like other senators, he felt some obligation to reflect the wishes of his constituents. And he would be up for reelection in 1920, with not only his own fortunes at stake but also those of the wartime coalition of anti–La Follette progressives and conservatives.

The stand that Lenroot took accorded with political realities in Wisconsin and Washington. More important, it accorded with Lenroot's concern that he be fair and thoughtful about a matter of unparalleled importance. Although Lenroot was critical of portions of the Covenant, the pro-League historian Denna Frank Fleming later judged his speech "easily the most impartial criticism of the Covenant that had so far been made. . . . It was very difficult to deny him any of the amendments he asked for, even though some of them soon proved in practice to be unnecessary."[50]

Lenroot approved the Covenant generally, as well as many of its specific provisions. But he quarreled with others, above all Article 10. He agreed that the United States should be primarily responsible for peace in the Western Hemisphere. If help was needed in Europe, America should respond, "but we should not be obliged to do so." Lenroot felt that only the negative guarantee should be binding— that is, the United States should not act as an aggressor. Lenroot also suggested that the domestic question of immigration should be specifically excluded from League jurisdiction; that the taking of a mandate should require legislative consent, and the mandate should be surrenderable at any time; and that a right of withdrawal after ten years should be included.[51]

McCumber gave the last significant address of the session, a speech that lasted four hours on 3 March. Although North Dakotans at the time were giving more attention to internal conflicts concerning the Nonpartisan League than they were to international affairs,

48. Merlin Hull to Woodrow Wilson, 13 February 1919, Wilson Papers; *Milwaukee Sentinel*, 12, 21, 23 February 1919.
49. *Milwaukee Sentinel*, 16, 23 February 1919.
50. Fleming, *League of Nations*, 141.
51. *CR* 65:3, pp. 4569–72 (28 February 1919).

and although Senator Asle Gronna reported getting a lot of anti-League mail, on balance McCumber's constituents were favorable, if vague, about the League of Nations. It did not matter to McCumber anyway. He was not up for reelection until 1922, and he felt so strongly about the League that he was willing to oppose the will of his constituents if need be.[52]

The contest was in an early stage, McCumber realized, but the Republicans who had spoken in the Senate following publication of the Covenant had been critical, some of them extremely so. McCumber wanted to show the country that the party was not united against the League.[53] Doubtless he wanted wavering Republicans to understand the same thing.

McCumber detailed the horrors of the recent war, calling for internationalism as a basis to prevent such a thing from happening again. His internationalism was based not on self-interest but on humanity, an obligation of the stronger to the weaker. Knox had contended that the United States could be depended on to come to the defense of civilization without being bound by League commitments. Yet as McCumber noted, the country had entered the war not to defend civilization but to defend her neutral rights. For the future, he wanted the nation to be committed in advance to repel the sort of attack Germany had made on France and Belgium. McCumber admitted imperfections in the charter and said that he expected changes would be made in light of senatorial criticism. He referred specifically to the Monroe Doctrine and to domestic questions.[54]

Although no other mild reservationist delivered a set speech during the period of Wilson's visit, one—Thomas Sterling of South Dakota—commented, as did moderates Selden P. Spencer of Missouri and Wesley L. Jones of Washington. Another moderate, Albert B. Cummins, the well-respected Senate veteran from Iowa, delivered a full speech. All of them wanted changes in the Covenant.[55] In this period, and for some months thereafter, the moderates differed little from the more conservative of the mild reservationists.

It was Lodge who had the last word. Near midnight on 3 March, as the session neared its constitutional end the following noon, Lodge

52. *Minneapolis Tribune,* 4 March 1919; *New York Tribune,* 6 March 1919; Morrison, "Senators from North Dakota," 272 n. 79, 274.

53. *CR* 65:3, p. 4872 (3 March 1919).

54. Ibid., 4873, 4876, 4878, 4880 (3 March 1919). The speech as a whole is on 4872–88.

55. Ibid., 3748–49 (19 February 1919), p. 4889 (3 March 1919); *New York Times,* 16 February 1919; *CR* 65:3, pp. 4875–76 (3 March 1919), pp. 4309–16 (26 February 1919).

got the floor. He offered a resolution stating the Senate's conclusion that "the constitution of the league of nations in the form now proposed to the peace conference should not be accepted by the United States" and that the League of Nations negotiations should be completed only after peace terms with Germany were agreed on. Several Democrats objected, and the Senate took no vote. But Lodge had accomplished his purpose: he put in the *Record* the names of thirty-seven Republican senators or senators-elect who supported the "Round Robin." The next day two other senators-elect adhered. Over a third of the Senate, Wilson and the world now knew, insisted on changes.[56]

Of the six men who emerged as mild reservationist leaders, five declined to sign: McCumber, Charles L. McNary of Oregon, LeBaron B. Colt of Rhode Island, Knute Nelson of Minnesota, and Frank B. Kellogg of Minnesota. But Lenroot signed, as did the remaining mild reservationists: Sterling, Frederick Hale of Maine, Walter E. Edge of New Jersey, and Henry W. Keyes of New Hampshire. Three moderates—Jones, William S. Kenyon of Iowa, and Arthur Capper of Kansas—withheld their signatures, but Cummins, Spencer, Reed Smoot of Utah, George B. McLean of Connecticut, and Charles E. Townsend of Michigan signed.[57]

Senator Frank B. Brandegee of Connecticut, instigator of Lodge's resolution, claimed that Kellogg and one or two others later expressed regret that they had not signed. To newsmen, Kellogg and Nelson criticized features of the Covenant; Jones said that he agreed with the idea of the Round Robin but that he never signed petitions; and Kenyon said that he had promised his constituents not to bind himself on the matter but that he would criticize the League draft in Iowa speeches. Thus, the opposition of the "middle grounders"— mild reservationists and moderates—was weaker than it seemed.[58]

The matter may be seen from a different perspective. The Round Robin represented a sort of common denominator, for it included several concessions to pro-Leaguers. The words *in the form now proposed* allowed senators who favored the League to sign. Surely there would be some changes in the Covenant, and not necessarily important ones. Also, the resolution expressed the desire "that the nations

56. Lodge, *The Senate*, 118–19.
57. Ibid., 120. George Norris, then considered pro-League, also refused to sign. By July Norris had become an irreconcilable. He is therefore not among the subjects of this study.
58. For Brandegee, see Chandler P. Anderson diary, entry for 13 March 1919, Chandler P. Anderson Papers, Library of Congress; *New York Tribune*, 5 March 1919.

of the world should unite to promote peace and general dis-armament."[59] Finally, though calling for a delay in considering the League, the resolution explicitly stated that the League question should be taken up by the peace conference once the treaty with Germany was concluded. Later on, the call for delay would be syn-onymous with opposition to the League, but this was not yet the case.

Following Wilson's return to Europe to resume treaty negotia-tions, those mild reservationists who were content with the League Covenant said little. But some of those who wanted changes spoke up. Although having no direct influence on events in Paris, these speakers were significant nevertheless. Their comments contrib-uted to the development of reservationism as a common denomi-nator for Senate Republicans and contributed also to the formula-tion of the terms that the mild reservationists as a faction within the Republican party would eventually offer to the Democrats as a basis for settlement. Lenroot and Kellogg, the two who would emerge as the most conservative of the mild reservationist leaders, were par-ticularly vocal.

When Kellogg made it known that he would present his views at a statewide Republican conference in St. Paul on 7 March, the an-nouncement attracted attention. Kellogg was a man of some attain-ments and was bound to exert influence. (In 1925, in token of his continuing high status, President Calvin Coolidge appointed him secretary of state.)

Raised on a Minnesota farm by parents of English ancestry, Kel-logg received only a sketchy formal education, then read law and was admitted to the bar in 1877. Though poor, Kellogg was well con-nected. The cousin of Cushman Kellogg Davis, Kellogg was brought into Davis's law firm, among the strongest in the state, when Davis went to the Senate in 1877. The firm represented major timber, rail-road, and mining companies, and Kellogg soon became part of the nation's elite of business and the bar.

A mild progressive in the era of Theodore Roosevelt, Kellogg acted as special prosecutor against the General Paper Company in 1905–1906, served as special counsel to the Interstate Commerce Commission in proceedings against railroad magnate E. H. Har-riman in 1906–1907, and steered the government's antitrust case against Standard Oil to a conclusion in 1911. The following year he

59. Fleming, *League of Nations*, 156.

became president of the American Bar Association. Kellogg supported Roosevelt's third-party presidential candidacy in 1912, but that was his only significant departure from regularity. Soon after, he helped reunite Bull Moosers and Republicans in Minnesota and secured his own election to the Senate in 1916, as an advocate of preparedness. Kellogg was very interested in international affairs and often visited Europe. He wanted to be on the Senate Foreign Relations Committee, and he seemed likely to get the post in the next Congress.[60]

In Minnesota during the war, even more than in the neighboring states of Wisconsin and the Dakotas, deep division developed between the large German-American population, along with anti-war socialists and Nonpartisan Leaguers, and a pro-war coalition of moderates and conservatives. Kellogg, representing the pro-war element, introduced in the Senate a resolution to expel Robert M. La Follette after La Follette made anti-war statements at a Nonpartisan League meeting in St. Paul. The intensity of feeling within his own state may have augmented Kellogg's already strong veneration for America's partner in the war, Great Britain, and may have encouraged his very strong hostility to the Germans, "the Hun."[61] To the extent that Kellogg supported the League, that support seems to have related in part to conditions in wartime Minnesota, which accentuated in Kellogg and others the desire to fulfill the purposes of the war.

As with Lenroot, the point should not be carried too far in Kellogg's case. His interest in international affairs antedated the war and related only partially to the special circumstances of his home state. So far as constituent pressure is concerned, in Minnesota, as in Wisconsin, the wartime patriots were not united behind the League, and those who backed it simply supplemented the conventional peace lobby.

Legendary in Washington for his fits of temper and his angry moods, Kellogg was also cautious to the point of occasional indecision. Later, as he agonized over the alternative reservation formulations, he earned the nickname "Nervous Nellie." Even before that,

60. Johnson and Malone, *American Biography*, supplement 2, pp. 355–57; Charles G. Cleaver, "Frank B. Kellogg: Attitudes and Assumptions Influencing His Foreign Policy Decisions," 2–3; Millard L. Gieske, "The Politics of Knute Nelson, 1912–1920," 324, 329; David Bryn-Jones, *Frank B. Kellogg: A Biography*, 119.

61. Carl H. Chrislock, *The Progressive Era in Minnesota, 1899–1918*, 145–81; idem, *Ethnicity Challenged: The Upper Midwest Norwegian-American Experience in World War I*, 58–59, 90–91; Cleaver, "Frank B. Kellogg," 6–7, 25–27, 31, 198.

some both in the Senate and outside considered him too sensitive to constituent opinion and therefore too erratic. Perhaps his pronounced stoop contributed to the unfavorable impression.[62]

Though respectful of constituent opinion, Kellogg did exert independent judgment about the League. In an area of expertise, and on an issue of transcendent importance, he was as much a leader as a follower. He deplored those he labeled "politicians," and he thought of himself as a "public servant." But he disliked Wilson and had a strong sense of party loyalty, and these feelings influenced his behavior despite protestations to the contrary.[63]

Before leaving Washington, Kellogg showed the text of his speech to Knute Nelson, the senior senator from Minnesota, and got Nelson's concurrence. Though neither senator had signed the Round Robin, and though both were aware of the strong pro-League sentiment in Minnesota headed by the Twin Cities newspapers, Kellogg—for himself and Nelson—staked out an equivocal position.[64] The importance of Kellogg's 7 March speech was enhanced by the presence at the party conference of national chairman Will Hays, who formally opened the 1920 Republican campaign. Hays's attendance lent to Kellogg's speech the color of party orthodoxy.[65]

Kellogg began on a positive note, pointing out that he had expressed himself in favor of a League in his 1916 campaign and had spoken for it in the Senate in December 1918. Typically for pro-Leaguers, he put the matter in the context of the sacrifices incurred in the war. Kellogg praised the pacific settlement provisions, but he proposed to exclude domestic questions, such as immigration policy, from League jurisdiction, and he urged that the Monroe Doctrine be protected. On the vital question of enforcement, Kellogg approved Article 16 sanctions for failure to abide by the decisions of arbitration. But he expressed grave doubts about Article 10. "I think only the most momentous circumstances and conditions which

62. Cleaver, "Frank B. Kellogg," 28, 41; Carter Field, *Bernard Baruch*, 195; Charles Hilles to Herbert Parsons, 8 July 1919, and Parsons to Hilles, 9 July 1919, Herbert Parsons Papers, Butler Library, Columbia University; Belle Case La Follette and Fola La Follette, *Robert M. La Follette, 1855–1925*, 1063.

63. Cleaver, "Frank B. Kellogg," 70–72, 214.

64. *Minneapolis Tribune*, 5 March 1919; Will Hays to Frank Munsey, 10 March 1919, enclosed in Ervin Wardman to Albert J. Beveridge, 10 March 1919, Albert J. Beveridge Papers, Library of Congress; Frank Kellogg to Henry Cabot Lodge, 13 March 1919, Lodge Papers; Raymond Clapper Diaries, entry for 18 March 1919, Raymond Clapper Papers, Library of Congress.

65. *Independent* 97 (29 March 1919): 433; *Minneapolis Tribune*, 6 March 1919.

threaten the peace of the world can justify our meddling in the affairs of Europe," he said.[66]

Hays was pleased. He wired the publisher Frank Munsey that since Kellogg had received Nelson's approval of the speech, and since neither had signed the Round Robin, "this will [add] two more senators against present draft."[67] Hays did not oppose the League; however, for the time being he hoped to unify the party on the basis of criticism of the Covenant.

For his part, Kellogg was glad to be inside the party tent. He promptly wrote Lodge of his speech, saying that his criticisms had gone over well. On returning to Washington, he commented that in the face of the strong pro-League feeling in Minnesota, critics would have a hard fight. At this stage of events, given the flaws in the draft Covenant, Kellogg could associate himself with its opponents without abandoning hope for the League.[68]

Lenroot took the same tack, but more pronouncedly. In a widely noted speech at the Commercial Club in Washington on 18 March, Lenroot angrily responded to Wilson's threat to coerce the Senate by tying the League to the treaty. Lenroot, sensitive about presidential dictation and congressional responsibilities, warned that if the treaty was unsatisfactory Congress might simply pass a joint resolution ending the war, thus leaving participation in the League for later determination. Further, if Wilson did not amend the Covenant to meet Senate objections, the Senate would propose amendments. Lenroot felt that the Senate, vis-à-vis the president, and the nation, vis-à-vis other countries, held the high cards. Neither should be coerced. Gilbert Hitchcock, ranking Democrat on the Senate Foreign Relations Committee, added to the importance of Lenroot's speech when he responded before the same forum on 1 April.[69]

At the end of March, Lenroot visited Wisconsin. On his return to Washington he said that Wisconsin people, by a three-to-one ratio, favored a League to prevent war but opposed the League as proposed. Speaking opposite Senator Hitchcock at the Economic Club in New York, he argued for an amendment concerning the Monroe Doctrine

66. *Minneapolis Tribune*, 8 March 1919.
67. Hays to Munsey, 10 March 1919, enclosed in Ervin Wardman to Albert J. Beveridge, 10 March 1919, Beveridge Papers.
68. Kellogg to Lodge, 13 March 1919, Lodge Papers; Raymond Clapper Diaries, entry for 18 March 1919, Clapper Papers.
69. *New York Tribune*, 19 March 1919; *New York Times*, 2 April 1919.

to be made in Paris; if not, he warned, the Covenant would be amended in the Senate.[70]

Moderates Kenyon, Spencer, and Capper also called for changes. So did Lodge, in a well-publicized debate with A. Lawrence Lowell. And irreconcilables, especially Borah, Reed, and Miles Poindexter of Washington, aggressively campaigned against the League.[71]

With the treaty not yet complete, and with both the country and the GOP already divided on the issue of the League, the middle grounders were still in the process of forming their positions, notwithstanding the speeches and comments of a few of them. Their thinking, as well as the cause of reservationism that they came to embrace, was advanced substantially by the 29 March publication of a letter from Elihu Root to Will Hays.

The seventy-four-year-old elder statesman enjoyed much prestige in the country, especially among Republican internationalists. Root had been a strong secretary of war for McKinley and Roosevelt; then, as secretary of state in Roosevelt's second administration, he had advanced the cause of international justice at the Second Hague Conference in 1907, had negotiated twenty-four bilateral treaties of arbitration, and had helped establish the Central American Court of Justice. For these services and others he had received a Nobel Peace Prize in 1912. Root had served in the Senate and had headed the Carnegie Endowment for International Peace, the American Society of International Law, and the American Bar Association.[72]

Prior to the publication of Root's letter to Hays, Root had privately sent specific suggestions for Covenant revision to Paris. Relying on the advice of David Hunter Miller, who was negotiating the details of Covenant revision, Wilson had rejected Root's ideas as having already been met or as lacking merit.[73] This rejection, though not immediately known, greatly augmented the importance of Root's letter to Hays.

70. *New York Times*, 2, 8 April 1919.

71. Ibid., 2 April 1919; *Providence Evening Tribune*, 4 April 1919; *St. Louis Post-Dispatch*, 11 March 1919; Miller, *Drafting of the Covenant*, 1:384–86; Ralph Stone, *The Irreconcilables: The Fight Against the League of Nations*, 78–83.

72. Richard W. Leopold, *Elihu Root and the Conservative Tradition*, 56–57; Martin David Dubin, "Elihu Root and the Advocacy of a League of Nations, 1914–1917," 440; Philip C. Jessup, *Elihu Root*, 321; Martin David Dubin, "The Carnegie Endowment for International Peace and the Advocacy of a League of Nations, 1914–1918," 345. Root had headed the Carnegie Endowment and the American Society of International Law since the inception of each.

73. Jessup, *Elihu Root*, 390, 395–96; Miller, *Drafting of the Covenant*, 1:298–300, 311, 377–82, 404; Walworth, *Wilson*, 2:301.

Root expressed the views of judicialists—international lawyers and scholars who dominated the American peace movement in the early twentieth century. Uncertain and divided on the subject of force, other than the force of public opinion, judicialists were united in looking to world law to provide order and peace on an international scale.[74] Viewing the Covenant from that perspective, Root found flaws.

After defending the prerogatives of the Senate, Root praised features of the Covenant. Then, however, he urged stronger provisions about making and using international law. He called for a reservation to deal with domestic questions and with the Monroe Doctrine. And he argued for limitation of Article 10 to a five-year period of postwar adjustment, after which a nation might end its obligation on one year's notice. Finally, Root urged the addition of review and withdrawal procedures.[75]

The response to Root's letter fulfilled Hay's fondest hopes. The letter won praise and support from a large and diverse audience. Newspapers acclaimed Root's ideas. The pro-League papers doubted the necessity of his suggestions but praised their spirit and acknowledged that they represented opinion that could not be ignored. Senators too endorsed the letter.[76]

The effect of Root's letter was compounded by another event. Three days earlier Charles Evans Hughes had spoken on the Covenant. He favored adherence to a League of Nations but urged seven amendments. These covered familiar subjects, already under review in Paris. One, however, was inadmissible from Wilson's standpoint: the elimination of Article 10. Hughes opposed permanent border guarantees. And recognizing the discretionary power of Congress to declare war, he did not want the country to be put in the position of going back on its word.[77]

Grudgingly and sparingly, Wilson yielded to the demands for revi-

74. C. Roland Marchand, *The American Peace Movement and Social Reform, 1898–1918*, 41–47, 56–57, 63, 120–23, 132; Dubin, "Carnegie Endowment," 358; Merle Curti, *Peace or War: The American Struggle, 1636–1936*, 204; Kuehl, *World Order*, 203–4.

75. Robert Bacon and James Brown Scott, eds., *Men and Policies: Addresses by Elihu Root*, 254–55, 258, 260, 265–68; Miller, *Drafting of the Covenant*, 1:379.

76. Jessup, *Elihu Root*, 394; Stimson Diaries, entry for 29 March 1919, Stimson Papers; *New York Tribune*, 1 April 1919; Beveridge to Munsey, 3 April 1919, Beveridge Papers; Kendrick, "The League of Nations," 109; Forrest Carlisle Pogue, Jr., "The Monroe Doctrine and the League of Nations," 85; *New York Times*, 1 April 1919.

77. David J. Danelski and Joseph S. Tulchin, eds., *The Autobiographical Notes of Charles Evans Hughes*, 210; Kendrick, "The League of Nations," 111–12.

sion, relying heavily on suggestions supplied by Taft and Hitchcock.[78] Some of the changes Wilson asked for met with ready agreement. But Wilson had to bargain hard for others, especially those concerning the Monroe Doctrine, and he had to make concessions on other treaty subjects.[79] Wilson's changes involved the Monroe Doctrine, the right of withdrawal, the exclusion of purely domestic questions from League jurisdiction, the unanimity rule in the Council, and protection against the imposition of mandate responsibilities on an unwilling member. For most of these subjects the negotiators agreed to the verbiage proposed by the American delegation, but for the controversial Monroe Doctrine issue British wording was accepted.[80] The changes soon proved insufficient to quell domestic criticism.

The main subject of criticism—Article 10—was not dealt with. Taft, though himself prepared to qualify this article, had not proposed a revision. Nor had Lowell. In any case Wilson was adamant. The Senate, he wrote, "would have to accept the vital Article 10 or reject the entire treaty and abide by the consequences." Another source of future difficulties involved the representation of British Empire countries. During the revision stage, negotiators agreed that British Dominions should be considered eligible for membership on the Council and that India, which was not self-governing, should nevertheless be a member of the League.[81]

When the revisers ignored Root's judicial proposals, they created a problem of a different sort. Unlike most other criticisms of the Covenant, these proposals were designed not so much to protect American interests and constitutional prerogatives as to create a better instrument for world peace. The judicial issues were not suitable for treatment by means of reservations, as were matters like Article 10 and the Monroe Doctrine. Yet the continuing weakness of the Covenant from the judicial standpoint nevertheless contributed to reservationism, by leaving Root dissatisfied and ready to assist Republicans who found fault with the revised Covenant.

78. Kendrick, "The League of Nations," 112–13; Miller, *Drafting of the Covenant*, 1:276–77, 374–75; *New York Times*, 12 March 1919.

79. Charles Seymour, ed., *The Intimate Papers of Colonel House*, vol. 4, *The Ending of the War*, 409; Miller, *Drafting of the Covenant*, 1:446–47; Bonsal, *Unfinished Business*, 181; Floto, *Colonel House in Paris*, 163, 191, 206–11; Tillman, *Anglo-American Relations*, 262–93.

80. Miller, *Drafting of the Covenant*, 1:336–37, 363, 425–26; Pogue, "The Monroe Doctrine," 79–81.

81. Taft to Henry L. Stimson, 9 March 1919, Stimson Papers; Lowell to Taft, 28 March 1919, A. Lawrence Lowell Papers, Pusey Library, Harvard University; Wilson quoted in James E. Hewes, Jr., "William E. Borah and the Image of Isolationism," 231; Miller, *Drafting of the Covenant*, 1:476, 489, 492–93.

Reassured by congratulatory cables from Taft and Hitchcock, Wilson thought that the distasteful work of revision was done. On 28 April, as chairman of the League of Nations Commission, he addressed a plenary session of the peace conference and explained the twenty-four changes that had been made, only some of them at his behest. The delegates approved, and the Covenant was ready for incorporation into the almost completed Treaty of Versailles.[82]

Lodge's immediate, privately expressed reaction was to fault the revised Covenant on several grounds. The new Article 21 read: "Nothing in this Covenant shall be deemed to affect the validity of international engagements, such as treaties of arbitration or regional understandings like the Monroe Doctrine, for securing the maintenance of peace." But in Lodge's mind the Monroe Doctrine was neither an "international engagement" nor a "regional understanding" but rather a unilateral American policy. He felt that the United States needed to retain the sole right to interpret it. The addition of Article 15 allowed the Council to define domestic questions, which Lodge found dangerous. Two years' notice for withdrawal seemed too long; Lodge thought that the mischief occasioning withdrawal would be done by then. And Lodge could not reconcile himself to the unmodified wording of Article 10. Nations would break their treaty commitment if called on to fight in some remote place. And if France was in jeopardy the United States would respond anyway— no universal commitment was needed.[83]

Even though Taft and the LEP quickly endorsed the revised Covenant, Lodge hoped to unify Republican senators on the basis of a fairly tough opposition stance.[84] With that in mind, he told the press that the Covenant would need "further amendments," and with whip Charles Curtis of Kansas, he wired Republican senators, asking them to withhold comment on the Covenant pending a party conference.[85] Such a conference might come very soon, Lodge knew, for vital legislation necessitated a special session, which in fact Wilson called on 7 May, to meet on the nineteenth. At the time, the distinction between *amendment* and *reservation* was not so sharply drawn by senators and observers as it would be later. Since the treaty

82. Walworth, *Wilson*, 2:420; Miller, *Drafting of the Covenant*, 1:495–98.
83. Garraty, *Lodge*, 364–65; Lodge to Elihu Root, 29 April 1919, Root Papers.
84. *Minneapolis Tribune*, 2 May 1919; *New York Tribune*, 1 May 1919; *New York Times*, 1 May 1919. The LEP launched a series of fifteen "ratification conventions" in New England and the Midwest, along with a barrage of speeches and publications. Charles DeBenedetti, *Origins of the Modern American Peace Movement, 1915–1929*, 21; Kuehl, *World Order*, 314.
85. Fleming, *League of Nations*, 196; *New York Times*, 30 April 1919.

was not yet completed, further changes in the Covenant might still be made without excessive delay. Even so, amendments would require the acquiescence of all parties to the treaty, which was not necessarily the case with reservations. Equally or more important than Lodge's use of the word *amendments* was the unstated implication that Republican senators would refuse to approve a treaty that did not include their previously developed program of amendments. Privately, Lodge hoped for still more—that the Senate would separate the treaty from the League and consider the treaty first.[86]

In case of trouble with the middle grounders, Lodge knew that the help of Elihu Root would be invaluable. Soon after the revised Covenant was made public, Lodge phoned Root twice, sent him a long letter, and sent two emissaries to see him. Root remained reassuringly critical.[87]

Irreconcilables had to be dealt with too, and early on 29 April Lodge met with Borah. Agreeing to support an amendment program, Borah retained the freedom to seek rejection of the League later and to try to commit the party to that course. Borah also agreed not to let internal party differences prevent the GOP from organizing the new Senate. The matter concerned Lodge, for the party's margin in the Senate would be small, forty-nine to forty-seven, and internal dissension was rife on domestic issues. Lodge's deal with Borah was neither firm nor altogether clear but was the best one Lodge could negotiate with the spirited senator.[88]

Lodge's efforts met with only partial success. His request notwithstanding, several senators commented on the Covenant before the party conference. Two of those who gave press statements became mild reservationists. Their comments, though brief, had several important effects, the most immediate of which was to put Lodge and other Republicans on notice that party unity could not be secured on the basis of an extreme anti-League program. The sen-

86. Robert La Follette to "My Beloved Boy," 10 May 1919, Robert M. La Follette Papers, La Follette Family Collection, Library of Congress; *St. Louis Post-Dispatch*, 18 May 1919; Hiram Johnson to Charles K. McClatchy, 13 May 1919, Johnson Papers.

87. Stone, *The Irreconcilables*, 90; Pepper, *Philadelphia Lawyer*, 124–25; Lodge to Root, 29 April 1919, Root Papers; George W. Pepper to Henry L. Stimson, 3 May 1919, Stimson Papers.

88. Stone, *The Irreconcilables*, 90–92; Lodge, *The Senate*, 146; Lodge to Beveridge, 30 April 1919, Beveridge Papers. The deal included Lodge's promise of thorough Senate deliberation, giving the irreconcilables time to mount their campaign and to work against the strong pro-League sentiment in the country (Hewes, "William E. Borah," 234).

ators were Charles L. McNary, by far the milder of the two, and Thomas Sterling, a less ardent and less active League supporter.

McNary was comparatively young, forty-five, and relatively new to the Senate. Appointed to fill a vacancy in 1917, he had been elected to a full term in 1918. In background, intellect, and temperament, he was well equipped for outstanding service. McNary was of eighteenth-century Scotch-Irish immigrant stock. His grandfather had headed a wagon company to Oregon in 1845. His father had died when Charles was nine, and the family was poor but close-knit, upstanding, and ambitious. McNary combined work and education throughout his youth and managed to work his way through Stanford University. A lawyer in public and private service, he also dabbled in business, agriculture, and education, serving as dean and law professor at Willamette College for a time. In 1913 he was appointed associate justice of the Supreme Court of Oregon. The appointment was well received; he was hailed as a man of "excellent record and character" who was blessed with "the most delightful personality" and the ability to make and keep friends.[89]

Though McNary formerly served as state Republican chairman, when he was appointed to the Senate he declared himself a progressive and not a "hide-bound partisan." In the Senate he proved true to the promise. Though a moderate progressive, he showed himself to be a senatorial type more than a strong factionalist. Presenting a pleasant appearance—six feet tall, slender, sandy-haired, blue-eyed, and clean-shaven—McNary excelled in personal relations and parliamentary issues. He rarely spoke in the Senate; when he did his style was expository and undramatic.[90]

In later life, McNary set out to avoid contentious issues unrelated to the interests of Oregon. But young McNary could not hold himself aloof from the League fight. It must have seemed to him that this was an issue in which his constituents were interested. Their pro-League opinion, reinforced by the state's leading Republican paper, the *Portland Oregonian*, seemed to him to be right and to warrant his active involvement.[91]

89. George Charles Hoffmann, Jr., "The Early Political Career of Charles McNary, 1917–1924," 54; Roger T. Johnson, "Charles L. McNary and the Republican Party During Prosperity and Depression," 14.

90. *Oregon Journal*, 30 May 1917, cited in Hoffman, "Career of Charles McNary," 51; McNary to Thomas B. Neuhausen, 1 October 1919, Thomas B. Neuhausen Papers, Special Collections Division, University of Oregon; Warren Harding to C. M. Idelman, 26 February 1920, Warren G. Harding Papers, Ohio Historical Society; Johnson and Malone, *American Biography*, supplement 3, pp. 496–97.

91. Johnson, "McNary and the Republican Party," 41–42; *Portland Oregonian*, 17,

Thomas Sterling was a farmer's son who became a lawyer. Born in 1851, he graduated from Illinois Wesleyan College in 1875, settled in South Dakota, and worked his way up in law and politics. From 1901 to 1911 he served as dean of the College of Law at the state university. Dignified, well-groomed, and conservative in appearance, he was elected to the Senate as a progressive Republican in 1913. At the start of his senatorial career, Sterling showed some independence, joining only five other Republicans in voting for the Federal Reserve bill. Gradually he moved to the right and to regularity, and in the 1920s he gave strong support to the Harding and Coolidge administrations. Wartime and postwar radicalism, which he opposed legislatively as a member of the Senate Judiciary Committee, may account in part for his transition, as well as for some of his international views.[92]

Sterling concerned himself with the postwar world and in December 1918, in a letter to a close friend, indicated his approach. Sterling was leery of the word *Enforce* in the title of the LEP. "That means an international army and armament, a part of which we will have to furnish and maintain and if our part is proportionate to our population and resources, it will form a large portion of such armament and we shall be subject to the possibility that the other members of this League will under certain conditions demand that the armament we furnish be turned against ourselves." But he strongly favored "a League to promote peace."[93]

By mid-January Sterling was ready to address the Senate. Some of his views clashed with Wilson's. Concerned about bolshevism in Russia and Germany, he backed Lodge and Knox in urging that discussion of the League be put off so that a peace settlement could be speedily made. And he was not prepared to coerce sovereign states. On the other hand, he favored an active American role in the postwar world. Sterling stressed the U. S. friendship with Great Britain, especially, and with France and Italy as well. He foresaw a peace that would rest on the continuation of the wartime relationship among these powers. He was one of the four that Hiram Johnson classed as "Senators from England." But in mid-April, before a home-state

---

19 February, 29 March, 14, 29 April 1919; *Oregon Journal*, 1 May, 16 September 1919; C. R. Forbes to Warren G. Harding, 28 February 1920, Harding Papers. The editor of the *Oregonian* was reported as for the League "with or without reservations."

92. *New York Times*, 27 October 1920; U.S. Congress, *Congressional Directory*, 66:1, pp. 106–7; Gilbert C. Fite, *Peter Norbeck: Prairie Statesman*, 96, 105, 115.

93. Thomas Sterling to Doane Robinson, 16 December 1918, Doane Robinson Papers, South Dakota Historical Resource Center.

audience, Sterling stressed avoiding European entanglements and retaining in Congress the right to declare war.[94]

McNary's comment on the revised Covenant preceded Sterling's. He was unequivocal. "In my opinion the covenant has been amended to meet all the legitimate objections raised against it," McNary said. "Whether it is perfect in all its details or not is insignificant as compared with the high principle it is calculated to serve, which in time will be perfected as far as human efforts can achieve and be as devotedly respected as the constitution of our own country. That feeling in itself will be sufficient to guarantee ever lasting peace."[95]

Sterling was more critical. "I believe Article Ten should be changed or amended, and that the reservation of the Monroe Doctrine should be made plain and unmistakable," he said. Yet Sterling, who at this time was variously seen as friendly to or doubtful of the League, approved other amendments. Most important, despite remaining doubts, he would not declare that he would vote against the Covenant as constituted.[96]

Two of the moderates who commented before the party conference was held also pointed toward a course less severe than that charted by Lodge. Charles E. Townsend said he thought the new draft would get "at least the qualified support of the Senate and the people." William S. Kenyon, a former judge who was well respected among his colleagues for legislative accomplishment and fair-mindedness, protested against Lodge's seeming effort to make a party issue of the League. He saw flaws still in the Covenant but said, significantly, "I believe certain dubious questions in it can be cleared up in the resolution of ratification." Kenyon was pointing toward reservationism, something short of the treaty amendment approach favored by Lodge.[97]

94. *CR* 65:3, pp. 1314–18 (13 January 1919); Johnson to Hiram Johnson, Jr., 16 February 1919, Johnson Papers; *Argus-Leader*, 12 April 1919.

95. *Portland Oregonian*, 30 April 1919.

96. *Minneapolis Tribune*, 9 May 1919; Sterling quoted in *New York World*, 8, 9 May 1919.

97. Townsend quoted in *New York Tribune*, 29 April 1919; Johnson and Malone, *American Biography*, supplement 1, pp. 465–66; Kenyon quoted in *New York World*, 3 May 1919. Privately, Kenyon approached the irreconcilable Democrat James Reed of Missouri and offered him a mailing list of twelve thousand and help in arranging a speech in Des Moines. According to Reed, Kenyon declined to speak himself on the grounds that it would be political suicide (Reed to Sterling E. Edmunds, 28 May 1919, in Thomas F. Eagleton, "James A. Reed and the League of Nations," 57–58). Kenyon was not a closet irreconcilable, but he did hope to sway the strong pro-League opinion of Iowa—advanced by the leading paper, the *Des Moines Register*—in the direction of reservationism.

Consensus eluded Lodge. Even the publication on 7 May of a summary of the treaty terms being offered to Germany did not help. Later, dissatisfied Italian-Americans and German-Americans would exert influence, as would disillusioned liberals. Already Irish-Americans were resentful that Wilson gave no hearing to those who sought Irish independence and, suspicious of the League as a British instrument, were becoming active on the irreconcilable side.[98] Provisions favoring Japan at the expense of China in the Shantung Peninsula would receive strong senatorial criticism when more widely and fully understood and publicized. But the first reaction of those senators who commented on the summary was preponderantly favorable, especially concerning the harsh treatment of Germany.[99] When Republican senators met in advance of the session, it was only to discuss matters of organization, not to take a stand on the League or on other aspects of the treaty. But Lodge did at least quell the progressive Republican rebellion against two Old Guard committee heads, partly by conciliating Borah with the makeup of the Senate Foreign Relations Committee. Lodge named Hiram Johnson to the committee.[100]

The "concession" suited Lodge's own purposes, for he wanted to pack the committee with anti-Leaguers. At the Republican conference of 14 May, Lodge was chosen party leader and was authorized to name the nine-member committee on committees. At the same conference, Republican senators agreed that the party ratio on the Foreign Relations Committee, the Finance Committee, and the Interstate Commerce Committee should be ten to seven. Lodge promptly named his friend Frank Brandegee head of the committee on committees. In practice, Lodge himself chose the four new Re-

98. Charles C. Tansill, *America and the Fight for Irish Freedom*, 302–3, 326–27, 330, 335; Peter Gerry, D. I. Walsh, Key Pittman, John B. Kendrick, and T. J. Walsh to Woodrow Wilson, 28 March 1919, Key Pittman Papers, Library of Congress; *CR* 66:1, pp. 729, 733 (6 June 1919); Stone, *The Irreconcilables*, 102–3; Kenneth R. Maxwell, "Irish-Americans and the Fight for Treaty Ratification," 638.

99. *Des Moines Register*, 9 May 1919; *Minneapolis Tribune*, 9 May 1919; *New York World*, 8 May 1919; *New York Times*, 11 May 1919. The treaty provided for demilitarization of part of the Rhineland and a fifteen-year inter-Allied occupation of that region; for French economic control of the Saar and its political alienation from Germany for at least fifteen years; for potentially stringent reparation terms; and, in connection with reparations, for German acknowledgment of guilt for the war. The victors stripped Germany of her colonies, not merely as the inevitable result of war but also on the grounds that Germany was not fit to govern them. Germany would be able to enter the League, but only after a probationary period.

100. Johnson to Hiram Johnson, Jr., and Archibald Johnson, 27 May 1919, Johnson Papers; Stone, *The Irreconcilables*, 96–98.

publican members of the Foreign Relations Committee, which was his prerogative as majority leader and prospective chairman of the committee. Two mild reservationists were among those frequently mentioned as likely prospects—Kellogg and Lenroot. Kellogg's claims were strongest, based on his background and his expression of interest two years earlier. But in a personal interview Kellogg refused to promise to back Lodge within the committee, and Lodge sent him a note saying that he could not be appointed. Later, Harding called on Kellogg and urged him to be a little more compliant, in the interests of the party. Kellogg refused.[101]

Lodge chose more-reliable men to join the committee for the first time: Harding, Hiram Johnson of California, George Moses of New Hampshire, and Harry New of Indiana. These four, together with holdovers Lodge, Borah, Brandegee, Knox, and Albert Fall of New Mexico, guaranteed Lodge a majority, even when the other Republican holdover, McCumber, joined with the Democrats. Lodge could be sure the committee would not recommend outright approval of the treaty.

Irreconcilables quickly took the offensive in the new Congress. The treaty was completed but not yet signed, and in deference to the Allies, Wilson withheld it from the Senate. But irreconcilables charged that it had been leaked to bankers. Borah inserted a copy supplied by the *Chicago Tribune* into the *Congressional Record*, opening the way for attacks on specific features.[102] Finally, on 10 June Knox introduced a new version of the resolution he had offered in December: to separate the League from the rest of the treaty and to defer consideration of the Covenant until later.

While the irreconcilables were holding center stage, people friendly to the League but not fully content with its charter increasingly talked of reservations.[103] On 30 May the influential Republican paper the *New York Tribune* editorially endorsed that approach. With terms already submitted to Germany, there seemed little chance of making further changes in the Covenant before Wilson came home with the completed treaty. Under those circumstances, the approach urged by Lodge—textual amendment of the Cove-

101. *New York Tribune*, 21 May 1919; Stone, *The Irreconcilables*, 97; Lodge to Kellogg, 28 May 1919, Lodge Papers; Bryn-Jones, *Frank B. Kellogg*, 113–14. Lodge also passed over a moderate, Kenyon, and compensated him with a different assignment (*Des Moines Register*, 8 May 1919; *Minneapolis Tribune*, 25 May 1919).

102. Stone, *The Irreconcilables*, 103–8; Kuehl, *World Order*, 313; George Juergens, *News From the White House: The Presidential-Press Relationship in the Progressive Era*, 245–46.

103. *Boston Herald*, 15 May 1919; *New York World*, 12 May 1919.

nant—implied time-consuming renegotiation with the Allies and possibly even with Germany. By contrast reservations, embodied in the Senate's resolution of ratification or in a separate resolution, could protect the United States equally well, without delaying the consummation of peace with Germany.

Central to the concern for speed was an economic consideration. Taft, who privately supported reservations but was committed to unreserved ratification in his official LEP capacity, agreed with Will Hays in a phone conversation that the Senate should approve the treaty in such a way that it would not go back to the peace conference. He told Hays, "If the impression got abroad that the senators, merely because they hate Mr. Wilson, were willing to defeat the treaty and postpone the . . . resumption of business, it would furnish Mr. Wilson with an argument that might embarrass the Republican party." Hays agreed.[104]

In the months that followed, proponents of the League would make much of the economic argument. A delay in peacemaking would in effect continue the Trading with the Enemies Act, would postpone the establishment of consulates in Germany, and in these and other ways would seriously hinder the resumption of trade with Germany. Meanwhile the Allied powers, having ratified the treaty, would be establishing long-term trade relations. Middle grounders not only proved receptive to this argument but also in many cases made it their own.

Some had additional reasons for wanting speedy ratification. Europe remained in distress and turmoil; the situation cried out for the normalization of economic and political relationships that only a peace settlement could bring.[105] In the United States, legislation was needed to accomplish the adjustment to peacetime conditions. For example, decisions had to be made about the railroad system, which had been taken over by the government during the war. It would not do for the Senate to be tied up in prolonged debate on the treaty. Finally, senators who on grounds unrelated to the matter of speed were committed to a moderately pro-League stance had political reasons for wanting to be done with the League issue and for not wanting to allow it to linger into the 1920 campaign. Republican voters were already divided about the League; as long as the issue

104. For Taft's support of reservations, see Taft to A. H. Vandenberg, 4 June 1919, William Howard Taft Papers, Library of Congress; William Howard Taft, Memorandum, 20 May 1919, Taft Papers.

105. See, for instance, *Providence Evening Tribune*, 4 April 1919; Irvine Lenroot to Nellie Nichols, 4 April 1919, Lenroot Papers.

remained prominent, some were bound to be discontented with the stance of their senator. Middle grounders, favoring compromise, were vulnerable. As Henry L. Stimson observed, "An issue submitted to a political campaign must necessarily be adopted in an extreme form one way or the other, and without compromise."[106] And neither the senators nor their party needed the issue. Domestic complaints abounded among the electorate, springing from the war and the dislocations of reconstruction; without the League question, 1920 looked very promising for the Republicans.

Mild reservationists were spurred to action by the challenge of the Knox resolution. The updated resolution called for an immediate peace treaty with Germany and, so far as the United States was concerned, a deferral of the League question until later. The resolution explained how this might be done and added that other nations, if they wished, might establish the League of Nations at once. It warned of "far-reaching covenants inimical to our free institutions" and implied that Article 10 represented an advance commitment that was in conflict with Congress's war-making power under the Constitution. The resolution advised the Peace Conference to so draw the treaty as to permit any nation to consider the League question at its leisure.[107]

There was no chance that Wilson would consent to any such change in the treaty. Taken in context, the resolution would serve only to commit the Republican party to a position of negation on the League. Those who feared this result of the resolution needed to explore further the reservationist alternative and perhaps to develop a specific program to which a bloc of senators might adhere. They needed also to ready themselves with amendments that might soften the terms of the Knox resolution if it was pushed to a vote and if it seemed likely to pass.[108] To accomplish these ends, two mild reservationists took the lead—Frank Kellogg and Fred Hale of Maine.

Hale was the son and grandson of senators. A slight, retiring bachelor who lived with his mother in a mansion near the Capitol, Hale had the broad cultural interests that befitted a graduate of Groton, Harvard, and Columbia Law School. He enjoyed golf and poker too, and the company of unpretentious colleagues like Warren Harding. Hale developed a lucrative law practice in Portland while dabbling

106. Stimson to Henry W. Rose, 20 January 1920, Stimson Papers.
107. *CR* 66:1, p. 894 (10 June 1919).
108. Nicholas Murray Butler to Frederick Hale, 12 June 1919, and to James W. Wadsworth, 29 July 1919, Nicholas Murray Butler Papers, Butler Library, Columbia University.

in politics. From 1912 through 1918 he served as Republican national committeeman and in 1916, at the age of forty-two, won election to the Senate. There he interested himself in naval affairs especially, and eventually he chaired the Naval Affairs Committee, as had his father, Eugene Hale.[109] He was leery of grandiose Wilsonian commitments. But he saw hope for the League if its pacific settlement provisions could be strengthened.[110]

Hale and Kellogg promoted an 11 June dinner at which a group of senators met with the president of Columbia University, and the scholar-politician Nicholas Murray Butler, who came to Washington for the occasion. The dinner was at Kellogg's, but Butler credited Hale as well as Kellogg for arranging it.[111] In addition to Hale and Kellogg, mild reservationists McNary and Edge, along with Harding, Spencer, and Joseph Frelinghuysen of New Jersey, were almost surely present. Butler probably also met with mild reservationists Sterling, Lenroot, and Keyes, as well as with moderates Capper, Kenyon, and Cummins.[112] Three of the most pro-League Republican senators— McCumber, Colt, and Nelson— were not present, perhaps because they were not yet ready to commit themselves to reservationism.

Before the dinner, Chandler P. Anderson, a distinguished international lawyer and a friend and protégé of Root's, was invited to lunch with Hale and Kellogg. Anderson understood the senators to say that

109. *CR* 88:1, p. 1837 (30 September 1963), p. 19071 (9 October 1963); "Memorandum to Dr. Herbert F. Margulies from Katharine F. Lenroot," 10 December 1968, in the possession of the author; Jonathan Daniels, *The End of Innocence*, 303; Harding to John Edwin Brown, 21 October 1919, to F. E. Scobey, 25 October 1919, and Harry Daugherty to Harding, 12 February 1919, Harding Papers.

110. *CR* 65:3, pp. 2598–99 (3 February 1919); *CR* 66:1, p. 1552 (23 June 1919).

111. Kellogg to Warren G. Harding, 9 June 1919, Harding Papers; Butler to Selden P. Spencer, 29 July 1919, Butler Papers; Nicholas Murray Butler *Across the Busy Years: Recollections and Reflections*, 2:197. Hale was a golfing friend of Butler's, and it was probably he who had brought Butler to Washington to meet with himself, Kellogg, and Harding in December 1918. (The personal relationships are made evident in Butler to Hale, 1 and 10 March 1920, and in Hale to Harding, 28 August 1920, Frederick Hale Papers, Syracuse University, and in Butler to Albert B. Cummins, 24 and 27 February 1920, Butler Papers. The meeting is noted in Kuehl, *World Order*, 296 and in Dubin, "Carnegie Endowment," 361.)

112. Kellogg to Harding, 9 June 1919, Harding Papers; Butler to Selden P. Spencer, 29 July 1919, Butler Papers; Butler, *Across the Busy Years*, 2:197; Kellogg to Butler, 19 November 1925, Frank B. Kellogg Papers, Minnesota Historical Society. Harding and Frelinghuysen became strong reservationists, but at this time their positions were neither clearly formulated nor widely known, and both were friends of Hale's. Harding was antagonistic to the League, but he wanted to seem "unprejudiced," and some senators thought he secretly favored the League very strongly (Harding to F. E. Scobey, 4 June 1919, Harding Papers; Charles Hilles to Col. Herbert Parsons, 5 June 1919, Parsons Papers).

they opposed the extreme position identified with Lodge, Knox, Borah, and Brandegee but favored reservations that would not require resubmission to the other signatories and that would protect American rights. Hale and Kellogg hoped that Anderson would spend an evening to discuss reservationism in detail. By way of preliminary, Anderson told them how he thought their plans might be effected through the other League members' silent acquiescence in the American reservations.[113]

Kellogg and Hale may have presented Anderson's view to Kellogg's other guests that evening, for Butler later endorsed it in a letter to Hays. The main topic, though, was specific reservations. Butler came to Washington with two reservations in hand, covering domestic questions and the Monroe Doctrine. He called them "declarations of interpretation" that would surely not require renegotiation and that would not open the door for other countries to make their own demands, causing "vexatious discussion and renewed delay." These interpretive reservations were to be embodied in the resolution of ratification. Before Butler presented his draft reservations to the senators, he discussed the treaty at some length. He probably talked about the powers of the president and of the Senate in treaty making. Then Butler offered his reservation proposals. The senators, in turn, impressed on Butler their concerns that the party should not take a wholly negative position on the League, that a reservation to Article 10 should be made in addition to the reservations Butler had drafted, and that something positive should be readied as an amendment to the Knox resolution.[114]

Butler returned to New York after midnight. On 12 June he sent Hale his reservation proposals, including a new one on Article 10, amendments to the Knox resolution, and a memo on the powers of the president and the Senate in treaty making. Butler's Article 10 reservation, which he presumed reflected the agreements of the previous night, was notably mild by later standards. It stated:

That if for the fulfillment of the obligation imposed by Article X of the covenant of the League of Nations, the Council of the League shall advise an act of war on the part of the United States, such act of war will only follow upon the exercise by the Congress of the United States of its constitutional power to declare war.[115]

113. Chandler P. Anderson Diary, entry for 11 June 1919, Anderson Papers.
114. Butler to Hays, 29 July 1919, to Frederick Hale, 12 June 1919, and to James W. Wadsworth, 29 July 1919, Butler Papers; Butler, *Across the Busy Years*, 2:197–200.
115. Butler to Frederick Hale, 12 June 1919, Butler Papers.

The reservation did not detail a point that critics of Article 10 later stressed: that Congress was in no way bound, legally or morally, to declare war or to use other sanctions.

In later years Butler exaggerated the importance of his evening with the senators. He thought that they had agreed on their course. They had not. Nevertheless, the dinner of 11 June was important. The middle grounders present at the dinner now understood that they were far from alone and now were much more willing to oppose the views of Lodge. More specifically, the dinner with Butler strengthened the middle grounders in their growing commitment to and understanding of reservationism and increased their wariness of the Knox resolution. By 18 June many of them had expressed their feelings, and Hiram Johnson blamed Butler. Furthermore, the reservations soon offered by Spencer and the amendments to the Knox resolution suggested by Hale were consistent with Butler's view.[116]

The movement to oppose the Knox resolution, begun by Kellogg and Hale when they arranged the Butler dinner, was continued by other mild reservationists. On 12 June the Foreign Relations Committee reported the resolution to the Senate. Two of the more conservative mild reservationists, both of whom were present at the meeting with Butler the night before, put stumbling blocks in the way of the resolution. Thomas Sterling introduced an alternative resolution, and Walter Edge issued a statement to the press. Sterling had been active before, but Edge had not.

Decades later Edge recalled that he had been a mild reservationist. He came to mild reservationism from the standpoint of a self-made businessman who continued to be concerned about the welfare of business while he served first as governor and then, at the age of forty-six, as senator. His advertising business had branches in London, Paris, and Brussels, giving him direct experience with European economic problems. Throughout the League conflict, Edge was deeply interested in the restoration of normal economic conditions and the promotion of trade. The Edge Act of December 1919 authorized new investment cooperatives to advance international trade and replace the War Finance Corporation.[117]

In all the League debates Edge plumped for a speedy settlement,

116. Butler to William Allen White, 1 September 1936, William Allen White Papers, Library of Congress; Johnson to Albert J. Beveridge, 18 June 1919, Beveridge Papers; Nicholas Murray Butler to Selden P. Spencer, 29 July 1919, Butler Papers.

117. Walter E. Edge, *A Jerseyman's Journal: Fifty Years of American Business and Politics*, 117; *New York Times*, 13 June 1919; U.S. Congress, *Congressional Directory*, 66:1, p. 64; Edge to Warren G. Harding, 26 August 1920, Harding Papers.

albeit one that would remain consistent with national interest. In his 12 June statement he approved the purpose of the Knox resolution but expressed some impatience with it, noting that the resolution was insufficient to accomplish the swift ratification that he wanted. The Republicans should decide what they would not approve, he said, and should notify the peace conference of the changes they wanted. He thought that the separation of the Covenant from the rest of the treaty was desirable but unlikely, so he hoped the conference would alter the Covenant to satisfy the Senate and end the danger of prolonged debate.[118]

Thomas Sterling took a more concrete step. He offered what the *New York Times* called "the first resolution of a qualifying nature to be presented." Sterling professed to favor the Knox resolution, yet his resolution offered an alternative and less extreme course. Strictly speaking, what Sterling proposed was a treaty amendment, for it was to be "attached to and become a part of said treaty and covenant." But the resolution referred to "the following express conditions or reservations" and thus may be taken as an early expression of reservationism. Since the treaty was not yet before the Senate, no true reservations could be adopted. Sterling's resolution cited America's special interest in the Western Hemisphere and said that with regard to Europe, Congress would decide about fulfilling obligations under Article 10.[119]

More forthrightly, two mild reservationist leaders expressed outright opposition to the Knox resolution—Porter McCumber in a speech and Charles McNary in a wire to the Oregon LEP. Behind the scenes, vote counters listed mild reservationists Kellogg, Lenroot, and Hale as opposed, along with moderates Jones, Spencer, Kenyon, and Capper.[120] As a result, when hoped-for reinforcements from dissident Democrats failed to appear, Lodge gave up. In the need to pass appropriations bills before 1 July, he found a convenient excuse for indefinitely postponing action on the resolution. Knox acquiesced, warning that he would later seek a vote.[121]

On 17 June it was announced in Paris that Germany had been given final terms, with the requirement that she reply by 23 June.

118. *New York Tribune*, 13 June 1919.
119. *New York Times*, 13 June 1919; *CR* 66:1, p. 1013 (12 June 1919).
120. *CR* 66:1, pp. 1264–76 (18 June 1919); *Oregon Journal*, 19 June 1919; Robert La Follette to "My dear lads," 16 June 1919, La Follette Papers; Gus Karger to William Howard Taft, 16 June 1919, Taft Papers; Philander Knox to Albert J. Beveridge, 18 June 1919, Beveridge Papers.
121. *St. Louis Post-Dispatch*, 20 June 1919; *Minneapolis Tribune*, 20 June 1919; *Portland Oregonian*, 22, 24 June 1919; *New York Herald*, 23 June 1919.

But with submission of the treaty imminent, the Republicans found themselves disunited in the country and the Senate. Lodge had hoped for more but now realized that only reservationism might unite the party. But even reservationism would need strong efforts, among both the enemies and the friends of the League. Otherwise, Lodge feared, the treaty might be ratified as presented.[122]

Lodge called on Elihu Root for a letter, this time along specifically reservationist lines. Anxious that his party do something positive, Root drafted a letter to Lodge for the use of the Foreign Relations Committee. He brought it to the Capitol on 20 June, and after a series of consultations and some revision, the letter was released to the press the following day. Lodge promptly endorsed Root's proposals.[123]

In his letter Root made a bow to the Knox resolution. Then, referring to his letter of 29 March to Hays, he said that his suggestions had not been considered. Yet there was much of worth in the Covenant, Root continued. Moreover, the condition of Europe required prompt action, he thought. Root proposed reservations. The first was by far the most drastic: the Senate would not consent to Article 10. Second, the right of withdrawal on two years' notice would not be dependent on any finding of the Council. That is, the Council could not block a withdrawal by saying that a nation had not met all its obligations. Third, Root offered wording that would protect America's use of the Monroe Doctrine and its control over domestic questions like the tariff and immigration.

More important than Root's specific proposals were his comments on the reservationist approach. Root said that his proposed reservations might become effective by tacit acceptance, that they would not require renegotiation. The comment met with widespread doubt. But at the suggestion of one or several of those with whom he conferred, he added that if senators doubted the effectiveness of the reservations, they could ask the four principal powers on the Council to state whether they objected. In any case, through reservationism America might protect her interests without delaying the consummation of peace.[124]

122. Henry L. Stimson Diary, Entry for 22 February 1920, Stimson Papers.

123. Root to Frank Brandegee, 8 June 1919, Root Papers; *New York World*, 21 June 1919; *New York Tribune*, 21 June 1919; Jessup, *Elihu Root*, 400–402; *New York Times*, 21 June 1919; Henry L. Stimson to Leonard Wood, 7 May 1919, Stimson Papers.

124. Jessup, *Elihu Root*, 401; Root to Henry Cabot Lodge, 19 June 1919, in Bacon and Scott, *Addresses by Elihu Root*, 269–77.

Lodge quickly followed up on the Root letter, meeting with all elements of the party. Anti-Leaguers were the easiest to deal with. They of course preferred reserved to unreserved ratification, which at the time seemed a strong possibility. Further, commitment to reservations did not preclude either the support of amendments to the treaty or a vote against the resolution of ratification even with amendments and reservations attached. Lodge further placated them with a pledge that would become important later: he would insist on the acceptance of reservations by the other major powers. For Lodge the middle grounders were the more difficult and dangerous, and he summoned Hays to help with them.[125] By 28 June, when the treaty was signed in Europe, Lodge had achieved only partial, though significant, success.

On 21 June "a prominent New England Senator," almost surely LeBaron Colt of Rhode Island, told the *Providence Tribune* that ratification with reservations would not require renegotiation, and he cited precedents to support that view. Moderates Capper and Spencer gave similar statements. And Kellogg privately told prominent New Yorkers that reservations were essential to ratification.[126] As of 28 June, most other middle grounders were also understood to favor reservations. But McNary and McCumber still refused to commit themselves to reservations, despite the urging of Hays.[127] And the Republicans came to no swift agreement on a specific program because some reservationists felt that Root's proposal to altogether eliminate Article 10 was too extreme.[128]

Woodrow Wilson, in private and public statements, stated his strong opposition to reservations.[129] Gilbert Hitchcock was acting minority leader for the Democrats in the absence of Thomas Martin, who was terminally ill. Taking his cue from Wilson, Hitchcock looked ahead to Senate action after the signing of the treaty and he rejected reservationism outright. He told reporters, "No compromise is possible on the league of nations." He foresaw the defeat of

125. *New York Tribune,* 25, 27 June 1919; *Portland Oregonian,* 27 June 1919.

126. *Providence Sunday Tribune,* 22 June 1919; *New York Tribune,* 28 June 1919; *St. Louis Post-Dispatch,* 28 June 1919; Kellogg to William Howard Taft, 21 July 1919, and to Nicholas Murray Butler, 19 November 1925, Kellogg Papers; Gus J. Karger to William Howard Taft, 14 June 1919, Taft Papers. One of those that Kellogg saw was Root, possibly before Root came to Washington on 20 June.

127. *New York Times,* 27 June 1919; Gus J. Karger to William Howard Taft, 28 June 1919, Taft Papers.

128. *New York World,* 23 June 1919; *New York Herald,* 23 June 1919; *New York Tribune,* 28 June 1919; *Independent* 99 (12 Ju July 1919): 40.

129. *New York Tribune,* 28 June 1919; *New York Times,* 28 June 1919; Wilson to Joseph Tumulty, 23 June 1919, Wilson Papers.

reservations by the Democrats aided by more than two Republicans. After reservations were defeated, no more than fifteen Republicans and one Democrat would vote against ratification. Reservations are like amendments, he said; League opponents could not agree among themselves, and much personal feeling had developed among them. "Senator Lodge, in trying to keep them together, favors them all. He is like a hen with a brood of chickens. He cannot keep them together and make them follow him, and he cannot follow each of them."[130] About a dozen of Hitchcock's colleagues privately gave the same assessment.[131]

But Hitchcock's strategy was already obsolete. The full treaty terms were authoritatively published on 28 June, revealing what seemed to be a shameful betrayal of China to Japan in connection with the former German rights in the Shantung Peninsula. Chinese delegates refused to sign. Under the circumstances, Wilson's extravagant praise for the treaty and his insistence on prompt and unreserved ratification served only to antagonize Republicans of all stripes.[132] McCumber and McNary, keystones in Hitchcock's strategy of seeking Senate rejection of reservations, announced on 29 June that they would support reservations, albeit "explanatory" or "interpretive" ones.[133]

Their decisions were important, and the senators took some trouble to explain them, privately and to newsmen. "I would prefer to vote for the League of Nations provisions just as they stand, but I am concerned about two things," McCumber wrote Taft on 2 July. "First: the ratification of the treaty and second: that when ratified it shall not be overturned in a year or two by the Congress."[134] McCumber, as well as McNary, decided that the adoption of reservations represented the minimum price for ratification; if the Demo-

130. *St. Louis Post-Dispatch*, 29 June 1919; *New York Tribune*, 28 June 1919.

131. Hamilton Holt to A. Lawrence Lowell, 30 June 1919, Taft Papers.

132. Baker and Dodd, *Public Papers of Woodrow Wilson*, 5:523–24; *New York Times*, 28, 29 June 1919; *New York Tribune*, 29 June 1919. Shantung terms had been known in general before, but the press had reported that Japan had promised to return political control to China in the near future; the text of the treaty made no mention of that. Chinese delegates were refused permission to speak at the signing ceremony. Wilson was himself unhappy with the Shantung terms. As he explained the matter to advisers, he acceded because the British and the French were bound by treaty to support Japan's claims, because Japan had given a verbal promise to yield political control of Shantung later, and because Japan threatened to quit the peace conference if denied these terms (Vance C. McCormick Diary, 119, Hoover Institution on War, Revolution, and Peace, Stanford University).

133. *New York Times*, 29 June 1919; *New York Tribune*, 29 June 1919.

134. McCumber to Taft, 2 July 1919, Taft Papers.

crats held all but James Reed and Thomas Gore, they would need the votes of nineteen Republicans for unqualified ratification. The votes seemed not to be there. McCumber explained his second point in a press statement. Reservations were needed concerning the Monroe Doctrine and domestic questions like immigration, racial equality, and the tariff; otherwise, some development in the future might impel the Senate to take action that would, in effect, take America out of the League.[135]

Staying with their party, McCumber and McNary hoped to moderate its position. McCumber called for only "explanatory reservations"; there should be none that would have the effect of nullifying the Covenant. Noting that Root had switched from his earlier position regarding Article 10, McCumber said that he could not accept the new Root proposal.[136] McNary declared:

I am satisfied with the treaty and the league of nations covenant as signed in Paris. . . . I believe the document will be ratified by the Senate in virtually its present form. . . . I have no objection to league opponents in the Senate being allowed to explain their constructions or interpretations of the treaty, but I certainly would object to any revision being attempted by the Senate that would materially change or nullify any portion of the document.[137]

Privately, McNary told Taft's informant, reporter Gus Karger, that "explanatory resolutions" covering the Monroe Doctrine and domestic questions might be necessary.[138]

McCumber, among the mildest of the reservationists and important because of the deepness of his concern and the constancy of his involvement, discussed his views and strategies in his letter to Taft. Immigration and tariff decisions, he thought, were patently domestic questions, so no nation would object to this being stated by the United States in a reservation. Thus such a reservation would not delay ending the war or joining the League. Similarly, a reservation on the Monroe Doctrine, if needed to get a two-thirds vote in the Senate, might be phrased in an inoffensive way, though some senators wanted to be truculent about it.

In his press statement McCumber had rejected Root's proposal to scrap Article 10 but had not himself suggested a specific reservation. He knew, though, that some reservation to the article was essential for ratification. On 1 July he had a long talk with Lodge and came

135. *New York Times,* 29 June 1919.
136. Ibid.
137. *New York Tribune,* 29 June 1919.
138. Karger to Taft, 1 July 1919, Taft Papers.

away convinced that Lodge would agree to "such a change in the Root program with reference to Article 10 as would insure the active participation of the United States in guaranteeing the territorial integrity and political independence of these newly created nations for such period of time as would be necessary to place them on their feet." He thought that the main fight would be against "the indefinite guaranty of the political independence and territorial integrity of the other nations from external aggression." As a last resort to secure ratification, McCumber was willing to yield the guarantee to intervene against aggression while retaining the negative guarantee to respect the territorial integrity of others. This, together with the agreement of each nation to submit before the Council any difference with another nation before resorting to war and to use boycott or war against a nation that does not do so, would "accomplish practically the same result." The pervasive objection that the Council might order the United States into war was "worse than specious." But McCumber added:

If it is necessary to meet the fears of some Senators in order to secure the two-thirds vote, I can see no serious objection to some proper statement in the resolution making clear to the world that Congressional action would be necessary to carry out the provision of the League and possibly even going a step further and asserting the right of the then Congress to pass its judgment as to the propriety or wisdom of engaging in a war.

McCumber explained to Taft why he was willing to make concessions on Article 10. "If we once get all of the nations by a cross compact to agree that all questions affecting the peace of the world shall first be submitted to the Council for advice and probably settlement, the other harsher features would never be called into activity."[139]

McCumber had previously spoken well of the negative guarantee, and he would do so again.[140] To be sure, the negative guarantee was for him a fallback position, one substantially supplemented by reliance on pacific settlement provisions backed by the sanctions of Article 16. Nevertheless, it is significant that he saw no great difference in consequences between this position and Wilson's, considering that the negative guarantee relied on the absolute, universal, advance commitment to joint military action. Either approach, he seemed to think, might serve as a cornerstone for world peace. But the point should not be pushed too far, for McCumber, more than

139. McCumber to Taft, 2 July 1919, Taft Papers.
140. *CR* 65:3, p. 4874 (3 March 1919).

other mild reservationists, did later battle to preserve the commitment to collective security under Article 10.

Although union with the Democrats for unreserved ratification would be a quixotic gesture, an effort to achieve two-thirds for ratification by a union of Democrats and nineteen or twenty Republicans seemed feasible. If necessary, McCumber would ignore his party's leadership in the undertaking. As of early July, that did not seem necessary. He came away from his talk with Lodge convinced that, as Gus Karger put it, "Lodge does not want to go so far as to defeat the treaty; he fears the political consequences if it is done by Republican votes."[141] Lodge, then, would not stand in the way of compromise. But to take advantage of the opportunity, McCumber and a few like-minded senators would have to accept reservationism.

The reservationist announcements of McCumber and McNary caused an immediate change in the thinking of Democratic leaders of the Senate as they made final preparations for receipt of the treaty. After a series of interviews, Britain's Sir William Wiseman wrote, "Democratic leaders are in favour of agreeing to some mild and vague reservation to the treaty which would satisfy the Republicans."[142] Even Hitchcock took that approach, though as acting leader he was reluctant to appear to seek compromise.[143] The Democrats were moving toward something that Wilson came to accept later—a resolution of "interpretations" separate from the resolution of ratification.

Meanwhile Lodge, increasingly taken with reservationism and fortified by word from Lord James Bryce that he thought England would not object to reservations, continued to press for the Root program. He won no full agreement mainly because of the proposed renunciation of Article 10.[144] But Kellogg was encouraged by reservationism's prospects, and he wrote Lodge to urge speedy action after the treaty was submitted. Lenroot, Cummins, and some others called on Lodge with the same message. They proposed that he take the lead in formulating a Republican program of reservations to be brought to the floor immediately, in lieu of long hearings in the Foreign Relations Committee. They would challenge the Democrats to ratify immediately or to take the blame for opposition and thus for

141. Karger to William Howard Taft, 2 July 1919, Taft Papers.
142. Sir William Wiseman, "Notes on the Political Situation in America," 5 July 1919, Sir William Wiseman Papers, Sterling Library, Yale University.
143. Gus Karger to William Howard Taft, 2 July 1919, Taft Papers.
144. Lodge to Root, 7 July 1919, and Bryce to Root, 6 June 1919, Root Papers. For an alternative program of reservations being considered by Lenroot, Senator William Calder of New York, and perhaps others, see Calder to Henry L. Stimson, 30 June. 1919, and William Crozier to Stimson, 18 July 1919, Stimson Papers.

obstructing economic recovery. The senators thought that the Republicans, with the possible exception of McCumber, could reach an agreement on such a program within ten days and that enough Democrats would join to produce a working majority.[145] The active involvement of the moderate Cummins was significant. The sixty-nine-year-old Iowan, in the Senate since 1908, had increased his influence as he retreated from insurgency and had recently been honored by his election as president pro tempore of the Senate.

Despite the encouraging signs of movement after 29 June, a substantial gap between Democrats and Republican reservationists remained to be bridged. Partisans divided on both the content and the form of reservations, as well as on what might happen if no compromise was reached and a reservationist resolution was voted on and defeated. Republican leaders sought pledges from senators that in such an event they would not vote for unreserved ratification.[146]

Problems lay ahead in any case but were compounded by the fact that Wilson, sailing home to lead the fight for ratification, was ill informed and badly advised about the situation in the United States, was overly optimistic, and was in a pugnacious mood. In the words of Lord Cecil, Wilson "despised the senatorial opposition, being confident that with his personality and great oratorical powers he would be able to crush Senator Lodge and other objectors."[147] Just before Wilson left France, Colonel House advised him to "meet the Senate in a conciliatory spirit." Wilson replied, "House, I have found one can never get anything in this life that is worth while without fighting for it." During his voyage only one of his advisers, Thomas Lamont, had any doubts about the prospects for the treaty in the Senate. The enthusiastic reception awaiting Wilson in the streets of New York and at Carnegie Hall reinforced reports of overwhelming support for the League among the people and among editors.[148]

145. Kellogg to Lodge, 7 July 1919, Lodge Papers; *Minneapolis Tribune,* 9 July 1919; *New York World,* 10, 9 July 1919.

146. "Confidential Memorandum," 1 July 1919, Parsons Papers; George Harvey to Albert J. Beveridge, 28 June 1919, Beveridge Papers. Senator Medill McCormick on 9 July claimed that the thirty-three votes were there, should a reservationist resolution be defeated (*Boston Herald,* 10 July 1919).

147. Lloyd E. Ambrosius, *Woodrow Wilson and the American Diplomatic Tradition: The Treaty Fight in Perspective,* 151-52; Arthur Walworth, *Wilson and the Peacemakers: American Diplomacy at the Paris Peace Conference, 1919,* 181-86, 192-93; Robert Cecil, *A Great Experiment,* 83.

148. House and Wilson quoted in Seymour, *Intimate Papers of Colonel House,* 4:487; Thomas W. Lamont, *Across World Frontiers,* 202-3; Leon H. Canfield, *The Presidency of Woodrow Wilson: Prelude to a World in Crisis,* 206; Link, *Woodrow Wilson,* 106-7.

As Wilson prepared to present the treaty to the Senate, the mild reservationists readied themselves to share center stage with him. Already, some of them had significantly influenced the course of events. Keyes, a modest freshman, had not acted, except to sign the Round Robin, and Edge, Nelson, and Colt had played only minor roles. But Hale and Sterling, and more particularly McCumber, McNary, Lenroot, and Kellogg, had been active. Mild reservationists had often worked in cooperation with moderates, who until October and November shared the views of the more conservative of them. Acting from diverse motives and expressing diverse views, the mild reservationists had finally come together in favor of reservationism. Most of them had opposed unqualified ratification, even after Wilson had brought about changes in the Covenant. At the same time, many mild reservationists had been instrumental in blocking the Knox resolution, and chiefly because of them Root had come forth to solidify reservationist feeling among Republicans. Borah and others would go further if they could, but even the irreconcilables would not initially oppose reservations. In any event, unless the Democrats joined them, the irreconcilables could not block either the adoption of reservations or treaty approval.

The mild reservationists had been effective but essentially negative, rejecting the extreme positions. Now they had the opportunity to do something quite positive, but exceptionally challenging. More realistic about ratification prospects than the League's chief proponent, Wilson, and more sincerely concerned about accomplishing ratification than their party leader, Lodge, this small minority among Republican senators needed to formulate a reservationist program on which they themselves could agree and then needed to use their bargaining power with Democrats and fellow Republicans to create for their program a two-thirds majority. Just agreeing among themselves would be no easy matter. When asked by Taft to take the lead, Kellogg aptly observed, "You forget that the Senators are all leaders."[149]

149. Kellogg to Taft, 21 July 1919, Kellogg Papers.

2 OPPORTUNITY LOST, 10 July–5 September 1919

*B*etween 10 July 1919 when Woodrow Wilson presented the treaty with Germany to the Senate, and 3 September, when the president began a speaking tour for the League, the mild reservationists sought to win a two-thirds majority for a compromise program. The senators failed and the president departed. On 4 September the Senate Foreign Relations Committee, having already approved forty-five amendments, adopted a tough reservation to Article 10. The best opportunity for compromise was lost. The fault did not lie with the mild reservationists; President Wilson had miscalculated. To a considerable extent, though, the extreme difficulties of the situation decided the outcome.

By the end of these weeks the mild reservationists were less mild than they had been and were no longer in close negotiation with Democrats. Within the Republican party, however, they remained a strong and active force. They worked for a party program on the League that they themselves could approve and that might attract Democratic support. Their leaders signaled their purpose with immediate criticism of the committee's proposed reservation to Article 10.

Reservationism had come into its own by July, but reservationists still confronted difficult questions. Should reservations be in the instrument of ratification or in a separate resolution? Should the reservations be merely "interpretive," stating the government's understanding of certain provisions, or should they be drastic, in effect amendatory? What subjects should they cover? Should other nations be required to accept the reservations explicitly, or only tacitly? If the reservations failed to pass, should reservationists reject the unreserved resolution of ratification? And should direct amendments to the treaty be made along with reservations? In considering each of these subjects, reservationists had to consider the extent to which a particular course would delay the conclusion of peace.

47

The mild reservationists paid close attention to tactics. Although the treaty continued to languish in the Foreign Relations Committee into September, senators looked ahead to the voting. The leaders of the rival parties sought the help of the middle grounders in trying to constitute a majority, which might control all votes preliminary to the final one on treaty approval, when two-thirds would be needed. Whichever group had a majority could frame the final resolution and put the onus of defeat on the other side. Republican friends of the League, in deciding how to align themselves, had to determine which alignment would produce the most satisfactory ratification resolution and which side was most likely to enlarge its number to achieve two-thirds.

Wilson's speech to the Senate on 10 July was far from his best. The president failed to provide long-awaited details about controverted issues such as Shantung, the Monroe Doctrine, Article 10, or reservations. Wilson did, at least, offer to make himself available to senators and the Foreign Relations Committee.[1]

Democrat Henry Ashurst of Arizona wrote that the speech put opponents "in a state of felicity. . . . His audience wanted raw meat, he fed them cold turnips." Of the Republicans who commented to the press, McCumber alone praised the speech. Spencer, Nelson, Smoot, Capper, and Edge were among those who faulted Wilson for failing to illuminate controversial matters. The blunt-spoken Edge took the occasion to restate an insistence on reservations and to predict that they would be voted.[2]

The president had been more forthcoming in a White House meeting with newsmen earlier in the day and in conversation with senators in the president's room of the Capitol after his speech. At his press conference, the first in two years, Wilson opposed reservations because all other signatories would have to assent and meanwhile the United States would remain in a technical state of war. Even if innocuous, reservations would have to be explained to other nations. Besides, there was no need for them. Wilson had made it clear in Paris that only Congress could declare war for the United States, a fact recognized in the use of the word *advise* in Article 10. If there was trouble in the Balkans or elsewhere, Wilson

1. *Providence Evening Tribune*, 12 July 1919; *Des Moines Register*, 11 July 1919.
2. George F. Sparks, ed., *A Many Colored Toga: The Diary of Henry Fountain Ashurst*, entry for 11 July 1919, pp. 98–99; *St. Louis Post-Dispatch*, 11 July 1919; *New York Herald*, 11 July 1919.

noted, the League Council would surely choose the nations best fitted to fight there.[3]

Surprisingly, Wilson disagreed with those who said that a simple majority could amend the ratifying resolution. He insisted that a two-thirds vote was needed. Wilson's interpretation was contrary to a Senate rule in effect since 1868 and conflicted with several precedents, as both Lodge and Hitchcock quickly pointed out.[4] It may be that Wilson was not talking about a reservation appended to the resolution of ratification but was referring to an interpretive resolution of reservations separate from the instrument of ratification. Such a resolution, Wilson understood, would require a two-thirds vote.[5] Whether or not he was misunderstood, during July and August the president entertained as a fallback position the idea of a separate, interpretive resolution, in case unreserved ratification could not be secured.

The fallback position was anachronistic, and Wilson's public insistence on unreserved ratification was still more unrealistic. Unfortunately, Wilson soon compounded the error when he bestowed his favor on Hitchcock as leader for the treaty in the Senate. When Claude Swanson of Virginia made the first address on the League following the submission of the treaty, observers thought that he had displaced Hitchcock as Wilson's spokesman.[6] But Wilson hastened to heal the seeming breach with Hitchcock, and thereafter Wilson dealt with the Senate through the Nebraskan.[7] A sixty-year-old, clean-shavenly handsome Omaha publisher, Hitchcock was the son of a senator and was himself a veteran of three terms in the House and service in the Senate since 1911. Yet as a speaker, Hitchcock was no match for the Republican's best, and he was not a distinguished tactician.[8] Insecure in his post as merely the acting minority leader during the illness of Thomas Martin, Hitchcock would not readily challenge Wilson's judgment or act independently among senators.

3. *Minneapolis Tribune*, 11 July 1919.

4. W. Stull Holt, *Treaties Defeated by the Senate: A Study of the Struggle Between President and Senate Over the Conduct of Foreign Relations*, 296; *New York Times*, 11 July 1919. Vice-president Marshall, however, later agreed with Wilson (*CR* 66:2, p. 2630 [9 February 1920]).

5. Not all authorities agreed—see the statement of Senator McCumber, *New York Times*, 20 August 1919.

6. *New York Herald*, 12 July 1919; *Minneapolis Tribune*, 12 July 1919.

7. *New York Herald*, 13, 15 July 1919; *Minneapolis Tribune*, 16, 19 July 1919.

8. *Boston Herald*, 28 February 1919; Robert Foster Patterson, "Gilbert M. Hitchcock: A Story of Two Careers."

Rejecting appeals for speedy action, the Senate Foreign Relations Committee read the full treaty and then, at the end of July, began extensive hearings. Meanwhile, the mild reservationists staked out their position. Hoping to achieve a quick and satisfactory ratification, they stood between Wilson with his followers and the anti-Leaguers, mostly from their own party. The mild reservationists wanted to find a basis for compromise between Democrats and Republicans and were willing to take the lead in negotiations. The two sides were far apart, so the task would be difficult, yet it was the best hope for ratification. In the process, some mild reservationists gave a fuller or at least more current exposition of their views than they had before.

Following Swanson's speech of 14 July, Kellogg spoke for the middle position. Swanson had suggested that reservations were not necessary because the Covenant covered the points at issue. So what would it harm, Kellogg asked, for the United States to state its understanding in its ratification? Key Pittman of Nevada, like Swanson a member of the Foreign Relations Committee, questioned Kellogg. In response Kellogg acknowledged that if a reservation changed the terms of the treaty, other signatories would have to accept it, directly or tacitly.[9]

Mild reservationists had a chance to talk directly with Wilson starting on 17 July and continuing throughout the month. After the Republican members of the Foreign Relations Committee ignored Wilson's invitation to the White House, the president decided to follow the advice of Hitchcock and John Sharp Williams of Mississippi who had suggested that Wilson meet with individual Republican senators to try for conciliation.[10] In all, Wilson saw twenty-three senators between 17 July and 1 August, talking with each one for forty-five minutes to over an hour. He saw all the mild reservationists except Hale, who was viewed by the LEP as "following Lodge."[11] Meanwhile Wilson postponed his projected speaking tour.

Wilson made no converts in these interviews. On the contrary, put in the limelight as the object of presidential pressure and persuasion, each Republican senator reaffirmed his devotion to reservations. At the same time, the senators were given occasion to clarify their views, for themselves and for their colleagues, simplifying the

9. Henry C. Ferrell, Jr., *Claude A. Swanson of Virginia: A Political Biography*, 124, 125; *CR* 66:1, pp. 2542–43 (14 July 1919).

10. Arthur Walworth, *Woodrow Wilson*, 2:343; Thomas A. Bailey, *Woodrow Wilson and the Great Betrayal*, 74.

11. W. R. Boyd to William S. Short, n.d. [20 June 1919], Lowell Papers.

task for those who would formulate a definite program. As a result of the interviews, Wilson now understood that he must compromise, but he still did not appreciate the extent of the compromise needed.

McCumber, the only pro-League Republican on the Foreign Relations Committee, came first. He said afterwards that the president had given him much confidential information but had not attempted to change his attitude. "I prefer the ratification of the treaty as it stands now. If it is necessary to obtain sufficient votes for its ratification I would accept explanations regarding some features that are now opposed."[12]

Wilson's second visitor, unlike McCumber, had been very quiet on the League but in an occasional interview had intimated his attitude.[13] He was LeBaron Colt of Rhode Island, who would become a leader of the mild reservationists. Colt was born in Massachusetts in 1846 to a mercantile family that included Samuel Colt, LeBaron's uncle, inventor of the revolver. Colt grew up in Hartford, graduated from Yale and Columbia Law School, and established his law practice in Bristol, Rhode Island. He served briefly in the General Assembly of Rhode Island, and from 1881 to 1913 he presided over various federal courts. He impressed legal contemporaries by the judicial quality of his mind and temperament, his knowledge, and his fondness for work. In 1913 Colt was elected to the United States Senate by the assembly and in 1918 by the people.

A tall, spare man, white-haired, clean-shaven, and dignified in bearing, Colt had humor and charm. Usually sedate, he occasionally gave way to emotion. Colt spoke little in the Senate, but he spoke well. He gained some status as an authority on legal and constitutional questions. A conservative Republican on domestic questions and closer personally to Taft than to Lodge, Colt was not much of a partisan. He gave the Wilson administration full support during the war—more so than did his party's leaders.[14]

Strongly interested in international law, world politics, and diplomacy, Colt approached the League question from a nonpartisan standpoint. Increasingly, he became attached to the League cause. The large Irish-American element in Rhode Island made support for

12. *Providence Evening Tribune*, 18 July 1919; *New York World*, 18 July 1919.

13. For an expression of Colt's early views, see *Providence Sunday Tribune*, 18, 25, May 1919.

14. Allen Johnson and Dumas Malone, eds., *Dictionary of American Biography*, 4:317–18; Leonard Schlup, "A Senator of Principle: Some Correspondence Between LeBaron Bradford Colt and William Howard Taft," 3, 4; *Providence Evening Tribune*, 6, 17 July 1919, 2 March 1919; *Minneapolis Tribune*, 11 January 1920; David Lawrence in *St. Louis Post-Dispatch*, 18 July 1919; Carter Field, *Bernard Baruch*, 195.

the League increasingly hazardous politically, but more so for the Democratic senator, Peter Gerry, than for Colt. Colt's position, evidently, was supported by a pro-League element within his own party, spearheaded by the state's leading paper, the *Evening Tribune* of Providence.[15]

Colt thought it best to state his views in the Senate before calling on the president. Since he had been reticent to that time and was classed as "doubtful," and perhaps also because he was so well respected, senators gave him close attention.[16] Colt argued for joining the League at least through the immediate postwar period, to "see through to the end the great undertaking upon which we embarked in entering the war." Afterwards, if the League worked and did not prove so dangerous as its enemies said, the country could continue as a member. Some features of the Covenant appealed to Colt. In particular he recommended the provisions for compulsory international conferences and compulsory arbitration to head off wars, and he approved arms reduction provisions too.[17]

But Colt also supported reservations. He suggested the possibility of limiting the duration of Article 10 to the period required to make the settlements of the peace conference secure. Later, after meeting with Wilson, Colt said that he would not risk the League for a minor reservation, such as one on the right of withdrawal. But if persuaded that a reservation to Article 10 was desirable, he would run the risk of other powers seeking reservations of their own, despite Wilson's warnings on that score.[18]

The third and last senator to see the president on 17 July was Knute Nelson of Minnesota. Not much involved in the League controversy to that point and rarely prominent afterwards as either a speaker or a negotiator, Nelson would prove to be among the more steadfast of the mild reservationists, as well as a leader among them in his own way.

Born in Norway in 1843, Nelson grew up on a Wisconsin farm and in May 1861 enlisted in the Union army. Though wounded and held prisoner for a month, he served until the expiration of his enlistment in July 1864. The intense patriotism of his youth did not fade but grew with the years. Nelson read law and joined the bar in 1867. He entered the Wisconsin Assembly the same year. After moving to Minnesota in 1871, where he combined farming and law, he quickly

---

15. *Providence Evening Tribune*, 17 February 1919, editorial.
16. *New York World*, 18 July 1919; *St. Louis Post-Dispatch*, 18 July 1919.
17. *CR* 66:1, pp. 2721–22 (17 July 1919).
18. Ibid.; *Providence Evening Tribune*, 18 July 1919.

entered politics and won election to Congress, then the governorship, and finally in 1895 the Senate. He was a trailblazer for Norwegian-Americans in politics.

Short, broad, and blue-eyed, with gray chin whiskers, Nelson was simple and humble in manner, loyal to his friends, the best- known politician in the state, "the grand old man of Minnesota." He was a party regular, but in the Progressive Era he supported lower tariffs, which were popular in his state. When war came, however, he broke with the Minnesota delegation to denounce and vote against the Gore resolution in 1916, which warned Americans off armed merchant ships. From the first, he regarded Germany as a menace to the United States and privately hoped the United States would join the Allies.[19] Once America entered the war, Nelson gave the administration strong support. Wilson helped in the movement to draft Nelson for another term in 1918, but the Democratic National Committee supported his opponent. Nelson then criticized Wilson as an "intense partisan." His energies and spirits flagging, Nelson would be eighty-two at the end of his term and would not run again.[20]

Though prone to fits of anger, Nelson was a careful, cautious man. Viewing the League in the context of the full treaty, he studied the treaty closely. By mid-June he was satisfied. Harsh provisions concerning German disarmament and reparations would keep Germany at peace for fifty years.[21] For Nelson, the League was an instrument to enforce the terms of the treaty. But anti-Germanism and a belief in war atrocity stories were not Nelson's only motivation for backing the treaty. A voracious reader of history, he was convinced that the old order had failed. As an immigrant concerned about Europe, he rejected isolationism and embraced the idea of world organization and collective security.[22] Economic considerations and a fear of Bolshevism also informed his views.

After his interview with the president, Nelson said that he strongly opposed the Shantung award and favored a reservation on the sub-

19. Martin W. Odland, *The Life of Knute Nelson*; Nelson to Scott C. Bone, 2 December 1919, Knute Nelson Papers, Minnesota Historical Society.

20. Johnson and Malone, *Dictionary of American Biography*, 13:418–19; Millard L. Gieske, "The Politics of Knute Nelson, 1912–1920," 17–29, 54; Odland, *Knute Nelson*, 288, 259; Nelson to W. S. Durnnel, 25 November 1918, cited in Gieske, "Knute Nelson," 556; 561–66. See also Carl H. Chrislock, *Ethnicity Challenged: The Upper Midwest Norwegian-American Experience in World War I*, 34, 52–55, 68, 84–85, 115.

21. Nelson to L. M. Willcuts, 17 June 1919, to Charles Grant Miller, 14 March 1919, to Frances E. Earlart, 24 March 1919, and to A. D. Stephens, 26 March 1919, Nelson Papers.

22. Gieske, "Knute Nelson," 612, 632–33.

ject. He had been known to support reservations on the Monroe
Doctrine, immigration, and Article 10, and he declared that he had
not changed his mind.[23] Nelson's talk of reservations was tactical,
done "for the sake of harmony." Republicans, with a few Democrats,
would adopt reservations, he thought, and then other Democrats
would accept the necessity of reservations and would create a two-
thirds majority.[24]

Nelson reiterated his support for reservations in a Senate speech
that evoked much comment. Reactions varied. An anti-League reporter for a leading Minnesota paper wrote that the speech ended the
hope of many Democrats that they could ratify without reservations
and that Nelson drew into line "with the general Republican viewpoint more wavering Republican senators." On the other hand, a few
weeks later Lodge wrote Elihu Root, "The most uncertain man is Nelson, who is not what he was but whose temper is entirely unimpaired."[25]

On 18 July Kellogg and McNary saw Wilson. Kellogg emerged
unimpressed by Wilson's understanding of the treaty and of the
influence of the League Covenant on the United States. He was stiff-
ened in his opposition to features of the treaty. McNary had a more
agreeable talk with the president. He found himself in general agreement with Wilson and told him that he favored certain interpretations but would not support "any reservation which might compel
the resubmission of the treaty."[26]

Four days later McNary gave a speech that was his first formal
statement on the League, his first significant speech in the Senate,
and his last address on the League.[27] He called for nonpartisan consideration of the treaty and said that such an approach would speed a
solution. To strike Article 10 or to "limit, alter, or modify the moral
obligation would . . . operate as an amendment," he said. Other
powers would then seek concessions. In essence McNary found the
Covenant quite safe. But to appease the doubtful, he was willing to
support interpretive reservations, in a separate resolution, covering
Congress's right to declare war under Article 10 and protecting from

23. *Minneapolis Tribune*, 18 July 1919; *New York Times*, 18 July 1919; *New York World*, 18 July 1919.

24. Nelson to Everett B. Wheeler, 27 August 1919, to Charles S. Mitchell, 19 July 1919, and to Edward W. Decker, 25 July 1919, Nelson Papers.

25. *Minneapolis Tribune*, 31 July 1919; Lodge to Root, 15 August 1919, Root Papers.

26. Chandler P. Anderson Diary, entry for 30 July 1919, Anderson Papers; *Portland Oregonian*, 19 July 1919.

27. Roger T. Johnson, "Charles L. McNary and the Republican Party During Pros-perity and Depression," 33, 35–36.

League intrusion the Monroe Doctrine and domestic questions. "While a work of supererogation, if found comforting, it would have its own reward."[28]

That McNary would accept "interpretations" pleased Democratic leaders. At the White House conferences Wilson had argued against anything that would require renegotiation, but he had also asked for suggestions that would not change the nature of the contract with other nations, implying that he would accept a compromise. A deal seemed possible. Cautiously, noncommittally, Wilson was exploring the possibilities of innocuous reservations.[29] Administration senators sought a compromise with the seven "Twilight zone" senators who had seen the president—the five mild reservationists plus Capper and Kenyon. Such a deal would leave the Democrats in command of a majority. Encouraged by his first seven interviews, Wilson appeared at the Capitol in a cheerful frame of mind. He said that misinterpretations and misunderstandings were chiefly responsible for opposition to the treaty and that he simply needed to "clarify counsels." He would continue to see senators and was thinking of abandoning his tour.[30]

Lodge would have none of it. Wilson had made no converts. "The best solution would be to carry the reservations by majority vote. We will take no explanatory interpretations such as the President has begun to talk about."[31] At the same time, according to anti-Leaguers thirty-five senators had pledged to oppose the Covenant without reservations and a few others might join the group. Anti-Leaguers noted that sentiment was drifting toward amendments. If the president won some Republicans for interpretations and battled for the treaty on that basis, he would endanger the whole treaty, one senator warned.[32] By the end of July Lodge was able to assure anti-League friends, "We have votes that will kill the treaty if proper reservations are not put on—I mean the real thing, such as you and I believe in." And he said: "Our list of men who will not vote for the treaty without reservations—and any reservations we have will be

28. *CR* 66:1, p. 2984 (22 July 1919).

29. *New York World*, 19 July 1919; *New York Herald*, 19 July 1919; *Boston Herald*, 19 July 1919; William Wiseman to Arthur Balfour, 18 July 1919, in E. L. Woodward and Rohan Butler, eds., *Documents on British Foreign Policy, 1919–1939*, 5:984–85; Wilson to Thomas Lamont, 17 July 1919, Wilson Papers, in Kurt Wimer, "Woodrow Wilson Tries Conciliation: An Effort That Failed," 425.

30. *Minneapolis Tribune*, 21 July 1919; *Boston Herald*, 19 July 1919; *Minneapolis Tribune*, 19 July 1919.

31. Lodge to Will Hays, 19 July 1919, Lodge Papers.

32. *New York World*, 29 July 1919.

the real thing and will change the treaty so far as we are concerned—
is growing. . . . We are getting very close to 40 pledged to go down
the line."[33]

For some of the seven who had already seen Wilson, the interviews had opened opportunities but had raised hazards. To all of
them, Wilson had seemed receptive to reservations. To those most
ardent for the League—Colt, McNary, Nelson, and McCumber—the
reservations that the president would accept, which were interpretive ones that would not be amendatory and would not require
renegotiation, squared with their own desires, which Kellogg shared.
But clearly Wilson wanted reservations, or "interpretations," in a separate resolution. Initially McNary agreed. Evidently the others had
doubts, and McNary soon changed his mind. Lodge had the votes to
reject the treaty if satisfactory reservations were not appended to the
resolution of ratification. Encouraging the Democrats, to the point
even of giving them a majority for a separate resolution, courted
disaster for the treaty, as well as political damage. Further, if the
strongest pro-League Republicans acted alone with the Democrats,
the remaining middle grounders would be weakened in their own
party councils.

The mild reservationists did what they had to do. Acting singly
and together, they drew up reservations "that might be made without injury to the treaty"; through Kellogg, they negotiated with
Lodge to get the fullest possible Republican support for their program; and they looked to Wilson to accept reservations publicly.
McCumber, McNary, and Kellogg took the lead, but Colt and Spencer,
a moderate, were among the "number of senators" active in the work.[34]

The president issued no public statement, but pressed ahead in
his missionary work with senators. On 22 July he met with Walter
Edge and two others. Edge said afterwards that he thought fair reservations would be promptly accepted abroad. "America should never
be a minority stockholder in an international corporation," the
business-minded senator said.[35]

The following day Thomas Sterling was one of Wilson's four call-
ers. Shantung was discussed at length in other interviews, but Sterling was more concerned about Article 10. He could not accept the

33. Lodge to James M. Beck, 29 July 1919, and to Louis A. Coolidge, 30 July 1919,
Lodge Papers.
34. Porter McCumber to William Howard Taft, 24 July 1919, Taft Papers; Kellogg
to Lodge, 22 July 1919, Lodge Papers; *Des Moines Register*, 27 July 1919; *New York
Times*, 24 July 1919; *Minneapolis Tribune*, 24 July 1919.
35. *Boston Herald*, 23 July 1919.

article without a reservation that allowed Congress to decide what part the nation would play in European conflict. Sterling again stressed Article 10 in a speech to the Senate on 4 August. Though in sympathy with much of the Covenant, he said that he could not vote to ratify without reservations.[36]

Among the last of the Republican senators to see Wilson was Lenroot, one of four invited for 30 July. Six days before, Lenroot had presented his views in detail in the Senate. He wanted Americans to know that most Republicans favored the treaty if reservations were adopted, and he urged the Foreign Relations Committee to report soon. His main objection was to Article 10, which could oblige the nation to fight in unjust wars. On this and on domestic questions he wanted "explicit reservations," although he was content with interpretive reservations on withdrawal and the Monroe Doctrine. On 30 July he told this to the president and said that these steps were prerequisites of ratification. Lenroot and the three others who saw Wilson that day concluded that he was beginning to see the need for reservations.[37]

Wilson saw two senators on 31 July and the final senator on 1 August. One of his 31 July visitors was Henry Keyes of New Hampshire, a fifty-six-year-old freshman senator who had been very quiet not only on the League but also on other questions, as was customary for newcomers to the Senate. After graduating from Harvard, he had given himself to politics, banking, business, and farming. Not wealthy and somewhat shy, he could not afford high-stakes golf and bridge, and in the words of his wife, Frances Parkinson Keyes, he "did not completely fit into the political picture."[38]

The League of Free Nations had been active in his state, and in February the legislature unanimously endorsed a League of Nations. On the other hand, Hiram Johnson was well received in Manchester in early July; Keyes's colleague Senator George Moses was highly critical of the Covenant and was on the way to becoming an irreconcilable; and the most influential publisher in the state, Frank Knox, was skeptical about the League, though not an irreconcilable.[39] From a political standpoint, then, Keyes stood to benefit by keeping

36. *St. Louis Post-Dispatch*, 23 July 1919; *New York Herald*, 24 July 1919; *CR* 66:1, pp. 3607–11 (4 August 1919).

37. *CR* 66:1, pp. 3090–95 (24 July 1919); *New York Times*, 31 July 1919; *New York Herald*, 31 July 1919.

38. Frances Parkinson Keyes, *All Flags Flying: Reminiscences of Frances Parkinson Keyes*, 108–10, 8, 13.

39. *Boston Herald*, 1 June 1919; *Manchester Union*, 23 May, 6 February, 11 July, 14 March, 4, 12 April, 23, 25 July 1919.

some distance from Wilson. But the position he adopted was that of a mild reservationist. Late in August Lodge noted that Keyes was not one of those pledged to vote against ratification if reservations failed.[40]

Following his talk with Wilson, Keyes told reporters that he had spent a pleasant hour but had not been converted. More than ever, he wanted reservations, "or to use the word I understand the President prefers, interpretations." If any language in the Covenant was unclear or subject to varying interpretations, "now is the time to record our interpretations or understanding."[41] Keyes's comments were not what Wilson had hoped to hear. Viewed from a different standpoint, however, the senator's use of the words *interpretations* and *understanding* as synonymous with *reservations* suggests that at this time, at least, Keyes sought nothing that would change the terms or meanings of the Covenant and that he might be counted on to support compromise on the basis of truly mild reservations.

As the White House interviews ended (partly because Wilson had to devote himself to urgent domestic problems), the mild reservationists were trying to formulate a reservationist program that they could agree on and that they could take to their colleagues. Their efforts were complicated somewhat by the public involvement of Taft and then of Hughes. On 24 July newspapers published leaked copies of two letters from Taft to Hays in which Taft presented six reservations, to be kept secret for a time but to be used as a basis for compromise after the Foreign Relations Committee's amendments and reservations had been defeated. Taft expressed the hope, as he had in direct correspondence with the senators, that McCumber, McNary, and Colt would join the Democrats in blocking anything destructive and that one of them would then present Taft's proposals.[42]

In the leaked letters Taft called for interpretive reservations within the resolution of ratification. The most controversial of the proposals—to limit Article 10 to a ten-year period, after which it might be renewed—he felt sure the Allies would accept. He construed it as an interpretation, not an amendment. Coming from the president of

40. Keyes, *All Flags Flying*, 136–37; Lodge to James T. Williams, Jr., 20 August 1919, Lodge Papers. Walter Edge remembered Keyes as a mild reservationist (Walter Evans Edge, *A Jerseyman's Journal: Fifty Years of American Business and Politics*, 117).

41. *Manchester Union*, 1 August 1919; *New York Times*, 1 August 1919.

42. *New York Times*, 24 July 1919; Taft to LeBaron Colt, 15 and 16 July 1919, to Charles McNary, 16 and 19 July 1919, and to Porter J. McCumber, 16 and 19 July 1919, Taft Papers.

the LEP, a man who had spearheaded the organization's campaign for unreserved ratification and who was the leading Republican advocate of the League of Nations, the letters caused a sensation.[43]

The LEP fell into rancorous disarray. After talking of a new national organization, Democratic leaders of the LEP headed by William Gibbs McAdoo and Vance McCormick secured a unanimous adoption by the LEP Executive Committee of a resolution reaffirming support for unconditional ratification. The Democrats also increased their propaganda efforts through the LEP machinery.[44] Taft could not and would not recant, and other Republicans in the LEP leadership, such as Lowell and Oscar Straus, backed him.[45]

For the moment, the publication of Taft's letters did no harm to mild reservationism and perhaps helped a bit. The mild reservationists were in consultation with Lodge, and at that time Lodge was seeking little more in the way of reservations than proposed by Taft. With Hays, who had issued his own reservationist statement that was similar to Taft's, Lodge saw reservationism as a basis for party unity, so long as reservations were in the resolution of ratification, as Taft proposed.[46] And the best chance for ratification was in this period, July and August.

Charles Evans Hughes, with Root and Taft one of the main luminaries of the Republican party, pitched in for a program of four reservations, writing a letter to Senator Hale dated 24 July and published 28 July. Lodge had asked for Hughes's help for reservationism earlier that month, and Hays had set out to get it. Hughes was at first inclined to go along with Root and advocate elimination of Article 10, but Hays persuaded him to seek only modification. With Root and Taft, Hughes argued for reservations in the resolution of ratification, but he also asserted that tacit acceptance by other signatories would suffice. Coming so soon after the pub-

43. Taft to Will Hays, 17 and 19 July 1919, Taft Papers. The source of the leak remains unclear. Some information is provided in Gus Karger to William Howard Taft, 23 July 1919, Taft Papers; in H. H. Kohlsaat to Woodrow Wilson, 7 August 1919, Wilson Papers; and in the *Boston Sunday Herald*, 27 July 1919.

44. *St. Louis Post-Dispatch*, 26 July 1919; William G. McAdoo to Woodrow Wilson, 31 July 1919, Wilson Papers; Elizabeth H. Bohn to Herbert Parsons, 11 August 1919, Parsons Papers.

45. Taft to William Short, 21 and 24 August 1919, and to Gus Karger, 24 August 1919, Taft Papers; Charles DeBenedetti, *Origins of the Modern American Peace Movement, 1915–1929*, 23.

46. Frank Kellogg to William Howard Taft, 28 July 1919, Kellogg Papers; Lodge to Hays, 19 July 1919, Lodge Papers; Will H. Hays, *The Memoirs of Will H. Hays*, 211–12; Hays to Albert J. Beveridge, 8 July 1919, Beveridge Papers.

lication of the Taft letters, Hughes's letter evoked only mild interest. But Kellogg, who had seen it in advance, thought it useful. Certainly it added weight to the program the mild reservationists were
developing.[47]

The efforts of the mild reservationists came to a head in two long
meetings held on 30 and 31 July in McCumber's office. Besides
McCumber and McNary, described by reporters as the leaders of the
group, the participants were Colt, Kellogg, Lenroot, and moderates
Cummins and Spencer, with Hale sitting in as an observer and liaison to stronger reservationists. Their purpose was to agree on the
wording of reservations covering the four topics suggested by Root.[48]

The group convened with the blessings of Lodge, who had met
with some or all of them at his home a few days earlier. Reportedly,
Lodge was angry with Borah for urging Democrats to vote against
reservations, and for that reason Lodge was accelerating his long-
standing efforts to get a party agreement on a specific program.
Lodge was already thinking of something more—amendments. And
in some other ways too he was not in full agreement with the mild
reservationists. But he remained concerned about uniting his party
against unqualified ratification. Since he knew that a few of the mild
reservationists held out against accepting the Root program as originally presented, with its repudiation of Article 10, he thought it
advantageous to get them to formulate a program themselves, clinch-
ing their opposition to unreserved ratification.[49]

The group of seven was a disparate lot, and its members found it
hard to agree, especially on Article 10. McNary wanted to leave the
article alone. Surprising to many, Colt wanted a strong reservation.
Cummins wanted to strike out the article altogether. Spencer vacil-
lated, having received much anti-League mail and having been told

47. Lodge to Elihu Root, 7 July 1919, Root Papers; Charles Hilles to William
Howard Taft, 17 July 1919, Taft Papers; Dexter Perkins, *Charles Evans Hughes and
American Democratic Statesmanship,* 79; Kellogg to William Howard Taft, 28 July
1919, Kellogg Papers.

48. McCumber to William Howard Taft, 31 July 1919, Taft Papers; *Minneapolis
Tribune,* 1 August 1919. Hale was also present when Kellogg met Chandler Anderson
for lunch on 30 July for discussions with Anderson about the specific wording of
reservations (Anderson Diary, entry for 30 July 1919, Anderson Papers).

49. Kellogg to Taft, 28 July 1919, Kellogg Papers; *New York World,* 27 July 1919;
Gus J. Karger to William Howard Taft, 31 July 1919, Taft Papers. Indicative of Lodge's
involvement are the following: Kellogg to Elihu Root, 21 August 1919, Root Papers;
Kellogg to William Howard Taft, 28 July 1919, Kellogg Papers; Chandler P. Anderson
Diary, entry for 30 July 1919, Anderson Papers; *New York Herald,* 31 July 1919; *New
York World,* 2 August 1919. Lodge expressed pleasure at the mild reservationist
efforts, in Lodge to Louis A. Coolidge, 2 August 1919, Lodge Papers.

by the state party chairman that opinion was running against the League. Disgusted, McNary said Spencer "flops around like a herring on dry land." Elected for a short term in 1918 "because of his church connections and general standing," Spencer faced uncertain reelection prospects in 1920. On 4 August Spencer left for Missouri to review the situation firsthand and to mend fences.[50]

When the seven reached an agreement on 31 July it remained tentative with respect to Article 10 and the senators understood that in any case the agreed-on reservations should be simply points of departure for negotiations with others. The seven agreed that the reservation program should become part of the treaty and not simply a separate resolution of interpretation. But they disagreed as to the character of their proposals. Some saw them as merely interpretive, whereas others felt that they modified treaty terms.[51] The difficulties and the divergences of interpretation were not surprising. McNary and McCumber saw reservations as a matter of practical necessity but not as inherently desirable; the others thought that reservations were necessary to protect the United States, and some of these senators protested at the use of the word *mild*.[52]

Indeed the seven came together for widely varying reasons. Each senator had mixed motives, of course, but the paramount goal for McNary, McCumber, and Colt was to advance peace through the League in the face of postwar turbulence and in the future. Lenroot, Spencer, and Cummins were in varying degrees concerned about peace but were also anxious to be done with the issue of the treaty, for reasons of politics and the need for domestic legislation. Kellogg shared the goals of both groups and strived as well for the normality of trade that peace would bring.

50. *Boston Herald*, 1 August 1919; *Minneapolis Tribune*, 1 1 August 1919; *CR* 66:1, p. 6926 (15 October 1919); *New York Times*, 5 August 1919; *CR* 66:1, p. 5957 (26 September 1919); *St. Louis Post-Dispatch*, 28 July 1919; *New York World*, 2 August 1919. Spencer also thought that national sentiment was swinging against the League (Spencer to Nicholas Murray Butler, 4 August 1919, Butler Papers). Gus Karger to William Howard Taft, 4 August 1919, Taft Papers; *St. Louis Post-Dispatch*, 27 June 1919; *New York World*, 5 August 1919. For the Missouri situation at this time, see the *St. Louis Post-Dispatch*, 27, 28 July, 1, 6 August 1919.

51. *New York World*, 3, 5 August 1919; *New York Times*, 4, 5 August 1919; *New York Tribune*, 2 August 1919. McNary, McCumber, and Colt considered their proposals to be interpretive (*Boston Herald*, 18 August 1919; Gus Karger to William Howard Taft, 21 August 1919, Taft Papers).

52. McNary to David Starr Jordan, 19 August 1919, David Starr Jordan Papers, Hoover Institution on War, Revolution, and Peace, Stanford University; McNary to William Gibbs McAdoo, 26 July 1919, William Gibbs McAdoo Papers, Library of Congress; McCumber to Henry White, 9 August 1919, H. White Papers; Theodore E. Burton to William Howard Taft, 21 July 1919, Taft Papers; *The World*, 5 August 1919.

Given the diffuseness of the group, it is not surprising that the members had trouble agreeing, that their agreements, especially on Article 10, were only tentative, and that they placed varying interpretations on their proposed reservations. What is surprising is that they agreed at all. The explanation lay in the willingness of McNary, McCumber, Colt, and Kellogg to make concessions to Lenroot, Spencer, and Cummins, who were closest to the center of the party. Beyond these three were others, chiefly middle grounders, whose votes were needed. Lodge already had his forty or more votes to defeat an unsatisfactory ratification. The mildest reservationists saw little point in joining with the Democrats to create a sterile majority. They needed twenty Republicans, in hand or in prospect, before they could effectively deal with the Democrats, and for that they had to make concessions.

The group did substantially advance its cause. However tentative, the senators agreed to the wording of reservations on Root's four topics. Reservations must be in the resolution of ratification—an important concession to necessity by McNary, in particular. The senators understood the importance of Shantung but hoped that the issue might be resolved by diplomacy—that Japan would soon set a date to restore the province to China—so they agreed to confine their reservations to matters in the Covenant.[53]

They agreed on tactics too. They would not immediately submit their reservations to either Lodge or Hitchcock but would instead try to expand their number. Once they had twenty, they thought, their group would control the situation. The twenty, united with forty-four of the forty-seven Democrats, could ratify. Most Republicans, under the leadership of Lodge, were expected to fall in line behind the program of reservations, with only the small band of irreconcilables expected to desert on the final vote—on treaty approval with the reservations attached.[54]

The least controversial reservations related to withdrawal and domestic questions. In each case, the proposed reservation asserted what the Democrats claimed was already implicit in the Covenant: the United States alone would judge whether it had met conditions for withdrawal after it had given two years' notice; and the United States alone would decide what constituted domestic questions, which would not be subject to League review. The third reservation, related to the Monroe Doctrine, stated, "The United States does not

53. *St. Louis Post-Dispatch*, 3 August 1919; *Portland Oregonian*, 3 August 1919.
54. *New York Times*, 1 August 1919; *New York Tribune*, 2 August 1919.

bind itself to submit for arbitration or inquiry by the Assembly or the Council any question which in the judgment of the United States depends upon or involves its long-established policy commonly known as the Monroe Doctrine, and it is preserved unaffected by any provision of the said treaty contained." The second reservation, to Article 10, was the most controversial. It stated:

That the suggestions of the council of the league of nations as to the means of carrying the obligations of Article X into effect are only advisory, and that any undertaking under the provisions of Article X, the execution of which may require the use of American military or naval forces or economic measures, can under the Constitution be carried out only by the action of the Congress, and that failure of the Congress to adopt the suggestions of the council of the league, or to provide such military or naval forces or economic measures, shall not constitute a violation of the treaty.[55]

McNary feared that the reservations might have gone too far, and he asked Taft's opinion. Taft thought that the four reservations did indeed go too far and objected especially to the one on Article 10, which he construed as denying any obligation.[56] Most senators disagreed with Taft, as later events showed. Certainly, by later standards all four reservations were "mild."

Republican senators responded warily. Newsmen reported the adherence of Nelson and of Arthur Capper, a publisher of farm journals who had served as state chairman of the LEP while governor of Kansas. But James Watson of Indiana, who was reported to favor the reservations, quickly recanted, and other Republicans held aloof for the time being.[57]

For the Democrats, Gilbert Hitchcock dismissed the compromise proposal and predicted unreserved ratification. His statement followed a conference with Wilson, and he knew that his uncompromising stance comported with Wilson's hopes. Beyond that, it reflected his own view, which he had maintained throughout the summer. One reason for his persistent optimism was a reliance on economic pressures. A month later, when he spoke in the Senate for unreserved ratification, Hitchcock stressed the economic advan-

55. *New York Tribune*, 2 August 1919. The text of the four reservations is in *CR* 66:1, p. 3690 (7 August 1919), as presented by Kellogg.

56. Gus Karger to William Howard Taft, 4 August 1919, and Taft to Karger, 15 August 1919, Taft Papers.

57. Homer E. Socolofsky, *Arthur Capper: Publisher, Politician, and Philanthropist*, 126; *Minneapolis Tribune*, 3, 4, 6 August 1919; *New York Times*, 3 August 1919.

tages of a speedy ratification. But the idea was not new and had already been stated when the seven Republicans made their proposals.[58]

Hitchcock had reason to hope for special help from liquor interests. The prohibition amendment to the Constitution would come into effect on 1 January 1920. Producers of whiskey, beer, and wine wanted to unload their stocks before then. Though wartime hostilities were long ended, wartime prohibition was still on. Just two days after he disparaged the mild reservationists' efforts, Hitchcock met with a representative of the whiskey makers. He said that until the treaty was approved by the Senate and signed by the president, and until the army was demobilized, Wilson would not lift wartime prohibition.[59]

Although Key Pittman shared Hitchcock's optimism, other Democrats did not. Following the tentative agreement among the seven Republicans, these Democrats cautiously talked with Republicans of compromise. It is not clear, however, whether they accepted the idea of reservations in the resolution of ratification or insisted on a separate resolution.[60]

On 6 August four LEP leaders—Vance McCormick, Oscar Straus, William Short, and A. Lawrence Lowell—met with the president, in the interests of compromise. Wilson said that he would be willing to respond to a letter from a middle grounder and that in his response he would explain that his construction of the Covenant coincided with their interpretations of the four controverted points. In his view, this letter would obviate the need for reservations. The LEP men then asked Kellogg to write the letter of inquiry. Kellogg said that reservations would be needed in any case, but he felt that such a statement by Wilson would be helpful. He would write the letter, in cooperation with Hitchcock, if his six colleagues approved. Nothing more came of it. Perhaps his colleagues did not approve, or perhaps Hitchcock, learning of Kellogg's conditions, scotched the plan. The absence from Washington of Spencer may have inhibited Kellogg. After that, Wilson looked toward a meeting with the Foreign Relations Committee as a vehicle for expounding his views.[61]

Mild reservationists had earlier hoped for a statement from Wil-

58. *New York Tribune*, 1 August 1919; *New York Herald*, 30 July 1919; *CR* 66:1, pp. 4726–31 (3 September 1919); Robert Lansing to Gary M. Jones, 4 August 1919, Robert Lansing Papers, Library of Congress.

59. *New York Times*, 3 August 1919.

60. Pittman to Hamilton Holt, 31 July 1919, Pittman Papers; *Des Moines Register*, 1 August 1919; *New York Tribune*, 8 August 1919.

61. A. Lawrence Lowell to William Howard Taft, 7 August 1919, Taft Papers; Oscar S. Straus, *Under Four Administrations: From Cleveland to Taft*, 428–29; Wimer, "Wilson Tries Conciliation," 428.

son, but the letter Wilson might have written would have accomplished little by that time. He could win no substantial number of Republicans with anything short of reservations, some of them "specific," in the resolution of ratification, and that he would not agree to. As of 7 August the minimum terms available to the administration—and it is far from certain that even these could have won ample Republican support—were those presented by Kellogg in his long awaited speech to the Senate. The terms were the four reservations prepared by the group of seven, to be incorporated in the resolution of ratification. Kellogg appended them in the *Record* at the end of his speech.[62]

Kellogg discussed the critical issue of renegotiation. He asserted, "Where either an amendment or a reservation clearly changes the meaning of the treaty it will require the instrument to be resubmitted to all other signatory powers." But there were precedents, he noted, for tacit acceptance. On reservations Kellogg, like most others, concerned himself chiefly with Article 10. He did not favor striking it out, as Root had suggested, because "it would not be a part of the treaty as between other nations." European nations had use for Article 10 in their intra-European relations, he thought. As to the United States, Kellogg acknowledged that the nation was interested in preventing Germany from becoming a menace and "in maintaining the stability of certain nations which have been formed through the results of this war. . . . But to perpetually guarantee the territorial integrity and political independence of every nation in the world in distant continents is quite another proposition." He wanted a reservation stating that Congress has the sole power to declare war and commit military and naval forces and that a failure to contribute would not be construed as a violation of the Covenant.[63]

The senator then talked of his hopes. "I am anxious that this treaty be ratified at the earliest possible date, the war ended, our soldiers returned home, and the country permitted to return to normal peace conditions." He did not think the League would end all war but recognized it as an experiment. He saw the League as consonant with the thrust of American policy over the previous twenty-five years toward "arbitration, international understanding, and pacific settlement of disputes." To reject the League would be to take a step backward.[64]

62. *Des Moines Register*, 27 July 1919; *CR* 66:1, pp. 3680–91 (7 August 1919).
63. *CR* 66:1, pp. 3691–93 (7 August 1919).
64. Ibid.

Following Kellogg's speech, Pittman argued that reservations would alter the contract and would require the assent of all signatories. Kellogg talked again of silent acquiescence, which he said had been the practice in the past. But Lodge declared his hope that when reservations were added the Senate would provide for overt acceptance by "at least the other four of the five principal allied and associated powers." He added: "There will be no question about it. They will accept them." Kellogg, responding to a question, again emphasized that a reservation would become binding on other parties once they put the "contract" into effect, and McCumber and Nelson agreed. But Brandegee, Poindexter, and Borah argued for explicit assent.[65]

During the following week of conferences and negotiations the League had its best chance in the Senate. A group of Democrats led by Swanson made an attractive offer to the mild reservationists, through McNary. Implicitly, Swanson accepted the Kellogg reservations and the requirement that reservations be in the instrument of ratification. Swanson said that if McNary could get twenty Republicans to support the Kellogg reservations, "the Democrats would join them in putting them over."[66] McNary had good reason to take these overtures very seriously, considering the source. Swanson had given the opening address on the League in July, and although soon passed over as presidential spokesman, he had continued periodically to consult with the president. Senators remembered the bad blood between Wilson and Hitchcock over the years and probably considered their rapprochement to be cosmetic.[67]

Other Democratic leaders joined in the compromise effort, trying to help McNary get his twenty and, as they viewed it, win ratification by letting the Republicans save face. Furnifold Simmons of North Carolina, Atlee Pomerene of Ohio, and Tom Walsh of Montana, members of the Foreign Relations Committee, pushed for compromise, as did the prospective party leader Oscar Underwood of Alabama, John Bankhead of Alabama, and Pat Harrison of Mississippi. They sought no prior commitment from Wilson; instead, they proposed to complete a deal and then offer it to him. But from

65. Ibid.

66. The words quoted are Gus Karger's (Karger to William Howard Taft, 11 August 1919, Taft Papers). Karger wrote that the Taft reservations were the basis of discussion, but events soon showed that this was not the case.

67. As late as 25 October, after Wilson had suffered a stroke, Warren Harding, commenting on the president's health, wrote, "I do not know that anyone in the Senate, outside of Senator Swanson, really knows the truth" (Harding to F. E. Scobey, 25 October 1919, Harding Papers).

Lowell, McNary got the impression that Wilson would accept a deal based on the Kellogg reservations.[68]

It remained for the mild reservationists, led in negotiations by McNary, to win over fellow Republicans. In their favor was a widespread public unhappiness about the delay in making peace. The issue of the high cost of living came to a head early in August. Railroad workers, still employees of the government under wartime law, demanded a wage boost to keep up with costs and threatened a crippling strike. Wilson capitalized on the situation. In an 8 August address to Congress on the high cost of living, the president linked that issue with the continuance of the legal state of war, and he urged speedy ratification. The wave of postwar strikes and accompanying evidences of radicalism augmented public unhappiness over the treaty delay.[69]

But though the public was growing impatient at the delay in ratification, it was also becoming less friendly to the League, as senators of various factions noted.[70] The anti-League drift sprang from a number of sources. Irreconcilables and Irish-American spokesmen stirred discontent, and Wilson refused to supply documents, including even the French Guarantee Treaty, requested by the Foreign Relations Committee and the Senate, providing anti-Wilson fodder for hostile senators. In addition the Shantung issue lingered as Japan made no promises and as Secretary of State Robert Lansing testified before the Foreign Relations Committee. He stated that at Paris he had thought the president need not give in to Japan on Shantung but that he had been largely ignored on that and on other matters.[71]

Senatorial ill will toward Wilson also hampered the mild reservationists. The president's reluctance to provide requested documents

68. *New York World*, 11, 18 August 1919; *St. Louis Post-Dispatch*, 21 August 1919; Robert Lansing Desk Books, 1919, entry for 22 November 1919, Lansing Papers; H. N. Rickey to William Short, n.d. (ca. 15 August 1919), LEP Papers; Gus J. Karger to William Howard Taft, 11 August 1919, Taft Papers.

69. *New York Times*, 1–9 August 1919; *New York World*, 1–9 August 1919. For comments on public concern about inflation, see William Gibbs McAdoo to Woodrow Wilson, 31 July 1919, and Huston Thompson to Wilson, 31 July 1919, Wilson Papers.

70. George Moses, in the *New York Herald*, 25 July 1919; Hiram Johnson to Franklin Hichborn, 31 July 1919, and to Hiram Johnson, Jr., and Arch Johnson, 23 August 1919, Johnson Papers; Henry Cabot Lodge to John W. Weeks, 31 July 1919, Lodge Papers; Selden Spencer to Nicholas Murray Butler, 18 August 1919, Butler Papers; Warren Harding to H. M. Daugherty, 25 July 1919, and to F. E. Scobey, 2 September 1919, Harding Papers; Ralph B. Levering, *The Public and American Foreign Policy, 1918–1978*, 44–45.

71. Walworth, *Wilson*, 2:346; Holt, *Treaties Defeated by the Senate*, 281; *Minneapolis Tribune*, 6–8 August 1919; Bailey, *Great Betrayal*, 82–83.

and his use of the cost of living situation as an excuse for another ratification appeal reinforced animosity. Lodge, who considered Wilson dangerous to American constitutional government and to the nation's independence and safety, was emotionally engaged. "Personal animosity to the President is the great influence against the treaty," Lansing wrote a friend early in August. But Nelson felt that there was something else, something more important to senators: "an unwillingness to mix in the local affairs of Europe." Earlier speeches by Sterling, Kellogg, and Lenroot, among the milder Republicans, illustrated this point.[72]

Despite Swanson's overture and the activity of other Democrats, most Republicans declined commitment pending a speech by Lodge announced for 12 August—Lodge's first address on the treaty since its submission to the Senate.[73] The speech gave scant comfort to the mild reservationists. Lodge took a reservationist position, but the burden of his speech was a criticism of the League as a new Holy Alliance that embodied dangerous and unrealistic commitments. Throughout, and especially at the end, he invoked American nationalism as a basis to oppose the "murky covenant."[74] For three minutes, in an unprecedented display that perhaps influenced senators afterward, Marine veterans and others in the galleries shouted and cheered. Down below, Republicans came up to shake Lodge's hand. Lodge was pleased with his effort, and even pro-Leaguers acknowledged the influence of his speech.[75]

In his speech and in private conferences, Lodge went beyond the program of the group of seven. He advocated reservations on the four conventional subjects, but not necessarily the wording submitted by Kellogg. Further, he urged a fifth reservation, one that would allow the Senate to confirm American representatives to the League. And as before, he insisted that Britain, France, Italy, and Japan formally assent to American reservations. Otherwise, reservations would be meaningless, he said, and he would not support them.[76]

72. Robert Small in *Minneapolis Tribune*, 17, 18 July 1919; Lodge to James M. Beck, 30 September 1920, and to Andrew F. West, 22 August 1919, Lodge Papers; Lansing to Gary M. Jones, 4 August 1919, Lansing Papers; Nelson to Soren Listoe, 2 December 1919, Nelson Papers.

73. Also, the mild reservationists awaited the return of Spencer (*Minneapolis Tribune*, 11 August 1919).

74. *CR* 66:1, pp. 3778–84 (12 August 1919).

75. *New York Times*, 13 August 1919; Lodge to J.D.H. Luce, 18 August 1919, Lodge Papers; W. H. Short to William Howard Taft, 14 August 1919, and Gus Karger to Taft, 21 August 1919, Taft Papers.

76. *CR* 66:1, pp. 3778–84 (12 August 1919); *New York World*, 16 August 1919.

But Lodge was not scuttling the party unity he had done so much to forge. Root, more than anyone else, had drawn the pro-League Republicans into the reservationist fold. The fifth reservation that Lodge now proposed had been included in Root's suggestions to Hays in his letter of 29 March, albeit at the suggestion of George Harvey.[77] And in his 21 June letter to Lodge, Root—again at the suggestion of others and only as one of several possibilities—had written of securing assent from the four main allied and associated powers. Without reminding him of the qualification, Lodge referred to Root's role as he requested further help from the elder statesman in dealing with Colt and Kellogg. Lodge wanted them to support "real reservations" and "above all . . . requiring the assent of the other four principal allied and associated powers before they become binding."[78] Clearly, Lodge was not ready to break with the mild reservationists or with Root, who had their confidence.

In the same regard, Lodge had been claiming, since 20 July, that he had assurances from a prominent British leader that Britain and France would readily accept American reservations on the conventional topics.[79] Probably he had in mind the letter from Lord Bryce that Root had passed on to him two weeks before. Whatever the source of his confidence, he felt that the mild reservationists could accept his proposals without risk to the treaty.

Despite Lodge's hardened attitude, McNary continued to confer regularly with him, seeking his personal support and his assistance in winning other Republicans.[80] Nor did the mild reservationists object when Lodge showed the Republicans a set of five reservations, not authored by him but a composite, that differed in some respects from their own.[81] From the first, they had not insisted on their wording but had viewed it as a starting point for negotiations with potential adherents.

Lodge and the mild reservationists were continuing what would prove to be a prolonged game of cat and mouse. Each needed the other, but their ideas and interests did not fully coincide. For party unity, and to honor his own convictions, Lodge was less than mild, but he hoped to draw the mild reservationists to him by promise and threat. The mild reservationists needed his help first to win twenty Republicans and then to win the rest, and they understood that he

77. Henry L. Stimson Diaries, entry for 29 March 1919, Stimson Papers.
78. Lodge to Root, 15 August 1919, Root Papers.
79. *New York Times*, 21 July 1919.
80. Ibid., 12, 15 August 1919; *Des Moines Register*, 13 August 1919.
81. *St. Louis Post-Dispatch*, 15, 16 August 1919; *New York Times*, 16 August 1919.

needed them to preserve majority control. But the mild reservationists realized too that Lodge was not entirely of their mind and that he responded to pressures from anti-Leaguers. Thus, just as he brought pressure on them through harsher proposals all the while conferring with them on reservations and stratagems, so they supplemented their cooperation with pressure. Specifically, soon after Lodge's speech five of them said that they would cooperate with Hitchcock in an effort to bring the treaty to the Senate floor, if the Foreign Relations Committee delayed further. Lodge decided, over the protests of Knox and Borah, to report the treaty in about three weeks.[82]

The relationship between Lodge and the mild reservationists had a sense of urgency at this time, for between 13 and 15 August the Swanson group of Democrats wooed Republicans with unprecedented ardor. They realized that a deal based on Kellogg's terms was the best they could do and that it had better be done swiftly, before the situation deteriorated further. Thus, what had earlier been a semiconfidential matter between Swanson and McNary now became a matter of public knowledge: if the Republicans could bring over twenty votes, the Democrats would at least present the possibilities to Wilson. For their part, despite Shantung and the other factors working against them, the mild reservationists found many of their Republican colleagues receptive to a deal because of their strong desire to end the matter and to address domestic problems, thereby avoiding blame for high living costs. As of 15 August, polls taken by McNary and Charles Curtis, the latter at the behest of Lodge, showed that eighteen Republicans would support reservations along the lines presented by the group of seven if the treaty could be brought promptly out of committee and ratified on that basis. Five others were in doubt. Some talked of a party conference to bring the treaty out of committee.[83]

Lodge denied that a deal based on mild reservations was in the works. "We are not licked yet," he said.[84] And indeed no agreement had been reached on the wording of reservations. Even so, Hitchcock considered Democrats and Republicans to be close to rap-

82. *Des Moines Register*, 14, 16 August 1919; Harry S. New to Albert J. Beveridge, 13 August 1919, Beveridge Papers; Jack E. Kendrick, "The League of Nations and the Republican Senate, 1918–1921," 194.

83. *New York Times*, 15 August 1919; *New York Tribune*, 16 August 1919; H. N. Rickey to William Short, n.d. [mid-August 1919], LEP Papers; Gus Karger to William Howard Taft, 21 August 1919, Taft Papers. Sterling was prominent among the eighteen. Karger thought Taft should talk with him, McNary, McCumber, Lenroot, and Kellogg.

84. *Boston Herald*, 15 August 1919.

prochement. But before going to the White House to discuss the matter with Wilson, Hitchcock talked with McNary and with another Republican identified only as "one of the treaty's staunchest friends."[85] The latter, probably McCumber, warned Hitchcock that ratification without reservations was impossible and that in the event of a vote on acceptance or rejection of the treaty as it stood, only three Republican votes could be counted for ratification. Hitchcock asked McNary for the results of the poll and reportedly was told that twenty to twenty-five Republicans favored ratification with the Kellogg reservations and that there was no chance for unqualified ratification.[86]

It is not known what advice Hitchcock gave Wilson. But other Democrats, including Lansing and McAdoo, had advised compromise, and Pittman had warned that most Democrats favored reservations.[87] Wilson was not swayed. In his discussion with Hitchcock he brushed aside the idea of an immediate deal and diverted the conversation to the dangers of the amendments that Foreign Relations Committee Republicans were talking of. Emerging from the White House, Hitchcock dutifully said: "In the opinion of the President, no compromise issue is now before the friends of the treaty and the League. This is not even the time to think of a compromise, much less to discuss it or negotiate it. The time for reservations to the treaty is still far off. There may have to be a compromise in the end, but at present that bridge is not being crossed."[88] Hitchcock also said that Wilson opposed even mild reservations on the grounds that Europe would think the United States was coming into the League halfheartedly.[89] This was more than a rationalization. Dubious of legalism, Wilson had from the first hoped for a new spirit in world affairs.[90] Wilson no doubt also feared prolonged renegotiation with attendant counter-reservations from other signatories while Europe remained in a state of turbulence. He had often warned of this in his interviews with senators. In addition, Wilson's personal good faith was at stake. He had assured his British and French colleagues that the Senate would approve the treaty.[91]

85. Ibid., 16 August 1919.

86. *New York World*, 16 August 1919.

87. Lansing Desk Books, 1919, entry for 11 August 1919, Lansing Papers; William Gibbs McAdoo, *Crowded Years: The Reminiscences of William G. McAdoo*, 514; Wimer, "Wilson Tries Conciliation," 433.

88. *New York Times*, 16 August 1919.

89. *Boston Herald*, 16 August 1919.

90. Sondra R. Herman, *Eleven Against War: Studies in American Internationalist Thought, 1898–1921*, 207–8.

91. Thomas A. Bailey, *Woodrow Wilson and the Lost Peace*, 184.

But Wilson had still another reason to oppose mild reservations. As McAdoo later recalled, Wilson had explained that if he showed any inclination to accept mild reservations, the opponents of the treaty "would immediately propose other and more objectionable reservations which it would be impossible to consider."[92] Wilson twice expressed this fear several weeks later, and in mid-August it already troubled him. He had grounds for worry. In the wake of Lodge's tough speech, the Foreign Relations Committee framed outright amendments to the treaty, and Lodge showed senators a new group of reservations. The senators seeking compromise had reached no firm agreement, and anti-Leaguers favored terms harsher than the Kellogg reservations. What Wilson might agree to as final terms of compromise could turn out to be only a starting point.

Wilson had an alternative. A day before Hitchcock called on him, the Foreign Relations Committee had accepted his invitation for a meeting at the White House on 19 August. Full transcripts of the meeting were to be made immediately available to newspapers. Thus Wilson could begin to take his case to the people. Soon he could start a speaking tour. Through the people, he hoped to win over recalcitrant senators.

But Wilson overlooked the growing public doubts about the Covenant, and he underestimated the strength of his organized antagonists. He did not realize that an appeal over the heads of the mild reservationists would serve not to win them but to antagonize them. Nor did he realize how fully committed the mild reservationists were to a program of reservations embodied in the resolution of ratification. He did not foresee that when cut off from Democratic negotiators, the mild reservationists would have to do their bargaining with anti-Leaguers, so that ultimately Wilson would be presented with a far less attractive package of reservations than the one now being discussed by Hitchcock. To Wilson, the deal Swanson and McNary had negotiated was both undesirable and uncertain. It was undesirable because the reservations would be in the resolution of ratification; it was uncertain because no specific wording had yet been approved by two-thirds of the senators. Even so, this was the best deal Wilson had any chance to make, and this was the best opportunity he would have to make it.

McNary and some of his colleagues would not be discouraged. They noted that Wilson objected to amendments, which required a

92. McAdoo, *Crowded Years*, 514.

new treaty with Germany, but that he did not make the same objection to reservations, and they pointed out that Hitchcock had not repudiated reservations altogether but had talked of crossing that bridge later. The reservations that Lodge was showing senators might become a basis of compromise. After talking with Lodge on the morning of 18 August, Kellogg wrote Lowell: "He signified his willingness to accept substantially the reservations which we drew. He wishes to change the reservation in relation to Section X, but I do not think it materially changes it as we wrote it." Lodge seemed anxious for ratification, and he thought that the treaty might be reported the following week. Mild reservationists took comfort also from the feelers that Democratic senators continued to put out. Indeed some of the Democrats professed to think that Wilson would yield to necessity and accept reservations.[93]

There was, however, a complicating factor—antagonism to the League and the treaty because of the Shantung provisions and the failure of either the Japanese or the American government to give acceptable guarantees to China. According to George Norris, it was a disgraceful deal, based on secret treaties and designed "to carve up the territory not of an enemy but of an allied friend." Japan, moreover, had a record of mistreating Koreans, including Christians. And the treaty set no date for the restoration of Shantung to China.[94] Several senators noted that they did not subscribe to the Kellogg reservations because nothing was said of Shantung.[95] Lodge was showing senators the draft of two outright amendments to the treaty, one of which would alter the Shantung provisions by substituting the name of China wherever Japan was referred to.[96] The other amendment would give the United States and the British Empire equal representation in the League.

Lodge's circulation of the amendments did not belie his intention to take soundings on a program of reservations or lessen the importance of that effort. Presenting the amendments to the Senate would serve as a unifying concession to irreconcilables and some other Republican senators and would be consistent with Lodge's own convictions. But if Senate votes on the amendments occurred in the context of bipartisan agreement on reservations, to be considered after the amendments were dealt with, those amendments would have scant

93. Kellogg to Lowell, 18 August 1919, Lowell Papers; *Minneapolis Tribune*, 17 August 1919; *New York Tribune*, 17 August 1919.
94. *CR* 66:1, pp. 2592–97 (15 July 1919).
95. *Minneapolis Tribune*, 17 August 1919; *Portland Oregonian*, 17 August 1919.
96. *Minneapolis Tribune*, 16 August 1919.

chance of adoption. Only in the absence of such an understanding did the amendments pose a serious problem for pro-League senators.

For the mild reservationists, then, the situation was very muddled on the eve of Wilson's meeting with the Foreign Relations Committee. If, despite Hitchcock's discouraging statement of 15 August, the president now showed himself ready for compromise on a realistic basis, he might well get it from the Republicans, as a result of the public's demand for peace. Otherwise, the mild reservationists would have to take up defensive positions to balk those who would capitalize on the growing doubts about the League.

At the meeting Wilson treated his visitors with courtesy and handled himself well, first presenting a prepared statement and then responding to questions. The meeting lasted three and a half hours, through the morning, after which the president invited his guests for lunch. He was willing to resume afterward, but the senators declined.[97]

In his statement Wilson urged prompt action, chiefly in the interest of resumed trade with the Central Powers. He saw no need for delay, claiming that all the suggestions made to him in February had subsequently been acted on at Paris. Taking up Article 10, he argued that the United States was doubly protected, first by her veto in the Council and second by the right of Congress to reject the advice of the Council, a right that he said had been understood by all signatories. Of course the United States would "undertake to respect and preserve against external aggression the territorial integrity and existing political independence of all members of the league." This constituted "a very grave and solemn moral obligation. But it is a moral, not a legal obligation, and leaves our Congress absolutely free to put its own interpretation upon it in all cases that call for action. It is binding in conscience only, not in law." He called Article 10 "the very backbone of the whole covenant. Without it the league would be hardly more than an influential debating society." Then Wilson offered a concession. He was favorable to interpretations "accompanying the act of ratification." But these must not be "part of the formal ratification itself." If they were, there would be a long delay, since all the nations would need to assent, including Germany. Other powers would offer their own reservations, some quite serious, and "the meaning and operative force of the treaty would presently be clouded from one end of its clauses to the other."[98]

97. Walworth, *Wilson*, 2:348, 352.
98. U.S. Congress, Senate, *Treaty of Peace With Germany: Report of the Conference Between Members of the Senate Committee on Foreign Relations and the President of the United States. At the White House, Tuesday, August 19, 1919*, 66th

In the questioning that followed, McCumber argued that acquiescence to reservations could be tacit, but Wilson objected. He admitted that he was not clear on the legal status of reservations, but he reiterated that reservations would only prompt counter-reservations and obscure the treaty's meaning.[99] Borah brought the questioning to the critical issue of Article 10 and Wilson's distinction between a moral and a legal obligation. Other senators joined in, and Wilson, responding to Harding, gave what would become a much discussed explanation.

Now a moral obligation is of course superior to a legal obligation, and, if I may say so, has a greater binding force; only there always remains in the moral obligation the right to exercise one's judgment as to whether it is indeed incumbent upon one in those circumstances to do that thing. In every moral obligation there is an element of judgment. In a legal obligation there is no element of judgment.[100]

The senators took up other matters. In response Wilson explained that he had learned of the secret treaties only after he had reached Paris and that he was disappointed with the Shantung provisions, which sprang in part from a secret treaty. He did not think that in a dispute between the United States and Great Britain, the British would have the assistance of other parts of the Empire that were members of the Assembly. He noted, "Diplomatically speaking, there is only one 'British Empire.'"[101] Questioned by Albert Fall, Wilson backtracked on his initial statement and acknowledged that since Germany was not initially to be a member of the League, it would not have to approve reservations to the Covenant.[102]

Afterward Hiram Johnson reported that Wilson had done well, and McCumber and the Democrats praised his performance. But Colt was not happy with Wilson's discussion of Article 10, calling it "inconsistent and irreconcilable," and Root found Wilson's explanation intolerable. Lodge felt that Wilson's performance "has not affected a single Senator but has strengthened us in the Senate. He made some admissions which, when understood, will prove very harmful to him."[103]

Cong., 1st sess., 1919, S.Doc. 76, pp. 3–10.

99. Ibid., 11–14.

100. Ibid., 19.

101. Ibid., 22, 30–31, 43–44.

102. Ibid., 17.

103. Johnson to Hiram Johnson, Jr., and Arch Johnson, 23 August 1919, Johnson Papers; *New York World*, 20 August 1919; Colt to Elihu Root, 2 September 1919, and Root to Colt, 28 August 1919, Root Papers; Lodge to James T. Williams, 20 August 1919, Lodge Papers.

Wilson had indeed made some slips and had presented unconvincing arguments on critical issues. Wilson's denial of foreknowledge of the secret treaties was a blunder. Not only had some of them crossed his desk, but the Bolsheviks had exposed them, and some had been published in American newspapers. The president's admission that reservations to the Covenant would have to be submitted to Germany hurt his cause too. Democrats in the Senate had argued otherwise, so Wilson's statement revealed an embarrassing lack of coordination with them.[104]

Wilson also erred when he argued against tacit acceptance of reservations. He was trying to make reservations in the resolution of ratification more difficult, not easier. In effect, however, he undermined the mild reservationists and helped those who insisted on formal acceptance by the Great Powers. Wilson ignored advice from the solicitor of the State Department, who had suggested that reservations need not be submitted to other governments for action by their parliaments but could be deposited at Paris.[105]

Wilson's main failure before the Foreign Relations Committee concerned Article 10. He saw the obligation under the article as central to the workings of the League and to the peace of the world. Others rejected the obligation, he knew. He tried to reconcile the irreconcilable through verbal legerdemain, chiefly through the distinction between a legal and a moral obligation. All he did was confuse the issue and give fresh impetus to demands for a clarifying and protective reservation. Wilson's argument—that the moral obligation, as distinct from a legal one, left open the door for judgment—did not go to the heart of senatorial objections. If the words of Article 10 committed the United States, and if the fact of aggression against a member was clear, surely judgment could not legitimately obviate the moral obligation—and Wilson had said that a moral obligation is superior to a legal one. In the same vein, although Wilson explained that the word *advise* had deliberately been used to recognize American constitutional processes, would Congress not be morally bound to follow that advice? To be sure, as Wilson pointed out, an American member of the Council would participate in giving the advice, but was that fact a protection only or might it not further obligate

104. Arthur S. Link, *Woodrow Wilson: Revolution, War, and Peace*, 78; John A. Garraty, *Woodrow Wilson: A Great Life in Brief*, 176; Walworth, *Wilson*, 2:351; Bailey, *Great Betrayal*, 86, 87. Link observed that Wilson was not in the habit of lying; he had the treaties in his possession before going to Paris but did not feel bound by them and felt no need to read them.

105. Lester Woolsey to Robert Lansing, 29 July 1919, Wilson Papers.

Congress to follow the Council's advice? Senators would not willingly delegate Congress's war powers to an official in the executive branch, that is, the American representative on the Council. Even if Wilson had done more to minimize the extent of the obligation under Article 10, difficulties would have remained, for the president could not guarantee how other nations would construe the article.[106] The basic difficulty was simply this: Wilson and the League Covenant had gone well beyond American internationalist thought regarding collective security and had slighted the legalistic side, for which there was a strong foundation in American thought and practice. Wilson approved the new commitment to coercion and collective security embodied in Article 10, and most senators, including the majority of the mild reservationists and all the moderates, would not accept such a commitment without substantial qualification.[107]

That Wilson had not gone far enough to meet the situation was demonstrated at the Capitol the following day. Prompted by Wilson's initial statement to the senators and acting entirely on his own, Pittman introduced a resolution of "understanding" that embodied the reservations Kellogg had offered but that was separate from the instrument of ratification.[108] He hoped that all nations on the League Council would adopt the same resolution, eliminating the need for renegotiation. Mild reservationists did not participate in the lively and well-attended debate, but afterward Colt, Kellogg, and McNary repudiated the scheme.[109]

Between 19 August, when Wilson met with the Foreign Relations

---

106. In practice, as it happens, within the League the extent of the obligation was debated for several years (Roland Stromberg, "The Riddle of Collective Security," in *Issues and Conflicts: Studies in Twentieth Century Diplomacy*, ed. George L. Anderson, 161).

107. Warren F. Kuehl, *Seeking World Order: The United States and International Organization to 1920*, 339–40. For further commentary on the problems associated with Article 10, see Stromberg, "Riddle of Collective Security," 160–62; John A. Garraty, *Henry Cabot Lodge: A Biography*, 368–69; Edgar William Schmickle, "For the Proper Use of Victory: Diplomacy and the Imperatives of Vision in the Foreign Policy of Woodrow Wilson, 1916–1919," 326–29; Melvyn P. Leffler, *The Elusive Quest: America's Pursuit of European Stability and French Security, 1919–1933*, 11–13, 16–17; John Chalmers Vinson, *Referendum for Isolation: Defeat of Article Ten of the League of Nations Covenant*, 21; Seth P. Tillman, *Anglo-American Relations at the Paris Peace Conference of 1919*, 126; and Link, *Wilson: Revolution, War, and Peace*, 119.

108. *New York Times*, 22 August 1919.

109. *CR*66:1, pp. 4035–36, 4048, 4050 (20 August 1919); *New York Times*, 21 August 1919; *New York World*, 21 August 1919; McNary to Thomas Neuhausen, 23 August 1919, Neuhausen Papers.

Committee, and 3 September, when at last he set out on his speaking tour, the mild reservationists found themselves increasingly on the defensive. The olive branch offered by Wilson and then by Pittman was too small. About a dozen Democrats negotiated with Lenroot, McCumber, McNary, and others, but without Wilson's backing they could offer little more than Pittman had.[110] Meanwhile, the majority on the Foreign Relations Committee adopted treaty amendments that posed a dilemma: some of them were patently popular yet were dangerous to the treaty. And the majority readied itself to adopt reservations harsher than those offered by Kellogg. In addition, anti-League sentiment received fresh fillips from the committee testimony of disgruntled ethnic groups headed by the Irish-Americans and from a notable Senate speech by Knox. The announcement that such irreconcilables as Johnson and Borah would take the stump at the same time as Wilson lessened prospects for a middle-ground settlement.

In the last ten days of August, Bernard Baruch tried to mediate a settlement, with the president's blessings. Baruch was the former head of the War Industries Board and had served Wilson in Paris. He was aided in the negotiations by Bradley Palmer, another Paris financial adviser. But since Wilson would yield nothing beyond reservations separate from the instrument of ratification, the mission failed.[111]

Mild reservationists told reporters that they had "information that in the end their plan would have democratic support." Colt and others told Gus Karger that they expected the president to yield on the inclusion of reservations in the ratification, since the proposed reservations merely explained what the president said was already in the treaty and would not require renegotiation. For the moment, however, the mild reservationists had to make do with hope for the future, while defending against immediate dangers.[112]

By a 9–8 vote on 23 August, the Foreign Relations Committee had approved, as a textual amendment to the treaty, the substitution of *China* for *Japan* in sections relating to Shantung, so that China would take over the properties and rights that had belonged to Ger-

110. _New York World_, 8 September 1919.
111. Chandler P. Anderson Diary, entry for 27 August 1919, Anderson Papers; Margaret L. Coit, _Mr. Baruch_, 292; Bernard M. Baruch, _Baruch: The Public Years_, 135–36; Jordan A. Schwarz, _The Speculator: Bernard M. Baruch in Washington, 1917–1965_, 151–52; Wilson to Thomas Lamont, 21 August 1919, Wilson Papers, cited in Wimer, "Wilson Tries Conciliation," 431.
112. _Des Moines Register_, 21 August 1919; Karger to William Howard Taft, 21 August 1919, Taft Papers.

many. In the days that followed, the committee approved amendments, sponsored by Albert Fall, to remove American representatives from nearly all the commissions set up to enforce provisions of the treaty; the Johnson amendment to give the United States as many votes as the British Empire in League affairs; and an amendment by George Moses to prevent nations involved in a controversy from taking part in the consideration or the settlement of the issue in the League Council, this directed against the British Empire. The committee also approved four reservations: the one on Article 10 went well beyond what the mild reservationists had proposed. The committee tabled other reservations for future consideration, along with a "preamble" that would require assent to the reservations by three of the four Great Powers.[113]

Of the ethnic groups that had complaints about the treaty, Irish-Americans received the most publicity because of their testimony before the committee. Before the president's speaking trip McCumber warned Wilson:

The most bitter opposition comes from the Sinn Fein followers in the United States, who have been misled by false assertions . . . (a) That Great Britain has six votes to our one in the settlement of international disputes; (b) that Great Britain has acquired millions of square miles of territory as the result of the war; (c) that we bind ourselves to come to the aid of Great Britain if Ireland, Egypt or India should rebel. The next serious opposition comes from that class of people to whom the mention of Japan is as a red flag to a bull.[114]

On the Senate floor Knox, not yet classed with the irreconcilables, called for a rejection of the treaty and a separate peace with Germany. He decried the harsh terms of the treaty and foresaw in the pact a source of endless trouble for the United States.[115]

Shantung was first, and for a time was foremost, in public attention and in the minds of senators and the president. The issue had been agitating for months when the anti-League majority on the Foreign Relations Committee began to lay the final groundwork for an amendment. On 14 August the committee decided to call four pro-China Oriental experts, plus William Bullitt, who had resigned from the peace commission. The testimony, hostile to the Shantung provision, began on 18 August. Lodge saw the political advantages of

113. Denna Frank Fleming, *The United States and the League of Nations, 1918–1920*, 326–29; *New York Times*, 5 September 1919.
114. McCumber to Wilson, 29 August 1919, Wilson Papers.
115. *New York Times*, 30 August 1919.

the issue, but beyond that he had long been fearful and suspicious of Japan. He felt strongly about the issue on its merits, and he was the one who offered the amendment in committee. Many senators predicted that the fate of the treaty would rest with the amendment.[116] Any amendment would change the treaty for all the nations involved and would require renegotiation. And the Shantung amendment in particular was bound to meet resistance—from Japan and others. Wilson, alarmed since mid-August when the prospect of an amendment had been raised, decided after the committee approved the amendment that he should not delay further in taking his case to the people. Starting in Columbus, Ohio, he would travel to the West, where public opinion was not so fully developed as in the East.[117]

In the Senate, McCumber spoke in opposition to the popular amendment three days after it was approved but weeks before the committee reported the action to the Senate. He had briefed himself thoroughly on Shantung and had made the subject his own in questioning witnesses at the hearings.[118] Countering a strong tide of sentiment, McCumber's speech was an act of courage as well as erudition. Statements seemingly friendly to Japan in particular went against the current. McCumber argued that the amendment would not help China but would only offend Japan and endanger the League. Even though Japan had moved into Shantung before the secret treaty with Great Britain, France, and Italy, Japan had had an oral agreement with them, McCumber conjectured, before the formal treaty. These nations could not accept the amendment.[119]

Charles Michelson, writing for the Democratic *New York World*, thought McCumber was more effective than Democratic senators. Hitchcock credited McCumber with putting "the final nail in the coffin of the Shantung thing." But Hitchcock's optimism was premature. Since Democrats Reed and Gore favored the amendment, and since five Democrats were still noncommittal as of a 25 August *Chicago Tribune* poll, much would depend on the mild reserva-

116. *New York World*, 15 August 1919; William C. Widenor, *Henry Cabot Lodge and the Search for an American Foreign Policy*, 327–28; Robert James Fischer, "Henry Cabot Lodge's Concept of Foreign Policy and the League of Nations," 226; *New York Times*, 25 August 1919.

117. Walworth, *Wilson*, 2:359; *Portland Oregonian*, 31 August 1919.

118. U.S. Congress, Senate, *Treaty of Peace With Germany: Hearings Before the Committee on Foreign Relations, United States Senate*, 66th Cong., 1st sess., 1919, S.Doc. 106, pp. 432, 464–65, 469–86, 559, 563–69, 572–77, 592–97, 610, 613, 617, 625, 633–37, 643.

119. *CR*66:1, pp. 4345–49, 4358–59, 4361 (26 August 1919).

tionists. According to the *Tribune*, only McCumber and McNary were committed against the amendment. However, at the end of McCumber's speech Nelson and Lenroot asked questions that suggested they opposed the amendment on the grounds that it would have no useful effect. Other powers had ratified or were in the process of ratifying the treaty with the original Shantung provisions.[120]

Emotions, already high, heated further in the wake of McCumber's speech. As a result, Nelson became more heavily engaged in the fight for ratification. On 27 August the highly strung Albert Fall took the floor to criticize the tone of McCumber's speech. McCumber and others, Fall said, tended to be impatient with critics of the treaty. Nelson interrupted, and Fall suggested that Nelson was in his second childhood. Nelson called him on that, and Fall apologized but started an angry colloquy with McCumber.[121] By then Nelson had been further aroused by Knox's speech, which had called the treaty too severe and had asked for a separate peace. Nelson somewhat heatedly told reporters, "The repudiation of the pending treaty of peace as advocated by Senator Knox . . . is an open invitation to Germany to attack France." Knox, he felt, would have America violate her pledges and leave helpless a world stricken by war. Lodge was led to wonder whether Nelson would even support reservations. He seemed "very violent about Germany."[122]

On the night of 30 August, a day after Knox's speech and just after his own statement, Nelson met with four other mild reservationists. Though for a long time sympathetic, Nelson was not in the habit of conferring with mild reservationist leaders. The event marked his emergence as one of the leadership group. Usually a party man, Nelson for many months had thought Republican leaders would accomplish ratification, at the price of innocuous reservations. By the end of August, however, he had become disillusioned with Lodge and Knox and was ready to steer an independent course. Lodge's speech of 12 August, he thought, could not possibly "breed compromise," and Nelson sadly concluded, "He is a great scholar and author, but he lacks the real element of a statesman." Knox's speech,

120. Hitchcock quoted in *New York World*, 14 September, 27 August 1919; *New York Times*, 26 August 1919; *CR*66:1, pp. 4348–49 (26 August 1919).

121. *CR*66:1, p. 4408 (27 August 1919); *Minneapolis Tribune*, 28 August 1919; *New York World*, 14 September 1919.

122. *New York World*, 31 August 1919; Lodge to Elihu Root, 3 September 1919, Root Papers.

surprising from "a man of his standing," seemed "a bid for the German vote."[123]

The five mild reservationists met to plot a common course of action in response to recent events—the reservation situation; Knox's renewed effort to separate the League and the treaty; the Fall, Johnson, and Moses amendments; and above all, the Shantung amendment. The senators believed that the Shantung amendment would come up first in the Senate and, if passed, could break the trail for other amendments.[124] At least one of them, Kellogg, had agonized over what to do before deciding to cast his lot against the amendment. Three others of the original group of seven—Cummins, Lenroot, and Spencer—held aloof, at least for the time being, though only Spencer was reported to waver respecting the amendment.[125]

The five mild reservationists agreed in their 30 August conference that they would oppose not only the Shantung amendment but also all others, as well as the Knox effort to have a separate vote on the Covenant. They agreed also to a substantial concession, one that they had earlier resisted: to frame a reservation on Shantung.[126] The reservation would appease their own feelings on the issue, and those of their constituents, and would help win other middle grounders to their position. But it might also open the door to more troublesome reservations.

On the strength of their commitment against the amendment and their concession to adding a reservation, the mild reservationists were confident that neither the Shantung amendment nor any other amendment would pass. One of them claimed seven to ten Republican votes against the Shantung amendment and from eighteen to twenty-two against others. But the prospective triumph was tainted. As McCumber told Taft, "How far we shall be compelled to go in the matter of reservations, in order to line up a sufficient number of Republican Senators to put the treaty through, is the real question." That question continued to plague the mild reservationists for some time, partly because, as Senator Harry New noted, the vote on Shantung promised to be very close. Senators and outside

123. Nelson's judgment of Lodge is in Nelson to L. M. Willcuts, 15 August 1919, and was repeated in a letter to William B. Mitchell, 2 September 1919, Nelson Papers; Nelson to S. Listoe, 3 September 1919, and to Edwin Mattson, 1 September 1919, Nelson Papers.

124. *New York Times*, 25 August, 1 September 1919.

125. Kellogg to Elihu Root, 21 August 1919, Root Papers; *New York Times*, 26 August 1919.

126. *New York Times*, 1 September 1919.

observers feared that many Democrats might defect, which would cancel the votes of middle grounders.[127]

The Shantung issue had gotten so much attention for such a long period that the mild reservationists did not fully focus on the problem of the Johnson amendment, which equalized American and British Empire voting strength. The Foreign Relations Committee adopted the amendment on 29 August. Some senators thought it a great stroke by anti-Leaguers.[128]

While organizing to fend off amendments, the McNary-McCumber group fought a rearguard action over reservations. Once more they played cat and mouse with Lodge; each side needed the other, but the two diverged at critical points of interest. The mild reservationists still hoped to use Lodge to win enough Republicans for a deal with the Democrats and thus create a two-thirds majority for the treaty. Lodge was much less interested in satisfying the Democrats; he hoped to unite the Republicans, and that would require a tougher program than the one put forth by the mild reservationists.[129]

Lodge's position was stronger than it had been a month before. Earlier there had been little chance of an outright ratification, but a resolution of reservations separate from the resolution of ratification had had a possibility of winning at least a majority. That danger was almost gone by the end of August. Anti-League feeling in the country and the Senate was stronger than before. Equally important, the Democrats, restrained by the president, now only tentatively sang their siren songs to the mild reservationists. Thus, the latter posed no credible threat of a breakaway from the body of the party. They were not powerless, however, for Lodge still needed them to keep the party together and perhaps to keep his majority. This last would depend on how many Democrats might defect to his side.

The relationship between Lodge and the mild reservationists was not without its tensions and animosities. Lodge complained to Root about Nelson, and he grew impatient with Kellogg, who had "turned out a perfect grist of amendments" and who, professing not to want to return to the Senate, seemed to ignore party interests. On the other

127. Ibid.; McCumber to Taft, 30 August 1919, Taft Papers; New in *New York Times*, 2 September 1919.

128. *St. Louis Post-Dispatch*, 3 September 1919.

129. Kellogg wrote Taft, with reference to the Hughes reservation to Article 10, "There are a large number of Senators on the Republican side who will not agree to that, and they want something even stronger than what I prepared" (Kellogg to Taft, 20 August 1919, Taft Papers).

side, Colt also confided in Root. He wrote: "I do not like the attitude of our Republican leaders in the Senate. They seem to be determined to kill the whole treaty. As I view it, their position is unwise both as respects our national honor and the future of our party." And McNary had developed a strong dislike for Lodge, according to Karger. Nelson's disillusionment with Lodge has been noted.[130]

Nevertheless, Lodge and the mild reservationists kept in wary contact on reservations. But Lodge worked more closely with Knox in framing reservations and with other Republicans on the Foreign Relations Committee.[131] By 3 September these Republicans, excepting McCumber, were ready to agree on a program of reservations, to be voted by the full committee the next day, coinciding with the start of Wilson's tour. As a counterweight, McCumber drafted a pledge refusing support to reservations that would send the treaty back. Its signers also reasserted their confidence in and support of the Kellogg reservations. Nelson, Colt, and McNary promptly joined McCumber in signing. Kellogg, who was away, had promised to sign and predicted that others would too. McNary thought that if enough Republicans signed, Lodge would have to accept mild reservations.[132]

Tacitly, the two sides compromised some of their differences. Committee action after so much delay represented a yielding by Lodge to mild reservationist pressure, though other factors influenced him too.[133] At the caucus of committee Republicans, the senators agreed to put off for a time a fifth reservation, which Lodge had been touting for some weeks, that would require Senate confirmation for any American delegate to the League Council.[134] On two of the four committee reservations, Lodge and Knox offered wording that was acceptable to the mild reservationists, and McCumber supported these with his votes. The reservations covered domestic questions and the Monroe Doctrine, though on the latter the committee reservation was somewhat stronger than Kellogg's. Further, al-

130. Lodge to Root, 3 September, 15 August 1919, and Colt to Root, 2 September 1919, Root Papers; Karger to William Howard Taft, 3 September 1919, Taft Papers.

131. *New York World*, 2, 3 September 1919.

132. Gus Karger to William Howard Taft, 3 September 1919, Taft Papers; *St. Louis Post-Dispatch*, 7 September 1919; *New York World*, 8 September 1919.

133. Frank Kellogg to Elihu Root, 21 August 1919, Root Papers; Lodge to Albert J. Beveridge, 19 August 1919, Beveridge Papers; Lodge to James T. Williams, Jr., 20 August 1919, Lodge Papers.

134. Warren G. Harding to F. E. Scobey, 2 September 1919, Harding Papers; *St. Louis Post-Dispatch*, 3 September 1919; *New York World*, 15 August, 5 September 1919.

though Lodge read in committee a preamble requiring the acceptance of reservations by three of the four Great Powers, something the mild reservationists had resisted, he did not push the matter to a vote.[135]

But Lodge and the committee majority did not satisfy the mild reservationists on other matters. McCumber objected to the majority's withdrawal reservation and refused to vote for it. Lodge, however, foresaw no trouble in compromising the matter.[136] Of greater consequence, McCumber also voted against the committee's reservation to Article 10. As events showed, Lodge hoped to get party backing for this reservation and thus adoption in the Senate. McCumber, soon backed by a few of his colleagues, resisted.

The conflict had been evident before committee action. Lodge had circulated among Republicans what would become the committee's reservation, a highly negative draft, whereas the mild reservationists had contended for their own proposal, which stressed merely the constitutional prerogatives of Congress.[137] The reservation voted by the committee stated:

That the United States declines to assume, under the provisions of Article X, or under any other article, any obligation to preserve the territorial integrity, or political independence of any other nation or to interfere in controversies between other nations members of the League or not, or to employ the military or naval forces of the United States in such controversies, or to adopt economic measures for the protection of any other country, whether a member of the League or not, against external aggression or for the purpose of coercing any other country, or for the purpose of intervention in the internal conflicts or other controversies which may arise in any other country, and no mandate shall be accepted by the United States under Article XXII, Part I, of the treaty of peace with Germany except by action of the Congress of the United States.[138]

The day after the committee vote, McCumber told the Senate that there was a difference between the committee reservation and Kellogg's, despite claims to the contrary. Both reservations would allow the United States to retain freedom of action, he said, but

the committee reservation by its most positive declaration that the purpose

135. *New York Times*, 4, 5 September 1919; *New York Tribune*, 7 September 1919; U.S. Congress, Senate, *Proceedings of the Committee on Foreign Relations, U, United States Senate, from the Sixty-Third Congress to the Sixty-Seventh Congress*, 170, 176; Frank Kellogg to Elihu Root, 11 August 1919, Root Papers.

136. Lodge to George Harvey, 5 September 1919, Lodge Papers. McCumber explained his objection in the Senate (*CR*66:1, p. 5357 [15 September 1919]).

137. *New York World*, 4 September 1919; *New York Tribune*, 4 September 1919.

138. *New York Times*, 5 September 1919.

of this Government will be non-interference with any kind of war or with any kind of threatened war invites and encourages such war. Our substitute reservation, leaving us in harmony with the other great nations in a general purpose to prevent such wrong and aggressive wars, although the Congress alone must determine whether and to what extent, if any, we shall interfere, discourages such criminal wars.[139]

After repeating the thought in other ways, McCumber concluded that the committee reservation was worse than striking Article 10 altogether. McNary, Colt, Kellogg, and Nelson stood with McCumber. Lenroot expressed fear that the committee reservation might interfere with the obligation to use the boycott under Article 16, and Spencer called it "unnecessarily drastic."[140]

Though Lodge tried to minimize his differences with the mild reservationists, he was aware of them. He was willing to risk some defections because he expected ample help from maverick Democrats. That prospect was strongly enhanced when John K. Shields of Tennessee voted in committee for three of the four reservations, abstaining on the one relating to Article 10. As a member of the committee, Shields could lead other Democrats to the committee's program, Lodge thought. With this accession, Lodge counted on five Democrats, and he hoped for more.[141] Then Kenyon, Capper, and Cummins announced that they would vote for the committee program, strengthening Lodge's hopes. Still, he would burn no bridges. Kellogg found him conciliatory and predicted a compromise that would unite the whole Republican party.[142]

Perforce, McCumber remained ready to seek compromise with Lodge. At the same time, he hoped for a deal with the Democrats. After organizing on 30 August, his five claimed that sixteen Republicans would support their program, and they took soundings among the Democrats on that basis. Some Democrats assured the group that if a program of interpretive reservations failed, they would come over to the mild reservationists. After the McCumber-McNary group pledged itself against anything that would require rene-

139. *CR*66:1, p. 4902 (5 September 1919).
140. *New York World*, 6 September 1919.
141. *New York Times*, 5 September 1919; Lodge to George Harvey, 5 September 1919, Lodge Papers.
142. *New York Tribune*, 5, 6, 7 September 1919; *New York World*, 6 September 1919; *Des Moines Register*, 7, 10 September 1919. The report about Kenyon and Capper is confirmed in Gus Karger to William Howard Taft, 5 September 1919, Taft Papers.

gotiation and in favor of mild reservations, McNary asked Karger to inform Hitchcock about the agreement.[143]

A possible compromise between the Democrats and the Republicans on the basis of a mild reservationist program depended on the president. Unfortunately, the best opportunity had already come and gone. A possibility remained, but with Wilson about to take his case to the people, administration Democrats had to put aside serious negotiation, and the mild reservationists had to accept the delay. Swanson, a visitor at the White House the day before Wilson left, came away deeply discouraged. He had urged the acceptance of reservations as earnestly as he could, and Wilson had listened attentively but had declined to commit himself.[144] Talking freely to Karger with a tongue loosened by alcohol, Swanson "deplored the fact that the President was in the hands of 'lickspittles' who dared not tell him the truth." If Wilson had yielded six weeks earlier, Swanson said, the president could have had reservations separate from the treaty. Now the reservations would have to be part of the treaty, and if Wilson waited much longer, he might have to accept amendments.[145]

Doubtless Hitchcock was one of the "lickspittles" Swanson had in mind. The day after Swanson's visit, the Nebraskan went to the White House to give a final report on the Senate situation and to receive Wilson's instructions. Hitchcock had listened carefully to Karger's message from McNary and had asked for permission to submit the information to Wilson. If he did so, he perhaps contributed to a false sense of optimism on Wilson's part. Afterward, telling reporters that the time for reservations had not arrived, Hitchcock asserted: "The so-called mild reservationists among the Republicans will aid us. Undoubtedly they can be persuaded to vote for the rejection of any reservation that jeopardizes the treaty itself. . . . The Foreign Relations Committee will bring the treaty into the Senate in such form that we will be able to poll our greatest possible strength against it."[146] Hitchcock thought that the committee's proposal of amendments would divide the Republicans and would drive the reservationists to his side. He believed that the latter would

143. *New York Times*, 1 September 1919; Karger to William Howard Taft, 3 September 1919, Taft Papers.

144. *New York Times*, 3 September 1919; George Wharton Pepper, *Philadelphia Lawyer: An Autobiography*, 129. At Lodge's funeral in 1924, Swanson told Pepper about his meeting with Wilson.

145. Karger to William Howard Taft, 5 September 1919, Taft Papers.

146. *New York World*, 4 September 1919.

come to see that reservations endangered the treaty partly because the major powers could not accept them, since the major powers feared that Germany, no longer under compulsion, would resentfully reject reservations. Hitchcock thought, rather vaguely, that amendments would fail and that once they did, the Democrats would come together with roughly twenty Republicans.[147]

Wilson realized that a time for reservations might come. He provided Hitchcock with four reservations, on the usual subjects. They were similar to Kellogg's and were to be included in the instrument of ratification. But Wilson did not authorize Hitchcock to disclose their authorship. As Hitchcock later recalled, Wilson still felt that if he agreed to reservations, "his enemies would make use of his yielding to demand more and more because they wanted not only to defeat the league but to discredit and overthrow him."[148] The accuracy of Hitchcock's recollection is supported by a contemporaneous comment of Wilson's. Six days before his conference with Hitchcock, the president wrote: "I must confess to a bit of discouragement about the way in which some of the men I have been dealing with have been acting. I have treated them with absolute frankness and as friends and cooperators, but they respond sluggishly, to say the least, and seem more and more to show themselves opponents on other grounds than those avowed."[149]

Hitchcock might have planned to use Wilson's reservations when he thought best, but evidently that was not to be soon. For the time being, the fight was against amendments and for outright ratification, as Hitchcock declared to reporters afterward. The following day, after the Foreign Relations Committee had adopted its four reservations, Hitchcock condemned the reservations as tantamount to amendments.[150]

In yielding on reservations in the instrument of ratification, Wilson had made a major concession. But the bargaining tactic of secrecy and delay was a dangerous one.[151] And the whole strategy was based on false premises: that Wilson's trip would help his cause; that the situation in the Senate would not get any worse during the

147. Hitchcock to William Howard Taft, 29 August 1919, Taft Papers.
148. Gilbert M. Hitchcock, "Events Leading to the World War" (13 January 1925), Gilbert Hitchcock Papers, Library of Congress. For the text of the reservations, see Bailey, *Great Betrayal*, 393–94.
149. Wilson to H. H. Kohlsaat, 27 August 1919, Wilson Papers.
150. *New York World*, 5, 9 September 1919.
151. Thomas Bailey observed, "Wilson had played this kind of game before . . . but it is a dangerous game—a game that demands that one have one's wits about one, and that one observes the play closely at every stage" (*Great Betrayal*, 172).

period of action on amendments; and that the mild reservations Wilson offered would suffice after amendments were disposed of.

Among the mild reservationists, McCumber and McNary shared the misguided optimism, for the moment. That made little difference. The Democrats were not ready to bargain in any case; had they been, these mildest of reservationists would have been entirely willing. As it was, the mild reservationists had just one course open to them: to negotiate with fellow Republicans, directly and through Lodge. On 5 September McCumber began the process by announcing to the Senate his own reservation proposals, as an alternative to the committee's. His reservations were mild enough, and sharply varied from the committee's on Article 10, as McCumber took pains to note. But unlike Wilson's draft, McCumber's covered six subjects, not four. To counter amendments, McCumber proposed additional reservations on Shantung and on British colonial representation.[152] As time went on, McCumber and his colleagues would have to yield still more and would move even further from what Wilson had thought would be the basis for a final settlement.

From the sad perspective of November, Senator Ashurst concluded, "The Pro-Leaguers had sinned away their day of grace by failing to compromise last August."[153] The mild reservationists, aided by moderates Cummins and Spencer, had given them the chance. The offer made in August by the mild reservationists was not that attractive to Wilson, whose preferences guided Democratic senators. He exaggerated the hazards of prolonged renegotiation; other powers were ready to accept American reservations to get the United States promptly into the League. But there was point to the president's feeling that American reservations would "chill our relationship" with fellow League members. Perhaps the world, rebuilding on new foundations, needed an act of faith from the United States.[154]

Yet the mild reservationists would or could offer no more. There were other senators in the background, but even referring only to the eight who took the lead in July and August, the operative word is *would*. Spencer, Cummins, Lenroot, Kellogg, and Colt each interpreted the reservations in his own way and decided that the Kellogg reservations in the instrument of ratification squared with his con-

152. Gus Karger to William Howard Taft, 5 September 1919, Taft Papers; *CR*66:1, pp. 4902–3, 5 September 1919.

153. Sparks, *Many Colored Toga*, entry for 19 November 1919, p. 116.

154. Stromberg, "Riddle of Collective Security," 162–63, 165.

victions. Only McCumber, McNary, and Nelson had to make tactical decisions. If they could have achieved ratification with no reservations at all, or interpretive ones in a separate resolution, they would have been content. They came to judge that their inclinations were not practical. They could have joined the Democrats in trying to create a majority for a separate resolution, thus putting the other reservationists in the embarrassing position of opposing the League. Arguably, they would have been followed by enough reservationists to produce the requisite two-thirds. But they had no assurance that their help would create a majority, since in addition to Reed and Gore there were four or five other Democrats who might insist on reservations in the instrument of ratification. More important, as of the end of July, when McCumber and McNary reached an agreement with their pro-League colleagues, Lodge had pledges from more than a third of the Senate to reject an unreserved ratification. And even McCumber and McNary had to agree that a separate resolution would not be binding on other nations and in that sense would not be protective of the United States. Under the circumstances, the proposal for the Kellogg reservations in the instrument of ratification was the best the mild reservationists could offer.

The offer, as conveyed by Hitchcock to Wilson on 15 August, was not clear-cut, for pledges were vague. But senators were being swept along on the tide of public sentiment for a speedy ratification, so presidential encouragement might very well have led to a definite agreement by a constitutional majority in late August. Had the Democrats joined with McNary's supporters, Republican holdouts would have been put in the uncomfortable role of obstructionists. It is hard to believe that at least three or four would not have come over. More likely, all but the irreconcilables would have. For Republicans, ratification represented a victory for the reservationism that they had developed and insisted on, and it would have ended a divisive issue.

The offer fashioned by the mild reservationists was realistic. It was not easily made. The original group of seven, joined soon by Nelson, had to reconcile strong differences among themselves. McCumber, McNary, and Nelson favored reservations only for the sake of expediency. Kellogg believed in reservations that would be protective, and he therefore favored putting them in the instrument of ratification. But he also wanted reservations mild enough to be construed as being merely interpretive, as clarifying the meanings in the Covenant that Wilson thought were already clearly stated. Colt sympathized with the views and purposes of his milder colleagues, but more than they he worried about Article 10. Lenroot, Cummins, and Spencer wanted somewhat stronger reservations than did the others. Their reservations would in effect alter the Covenant as it related to some of America's rights and obligations. Moreover Spencer, in frank deference to constituent opinion, was reluctant to commit himself very definitely.

For all of them, the League was a logical extension of America's wartime role. The League would complete a patriotic obligation—to those Americans who had died and to the Allies. Nelson, McCumber, and perhaps Cummins felt most strongly about the iniquities of Germany and the continuing menace the country posed. Cummins would go no further, but the others agreed that the postwar situation was deeply unsettled and that the United States should contribute to stability through the League.[155] However, the eight differed among themselves concerning the extent, duration, and nature of America's proper commitment. McNary, and to a lesser extent McCumber and Nelson, favored the long-term collective security commitment of Article 10. Colt, and perhaps Kellogg, saw the article as chiefly useful for the postwar period. Lenroot, Cummins, and Spencer were in varying degrees dubious about Article 10, putting their faith in international law, pacific settlement, and disarmament. Even those who had more hopes for Article 10 shared that faith, which lay in the mainstream of Republican internationalist tradition.

There were common denominators. The original seven, and those who subsequently joined them, all wanted to enter the League. They wanted speedy action in the United States and therefore disapproved of obstacles that would require prolonged renegotiation abroad. They supported reservations that were relatively mild—some senators following their convictions, others viewing expediency. They agreed too that the reservations must be in the ratification resolution.

After Wilson rejected the mild reservationist initiative, and after the anti-Leaguers launched a counteroffensive through the Foreign Relations Committee, accompanied by a movement of public opinion away from the League, the mild reservationists took up defensive positions. By the end of August their role, as they saw it, was to limit damage, pending a change in Wilson's attitude. Specifically, they needed to block amendments to the treaty, such as the amendment on Shantung, as well as destructive reservations. The compromises embodied in the Foreign Relations Committee's four reservations showed that the mild reservationists were achieving some success at

155. *CR*66:1, p. 5957 (26 September 1919).

the start of the new phase of the battle. At the same time, their talk of new reservations to counter amendments indicated that their defense involved strategic retreat.

Under the new circumstances, individual roles changed, and the makeup of the group began to alter. Briefly, in September, McCumber, a leader with McNary from the start, became yet more important as staunch resistance superseded conciliation. And in that context Nelson stepped forth. Meanwhile Cummins, Spencer, and Lenroot distanced themselves from the other five, though the matter was far from clear-cut and, in Lenroot's case, was only temporary.

Cummins may have acted with the others for a speedy settlement so that Congress could turn its attention to serious domestic issues. This is speculative, but the grounds for reasonable speculation are substantial. Cummins was concerned about the railroad situation and the landmark bill that, as chairman of the Interstate Commerce Committee, he was fashioning. But he did not disguise his doubts about Article 10 and other phases of the treaty. When the opportunity for quick agreement passed, it was natural that Cummins began to drift away from the others and toward Lodge.

Spencer had hoped for a speedy ratification, on the basis of compromise, partly for the sake of the nation and the world and partly to be done with the issue. When the issue persisted, he aligned himself with Republicans of Missouri, who pressured him strongly against the League. Had he disguised his motives, one might now accuse him of cowardice. Since he did not, his actions must be attributed, in part at least, to the conviction that a senator should faithfully reflect the predominant opinion of his constituents, particularly those of his own party.

Lenroot too was respectful of home-state opinion and was concerned about reelection in 1920. But on matters of great importance, such as the League, he believed it the duty of a senator to vote his informed convictions. His brief aloofness during the end of August and the first days of September probably reflected indecision and characteristic caution in the face of the changing situation.

If the *New York Times* was accurate, all the middle grounders were, fleetingly, mild reservationists in mid-August; that is, all were prepared to support a compromise resolution of ratification based on the Kellogg reservations.[156] Whether or not that was so, only some reaffirmed and clarified their commitment to a mild reservationist course in the critical days of October and November, thus distin-

156. *New York Times*, 3 October 1919.

guishing themselves from the moderates. In the main, the moderates remained distinct from the strong reservationists and the irreconcilables and were an important element to the mild reservationist leaders and to Lodge in vote-counting calculations. Before all such calculations could be made, however, President Wilson would embark on his speaking tour. It was left to Wilson either to open the door to negotiation across party lines or to force the mild reservationist leaders to make the best deal possible with those to the right of them in the Republican party.

3 COMPROMISE AND CONFRONTATION
Article 10 and the Battle on Amendments, 4 September–6 November 1919

Woodrow Wilson's speaking tour failed. Far from winning the support of senators, Wilson antagonized many. When compromise was overdue, he showed himself unyielding. Then the strain of the trip broke his fragile health. Mild reservationists, however, remained central figures. Not numerous enough to create a two-thirds majority for ratification, they did hold a balance of power because their votes could give a majority to either Hitchcock or Lodge in voting on amendments and, later, on reservations.

Through September and most of October, Hitchcock, following Wilson's lead and his own judgment, avoided compromise negotiations with Republicans. By 21 October, when the Foreign Relations Committee again considered reservations, it was too late. The Republicans, divided among themselves on amendments, had coalesced on an enlarged program of reservations, inaptly dubbed the "Lodge reservations."

While Hitchcock had waited, in September a leadership group of six mild reservationists had agreed with Lodge on a reservation to Article 10. Then, as amendments came up in the Senate, they parted from Lodge to woo fellow middle grounders to oppose amendments. In the process, they had to promise additional reservations. Later, the mild reservationist leaders claimed that the reservations had been made by the friends of the treaty, not its enemies. Mild reservationists were, in fact, the principal authors of the "Lodge reservations." Those reservations, however, could not be characterized as mild.

To some extent, the mild reservationist leaders became somewhat less mild in their opinions, and according to Lodge's informed judgment, a key member of the group, Lenroot, had never been mild.[1] More important, they accommodated to the increasingly hardened attitude of Republican colleagues. Whereas most of the leaders compromised as a matter of necessity, the senators whom they won over in the fight against amendments, men like Hale and Edge, favored strong reservations as a matter of conviction. Yet these opponents of amendments and of reservations that would destroy the League were called *mild reservationists* by reporters and by their colleagues. The term *reservationist* would have been apter. But the term *mild reservationist*, having come into use earlier, persisted. If it was not fully descriptive, neither was it meaningless. Those to whom it was applied did indeed seek milder solutions than those who would amend the treaty, or destroy it.

Nelson, who had joined the group in late August, continued as a leader, and Lenroot also renewed his commitment, whereas Cummins and Spencer fell away. Among the six leaders—McCumber, McNary, Colt, Nelson, Kellogg, and Lenroot—roles changed. Gradually, starting in late September, Kellogg and Lenroot replaced McCumber and McNary as the principal leaders—serving as spokesmen, formulating strategy, drafting reservations, and negotiating with senators. The shift reflected, among other things, the change in the mild reservationists' position. So long as a deal involving twenty Republicans and forty-four Democrats had seemed feasible, McCumber and McNary, who were closest to the Wilsonian viewpoint, had been foremost. When the mild reservationist leaders found themselves trying to deal not with the Democrats but with fellow Republicans, directly or through Lodge, Kellogg and Lenroot proved most effective.

The strongest backers of the proposal to substitute reservations for amendments were Hale, Edge, Sterling, and Keyes. Their ideas on the nature of suitable reservations did not differ from those of moderates such as Spencer and Cummins, yet at a critical stage in the fight against amendments, these senators explicitly associated themselves with the mild reservationist leaders to bring into being the mild reservationist faction.

Wilson made a great mistake when he decided to take his trip, and he blundered in the course of his tour. Traditionally wary of executive encroachment, senators had acquiesced in Wilson's wartime autocracy. But they had reacted wrathfully when he had declined to seek their advice about the treaty of peace, had failed to keep them

1. Lodge to Frederick Gillett, 26 July 1920, Lodge Papers.

informed as he had promised, and by entwining the League with the peace treaty had sought to coerce their consent. Now, going over their heads to the people, he renewed that offensive tactic. In the minds of some senators and observers, the tour presaged a bid for an unprecedented third term as president.[2]

Wilson hurt his case when he insulted senators, gave unsatisfactory explanations, and misstated facts. Rejecting reservations, and in particular the compromise on Article 10, he pitted himself against the very senators he most needed to attract—the mild reservationists. On the stump, Wilson addressed himself to his audiences, no longer to the senators. But public pressure on the Senate never developed. To senators, Wilson's words seemed emotional, vague, derisive, uncompromising, and self-glorifying.

In his early speeches, Wilson referred to his opponents as "contemptible quitters" who were "ignorant of the treaty" and "incapable of altruistic purposes." He announced the opposition of the "pro-German element" and said that the choice was "between the League of Nations and Germanism." He challenged Senate opponents to "put up or shut up." Wilson made a strong emotional appeal for the Covenant in its present form and denounced reservations as "an assent with a big but. We agree—but."[3]

Senators awaited the results of the tour as though it were an election. The mails and newspapers, however, would bring only partial returns. The real results of the trip would be registered by those senators that Wilson hoped to pressure through his speeches in their home states. The first to report, in Senate speeches delivered on 9 and 10 September, were Spencer of Missouri and Kenyon of Iowa. Both reacted more harshly to Wilson's speeches than colleagues had anticipated.[4]

Speaking on the ninth, Spencer denied that the choice was between acceptance and rejection, as Wilson had said. He disclaimed any sympathy for changes designed to kill the treaty "or to so complicate the situation as to destroy or endanger its ratification." But there must be reservations, to protect American independence. He doubted that there would be a delay in acceptance, "either by express approval or by acquiescence."[5]

Kenyon spoke the following day, at greater length and with more

2. Herbert Parsons to Major Ralph Glyn, 15 September 1919, Parsons Papers.
3. Ray S. Baker and William E. Dodd, eds., *The Public Papers of Woodrow Wilson: War and Peace, Presidential Messages, Addresses and Public Papers (1917–1924)*, 5:37–40, 42, 47, 51, 615, 619, 623–24, 631.
4. *New York World*, 8, 15 September 1919; *New York Tribune*, 10 September 1919.
5. *CR* 66:1, pp. 5078–79 (9 September 1919).

passion. He commanded more attention than Spencer, since he had not yet addressed the Senate on the treaty. Kenyon also had been in the Senate longer than Spencer, was more influential, and usually acted in concert with Cummins, his veteran colleague.[6] Early in his speech Kenyon attacked Wilson's statement, made in Iowa as in Missouri, that the Senate must either take the treaty now before it or have none at all. This he called "an unfair and false issue." Nor would he be influenced by the appeal for a speedy ratification to resume regular trade relations with Germany. With both sarcasm and outrage, Kenyon condemned the Shantung provisions, decried Wilson's use of the high cost of living as an argument for hasty ratification, denounced executive autocracy, and defended senatorial prerogatives on treaties. He declared himself for strong reservations in the resolution of ratification and ended by announcing his support of the Johnson amendment, "to equalize the voting power of Britain and the United States."[7]

Comments by other senators gave further indication that so far Wilson had failed. Senators reportedly took "keen interest" in the president's declaration that some of them were "contemptible quitters," and one of them, Reed Smoot, promptly described Wilson as "the self-appointed modern dictator of the world's affairs."[8] Charles Townsend of Michigan, quiet to that time but soon to become more active, followed Kenyon's speech by inserting in the *Congressional Record* an editorial by Arthur H. Vandenberg that criticized Wilson for his language and unbridled internationalism. Townsend commented that he had been led to expect that Wilson would give to the people information that he felt no responsibility to give the Senate, but Townsend had not found any such information in Wilson's early speeches.[9] And Democrat Henry Ashurst wrote in his diary: "Opposition to the Treaty is increasing here and unless checked (how, I do not know) the heat of popular resentment will consume the Treaty, root and branch. A President who essays a speaking trip is assured of audience, but W.W. has made no converts to the Treaty."[10]

6. *New York Tribune*, 11 September 1919.

7. *CR* 66:1, pp. 5149–55 (10 September 1919).

8. *New York World*, 7 September 1919; Reed Smoot to C. W. Nibley, 8 September 1919, in Milton R. Merrill, "Reed Smoot, Apostle in Politics," 308.

9. *CR* 66:1, pp. 5156–57 (10 September 1919). Lenroot, visiting in Milwaukee, criticized Wilson for his offensive style and for misrepresentation, especially about Article 10; Harding judged from reports from all over the country that the trip was failing (*Milwaukee Sentinel*, 12 September 1919; Harding to Malcolm Jennings, 12 September 1919, Harding Papers).

10. George F. Sparks, ed., *A Many Colored Toga: The Diary of Henry Fountain*

Wilson had played into Lodge's hands. Continuing to seek agreement among Republicans on reservations, Lodge laid down a party line in his 10 September report for the majority on the Foreign Relations Committee. Caustically, Lodge shifted the blame for delay to the executive, which had withheld information. He noted the current trade with Germany, despite the lack of consuls. And he argued that amendments could be considered at the peace conference, which remained in session in Paris, thereby preventing more delays. Germany, a nonmember, need not be consulted about Covenant amendments and could swiftly be brought in to consent to other amendments.

After listing proposed amendments and reservations, the majority report stated, "This covenant of the League of Nations is an alliance and not a league, as is amply shown by the provisions of the treaty with Germany, which vests all essential power in the five great nations." The League as it stood was dangerous. The amendments and reservations would "guard American rights and American sovereignty" and would be accepted abroad, "for without us their league is a wreck and all their gains from a victorious peace are imperilled."[11]

Despite McCumber's refusal to sign the report, Republicans tended to adhere to it. The majority report pointed the way for the largest faction among Senate Republicans, the strong reservationists. Some of these—Joseph Frelinghuysen, James Wadsworth, Warren Harding—spoke like irreconcilables in debate. Seven of them did not say a word on the Senate floor during the prolonged debates on the League but were content to follow the majority leader.[12]

Two days after the filing of the majority report, and just three days before the treaty became the unfinished business before the Senate, friends of the League sustained another sharp blow. Closing out its hearings, the Foreign Relations Committee took testimony from William C. Bullitt, a twenty-eight-year-old State Department employee who had worked for the peace commission until May, when he had resigned in protest over treaty terms. Now Bullitt made headlines with the disclosure that at Paris, Secretary of State Lansing, one of the commissioners, had told him that the treaty as a whole was bad and the League was useless. Lansing repaired the damage only a little on 29 September, when he came out for ratification of

---

Ashurst, entry for 12 September 1919, p. 105.

11. *CR* 66:1, pp. 5112–14 (10 September 1919).

12. David Mervin, "Henry Cabot Lodge and the League of Nations," 210.

the treaty as written. In Paris, General Tasker Bliss quietly declined to sign a statement designed to show that all the commissioners had approved the treaty.[13]

The drift of opinion away from the League in September was spurred by a strong speaking campaign by irreconcilables. Johnson, Borah, Poindexter, and Medill McCormick spoke in most of the same states as did Wilson and in some others as well. Johnson, who with Borah was the most effective of the group, took the longest tour. Since Johnson was a presidential aspirant, the speaking tour suited his purposes well. On balance the senators did not draw as many people as did the president, but they did attract large and enthusiastic crowds.[14]

The Friends of Irish Freedom was one of two organizations that provided financial backing, rented halls, publicized meetings, hired bands, and applauded the speakers. But the Irish-Americans were not solely dependent on irreconcilable senators. They held their own mass rallies against the League in September and on into October, and they intruded on Wilson's meetings, passing out anti-League pamphlets and publishing anti-League ads.[15] Their opposition to the League was perhaps rekindled by the strong testimony of their leaders at the end of August, by the emergence of the treaty in the Senate, and by the fact that the Johnson amendment to equalize voting with Great Britain seemed to be the Senate's first order of business. Wilson's private secretary, Joseph Tumulty, and Senators Tom Walsh and James Phelan had for some time urged Wilson to speak out on the issue of Irish independence, but he had not. Finally, near the end of his tour Wilson discussed questions concerning Ireland, but did not declare for self-determination. Irish-Americans were mainly Democrats, but Republicans courted them.[16]

More circumspectly, German-Americans also expressed their opposition to the League during Wilson's tour. Earlier hopeful of the League, they had begun to react strongly against it after German objections to treaty provisions had been ignored and Germany had

---

13. Ralph Stone, *The Irreconcilables: The Fight Against the League of Nations*, 138; Denna Frank Fleming, *The United States and the League of Nations, 1918–1920*, 367; Frederick Palmer, *Bliss, Peacemaker: The Life and Letters of General Taskar Howard Bliss*, 420.

14. Stone, *The Irreconcilables*, 131–33.

15. John Bernard Duff, "The Politics of Revenge: The Ethnic Opposition to the Peace Policies of Woodrow Wilson," 171–72; Stone, *The Irreconcilables*, 131; Charles C. Tansill, *America and the Fight for Irish Freedom*, 336.

16. Duff, "Politics of Revenge," 164, 173–74; Herbert Parsons to Major Ralph Glyn, 17 September 1919, Parsons Papers.

been forced to sign the treaty. The continuance of the food blockade against Germany until 12 July shocked German-Americans too. The Steuben Society of America, formed in May 1919, opposed the treaty and the League in its periodical, and the German-American press, encouraged by other anti-Wilsonians, became increasingly bold in its criticisms. Now the German-American press greeted Wilson with icy hostility as he swung through their territory in the Midwest and Great Plains. When Wilson countered with charges of disloyalty, he only increased their sullen opposition.[17]

Public support for the League had been broad but shallow. Some of it now crumbled under the pounding of critics. And some League supporters simply became less ardent as they turned to other concerns, such as the rising costs of living. The public was distracted and alarmed by postwar strikes, including the shocking Boston police strike in September and the huge steel strike; by radicalism, associated with the strikes; by the Communist party and other voices of discontent in the United States; and by bolshevism overseas.

In the face of the hardening tendency, the mild reservationists might have expected Democratic leaders to try to negotiate with them before the situation deteriorated further. Indeed, Furnifold Simmons of North Carolina, a member of the Foreign Relations Committee and a strong administration man high in party councils, talked compromise among his Democratic colleagues and on 8 September came out for "some concessions in the way of reservations . . . conservative reservations of an interpretive nature." Simmons's fellow North Carolinian, Lee Overman, supported him, as did Atlee Pomerene of Ohio, another member of the Foreign Relations Committee. Pomerene telegraphed Wilson, warning of harsh reservations to come unless the Democrats promptly dealt with the mild reservationists.[18]

But Gilbert Hitchcock did not take the reservationist path. His minority report, filed on 11 September, left no room for compromise and warned of the economic costs of a delay in ratification. And John Sharp Williams of Mississippi, a member of the committee and an able spokesman, was equally uncompromising in a speech supporting the minority report. Hitchcock met periodically with McCumber, but he refused to negotiate in any definite way. He still hoped

17. Duff, "Politics of Revenge," 132–47, 175; *New York World*, 9 September 1919; Archibald John Dodds, "The Public Services of Philander Chase Knox," 476–77.
18. *Des Moines Register*, 9 September 1919; *Portland Oregonian*, 8 September 1919; *New York World*, 10 September 1919; *New York Tribune*, 10 September 1919; Baker (Newton?) to Joseph Tumulty, 15 September 1919, Wilson Papers.

that the fight among Republicans over amendments would weaken the opposition and ease the way to compromise on favorable terms.[19] Hitchcock reassured Wilson along these lines, as did Pittman and Postmaster General Albert Burleson. The LEP gave further encouragement by endorsing unreserved ratification.[20]

As Wilson proceeded on his tour, he yielded nothing of substance. He minimized the obligations in Article 10 and said again that the Council could only advise and that the United States had a veto, but he still called Article 10 the heart of the Covenant. He agreed to a separate resolution of interpretations while also denying the need for even that. But a reservation that constituted a condition to ratification would have to go back for renegotiation with all parties, including Germany. And he deemed any reservation that sought special privilege for the United States so offensive that he would rather stay out of the League altogether. He spoke well of the mild reservationists but asked that they "forget the details" and stand with him.[21]

Rebuffed by Wilson and Hitchcock, the mild reservationist leaders—particularly McCumber, McNary, Kellogg, and Lenroot, supported by Colt and Nelson—chose to negotiate with Lodge, who acted for himself and as liaison to other Republicans. The GOP had long since unified on the idea of reservations embodied in the resolution of ratification, though many Republican senators reserved the right to ask for amendments or outright rejection. The Foreign Relations Committee, headed by Lodge, had brought forth specific reservations on the four agreed-upon subjects. With the 1920 elections in sight and with Wilson a possible Democratic candidate, mild reservationists who held aloof from the party program would stand alone, with no hope of mustering the twenty Republicans needed to ratify. And negotiation with Lodge did not preclude a deal with Hitchcock, at least not during the early stages of the Lodge negotiations. Should the Democrats decide to compromise, and should the irreconcila-

19. *New York Tribune*, 12 September 1919; Jack E. Kendrick, "The League of Nations and the Republican Senate, 1918–1921," 215; *New York World*, 9, 10, 12 September 1919; *St. Louis Post-Dispatch*, 8 September 1919; Cochran (William Cochran) to Joseph Tumulty, 11 September 1919, Wilson Papers.

20. Earl Gaddis (secretary to Senator Hitchcock) to Joseph Tumulty, 7 September 1919, Forster to Tumulty, 8 September 1919, Cochran to Tumulty, 11 September 1919, Burleson to Wilson, 13 September 1919, Wilson Papers; *St. Louis Post-Dispatch*, 15 September 1919. Neither Taft nor Lowell approved the uncompromising course of the LEP Executive Committee (Taft to Gilbert Hitchcock, 2 September 1919, and Lowell to Taft, 12 September 1919, Taft Papers).

21. Baker and Dodd, eds., *Public Papers of Woodrow Wilson*, 6:129–30, 225–27, 254, 258 on Article 10; 6:129, 142, 148–49, 192, 212 on reservations; and 6:214 on mild reservationists.

bles balk at a reservationist program, Lodge could serve as the necessary emissary to some of the magical twenty Republicans. In addition, as the battle on amendments neared, featuring the popular
Johnson amendment, mild reservationist leaders knew that they
would have their best chance of winning allies if they remained
cooperative to a party program of reservations. Nor were they impervious to the call for party unity or to personal resentment at Wilson's stance and his tactics.

Lodge knew he held high cards. By early September he counted at
least six Democrats supporting his full reservation program.[22] These
Democrats were not like Simmons, Pomerene, or Overman, men
who would accept mild reservations as a matter of expediency. They
were men who believed in strong reservations or who were under
strong constituent pressure: Reed; Shields; Thomas Gore of Oklahoma; Charles Thomas of Colorado, who deplored the labor section
of the treaty; Hoke Smith of Georgia, an able, sincere, and independent man and an enemy of Wilson's; and David Walsh of Massachusetts, who was strongly pressured against the League by his Irish-
American constituents.[23]

Lodge revealed his own inclinations when he urged former Senator Albert J. Beveridge, an irreconcilable and a strong speaker, to
take the stump sooner than he had planned. That is not to say that
Lodge hoped to kill the League, though possibly at this time he did,
but that he wanted strong reservations and some amendments and
saw criticism of the Covenant as conducing to their adoption.[24]
Still, Lodge was willing to compromise with the mild reservationist
leaders. He had to consider a warning from Root not to alienate them
and, by implication, Root. Also, Lodge needed full party unity if he
was to put the blame for killing the treaty on the Democrats. And
given all the factors working in the anti-League direction in Sep-

22. Lodge to James T. Williams, Jr., 6 September 1919, and to George Harvey, 11
September 1919, Lodge Papers.
23. John A. Garraty, *Woodrow Wilson: A Great Life in Brief,* 155; H. B. Learned,
"The Attitude of the United States Senate Towards the Versailles Treaty, 1918–1920,"
in *A History of the Peace Conference of Paris,* ed. H.W.V. Temperley, 415; Dewey W.
Grantham, Jr., "The Southern Senators and the League of Nations, 1918–1920," 189.
24. Lodge to Beveridge, 9 September 1919, Beveridge Papers. On Lodge's hardening attitude in this period, see William C. Widenor, *Henry Cabot Lodge and the
Search for an American Foreign Policy,* 335–36, 342. See also Lodge to Lord Bryce,
8 October 1919, to Arthur W. Hatch, 10 October 1919, and to James T. Williams, Jr.,
15 October 1919, Lodge Papers.

tember, Lodge knew that he would not have to yield anything vital in a compromise bargain.[25]

Through Kellogg, Lodge initiated negotiations, which were held intermittently throughout the second and third weeks of September. McCumber, McNary, Lenroot, and Kellogg drafted a series of revisions to the Foreign Relations Committee's Article 10 reservation and proposed them to Lodge, through Kellogg. Lodge bargained with them on behalf of himself and his party colleagues, but toward the end he occasionally withheld assent on the grounds that others must be consulted.[26] The two sides reached an agreement on 22 September in a meeting between Lodge, McCumber, and Kellogg. Formally, the deal was still tentative, since Lodge could not commit the others. And indeed, the mild reservationists subsequently won slight changes in the reservation. Essentially, though, the reservation was the Republican party's solution to the Article 10 dilemma and was the one voted on by the Senate in November.[27]

Although the reservation was produced by Republicans, McCumber in particular saw it as a basis for compromise with the Democrats. Breaking what Kellogg construed as a confidence, he revealed the reservation to the LEP, whose leaders transmitted it to Wilson.[28] The reservation stated:

The United States assumes no obligation under the provisions of article X to preserve the territorial integrity or political independence of any other country or to interfere in controversies between other nations whether members of the league or not or to employ the military or naval forces of the United States under any article of the treaty for any purpose unless in any particular case the Congress which under the Constitution has the sole

25. Root to Lodge, 10 September 1919; see also Root to Lodge, 26 September 1919, both in Root Papers; *New York World*, 15 September 1919; Lodge to James T. Williams, Jr., 6 September 1919, and to George Harvey, 11 September 1919, Lodge Papers.

26. Kellogg to Elihu Root, 11 September 1919, Root Papers; Gus Karger to William Howard Taft, 10 September 1919, William Short to Taft, 15 September 1919, Karger to Taft, 17 September 1919, Memo, Charles D. Warner to Mr. Rickey, enclosed in Talcott Williams to Taft, 19 September 1919, Short to Taft, 22 September 1919, Taft Papers; Lenroot in *CR* 66:2, p. 4214 (12 March 1920); Vance McCormick to Woodrow Wilson, 18 September 1919, Hitchcock Papers; *New York World*, 16, 18 September 1919.

27. Chandler P. Anderson Diary, entry for 21 September 1919, Anderson Papers; William H. Short to William Howard Taft, 22 September 1919, and Talcott Williams to Taft, 1 October 1919, Taft Papers; Henry Cabot Lodge to Elihu Root, 29 September 1919, Root Papers; *New York Times*, 28 September 1919.

28. *New York Tribune*, 28 September 1919; Chandler P. Anderson Diary, entry for 2 October 1919, Anderson Papers; H. N. Rickey to (Joseph) Tumulty, n.d. [22 September 1919], and Rickey to William Short, 25 September 1919, LEP Papers.

power to declare war or authorize the employment of the military or naval forces of the United States shall by act or joint resolution so declare.[29]

Though not wholly satisfactory to all the mild reservationists, least of all to McCumber, the reservation seemed to them to be better than the committee's in several ways. The committee's reservation had refused any commitment not only on the use of the armed forces but on "economic measures" as well. The boycott was one coercive device that Articles 16 and 17 stated was to be used to induce pacific settlement. For Lenroot, Colt, and Taft, a major complaint with the committee's reservation was its refusal to commit to boycott. The problem was eliminated in the compromise version.[30]

The words *which under the Constitution has the sole power to declare war or authorize the employment of the military or naval forces of the United States* were inserted at the urging of several mild reservationists who thought that, as Lenroot later explained it, "the recital would meet with more favor from our associates than if the recital were omitted." That is, a statement of constitutional limitations would seem to other League members less a rebuff than would a bald statement of unwillingness to commit the United States in advance.[31]

Lodge made another concession to McCumber before the deal was struck. In the late stages of the negotiation, Lodge had proposed that the new reservation should disavow obligations under Article 10 unless Congress should "otherwise specifically determine." In place of these final words Lodge agreed to *by act or joint resolution so declare.* McCumber felt that Lodge's original wording could be taken to mean that the United States would not support the side that would repress aggression.[32]

This seemingly trivial change was related to the mild reservationists' principal objection to the original committee proposal. They felt that it in effect declared a policy of noninterference, of contempt for all Council advice, instead of a mere refusal to be bound either legally or morally in advance of congressional action.

29. William H. Short to William Howard Taft, 22 September 1919, Taft Papers. It may be compared with the committee's reservation (see p. 85).

30. Henry Cabot Lodge to George Harvey, 11 September 1919, Lodge Papers; William Howard Taft to Gus Karger, 16 September 1919, Taft Papers.

31. *CR* 66:1, p. 7949 (4 November 1919). Lenroot explained the wording, but he did not approve it.

32. Memo, Charles D. Warner to Mr. Rickey, n.d., enclosed in Talcott Williams to William Howard Taft, 19 September 1919, and Porter McCumber to Frank Kellogg 16 September 1919, enclosed in Gus Karger to Taft, 18 September 1919, Taft Papers.

Some of the mild reservationists reportedly thought that the spread of bolshevism might warrant intervention. When mild reservationists had first raised the objection, Lodge had denied that he intended to chart a course of pacific isolationism, and he had agreed to verbal changes to meet the objection. The revised reservation did that, to the satisfaction of the mild reservationists. It was, in fact, substantially different from the committee's in that it stressed constitutional limitations only, whereas the committee's downplayed the constitutional aspect and seemed to stress a policy of aloofness from international involvement. Despite the concessions that McCumber, especially, received from Lodge, the reservation was still a tough one. Disavowing obligation, it satisfied Lodge.[33]

Strong party pressure clearly influenced the mild reservationists. Nevertheless, only McCumber and McNary got much less than what they wanted. Nelson took no part in the negotiations, and the other three leaders had openly opposed the obligation in Article 10. They had objected to the committee reservation not because it rejected that obligation but because it struck at the boycott and sounded isolationist in tone. On these matters they had been mollified. Some among them thought the new wording too drastic, yet on balance the reservation did no violence to their views.[34]

McCumber, whose 15 September minority report on the treaty attacked Lodge's report for its sarcastic tone and for its substance, yielded only as a matter of expediency. Having gotten as much as he could from Lodge, he had nowhere else to turn. McCumber would have kept the obligation if he could have. He viewed the compromise as an amendment. But he was pleased that the negative guarantee remained—that each nation pledged to respect the territorial integrity and political independence of other nations. If that were honored, he thought, there would be no need to intervene to protect weaker nations.[35]

What significance did the Republican agreement have for the future functioning of the League? Quite apart from the agreed-on reservation, the Covenant itself, combined with certain facts of world politics, offered the prospect of only a weak system of collec-

33. Lodge to George Harvey, 11 September 1919, Lodge Papers.

34. Gus Karger to William Howard Taft, 13 September 1919, Williams to Taft, 22 September 1919, Karger to Taft, 8 and 10 September 1919, Williams to Taft, 1 October 1919, Taft Papers; T. B. Neuhausen to Charles McNary, 22 September 1919, Neuhausen Papers; *Portland Oregonian*, 21, 28 September 1919; H. N. Rickey to Joseph Tumulty, n.d. [September 1919], LEP Papers.

35. *CR* 66:1, pp. 5356–59 [15 September 1919]; H. N. Rickey to Joseph Tumulty, n.d. [September 1919], LEP Papers; *Portland Oregonian*, 16 December 1919.

tive security. The reservation, if adopted as part of the ratification, would have virtually destroyed even that. It struck at two key ingredients of collective security: predictability and universality. By severely lessening the first, the reservation in effect would have dealt a sharp blow also to the second. And the United States by its action would in all probability have caused Great Britain to follow suit, if not with a reservation then with a narrow interpretation of Article 10 within the League Council.[36]

The importance of the reservation is lessened because it is unlikely that a strong system of collective security would have developed even if the United States had ratified without the reservation to Article 10. Whereas Germany would soon enter the League, the Soviet Union would not, so universality would have been lacking. And there were ambiguities in the wording of Article 10 that left the door open to self-serving interpretation by those countries expected to provide security, chiefly the United States and Great Britain.[37] Quite apart from any reservation, moreover, the American Constitution left ultimate discretion to Congress. Under those circumstances, and given the strong tradition of isolationism in America, the element of predictability would have been lacking even without the reservation. The reservation, then, did not in and of itself destroy the possibility of collective security. But had it been adopted as part of the ratification, it would have greatly weakened an already imperfect system.

It is not clear if the mild reservationists fully realized the influence of the compromise reservation. Kellogg in particular liked to say that by making reservations instead of amendments, the United States would leave the Covenant intact for other members. But that clearly was not the case in this instance. At least some of the mild reservationists, headed by Kellogg and Lenroot, were perhaps indifferent, for the features of the Covenant that appealed to them did not include the system of collective security. For them, and to a lesser extent for the other leaders, the deal was worth making because it promised to keep intact the negative guarantee, the system of pacific settlement backed by sanctions, the system of world con-

36. Inis L. Claude, Jr., *Swords Into Plowshares: The Problems and Progress of International Organization,* 253, 256; George W. Egerton, *Great Britain and the Creation of the League of Nations: Strategy, Politics, and International Organization, 1914–1919,* 191–92; Alfred Zimmern, *The League of Nations and the Rule of Law, 1918–1935,* 325–28; Widenor, *Henry Cabot Lodge,* 337.

37. Zimmern, *League of Nations,* 240–42. The words *undertake to* were weaker than the alternative, *guarantee.* And the second sentence relating to advice from the League Council left it for each nation to act or not act on that advice.

ference on threat of war under Article 11, and disarmament possibilities. All the mild reservationists believed that if the president would but acquiesce in the reservation to Article 10, these other features of the Covenant could be preserved.

Wilson had been forewarned. On 18 September Vance McCormick, a member of the LEP Executive Committee, wired Wilson a copy of what he thought was the final draft of the compromise reservation. Although the draft turned out not to be final, it was close. The reservation was so confidential, McCormick reported, that it had not been shown to Hitchcock. "Please communicate to Senator Hitchcock confidential information received from Vance McCormick," Wilson wired his executive secretary, "and say to him that I should regard any such reservation as a practical rejection of the Covenant."[38]

Having received the somewhat revised compromise agreement of 22 September, Wilson decided to publicly reject it. Speaking in the Mormon Tabernacle the next day, Wilson launched a frontal attack on reservations. Would the country see the war through or not? He had found on his trip that the vast majority of Americans favored the League. "One by one the objections have melted away." Withdrawal, domestic questions, the Monroe Doctrine—they were all adequately dealt with in the Covenant. "The forces of objection being driven out of one position after another are now centering upon the heart of the League itself." He added, "Reservations are to all intents and purposes equivalent to amendments." The people did not want them, and if adopted, reservations would have to go to all treaty signatories, including Germany.[39]

Then Wilson read to his audience the text of the compromise reservation to Article 10. "That is a rejection of the Covenant," he said. "That is an absolute refusal to carry any part of the same responsibility that the other members of the League carry." Discussing the importance and value of Article 10, Wilson emphasized the American veto, the powers of congress, and the likelihood that in the event of aggression the Council would call on nations closest to the theater of war. Then he resumed his attack on the reservation. The last part, concerning the powers of Congress, was common knowledge and thus was not needed. What he objected to was the denial of obligation. The president reiterated his point in equally strong terms at

38. Vance McCormick to J. P. Tumulty, 18 September 1919, and W. W. (Wilson) to (Rudolph) Forster, 19 September 1919, Wilson Papers. Forster complied with Wilson's request (Forster to Hitchcock, 24 September 1919, Hitchcock Papers).

39. Baker and Dodd, eds., *Public Papers of Woodrow Wilson*, 6:349.

Cheyenne, Denver, and Pueblo, where illness brought his tour to an end.[40]

The mild reservationist leaders were profoundly shaken by Wilson's remarks at Salt Lake City. They were disturbed not only by his threat to the treaty but also by his interpretation of Article 10, which seemed to retract earlier assurances of Congress's powers. The six leaders and Hale agreed on 24 September that in light of Wilson's interpretation, reservations must be strong. Lenroot was deputized to say so to the Senate that afternoon.[41]

Lenroot spoke briefly. He quoted the reservation that Wilson had read at Salt Lake City and Wilson's condemnation of it. He then rejoined, "Unless a reservation substantially such as that read by the President is incorporated as part of the ratification resolution, this peace treaty is not, in my judgment, going to be ratified by the Senate." Next Lenroot quoted Wilson as having said, at Salt Lake City and earlier at Indianapolis, that nothing could be done "without the consent of the United States"—that no independence of judgment would be sacrificed under Article 10.

> The President of the United States must take one of the two horns of the dilemma that he is in. If the United States remains a free agent under the provisions of the article as it stands, the reservation that is proposed can not cut the heart out of the covenant. If it is a free agent, it can do no harm. If it is not a free agent, then the President—I do not say intentionally—has been misstating to the country the effect of article 10.[42]

Lenroot stated that, technically speaking, Congress had to act before the United States could go to war. But Wilson, by pushing for the ratification of the treaty with Article 10 in its present form, was now asking the Senate "to pledge the solemn word of the United States that whenever the occasion arises it will engage in war, if necessary, to preserve the territorial integrity of any member of the league from external aggression." Wilson had occasionally suggested that the United States could act only on the advice of the Council, Lenroot observed. "[But] the President must know that the undertaking in Article Ten to respect and preserve the territorial integrity and political independence of every member of the league against

40. Ibid., 350–53, 382, 390, 412, 415.
41. Kellogg to Taft, 25 September 1919, Kellogg Papers; Gus Karger to William Howard Taft, 23 September 1919, Taft Papers; *New York Tribune*, 26, 27 September 1919; *Milwaukee Sentinel*, 26 September 1919.
42. *CR* 66:1, p. 5912 (25 September 1919).

external aggression is a promise irrespective of any advice of the council."[43]

In speeches the following day, Cummins and Hale condemned Article 10 and called for strong reservations. Lodge responded to Wilson's rejection of the compromise reservation by saying that fifty-four senators backed it.[44] Had Wilson retained his health, he might eventually have agreed to meaningful compromise on Article 10 and on lesser questions. But his physical collapse on 25 September separated him from his advisers. His earlier rejection of the Republican compromise reservation to Article 10 and his construction of that article as carrying military obligation effected a deadlock.

After his breakdown at Pueblo, Wilson was hurried back to Washington. Not until 10 February 1920 did anyone disclose the nature of his illness or its seriousness, and indeed he seemed somewhat better by the time he reached the capital. Democratic senators, in the wake of Lenroot's speech and related events signaling Republican agreement, hoped to see Wilson soon to describe the situation and the need for compromise.[45] They did not get the chance, for he suffered a severe stroke on 2 October. By the end of the month, his mind was "relatively clear; but he was physically enfeebled, and the disease had wrecked his emotional constitution and aggravated all his more unfortunate personal traits."[46] On the advice of one of his doctors, Mrs. Wilson undertook to shield him from every person or document that might cause anxiety. The last information that Wilson had been given—received during the final stages of his trip—had been encouraging, as were the cheers of the crowds. These were the mis-

43. Ibid.

44. Ibid., 5952–57, 5985 (26 September 1919); *Minneapolis Tribune*, 29 September 1919.

45. George Juergens, *News From the White House: The Presidential-Press Relationship in the Progressive Era*, 258–61; Edwin A. Weinstein, *Woodrow Wilson: A Medical and Psychological Biography*, 353, 355; *St. Louis Post-Dispatch*, 26 September 1919; *Des Moines Resister*, 30 September, 2 October 1919; *New York Tribune*, 27, 28 September 1919.

46. Arthur S. Link, *Woodrow Wilson: Revolution, War, and Peace*, 121. According to some authorities, health problems plagued Wilson for some time and help to explain unwise actions on the treaty since the spring of 1919 (Weinstein, *Woodrow Wilson*; Edwin A. Weinstein, James W. Anderson, and Arthur S. Link, "Woodrow Wilson's Political Personality: A Reappraisal," 585–98. For a sampling of a conflicting view, see Michael F. Marmor, "Wilson, Strokes, and Zebras," 528–35, and Alexander George and Juliette George, "Woodrow Wilson and Colonel House: A Reply to Weinstein, Anderson, and Link," 641–65. See also Bert Edward Park, *The Impact of Illness on World Leaders*.

leading impressions that Wilson retained in the months that followed.[47]

Senate Democrats suffered a leadership gap during Wilson's illness. Hitchcock could hardly take it on himself to deviate from the strategy that he had earlier developed and that Wilson had approved. He would postpone the question of reservations until amendments had been acted on. Meanwhile, he told Tumulty on 29 September, he had no matter to put before the president that could not wait until he had recovered.[48] The mild reservationist leaders agreed on the urgency and importance of the amendments. But far from putting aside reservations, as Hitchcock did, they developed new ones, to counter the challenge of the amendments.

Although still in doubt and disagreement concerning the legal effect of reservations, mild reservationist leaders understood that amendments would require full renegotiation and would cause a great delay in formally ending the war. On the strength of that argument, principally, and with the promise of reservations on the subjects covered by the amendments, they were able to win enough Republican allies to defeat the amendments. Victory did not come easily, and for a time the strongest of the amendments, Hiram Johnson's, seemed destined to pass. Indeed it was so attractive that Kellogg and Lenroot approached the subject with extreme caution. Paradoxically, these two led the mild reservationists in the formulation and the negotiation of reservation alternatives to amendments and in floor debates.

Preliminary skirmishes on the Johnson amendment had begun while the mild reservationist leaders were still negotiating the Article 10 compromise reservation. The Senate took up the treaty in open executive session on 16 September. The clerk began to read the 537-page treaty into the record, starting with the first section, the League Covenant. When Article 3 was reached that day, the Johnson amendment to it was in order, but Lodge asked that it be passed over for a time, since Johnson and others were on the stump.[49] On 22 September James Reed gave the amendment a strong send-off with a

47. Edith Bolling Wilson, *My Memoir*, 289; Albert Burleson to Wilson, 22 September 1919, (Rudolph) Forster to (Joseph) Tumulty, 23 September 1919, Gilbert Hitchcock to Tumulty, 24 September 1919, Joseph T. Robinson to Wilson, 25 September 1919, Wilson Papers.

48. *Portland Oregonian*, 30 September 1919.

49. *New York World*, 11 September 1919; *Minneapolis Tribune*, 17 September 1919.

powerful four-hour speech before almost the whole Senate, about a hundred House members, and full galleries. He created something of a sensation when he read a memorandum from Wilson, Lloyd George, and Clemenceau assuring Canadian Prime Minister Robert Borden that Britain's self-governing dominions were eligible to sit in the Council. The memorandum, written in May, had been published in Canada but had been little noticed in the United States. Contradicting statements that Wilson had made on his tour and that Reed now quoted, the memo advanced the cause of the Johnson amendment, which would equalize American and British voting power not only in the Assembly but also on the Council.[50] Political leaders divided in their predictions of the outcome but agreed that the vote, which might come within days, would be close. Both sides understood that if the Johnson amendment passed, other amendments might also win adoption.[51]

It is hard to imagine that members of the League other than Great Britain would agree to give the United States six votes in the Assembly. Nevertheless, Americans hailed the amendment. The widespread public hostility toward Great Britain reflected in the popularity of the Johnson amendment resulted from more than the Old World animosity of such ethnic groups as the Irish-Americans and the German-Americans, though that contributed. Anglophobia tied in with American nationalism, since England had been the enemy in the American Revolution, in the War of 1812, and, to a degree, even in the Civil War. Beyond that, American democrats saw Britain as the world's bastion of aristocracy and imperial domination.[52]

Republican middle grounders could determine the outcome. Lodge, anxious that the amendment not be beaten by Republican votes, additionally pressured some of them. He thought that McCumber, McNary, Nelson, and Colt were hopeless but that their votes would be offset by defecting Democrats.[53] Cummins followed

50. Thomas F. Eagleton, "James A. Reed and the League of Nations," 61–64; *New York Tribune*, 23 September 1919; Stone, *The Irreconcilables*, 134; *New York Times*, 23 September 1919.

51. Breckenridge Long to Joseph Tumulty, 23 September 1919, Wilson Papers; Nicholas Murray Butler to William M. Calder, 24 September 1919, Butler Papers; William H. Short to William Howard Taft, 22 September 1919, and Talcott Williams to Taft, 22 September 1919, Taft Papers.

52. *New York Tribune*, 19 September 1919; Henry L. Stimson Diaries, entry for 24 September 1919, Stimson Papers; Walter Heineman to Irvine Lenroot, 23 September 1919, in "Corres. between W. B. Heineman . . . General L. C. Boyle, and (William) Borah," William E. Borah Papers, Library of Congress; Duff, "Politics of Revenge," 160, 177.

53. Lodge to John M. Weeks, 22 September 1919, Lodge Papers; Chandler P.

Kenyon in announcing for the amendment, but some other senators, although cautious of the amendment's political attractiveness, feared its adoption. As Harding explained the attitude of some of his colleagues: "The objection to sanctioning such an amendment among the earliest changes made, lies in the fact that one amendment to the text of the League Covenant would open the way for numerous amendments which would tend to wreck the whole league scheme. A very considerable number of reservationists do not want to adopt such a course." But there was something else. Edge, reflecting a common view among the middle grounders, wrote Root that he preferred reservations to amendments "in order to save time by avoiding reference of the Treaty to the conference." In a Senate speech Hale expressed himself for strong reservations in preference to amendments and also stressed the need for haste. The continuing unsettled conditions in Europe, joined with the desire to resume full economic relations with Germany and to end wartime legislation, explains the strong and pervasive desire for a formal consummation of peace.[54]

Mild reservationist leaders conferred among themselves and with other senators in the week of 17–24 September. Though not all of them would commit themselves against the Johnson amendment, Kellogg, Lenroot, Edge, McNary, and Spencer drafted reservations on the "six vote" question, as McCumber already had done.[55] Colt, Nelson, Capper, and Sterling also studied reservation possibilities. Kellogg judged that none but the toughest of the reservation proposals, Lenroot's, could sidetrack the Johnson amendment. Edge agreed that Lenroot's reservation was good, better than his own. Lenroot's reservation stated that the United States would not be bound by any League decision in which the British Empire either cast more than one vote or voted when party to the dispute.[56]

Using reservationism as a weapon against the Johnson amendment, on 25 September Lenroot, representing the other mild reservationist leaders and Hale, told Lodge and Swanson that his group opposed immediate consideration of the amendment and, if need be,

Anderson Diary, entry for 21 September 1919, Anderson Papers.

54. *CR* 66:1, pp. 5957, 5985 (26 September 1919); Harding to F. E. Scobey, 27 September 1919, Harding Papers; Edge to Root, 26 September 1919, Root Papers.

55. Gus Karger to William Howard Taft, 24 September 1919, Taft Papers; *St. Louis Post-Dispatch*, 21 September 1919; Edge to Elihu Root, 26 September 1919, Root Papers; *Portland Oregonian*, 28 September 1919.

56. *New York Times*, 25 September 1919; Kellogg to William Howard Taft, 25 September 1919, Kellogg Papers; Walter Edge to Elihu Root, 26 September 1919, Root Papers.

would vote against taking it up. The group wanted time to win agreement on a reservation instead of the amendment. Johnson had returned to Washington expecting a vote, so Lenroot told Lodge that if the Johnson amendment was moved from the top of the list to the bottom, his group would promise Johnson at least four days' notice of a vote. Thus, Johnson could return to the stump and take his campaign to the West Coast. In effect, Lenroot threatened the defeat of the amendment if action on it was not postponed. Lodge had reason to fear the votes not only of the seven senators that Lenroot represented but also those of Edge, Townsend, and perhaps others.[57]

By then several Democrats, under strong pressure from Wilson, had returned to the fold, so Lodge could count on no more than three Democrats for the amendment. Thus, the mild reservationists held a commanding position. Furthermore, Senator Boies Penrose of Pennsylvania, who had been ill, had returned to Washington to express a sentiment that was widespread among conservative Republicans—that they should not help Johnson advance his presidential hopes.[58] Unhappy at the delay, Johnson warned that he would not let the temporary postponement become a permanent one, no matter how many Republicans preferred a reservation. Meanwhile, however, the weak Fall amendments moved to the head of the list, giving a tactical advantage to those who opposed all amendments. Hays, close to the situation in Washington, predicted that all amendments would fail. With some justification, McNary claimed that the mild reservationists caused the popular Johnson amendment to go over.[59]

If mild reservationists had not ended the battle on the Johnson amendment, they had won a principal engagement. In so doing, they advanced reservationism as an alternative. Taking the lead in formulating possible reservations to cover the subject, they negotiated with other Republicans. So it was also with the Fall amendments. These amendments would have withheld American participation in commissions created under the treaty and would have declined American commitment to help enforce certain provisions of the treaty. Mild reservationists spearheaded the opposition to and clinched the

57. *New York Times*, 26 September 1919; *New York World*, 26 September 1919; Charles P. Hilles to William Howard Taft, 1 October 1919, Taft Papers.

58. Talcott Williams to William Howard Taft, 27 September 1919; Gus Karger to Taft, 24 September 1919, Taft Papers; *New York Tribune*, 25 September 1919.

59. *New York Times*, 26 September 1919; Henry L. Stimson Diaries, entry for 25 September 1919, Stimson Papers; McNary to William Howard Taft, 26 September 1919, Taft Papers.

defeat of the amendments with the promise of some reservations. Before an almost full Senate chamber and packed galleries, on 2 October Lenroot reassured colleagues about reservations that would follow, and several senators went on record for reservations instead of amendments.[60] By the end of the day all but one of the thirty-seven Fall amendments had been rejected, and the last one was turned down two weeks later.

The key vote was on the first Fall amendment. It lost, 58–30.[61] Acting with the Democrats, seventeen Republicans, all middle grounders, accomplished its defeat. Of the middle grounder group, only George McLean of Connecticut voted for the amendment. The vote on this amendment, and on the other Fall amendments, was significant in several ways. Middle grounders showed themselves to have a commanding position so far as amendments were concerned. But the pro-amendment group mustered more than a third of the Senate, including those paired and those absent and not paired. Unreserved ratification was now out of the question; reservations became certain; and it became clear that reservations would have to meet the requirements of some of the pro-amendment group as a condition for ratification.

As an immediate aftermath, Lenroot, McNary, Capper, Smoot of Utah, and the New Hampshire irreconcilable George Moses set to work on reservations to cover the Fall amendments. Already Kellogg, at first alone and then with Chandler Anderson, had drafted a reservation that met with Lodge's approval.[62] The eighth reservation adopted by the Foreign Relations Committee on 23 October in part fulfilled the promises of Lenroot and Kellogg. American participation in commissions would be determined by law, and representatives would be confirmed by the Senate.[63] As Lenroot had noted in debate, the reservation to Article 10 concerning the use of the armed forces also met some of the purposes of the Fall amendments.

The middle grounders' defeat of the Fall amendments gave no indication how they would vote on the far more popular Johnson amendment. Though it had been shifted to the bottom of the list for Senate action, once the Fall amendments had been decided senators

60. *St. Louis Post-Dispatch*, 3 October 1919.
61. *CR* 66:1, p. 6269 (2 October 1919).
62. *New York Times*, 3 October 1919; Kellogg to Lodge, 9 September 1919; Lodge to Kellogg, 9 September 1919, Lodge Papers; Chandler P. Anderson Diary, entry for 21 September 1919, Anderson Papers; Lodge to Elihu Root, 3 December 1919, Root Papers.
63. As renumbered later, this became the seventh of the "Lodge reservations" voted on 19 November.

and observers gave the Johnson amendment their immediate attention because it was the most formidable of the committee amendments. As of 3 October, when William Howard Taft arrived in Washington to assess the situation and to use his influence against the
Johnson amendment, two senators seemed to hold the key to the
situation. Observers counted McNary, McCumber, Colt, and Nelson against the amendment but Democrats Reed, Gore, and David
Walsh for it. If party lines held, apart from these defections, the Senate vote would be 48–48, and the vice-president would cast the
deciding vote against the amendment. But Kellogg and Shields were
thought to be in doubt. If both supported the amendment, it would
pass.[64]

Taft met with McCumber, McNary, Kellogg, and Colt, as well as
with Hitchcock and Oscar Underwood of Alabama. It had become
apparent that Thomas Martin would not resume his Senate duties,
which were now shared by the rivals for the succession to minority
leader, although Hitchcock continued as the spokesman on foreign
relations. In the main, the senators confirmed press reports, and
Taft came away fearful of the outcome, on two scores. The prospective vote on the Johnson amendment would be perilously close—a
single vote might determine the result. And to counter the amendment, some mild reservationists would support Lenroot's draft of a
reservation that Taft found unduly drastic. The more immediate
problem was the amendment, and Taft's best hope seemed to be Kellogg, though the Minnesotan spoke irately of Wilson and impressed
McNary as being unreliable. Hale, Lenroot, Keyes, Edge, Capper,
and Townsend were others with whom there was some hope, Taft
learned.[65] Taft asked Colt to argue the case with Kellogg, and he
wrote directly to the senator pleading with him to save the treaty.
Kellogg remained noncommittal to the end, but he did finally vote
against the amendment. Then he replied to Taft, saying he had never
intended to vote for it and asking where Taft had gotten the idea that
he would.[66]

How Kellogg would have voted had there been no satisfactory
understanding about a reservation is unknowable. Throughout the
period, he opposed the amendment and hoped for its defeat. He was
inclined to vote against it even before he saw Elihu Root at an Ameri-

64. *Minneapolis Tribune*, 1 October 1919; *New York Tribune*, 6 October 1919;
New York World, 13 October 1919; *New York Times*, 13 October 1919.
    65. Taft to A. Lawrence Lowell, 5 October 1919, Taft Papers.
    66. Taft to Colt, 5 October 1919, and to Kellogg, 11 October 1919, Taft Papers;
Kellogg to Taft, 27 October 1919, Kellogg Papers.

can Bar Association meeting in Boston in early September. Root, a man Kellogg highly respected and sometimes consulted, strengthened his conviction by stressing the preferability of reservations to amendments. Amendments could cause America's exclusion from the treaty through the action of other nations, and Wilson would be relieved of his responsibility for a bad treaty. On the other hand, Wilson had acknowledged the reasonableness of clarifying reservations. If the treaty was defeated because of them, Wilson would be responsible. Chandler Anderson, Root's protégé, later reiterated the view, and Kellogg agreed. The Minnesotan thought Lodge and Brandegee saw the point too.[67] That they continued to support the amendment may have contributed to Kellogg's hesitancy in announcing his opposition.

Until the middle of October the issue remained in doubt. Taft continued to try to influence senators, but with little apparent effect.[68] The organization he ostensibly headed, the LEP, had not followed his lead in endorsing reservations, so it was not in a strong position to influence Republican reservationists. Indeed an LEP telegram soliciting thousand-dollar contributions for pro-League, anti-reservation propaganda antagonized some of them.[69] McCumber delivered what a historian has described as the strongest and best speech in defense of League voting provisions. He suggested a reservation to make it doubly clear that the British Empire would have only one vote when any part of it was involved in a dispute. But he aroused little interest.[70]

To nose-counters, the more important statements came from previously uncommitted moderates. Before the vote on the Fall amendments, Capper announced his support not only for the four committee reservations but also for the Shantung and Johnson amendments. On the following day, 3 October, Wesley Jones endorsed the Johnson amendment, in terms similar to those used by Cummins a week earlier.[71] Six days later, before a closely attentive Senate, Democrat

67. Chandler P. Anderson Diary, entry for 1 October 1919, Anderson Papers.

68. *Des Moines Register*, 13 October 1919; Warren Harding to F. E. Scobey, 8 October 1919, Harding Papers; Charles Townsend to William Howard Taft, 9 October 1919, and Taft to Gilbert Hitchcock, 7 October 1919, Taft Papers; Homer E. Socolofsky, *Arthur Capper: Publisher, Politician, and Philanthropist*, 130.

69. Philip Bennett, Financial Secretary, to "Dear Co-Worker," 29 September 1919, Jordan Papers; *Des Moines Register*, 21 September 1919; *CR* 66:1, p. 5937 (26 September 1919).

70. Learned, "Versailles Treaty," 414; *CR* 66:1, pp. 6439–43 (6 October 1919); *Portland Oregonian*, 7 October 1919.

71. *New York Tribune*, 3 October 1919; William Allen White to Arthur Capper,

Walsh of Massachusetts emotionally spoke for a League that would do justice to the oppressed, and he criticized the Covenant. Theretofore an administration loyalist who had urged patience on his fellow Irish-Americans, Walsh in effect declared his independence from Wilson on the Johnson amendment and on other treaty issues. His speech came only days after the Democratic state convention in Massachusetts had called for ratification with an equal voting amendment and with measures to advance Irish independence. In the wake of rumors that Kellogg had decided to vote for the amendment, Walsh's speech seemed to give the amendment a two-vote majority.[72]

Most middle grounders remained noncommittal, but three edged warily toward the amendment. Opponents of the Johnson amendment had had hopes for Lenroot and Townsend, who were thought to be undecided, and for Spencer, who in early September had criticized the Johnson amendment.[73] But in brief Senate remarks, Lenroot pointed out that the Johnson amendment would not fully accomplish its purpose of equalizing the voting with Great Britain. When the United States was party to a dispute, it could not vote, whether it had one vote or six, whereas the British Empire would retain its six votes. But he did not claim that the amendment would be utterly useless, and he drew a sharp distinction between amendments to the Covenant and those to other parts of the treaty. The League Covenant would take effect as soon as Britain, France, and Italy ratified the treaty, and those three nations, acting under the terms of the Covenant, could amend the treaty. Thus amendments to the Covenant would not require prolonged renegotiation with all signatories, and Germany would not be involved, in Lenroot's view. He proposed, therefore, to consider amendments to the Covenant on their merits.[74]

Outside the Senate chamber, Lenroot continued to push for his reservation. In a political sense, the reservation remained an alternative to the Johnson amendment. But for Lenroot himself, and for

---

21 August 1919, in Walter Johnson, ed., *Selected Letters of William Allen White, 1899–1943* (New York: Henry Holt and Company, 1947), 200–201; Socolofsky, *Arthur Capper*, 126–29. One of the leaders was Capper's Kansas colleague, Charles Curtis; *CR* 66:1, pp. 6332–38 (3 October 1919). For Cummins's speech, see pp. 5952–57 (26 September 1919).

72. *Des Moines Register*, 10 October 1919; Louis L. Gerson, *The Hyphenate in Recent American Politics and Diplomacy*, 109; *Portland Oregonian*, 5 October 1919; *Minneapolis Tribune*, 8, 11 October 1919; *New York Tribune*, 11 October 1919; *Providence Evening Tribune*, 11 October 1919.

73. *St. Louis Post-Dispatch*, 6 September 1919.

74. *CR* 66:1, p. 6445 (6 October 1919), p. 6273 (2 October 1919), p. 6450 (6 October 1919).

those who accepted his logic, the door was open to support for both the reservation and the amendment. To what extent Lenroot was moved by political considerations is not known. But it is clear that he faced a very difficult reelection fight in 1920, that Senator La Follette would use all his power to defeat Lenroot, that the La Follette forces were lining up against the League, and that anti-League sentiment was gaining in Wisconsin.[75]

Taft made no direct appeal to Lenroot, who had been an insurgent antagonist during Taft's presidency, though he tried to reach him through the unlikely agency of Hitchcock. Taft did write directly to Senator Townsend of Michigan. Townsend had supported a reservationist compromise in August and had voted against all but one of the Fall amendments. A moderate, he had been quiet on the treaty and the League up to that time, probably at least partly because of his wife's illness.[76]

Born on a Michigan farm in 1856, Townsend grew up in poverty. Largely self-educated, he was almost forty before he was admitted to the bar. He won election to the House of Representatives in 1902 and to the Senate in 1910, and he gained some prominence in both bodies in connection with railroad legislation. Townsend was a skilled debater and a moderate progressive.[77] On 28 August, mainly for the benefit of his constituents, Townsend gave his general position on the treaty. He opposed worldwide entanglements but approved of international arbitration, and he wanted the treaty ratified. America should be protected, however—by reservations if possible, by amendments if necessary. But he did not favor the Shantung amendment because it was also an entanglement.[78]

In response to Taft's appeal, Townsend gave an updated statement of his position. "I do not think that many of the reservations which have been proposed would necessarily send the Treaty back to conference and I am in favor, just as far as it is possible, to secure what we want through reservations," he wrote. But he described himself as "troubled" about the Johnson amendment. The treaty provision

75. *Milwaukee Sentinel*, 11 October 1919; *Minneapolis Tribune*, 11 October 1919; La Follette to "My Dear Pards," 21 June 1919, La Follette Papers; Clara Lenroot to Nellie Nichols, 21 August 1919, Lenroot Papers; W. W. Powell to William H. Short, 28 August 1919, LEP Papers.

76. Herbert F. Margulies, *Senator Lenroot of Wisconsin: A Political Biography, 1900–1929*, 84–85; Taft to Hitchcock, 7 October 1919, and Townsend to Taft, 9 October 1919, Taft Papers; *CR* 66:1, p. 4453 (28 August 1919). Townsend's wife died in early 1920.

77. *Washington Post*, 4 August 1924.

78. *CR* 66:1, pp. 4453–55 (28 August 1919).

on voting seemed inequitable, though as Taft had suggested, the United States seemed unlikely to suffer from it. "It is, however, a very difficult matter to explain to the people," Townsend continued. "They are not willing that any country on earth shall be regarded as superior to their own and no one can convince them to the contrary." On 18 October Townsend implied his decision: he had printed in the *Congressional Record* a newspaper article favorable to the Johnson amendment, and he praised the author of the article.[79]

Spencer, the third middle grounder moving toward the amendment, remained under pressure from Republican politicians in Missouri, some of whom used the League issue as a weapon against him. His political friends managed to head off a full-scale party convention, but they could not prevent the State Central Committee from urging him to support the Foreign Relations Committee's reservations and amendments. Although not committing his vote, Spencer thanked the committee for its directions.[80]

Backers of the Johnson amendment counted on reluctant help from many of the middle grounders because of constituent opinion. Even so, their position was insecure. Unless another Democrat or two joined them, an unlikely prospect, if only one Republican defected and joined the four Republicans counted in opposition, the amendment would be killed. And Kellogg remained uncommitted while newsmen speculated that Spencer and Smoot were also in doubt.[81]

The coup de grâce came from an unexpected quarter. On 16 October, in final debate on the Shantung amendment, Fred Hale announced that he would oppose all amendments, including Johnson's. He had been counted as favoring amendments, and Lodge in particular thought that Hale, as a Rooseveltian nationalist, belonged with the strong reservationists.[82] But Hale's action should have

79. Townsend to Taft, 9 October 1919, Taft Papers; *CR* 66:1, pp. 7105–6 (18 October 1919).

80. *St. Louis Post-Dispatch*, 9–11 October 1919). When in September a friend suggested that Spencer be the speaker at a Missouri Republican club banquet, the name was "hooted down unanimously." Meanwhile, a canvass of four thousand Republican voters in the state found the vast majority against the League in any form. Hiram Johnson had been very well received in St. Louis that month, and the city was known for its "Wilson-hating German Republicans" (E. Mont Reily to Warren G. Harding, 15 September 1919, Harding Papers; *St. Louis Post-Dispatch*, 13 September 1919; Eagleton, "James A. Reed," 29). On the other hand, the *St. Louis Globe-Democrat* was taken by many as a Republican party organ in the state, and it favored the League with reservations (*St. Louis Post-Dispatch*, 8 October 1919).

81. *Providence Evening Tribune*, 13 October 1919.

82. *St. Louis Post-Dispatch*, 16 October 1919; Alice Roosevelt Longworth, *Crowded Hours*, 199, 289, 291.

occasioned no surprise. True, he had spoken bluntly about defects in the treaty and the Covenant and about Wilson. But since December 1918, when he and Kellogg had brought Nicholas Murray Butler to Washington for consultations, Hale had actively sought speedy ratification and had consorted with the mild reservationist leaders. Now, in the Senate, he argued against amendments. He thought that a reservation could protect American rights against British over-representation as well as or better than an amendment could. And a single amendment "nullifies the benefit that we shall get from the reservation play and may jeopardize the ratification of the treaty, and I do not want to see it so jeopardized." Hale remarked on the spirit of recrimination that had descended on the Senate, and he responded to those who called the middle grounders weak-kneed. Anyone who, like himself, had worked out a plan and followed it was innocent of the charge, he said. Finally, he called for night sessions, to hasten action.[83]

Though not explicit, two other previously uncommitted senators implied their opposition to the Johnson amendment. Kellogg and Sterling, speaking in the Senate against the Shantung amendment, praised reservations as preferable to amendments. And Colt caused no surprise when he spoke against the Johnson amendment.[84] Less conspicuously, the quiet New Hampshire freshman Henry Keyes announced his intention to vote against the Johnson amendment and the Shantung amendment as well, provided adequate reservations on those subjects were available. He disclosed his decision to Frank Knox, the influential Manchester editor-publisher. Referring to Johnson's proposal, Keyes said that he did not want to delay the restoration of normal conditions in the world, a delay entailed in treaty renegotiation. He did not like the unequal voting of Great Britain and the United States in the Assembly, but he was confident of an adequate reservation on the subject. Only if disappointed in that expectation would he vote for the amendment.

Keyes was more definite about opposing the Shantung amendment, though he favored a reservation to deal with the "unconscionable steal." Knox, quite critical of the Covenant, nevertheless approved Keyes's position. He did not want to abandon the Allies while the job was half done.

Keyes liked Hale and McNary, and he respected Kellogg and Lenroot. One or more of these men, through public and private remarks,

83. *CR* 66:1, pp. 6991–92 (16 October 1919).
84. Ibid., 6990, 6995 (16 October 1919), pp. 6925–27 (15 October 1919).

may have fortified his confidence in the reservationists' alternative to amendments.[85]

Before the Johnson amendment could be finally put to rest, the Senate had to deal with the Shantung amendment. Actually, six amendments were involved, each restoring German economic rights to China instead of to Japan, but the six were treated as one and were to be voted en bloc. As voting loomed near, everyone agreed that the amendment would be defeated by the votes of middle grounders, but the margin remained in doubt. The debate proved heated, as backers of the amendment showed aggravation with those middle grounders who, though deploring the Shantung provisions, wouldn't vote to amend them. "Whenever a reservationist opened his mouth," a reporter wrote, "a group of the amendment's supporters pounced upon his utterances with merciless retorts."[86]

McCumber, a master of the subject, reviewed it once again in a full and able speech that answered the speech by Lodge, the amendment's ardent sponsor. McCumber urged his colleagues to give Japan time to act justly. He aroused the ire of Reed when he said that many senators had become more solicitous of Germany than of friends who had helped defeat Germany. The fiery Reed challenged him to name the senators and called McCumber to order. Ruled against by the presiding officer, Senator Lewis Ball of Delaware, McCumber disparaged the ruling. Then he proceeded with his speech. A month earlier he had suggested a reservation, but he made no mention of it now. In that respect, and in his relatively friendly attitude toward Japan, McCumber separated himself from many of those he hoped to influence.[87]

It was Lenroot who, on the following day, 15 October, spoke to and for the middle grounders. He agreed with the general denunciation of the Shantung provisions. But he would pay no heed to senators like Reed and Borah who, even if they got an amendment to protect China, would later vote against the treaty, thus abandoning her. An amendment would do no good, he argued, but would simply keep the United States out of the treaty. Britain, France, and Italy were bound by treaty to support Japan's claims; they could not

85. *Manchester Union*, 16 October 1919, 5 February 1920; Frances Parkinson Keyes, *All Flags Flying: Reminiscences of Frances Parkinson Keyes*, 135. Earlier, Knox praised the Massachusetts Republican platform when it called for ratification without amendments but with reservations (*Manchester Union*, 6 October 1919).

86. *Minneapolis Tribune*, 16 October 1919.

87. *CR* 66:1, pp. 6880–83 (14 October 1919); *Minneapolis Tribune* (15 October 1919).

accept the amendment. "The fact is, and we might as well face it very frankly," Lenroot said, "that we are confronted with the proposition that if we adopt these amendments the United States is out of the treaty entirely; that is the issue. I can not give my consent to the position that I am unwilling to make peace with Germany unless Shantung is restored to China." Speaking with apparent authority, Lenroot advanced the reservationist alternative. "I want to assure the Senate," he said, "that they will later on have an opportunity to vote for a . . . reservation. If no other reservation is proposed, I shall offer a reservation substantially in this form: "The United States withholds its assent to Articles 156, 157, and 158, and reserves full liberty of action with respect to any controversy that may arise under said articles." Lenroot would not insist on the exact wording, however. Then he defended the reservation against Borah's charge that it would be useless. It would, Lenroot said, leave the United States free of complicity in the "crime" and free to act for China.[88]

Earlier that day, Colt and Spencer and Democrats Shields and Thomas had come out against the amendment and for a reservation. Spencer's remarks are most noteworthy. Deviating from the directions of the Republican State Central Committee, Spencer criticized the amendment as a "verbal bubble" that would accomplish nothing. Moreover, he said, the amendment constituted meddling in the Far East, the kind of meddling that he and other moderates deplored and for which they condemned Article 10. Reed, clashing with his colleague from Missouri for the first time in the treaty battle, pointed out that if the amendment was adopted, the matter would go back to the other signatories. Spencer replied, "It is for the very purpose of preventing, unless it is absolutely necessary, such amendments as will carry the treaty back that I prefer the reservations."[89]

On 16 October, at the start of what proved to be a six-and-a-half-hour debate preliminary to a vote, Kellogg reinforced Lenroot's pledge. He endorsed the reservation that Lenroot had proposed, and he made known to the Senate another very similar one that Root sent him in September. With Lenroot and others, Kellogg condemned the amendment as impracticable, since other nations would not agree to it. The treaty was far from perfect, he concluded, but he urged the Senate to approve it and end the war.[90]

Other senators wanted to explain their forthcoming votes to col-

88. *CR* 66:1, pp. 6951–52 (15 October 1919).
89. Ibid., 6947–48 (15 October 1919).
90. Ibid., 6989–90 (16 October 1919); Root to Kellogg, 8 September 1919, Root Papers.

leagues and constituents. Among them were several middle grounders who proposed to vote against the amendment. Hale would not
have the nation left out of the treaty because of Shantung, much as
he deplored the provision. Townsend and Sterling argued that the
amendment would be rejected abroad and would accomplish nothing, whereas a reservation would express America's views.[91] Implicitly, Sterling distinguished between the Shantung amendment,
which he opposed, and the Fall amendments, some of which he had
supported, on the grounds that though both would cause delay, only
the former was unacceptable to the other signatories.

McCumber next got the floor to elaborate on his earlier arguments. This time, though, he took note of his own reservation proposals—which would hold Japan to her promise to return Shantung
to China.[92] To some extent, on Shantung as on equal voting, he was
emulating Lenroot in offering the middle grounders a reservationist
alternative. To a greater degree, though, he was playing a lone hand for
a mild reservationist position that was anachronistic. Anti-amendment middle grounders like Townsend, Hale, Sterling, and others were
making it clear that they wanted reservations at least as strong as those
offered by Lenroot.

Smoot spoke when McCumber had finished. He had not spoken
on the treaty to that time and did not propose to talk at length now.
It may be presumed, though, that his colleagues gave him more than
ordinary attention, for his stance was very much in doubt. Heber J.
Grant, president of the Mormon church, reflected Utah sentiment
in his staunch support of the League. Smoot, on the other hand, saw
no likelihood that the League would bring peace in Europe. An apostle of the Mormon church, he based his judgment on his own reading
of the Book of Mormon and *Doctrine and Covenants*. In defiance of
Grant and others Smoot had backed reservations, and had written
Hays that he would vote for reservations and then for the League. He
had not, however, taken a position on amendments.[93]

Smoot told the Senate that the Shantung amendment was the
most difficult treaty question for him to decide. He wanted to register his opposition to the treaty provisions. But he thought that a
reservation would serve as well as an amendment, and he proposed
wording substantially like Lenroot's. Yet he would not yield to
Utah's pro-League opinion, especially since he knew that some

91. *CR* 66:1, pp. 6991, 6993–95 (16 October 1919).
92. Ibid., 6997 (16 October 1919).
93. Merrill, "Reed Smoot," 300, 312–16, 331.

attitudes were shifting as a result of his own criticisms. He announced that in no case would he vote for the treaty in its present form.[94]

Finally the senators voted. They rejected the amendment, 35–55. The three Democrats who voted for the amendment—Reed, Gore, and David Walsh—were considerably outweighed by the fourteen middle-ground Republicans who opposed it—Colt, Cummins, Hale, Kellogg, Kenyon, Keyes, Lenroot, McCumber, McNary, Nelson, Smoot, Spencer, Sterling, and Townsend. Edge, not voting, was announced as opposed. Earlier he had criticized the amendment as bringing an unnecessary entanglement. Those middle grounders who voted for the amendment were McLean, Capper, and Jones.[95] Though the Republicans opposing the Shantung amendment held no formal meeting, in public and private comments they made their positions known in advance and thus reinforced one another. Each knew that he was not alone and that his vote would not be quixotic.

Afterward, Democrats rejoiced at the bigger than expected margin. But "battalion of death" senators noted that they, the irreconcilables, abetted by others, had mustered thirty-five votes exclusive of two friendly absentees—more than enough to kill the treaty unless strong reservations were added.[96] In the wake of the Shantung vote, the issue between the parties concerned the character of reservations—whether they would be strong or mild. Indeed that had been the issue for some time, but Democratic leaders, following Wilson, were slow to acknowledge it.

While the Foreign Relations Committee resumed considering reservations, the Senate finished work on the amendments, starting with Johnson's. Though the Johnson amendment was seen as doomed, its proponents, headed by Hiram Johnson, did not propose to give up or to spare embarrassment to the opposition. Some of the middle grounders who planned to vote against the Johnson amendment gave their reasons and advanced the Lenroot reservation as a better alternative. Kellogg commented that despite the six votes for the United States proposed by Johnson, in a dispute with the British Empire, the United States would have no votes under the terms of the Covenant. And in a dispute with an outside nation, the British Empire would still have six votes. The Lenroot reservation better protected Amer-

94. Ibid., 318, 327; *CR* 66:1, p. 6997 (16 October 1919).
95. *CR* 66:1, p. 7013 (16 October 1919), p. 6131 (30 September 1919), p. 7103 (16 October 1919).
96. *St. Louis Post-Dispatch*, 17 October 1919; *Des Moines Register*, 17 October 1919.

ica and met the problems addressed by both Johnson's amendment and George Moses's, which remained to be acted on. Under the Lenroot reservation, which Kellogg read, the United States would not be bound by any vote in which the British Empire cast more than one vote; in a dispute with a member of the Empire, the United States would not be bound if the Empire cast any votes. The reservation, Kellogg added, would not require other members of the League to change the treaty between themselves—the great advantage of a reservation over an amendment.[97]

Lenroot followed on the next day, 23 October, with a frequently interrupted speech that, in the opinion of the *New York Tribune*'s Carter Field, killed the Johnson amendment. Lenroot, as before, acknowledged that the amendment would accomplish good under some very limited circumstances, and he reiterated the view that when the League came into effect the members could amend it, without consulting Germany. Thus he justified his own prospective vote for the amendment. The burden of his speech, however, was how ineffective the amendment would be and how his reservation would meet the same need.[98]

Colt, Edge, and McCumber joined the anti-amendment chorus. The first two urged that the Lenroot reservation be substituted for the amendment, whereas McCumber wanted something softer. Colt made the point that for the United States to get six votes, the charter would need to be completely rewritten. Edge, also concerned about expedition, said that business was being delayed because of uncertainty and that the United States was "losing its advantageous position in the race for world trade." McCumber minimized the importance of Britain's six votes and defended the rights of Canada.[99]

Moderates were not willing to vote against the Johnson amendment, even with its limited effectiveness. Somewhat apologetically, Townsend noted that he had consistently opposed amendments. But the Johnson amendment was different. "It is largely sentimental; but, sir, it is the sentiment of patriotism and national respect." He thought that other nations would accept it; in any case, he had to vote for it as a matter of national honor.[100]

97. *CR* 66:1, pp. 7325–28 (22 October 1919).

98. *New York Tribune*, 24 October 1919; *CR* 66:1, pp. 7361–66 (23 October 1919).

99. *CR* 66:1, pp. 7367–73 (23 October 1919). Edge had been in correspondence with Elihu Root, and the latter may have strengthened Edge's opposition to the Johnson amendment and other amendments (Root to Edge, 1 and 7 October 1919, Root Papers).

100. *CR* 66:1, pp. 7497–98 (25 October 1919).

The debate meandered along for several days. Then, during a lull Hitchcock suggested that a time for a vote be set, and Lodge asked for an immediate vote. A number of senators were absent, but the vote was held. The amendment lost by a deceptively close vote, 38–40. Of those absent and paired, or not voting, six senators favored the amendment, whereas twelve senators, Democrats, opposed it. Nine Republicans voted against the amendment—mild reservationists Colt, Edge, Hale, Kellogg, Keyes, McCumber, McNary, Nelson, and Sterling.[101]

Afterward the nine Republican opponents of the amendment issued a statement: the interest of the United States could and should be safeguarded by an effective reservation, and they pledged to vote for one. "Further, that in the interests of expediting action, and to bring about a final ratification of the peace treaty with Germany, with effective reservations, we will vote against all amendments to the treaty."[102] The Senate was almost finished with the committee's amendment proposals, but the statement doomed the one that remained—Moses's—as well as amendments offered by individual senators and any new ones that the committee might approve. For the nine senators, the statement lent the force of consistency to their politically risky votes against the Johnson amendment.

The action of the nine did not come without conditions, however. Taft was concerned about the character of the reservations recently voted in the Foreign Relations Committee, and he had written several mild reservationist leaders. Following the vote on the Johnson amendment, Colt, McNary, and Kellogg replied. Telling Taft of the nine votes against the amendment, Kellogg added, "Of course we will have to adopt some reservations or else we would not have had as many votes." McNary, explaining reservationist negotiation with Lodge during October, said, "The truth of the matter is that the first task of the mild reservationists was to defeat all amendments." The unstated implication of both was that concessions had been necessary, not only to reservations but to the character of those reservations.[103]

Before the Senate could act on reservations, it had to dispose of the remaining amendments: the one from committee, authored by George Moses, and others submitted by individual senators. These were already doomed and were quickly rejected—by the nine mild

101. Ibid., 7548 (27 October 1919).
102. *Minneapolis Tribune*, 28 October 1919.
103. Kellogg to Taft, 28 October 1919, McNary to Taft, 28 October 1919, Colt to Taft, 25 [27] October 1919, Taft Papers. Colt's letter concerned other aspects of the situation.

reservationists who had pledged themselves against all amendments, joined now by most of the moderates.[104]

With the amendments disposed of, the Senate was prepared to act on reservations. A revised program was ready, having been approved by the Foreign Relations Committee between 22 and 24 October. A Republican program, elaborated in intraparty negotiations in the first weeks of October, it followed up on earlier negotiations. The Democratic leadership had continued to hold aloof, and Lodge, not unhappy at that, had achieved a high degree of consensus in his party and among some dissident Democrats. By 20 October he was able to boast to the press that "a decisive majority" of the Senate was united behind reservations that would protect the peace, safety, sovereignty, and independence of the United States and that would "Americanize the treaty." He counted on all Republicans and six Democrats.[105]

The reservation program, some of it developed in direct response to amendments, was in considerable part the work of Lenroot and Kellogg. Their effort, however, reflected the necessity of accommodating strong reservationism for the middle grounders, whom in effect they represented, and for Lodge's followers and the irreconcilables, who backed even stronger reservations. The resultant reservationist program was both stronger and fuller than what the mild reservationists had expected in August.

When Wilson had returned from his tour, before the extent of his illness was appreciated, many Democratic senators had hoped to put the need for compromise before him. When that had proved impossible, Hitchcock, in consultation with Underwood and perhaps others, had acted on his own. Maybe it was already too late, but in retrospect his failure to even try to come to terms with the middle grounders in October seems mistaken. It was, however, understandable.

Underwood explained his thinking to Taft on 3 October. The leadership could count on forty Democrats to vote for the treaty without amendments or reservations. But as soon as the possibility of reservations was broached, the forty would divide, some wanting additional reservations or their own reservations. According to Underwood's plan, after amendments were defeated, the Democrats

104. *CR* 66:1, pp. 7679–80, 7683–86, 7692 (29 October 1919), p. 7942 (4 November 1919), p. 7969 (5 November 1919), p. 8013 (6 November 1919).
105. *St. Louis Post-Dispatch*, 20 October 1919.

would try to get ratification without reservations. If the Republicans insisted on reservations that the Democrats could not accept, the Democrats would vote against the resolution. That would not kill the treaty but would open the way for a compromise on reservations. Hitchcock, though privately pessimistic early in the month, adhered to the same plan. With Tumulty, Wilson's secretary, Hitchcock boldly announced that the Democrats would reject the treaty if drastic reservations were attached. Swanson acquiesced, discouraged by Wilson's adamancy on his tour. Vance McCormick, one of the principal Democrats in the leadership of the LEP, supported the uncompromising stand of the Senate leaders despite contrary advice from Harry Rickey of the LEP's Washington staff. According to McCormick, the Republican reservation proposals were really amendments, and after the Republicans failed to agree among themselves on reservations, unreserved ratification would come.[106]

During October, better than expected results on amendments encouraged the Democrats. At the same time, some of them hoped that pressure, especially from the business community, would help the Democrats to drive a bargain later.[107] Although businessmen had not been part of the "peace lobby" earlier, they increasingly chafed at the delay in establishing peace and resuming orderly trade.

Those Democrats who had hoped to see Wilson and warn him found their hands tied. Hitchcock too was constrained by Wilson's illness. Irresolute, and uncertain in his position of leadership, he could not easily deviate from the last instructions he had received from the president. Hitchcock did meet at least once with mild reservationist leaders, but nothing came of it. Two or three of these Republicans, surely McCumber among them, wanted to talk with Wilson but could not.[108]

The mild reservationists, then, had to treat with their fellow Republicans in developing a program of reservations that could command a majority in the Senate. Their task was twofold: to deal with Lodge in firming up and refining understandings of the four original reservations, as well as of some new and lesser ones that flowed from

106. Taft to A. Lawrence Lowell, 5 October 1919, Taft Papers; Hitchcock to William Jennings Bryan, 4 October 1919, William Jennings Bryan Papers, Library of Congress; *New York Times*, 8 October 1919; Lloyd E. Ambrosius, *Woodrow Wilson and the American Diplomatic Tradition: The Treaty Fight in Perspective*, 198; H. N. Rickey to William Short, 16 October 1919 (copy to McCormick), and McCormick to Rickey, 17 October 1919, LEP Papers.

107. *St. Louis Post-Dispatch*, 30 September, 3, 17 October 1919; *New York Tribune*, 9 October 1919.

108. Fleming, *League of Nations*, 389; *New York World*, 13 October 1919.

the Fall amendments and the widespread desire to assert legislative prerogatives; and to develop and secure support from the middle grounders for reservations on Shantung and equal voting, subjects on which Lodge was committed to amendment and was constrained from reservationist negotiation.

Article 10 remained the big issue. Mild reservationists had reached a tentative agreement with Lodge in September, but Taft feared that the wording might be construed as disavowing the boycott under Article 16. He expressed his fears to mild reservationist leaders during his visit to Washington and to A. Lawrence Lowell by letter. Lowell, part of a delegation of LEP leaders, consulted with McCumber and others and then met with Lodge, who agreed to two small verbal changes. Colt, meanwhile, flirted with a much milder reservation, which he understood the Democrats would support. But he received no encouragement from his mild reservationist colleagues, who evidently told him that the compromise as revised was the best they could get.[109]

Lenroot and Kellogg did most of the work of writing the reservations and negotiating with Lodge and other Republicans. As Lenroot wrote the sociologist Edward A. Ross, he gave the subject of the League and the treaty "more study and thought . . . than any public question that has ever come before me." And he told his sister in November that he was tired, "as I have been on the inside of everything and it has kept me on the jump." During Lenroot's reelection campaign in 1920, Capper said that Lenroot had "had the largest part in drafting the reservations in their final form." Another supporter, probably editorializing on the basis of a conversation with Lenroot, claimed that Lenroot had written eight of the reservations and had helped with the others. Kellogg's reservationist activity, attested to by McNary, is evidenced in his correspondence and in some of his Senate statements promising reservations in place of amendments.[110]

109. *Des Moines Register,* 5 October 1919; Taft to Lowell, 28 September 1919, and Porter McCumber to Taft, 24 October 1919, Taft Papers; Harry N. Rickey to William Short, 6 October 1919, LEP Papers.

110. Soon after Lodge announced the achievement of consensus, and the Foreign Relations Committee approved fourteen reservations, McNary wrote Taft, "Nearly all the Republicans will vote for the reservations proposed by the Committee, inasmuch as four mild reservations were accepted bodily and much discussion was indulged in by Senators Lodge, Kellogg, Lenroot and others, so that there is a sort of feeling that the reservations finally proposed are as good as could be had in order to constitute a meeting ground" (McNary to Taft, 28 October 1919, Taft Papers). Lenroot to Ross, 20 October 1919, Edward A. Ross Papers, State Historical Society of

It was natural that Lenroot and Kellogg took the lead in reservationist negotiation with Lodge. Both men were skilled and willing legislative draftsmen. In conviction, the two stood closer to Lodge than did McCumber, Colt, or Nelson; they were best equipped to bridge the gap between the mild reservationist leaders and those senators who were willing to oppose amendments on the promise of adequate reservations. Indeed the most active of these senators, Fred Hale, was a friend of both Kellogg's and Lenroot's. Despite rejecting Kellogg for membership on the Foreign Relations Committee, since early in July Lodge had consistently sought out Kellogg as one who might lead and act for his faction. It would have been strange had the two ceased their collaboration in October. Kellogg also commended himself to Lodge by his associations. He worked closely with Root's protégé Chandler Anderson, and the reservations the two agreed on undoubtedly had the valuable backing of Root. In addition, Kellogg—with Root, Anderson, Hale, and many others—was part of the Rooseveltian circle, people who had worked for Lodge's sainted friend and who shared many of Roosevelt's ideas and attitudes.[111]

Lenroot was a natural emissary to Lodge. Both Roosevelt and Augustus Peabody Gardner, Lodge's late son-in-law, had commended Lenroot to Lodge. Collaborating with Roosevelt, Lodge had taken a lively and helpful interest in Lenroot's election to the Senate in 1918. He admired Lenroot for his vote for war in the House of Representatives and then for his strong support of the war effort, at the cost of a break with La Follette and others. That Lenroot, though a mild reservationist, did not consort with Taft perhaps strengthened his position with Lodge. And the majority leader found Lenroot appreciative of the need for party unity behind a reservationist program. For his part, Lenroot believed—in light of the attitude of Wilson and his followers—that satisfactory ratification could come only through Republican unity behind reservations and that only Lodge could forge such unity.[112]

Wisconsin; Lenroot to Nellie Nichols, 16 November 1919, Lenroot Papers; Capper quoted in *Superior Telegram*, 28–29 August 1920; *Caspar Daily Tribune*, n.d., quoted in *Milwaukee Sentinel*, 21 July 1920; McNary to William Howard Taft, 26 October 1919, Taft Papers; Frank Kellogg to Henry Cabot Lodge, 3 October 1919, Lodge Papers; Chandler P. Anderson Diary, entry for 1 October 1919, Anderson Papers.

111. Alice Roosevelt Longworth referred to Hale and Kellogg as "old friends" (*Crowded Hours*, 289).

112. Margulies, *Lenroot*, 229–48; Lenroot to John B. Sanborn, 2 October 1919, LEP Papers; Lenroot to E. A. Ross, 20 October 1919, Ross Papers. Asked about Lenroot as a possible speaker on Roosevelt's birthday, Lodge said, "Lenroot would be excellent" (Lodge to R. M. Washburn, 8 October 1919, Lodge Papers).

Documentation for the writing or revising of specific reservations is fragmentary. But this much is clear: Lenroot and Kellogg's
greatest bargaining power concerned Shantung and equal voting.
The supporters of amendments could not turn to reservations on
those subjects until after the amendments had been acted on, at
which point Lenroot and Kellogg had already won middle-ground
support for reservations written by Lenroot. In the aftermath, the
Foreign Relations Committee accepted Lenroot's reservation on
Shantung.[113] Acting before Senate action on the Johnson amendment, the committee could not propose an equal voting reservation, but the Senate later accepted Lenroot's. Lodge asked that
no changes be made in the Monroe Doctrine reservation and that
only technical changes be made in the domestic questions reservation, which had been written by Kellogg. Of the four original reservations, only the one on withdrawal underwent important change
in October: new wording left the withdrawal decision wholly to
Congress.

Other reservations, on lesser topics, were also drawn, primarily to
defend the prerogatives of Congress against the president. Kellogg,
aided by Anderson, had collaborated with Lodge on secondary reservations of this sort in September and early October.[114] Although
Democrats and some pro-League Republicans found these reservations to be offensive in tone, they were acceptable to Lenroot and
Kellogg. These two shared the widespread hostility toward Wilson
and the strong concern of the Senate for restoration of its powers.
Furthermore, the reservations, though far from mild in tone, fell
within what had become the basic criterion for "mild reservations."
As laid down by Taft and adhered to by mild reservationists, these
were, "reservations that will be accepted by the Allies through the
exchange of notes and negotiations . . . [and] reservations that
would not require resubmission of the treaty to the other nations."[115] Not stated in Taft's definition, but understood by the mild
reservationists, was that in many cases the reservations would be
more than interpretive—they would change the treaty. But the
changes, disavowing specific obligations, would concern only the
United States. Since they did not alter the relations between other

113. Porter McCumber to William Howard Taft, 24 October 1919, Taft Papers;
Milwaukee Sentinel, 2 December 1919.
114. Chandler P. Anderson Diary, entry for 21 September 1919, Anderson Papers.
115. *New York World*, 4 October 1919. Unnamed mild reservationists used the
same criterion, as did McCumber (*Providence Sunday Tribune*, 5 October 1919; *New
York World*, 27 September 1919).

signatories, the reservations—unlike amendments—would not require full renegotiation.[116]

Through October, McCumber took a lively interest in prospective reservations. But since he was not representative of the middle grounders, he lacked bargaining power with Lodge. On one subject, however, McCumber did agree with critics of the treaty. He disliked the provision for an international labor organization with quasi-governmental powers. It was McCumber who wrote the labor organization reservation that the Senate adopted.[117]

Several months later William Short, secretary of the LEP, went over the reservations one by one with Lenroot, Kellogg, and McNary. He emerged from the conference convinced "that Mr. Lodge wrote none of them and that none of them were written by members of the Death Battalion." Still later, William Borah wrote a journalist, "I was not a reservationist and paid little attention to the different shadings which the different Senators gave to their reservations." Lenroot, among others, asserted that the reservations had been written by the friends of the treaty, not by its enemies. But the mild reservationist leaders did not work from a position of strength. The terms needed to satisfy their middle grounder friends, let alone the Lodge supporters, had to be harsher than those used in August. Furthermore, Lenroot and Kellogg agreed to support a preamble—although they were ready to bargain it away later—requiring three of the four major powers specifically to assent to American reservations. Lodge thought that the Allies could promptly agree by cable. Hiram Johnson, even though defeated on some questions concerning reservations, considered the total package to be "strong." As Short summarized the matter, "There appears to be much justification for the contention that reservations as they stand are the result of compromise."[118]

As of 20 October, the deal among Republicans and their few Democratic allies was neither firm nor complete. The Foreign Relations

116. Kellogg later said, "The principal object of adopting reservations instead of amendments was that the reservations should apply to this country alone and might be accepted by the other powers without disturbing the relations between those countries" (*CR* 66:2, p. 3611 [28 February 1920]).

117. Fleming, *League of Nations*, 84; *CR* 66:1, pp. 8640–41 [17 November 1919], p. 8730 [18 November 1919].

118. "Report of W. H. Short on Treaty Situation in Washington . . . January 8th and 9th," enclosed in Short to William Howard Taft, 10 January 1920, Taft Papers; Borah to William Hard, 26 November 1924, Borah Papers, in Kendrick, "League of Nations," 253; *Milwaukee Sentinel*, 2 December 1919; *CR* 66:2, p. 535 [13 December 1919]; *Minneapolis Tribune*, 20 October 1919.

Committee had not yet acted, and its members gave no blank checks. Irreconcilables, focusing on amendments, had not yet been fully heard on reservations. So far as the mild reservationist leaders were concerned, McCumber had actively negotiated in late August and in September, but less so in October. He felt bound to support compromises on the four original topics and to back a mandates reservation that was an offshoot from the original Article 10 reservation, but he was not otherwise committed.[119] In fact he was determined to push several alternative reservations of his own. And even his commitment to the original four was not definite, since a change in the withdrawal reservation did not meet his approval. Nelson too later thought it honorable to seek amendment to several "Lodge reservations." Even so, Lodge and Lenroot had not been wrong in claiming substantial agreement among Republicans. Dissidents, on the left and the right, would still be heard from. But all Republicans saw the need for party unity to create a majority for their program, and they understood that the package Lodge took to the Foreign Relations Committee was the product of painstaking compromise.

The mild reservationist leaders, as well as their middle grounder associates, thought that much of the job was finished. Presumably the committee would in substance approve the compromise package of reservations. If the Democrats would accept it, ratification was assured. The middle grounders could guard against irreconcilable efforts to tamper with the reservations or to add new and dangerous ones, but beyond that there was little more they could do, except try to persuade the Democrats to accept.

The reservations were stronger and more numerous than those the mild reservationists had offered in August. But there could be no turning back. Wilson had gambled and lost. Eschewing negotiation with the middle grounders, he had tried to coerce them through a public appeal. But instead of growing, public support for the Covenant had lessened.[120] Moreover, the president's ill-chosen words had antagonized many of those Republicans whose help he needed. During Wilson's absence, the mild reservationist leaders had brought about a compromise on Article 10. Wilson had summarily rejected it. Disabled and removed from control after that, he had left his lieutenants in the Senate a mandate to stand pat. The mild reservationist

119. *CR* 66:1, p. 8418 (13 November 1919).
120. Lodge to Mrs. Charles Prince, 16 October 1919, Lodge Papers.

leaders had had no recourse but to seek compromise within the Republican party.

Their task was part negotiation, part confrontation. Not wholly united among themselves, the mild reservationist leaders nevertheless had directed a successful campaign against the amendments. In the process, Lenroot and Kellogg in particular had promised relatively strong reservations on the subjects covered by the amendments and had announced reservations that were satisfactory enough to serve the immediate purpose. Meanwhile, the same senators, representing themselves and the other middle grounders, had negotiated with Lodge on the rest of the reservation program. If the results were not mild in an earlier sense, they at least reflected the thinking of the moderates and of the more conservative mild reservationists. Some Democrats disagreed about the intrinsic merits of the reservations but thought that the total program achieved their basic goals: to satisfy a majority in the Senate; to give adequate protection to the United States internationally; and to avoid time-consuming renegotiation.

The increasing prominence of Lenroot and Kellogg reflected the new mood of the country and of the middle grounders and the new situation in the Senate. More conservative on the League than McCumber, Lenroot and Kellogg were better able to work in a situation in which negotiation was intraparty rather than interparty. McCumber, as the second-ranked Republican on the Foreign Relations Committee, had served as a leader in early September, spearheading opposition to Lodge's original Article 10 reservation. He remained active now, but in a different role. He made himself the expert among opponents of the main amendments, and he stood for the possibility of mild reservations on the subjects of those amendments. Increasingly, he stood alone. Nelson contributed some oratory, and Colt added some analysis and perhaps some help with reservations.[121] But for the most part, they, with McNary, took secondary roles, supporting Lenroot and Kellogg.

The full mild reservationist faction emerged in this period: the six leaders—McCumber, McNary, Colt, Nelson, Kellogg and Lenroot—plus Hale, Edge, Keyes, and Sterling. All except Lenroot voted against the Johnson amendment and effectively killed remaining amendments by their declaration of opposition and by their

121. *New York World*, 2 October 1919; *Providence Sunday Tribune*, 12 October 1919.

votes.[122] Sterling had earlier voted for three of the Fall amendments, but in opposing the Johnson amendment, he had bucked the tide of public opinion. And in declaring against all further amendments, he strongly contributed to accomplishing the overall purpose of the mild reservationists: ratification of the treaty in such form as to preclude renegotiation while protecting the United States. The statement of the nine, it might be noted, had implications not only for further amendments but also for the character of reservations that might be adopted. If prolonged renegotiation was to be avoided, the reservations would have to be acceptable to the principal powers.

Lenroot did not join the nine, for unlike them, he had voted for the Johnson amendment and was prepared to vote for the amendment, in a revised form, again. Yet by his leadership in developing a widely accepted reservation on equal voting and by his speeches claiming that the amendment would have limited effectiveness, Lenroot did as much as any other senator to encompass the amendment's defeat. In further extenuation, one might note the distinction that Lenroot drew between the Johnson amendment and most of the others—that once the League was brought into being by Britain, France and Italy, these nations could amend the Covenant, without fresh referral to the peace conference. Others did not draw this distinction, but Lenroot found it persuasive.

Despite this qualification, because Lenroot did vote for the Johnson amendment it would be hard to include him among the mild reservationists were it not for other factors. First, he voted against the other amendments; second, more than any other senator, he offered realistic reservationist alternatives to all the major amendments, alternatives that were essential to the defeat of those amendments. It is relevant too that he had the confidence of the other mild reservationists in his negotiations with Lodge. Kellogg worked with him, and McNary and others accepted the results on the strength of his and Kellogg's participation. Many years later, replying to a student, Lenroot said that he had indeed been a mild reservationist.[123]

At the other end of the middle-ground spectrum, three moderates separated themselves from the rest by their votes on amendments. McLean voted for all of them; Jones supported twelve of the thir-

122. See Appendix 1.
123. Lenroot to Mary Becker, 31 January 1946, Lenroot Papers.

teen; and Capper, after opposing the Fall amendments, supported the others. The remaining moderates—Cummins, Kenyon, Smoot, Spencer, and Townsend—had mixed records. The differentiation between mild reservationists and moderates, evident in their actions on amendments, was confirmed when reservations reached the Senate floor in November.

4 REJECTION OF THE TREATY, 22 October–19 November 1919

*B*etween 22 and 24 October, the Republican majority on the Foreign Relations Committee, overriding Democratic alternatives, adopted an enlarged program of reservations. For the most part, the reservations reflected compromise within the party.

Though the mild reservationists had taken the largest part in preparing the program of reservations, they were not committed to it fully. The committee proposed two reservations that had not been the subjects of prior negotiation and that seemed unnecessary or extreme. And, in advance of Senate consideration of the reservations, the mild reservationists felt free to seek a modification in the preamble. One subject remained altogether open, for the committee would not offer a reservation on equal voting while amendments on that subject were before the Senate. In the main, though, the mild reservationists were committed to the committee program. Even McCumber and Nelson, both of whom reserved a fair measure of independence, felt bound to the chief features of the party's program. Thus, when the Senate began action on the reservations on 6 November, the adoption of a Republican program was assured.

For the mild reservationists, several problems remained. First, they needed to defeat destructive amendments to certain reservations, especially the reservation to Article 10, and destructive or superfluous reservations emanating from the committee and from individuals. Second, they had to win over enough Democrats to get a two-thirds majority for the resolution of ratification.

While the Senate adopted reservations in Committee of the Whole, the Democrats held aloof from serious negotiations. Toward the end, though, as the final day of voting approached, they became more active. Yet their strategy remained what it had been for some time—to seek a deal with the mild reservationists after the resolution embodying the "Lodge reservations" had failed to win two-thirds. It behooved the mild reservationists to persuade the Democrats that the plan could not succeed, that they would remain loyal to the "Lodge reservations," and that the Democrats would have to accommodate to that fact. At the same time, since the Democrats were not likely to acquiesce totally, the mild reservationists needed to leave the door open a little, for compromise on the preamble and for reconsideration after the initial vote.

The mild reservationists were not wholly united in approaching these problems. McCumber, acting largely on his own, tried to make the reservations milder. Lenroot, with fuller support, took a harder line in defense of the committee reservations and of his own equal-voting proposal. Indeed he emerged as a spokesman for both the mild reservationists and, on certain matters, for Lodge.

In the end the Democrats left the decision to Wilson. In a letter to senators of his party, read to them hours before the final debate was to start, the president rejected the "Lodge reservations." In their oratory, and by their votes on that day, 19 November, the mild reservationists did what they could for ratification, although they knew that for that day at least, chances were virtually nil. They hoped, however, to further impress on the Democrats that Republican lines were solid. In the process, by some of their speeches and votes and by action in their own caucus, the mild reservationists further identified themselves. If they caused no radical redefinition of the term *mild reservationist* from what the events of October had dictated, they at least provided additional evidence as to the meaning of the term.

A day before the 22 October meeting of the Foreign Relations Committee, which would act on reservations, McCumber offered in the Senate seven reservations, which he represented as the results of intraparty compromise. Some of them, notably the reservation to Article 10, were indeed that. Others, however, were McCumber's alone. Off the Senate floor, McCumber insisted that it was up to Republican friends of the treaty to win over enough Democrats to ratify, without the support of Hitchcock and his followers or of the irreconcilables.[1] McCumber surely knew that the plan's prospects for success, either in winning his mild reservationist colleagues to it or in dividing the Democrats, were not great. Under the circumstances, he could not afford to withhold support for much of his party's reservationist program.

1. *CR* 66:1, p. 7269 (21 October 1919); *New York Tribune*, 21 October 1919.

Hitchcock did not know what to do about the Republican program, which at last he had to face up to, so he convened a meeting of fifteen Democrats, mainly members of the Foreign Relations Committee, to plot a course. John Shields, a sincere advocate of reservations, urged his colleagues to make an immediate deal with the Republicans. He and others warned of breakaways within the Democratic ranks. But the reservation to Article 10 that McCumber had read, which was virtually identical to the one Wilson had unequivocally rejected, suggested that the Republican program would not be one the president could accept. Encouraged by the defeat of the Shantung amendment, Underwood professed optimism for unreserved ratification. Hitchcock knew better, but he thought it wise to hold off on compromise efforts at least until he could see Wilson. At the very least, he wanted to wait to see what sort of reservations the Republicans would put forth. And he thought there still would be time for compromise after a Republican resolution of ratification, embodying the party's reservations, was beaten by Democratic and irreconcilable votes. The meeting came to no conclusion.[2]

When on 22 October the committee acted on most of Lodge's slate of reservations, Hitchcock presented some alternative reservations as substitutes, and he offered amendments to Lodge's proposals. Hitchcock closely followed the draft of reservations that Wilson had given him before his tour, but the senator did not reveal their source or give them much emphasis.[3] Not surprisingly, all Democratic motions failed.

McCumber opposed parts of the program Lodge presented but, when unsuccessful in effecting changes, he supported most of the reservations on final vote. He did get committee support for his own reservation on the international labor organization. More important, he blocked an effort by Knox to alter the reservation to Article 10. Most Republican senators, he thought, along with enough Democratic senators to make a majority, wanted to broaden the reservation so that, in addition to repudiating any commitment to use the armed forces under Article 10, it would also eliminate any obligation to use the boycott. McCumber argued that Lodge's reservation, the product of the negotiations of September, was the reservation that the party could agree on. Lodge supported him, and Knox did

2. *New York Times*, 22 October 1919; *New York World*, 22 October 1919; *Birmingham News*, 20 October 1919, in Evans C. Johnson, *Oscar W. Underwood: A Political Biography*, 270.

3. Jack E. Kendrick, "The League of Nations and the Republican Senate, 1918–1921," 233.

not force the issue.[4] Successful in maintaining the agreed-on program, McCumber was powerless to alter it, and the "Lodge reservations" went through, largely unchanged. In all, the committee approved sixteen reservations; however, McCumber's required slight rewording, so for the committee Lodge reported just fifteen to the Senate on 24 October, and McCumber offered his individually. The committee left open the matter of equal voting.

The first reservation came to be the center of controversy for a time. It was the preamble. Later, while still part of the Republican program, it was denied a number, and the numbers of all the reservations that followed were changed accordingly. The reservation, as proposed and adopted, read:

The committee also report the following reservations and understandings to be made a part and a condition of the resolution of ratification, which ratification is not to take effect or bind the United States until the said following reservations and understandings have been accepted as a part and a condition of said instrument of ratification by at least three of the four principal allied and associated powers, to wit: Great Britain, France, Italy, and Japan.[5]

McCumber tried to amend by striking the requirement for acceptance but lost by a vote of 10–7, Shields voting with the Republicans, as he did on most votes. McCumber then sided with the minority in voting against the reservation. Lodge explained to mild reservationists that the requirement was demanded by several strong reservationists, who otherwise would not vote for ratification.[6]

Of the committee's original four reservations, covering the basic subjects suggested by Root, the only one substantially modified since committee action in September related to withdrawal. In one respect the reservation was somewhat softened from the bald statement, to which McCumber had objected, that the United States "reserves to itself the unconditional right to withdraw from the league of nations." The new reservation said that the United States construed Article 1 of the Covenant to mean that in case of notice of withdrawal, under the Article the United States alone would judge whether it had fulfilled its obligations. This was consistent with Wilson's explanation of the withdrawal article. However, the reser-

4. McCumber to William Howard Taft, 24 October 1919, Taft Papers.
5. U.S. Congress, Senate, *Proceedings of the Committee on Foreign Relations, United States Senate, from the Sixty-Third Congress to the Sixty-Seventh Congress,* 189–91.
6. Ibid., 191; Talcott Williams to William Howard Taft, 31 October 1919, Taft Papers.

vation specified that notice of withdrawal might be given by a concurrent resolution of Congress, which, unlike a joint resolution, did not require the president's signature. The change followed a proposal by Democrat Hoke Smith and was subsequently defended by Lodge and others as a concession to Smith for his support of other reservations.[7]

The third reservation, eventually renumbered as reservation 2, was the notable reservation to Article 10. Democrats offered two substitutes and an amendment. One of the substitutes was Hitchcock's, drawn from Wilson's proposal. McCumber voted against the Democratic proposals. Then, after warding off the threat from Knox to carry the denial of obligation beyond Article 10, he supported Lodge's proposal, which was adopted.[8]

The fourth reservation said that no mandate would be accepted except by action of Congress. In September the committee had included the subject in its reservation to Article 10. It now passed unanimously. On the domestic question issue, Hitchcock offered a substitute but got only four votes. By 11–6, with McCumber among the majority, the committee then approved Lodge's proposal. This was a slight elaboration of Kellogg's, which the committee had approved in September. The next reservation, on the Monroe Doctrine, was identical to the one the committee had proposed in September. McCumber and his colleagues had agreed to it then, and the senator supported it still. It was approved, 11–6.[9]

The Shantung reservation provoked extended argument. As presented by Lodge, the seventh reservation began with what Lenroot had proposed but then went further. It read:

The United States withholds its assent to articles 156, 157, and 158, and reserves full liberty of action with respect to any controversy which may arise under said articles between the Republic of China and the Empire of Japan, and the United States declines to recognize the validity of any rights, titles, or interests which Germany purports by the said articles to renounce in favor of Japan.

After a Hitchcock substitute failed, McCumber offered his own amendments. He argued that Lenroot's wording was tantamount to saying that the United States "rejects," and he proposed instead the

7. *CR* 66:1, pp. 6271–72 (2 October 1919); Henry Cabot Lodge to Elihu Root, 3 December 1919, Root Papers.
8. *Proceedings of the Committee on Foreign Relations*, 192; McCumber to William Howard Taft, 24 October 1919, Taft Papers.
9. *Proceedings of the Committee on Foreign Relations*, 192, 193.

words *refrains from entering into any agreement with reference to matters contained in* in place of *withholds its assent to.* He also tried to strike everything after the word *arise* and to substitute *in relation thereto.* McCumber's amendments lost. Discussion, however, evidently convinced Lodge and Knox that it was imprudent to go beyond Lenroot's wording, which, as McCumber later confided, had the support of Colt, Kellogg, and many Lodge followers. Knox therefore moved to strike all the wording after *Empire of Japan.* By 7–5, the committee approved the change, with Lodge, Knox, Harding, McCumber, and three Democrats out-voting five irreconcilables. Only partially satisfied, McCumber reserved the right to move a change in the Senate.[10]

Swiftly, the committee adopted four more reservations and passed over two, before adjourning for the day. Relatively minor compared to those already acted on, three of the lesser reservations had an important theme that linked them to portions of the reservations on Article 10 and on withdrawal. These three reservations were less concerned to protect America against unwise entanglements than to preserve the powers of Congress against the assertions of the president. Wilson's serious illness did little or nothing to soften feelings, for health bulletins were vague and the effort to run the country from a sickbed or through an appointed regency further evidenced apparent presidential contempt for constitutional processes.[11]

The eighth reservation expressed legislative prerogative for representatives to the League and to commissions. It was passed over for the day. The ninth, swiftly adopted, made clear America's understanding that the Reparations Commission could not interfere with German-American trade except with the approval of Congress. The tenth reservation rejected financial obligation to the League, "unless and until" Congress appropriated the money.

The other reservations approved that day did not relate to congressional powers but attempted protections and technical clarifica-

10. *Current History* 11 (November 1919): 227; *Proceedings of the Committee on Foreign Relations,* 194–95; McCumber to William Howard Taft, 24 October 1919, Taft Papers. On the Knox amendment, the *Proceedings* omit McCumber's name. The list of those voting for the amendment includes only six, but the total of seven is given, so evidently McCumber voted for it.

11. W. Stull Holt, *Treaties Defeated by the Senate: A Study of the Struggle Between President and Senate Over the Conduct of Foreign Relations,* 305; Raymond B. Fosdick, *Letters on the League of Nations,* 45; Jonathan Daniels, *The End of Innocence,* 291; Talcott Williams to William Howard Taft, 19 September 1919, Taft Papers; Warren G. Harding to A. E. Houston, 2 January 1920, Harding Papers; David Lawrence in *St. Louis Post-Dispatch,* 13, 25 October 1919.

tions. The eleventh said that the United States, if it agreed to arms limitations proposed by the League Council, reserved the right to increase its arms if threatened by war or invasion. At Shields's request, the twelfth reservation was passed over. It would clarify boycott obligations without seriously impairing them. The thirteenth reservation, the last one approved that day, would allow Americans to contest decisions of the Alien Property Custodian.[12]

The committee completed action the following day, 23 October. First, members heard James Reed testify at length for a reservation that would permit the United States to withhold from consideration by international tribunals any question that it thought affected its "national honor or interest." They returned to the subject later. Turning first to the remaining Lodge proposals, they took up the eighth reservation, passed over the day before, and McCumber offered a substitute. Much shorter, less comprehensive, and less offensively worded than the one Lodge offered, it nevertheless would have guaranteed Congress's rights in determining who would represent the United States in the League and its commissions and in specifying the extent of that representation. Only Democrat Atlee Pomerene supported it. In the vote on the original proposal, McCumber joined the Democrats in opposition, but they lost. The reservation, countering the Fall amendments, was the work of Kellogg and Chandler Anderson, and Kellogg later presented it in the Senate.[13]

According to the record of *Proceedings*, the committee next approved a new reservation, offered by McCumber, that the United States not be represented in the International Labor Organization unless Congress so authorized and that any representative would require Senate confirmation.[14] Though the reservation fit the pattern of those asserting congressional powers, McCumber's main purpose was to limit association with the I.L.O.

Then the committee approved a reservation by Shields, despite McCumber's opposition. This reservation, not part of Lodge's original program or the subject of any known prior negotiation with mild reservationists, said that the United States declined any trusteeship or other responsibility for those overseas possessions of Germany for which Germany had renounced title to the principal Allied and associated powers.

12. *Proceedings of the Committee on Foreign Relations*, 195.
13. Ibid., 196; Henry Cabot Lodge to Elihu Root, 3 December 1919, Root Papers; *CR* 66:1, p. 8564 (15 November 1919).
14. *Proceedings of the Committee on Foreign Relations*, 196.

Next, by unanimous consent, on the motion of Albert Fall the committee reconsidered reservation twelve. Evidently, contrary to the *Proceedings*, it had been approved earlier. Fall spotted an important oversight and offered the insertion of wording that would better express the purpose of the reservation. As first presented to the committee by Lodge, the wording seemed to challenge all boycott obligations. It read: "The United States reserves the right to permit, in its discretion, the nationals of a covenant-breaking State, as defined in article 16 of the covenant of the League of Nations, to continue their commercial, financial and personal relations with the nationals of the United States."[15] Fall's amendment, approved without record vote, inserted after *League of Nations* the words *residing within the United States or in countries other than that violating said article 16.* The amended reservation, passed by voice vote, was innocuous, and it accorded with understandings between Lodge and the mild reservationists.

That is not to say that the committee confined itself entirely to matters previously agreed on. In addition to the Shields reservation concerning German possessions, on motion of Shields the committee authorized Lodge to draft and favorably report a reservation on "the national honor or vital interests" of the United States, as proposed by Reed. Lodge, who had long favored such a limitation on international arbitration, supported the motion, and it passed.[16]

The Senate learned of the committee's action on reservations as it prepared to vote on the Johnson amendment. On 27 October nine Republicans accomplished the defeat of the amendment, as previously noted. After announcing their opposition to all other amendments, they next turned their attention to the committee's reservations. Their coalescence, coming at the start of what seemed to be the last act of the long drama, was significant, for they were in a position to control the situation. The nine senators were Colt, Kellogg, Nelson, McCumber, McNary, Hale, Edge, Keyes, and Sterling. They were joined now by Lenroot, who had voted for the Johnson amendment and therefore was not part of the original caucus. The rather loosely knit organization of the mild reservationists was thus made complete.[17]

Following committee action on the reservations, A. Lawrence

15. Ibid., 191.
16. Robert James Fischer, "Henry Cabot Lodge's Concept of Foreign Policy and the League of Nations," 99–105, 115–17.
17. Talcott Williams to William Howard Taft, 31 October 1919, Taft Papers. Williams, listing the group, failed to name Nelson, an oversight on his part.

Lowell came to Washington and, accompanied by Talcott Williams, on 29 October met with six of the group—Colt, Hale, Kellogg, Lenroot, McCumber, and McNary. The senators, speaking for themselves and noting the positions of those of the group not present, disclosed how they would vote and forecast the outcome for each reservation.

The mild reservationists were not fully united. McCumber, and perhaps Colt, would not support the preamble, and McCumber would seek modification in the Shantung reservation. Equal voting, not yet acted on in committee, was not discussed, but McCumber had already made it clear that he would seek something softer than Lenroot's reservation. On the minor reservations, mild reservationist votes might scatter. But in the main, the mild reservationists were in agreement. Most would back the preamble, since it was the price demanded by several strong reservationists in exchange for their support of ratification. They would also support the major reservations covering the four issues raised by Root, plus the non-controversial mandates reservation. All but two or three would support the Shantung reservation, and it would pass with the help of some Democrats. But none of the mild reservationists would vote for the Reed reservation on matters of national honor or interest, and that dangerous reservation would not pass.[18]

The committee reservations came under widespread criticism for their tone and content. Mild reservationist leaders responded somewhat defensively. To Taft, whose first reaction to the reservations was dismay, Colt wrote that final decisions had not yet been made; McNary suggested that he might yet vote with the Democrats on milder reservations; and McCumber sought Taft's aid in modifying the Shantung reservation.[19] At the same time, and in the same defensive vein, they argued that the reservationist program was the best that could be expected under the circumstances and that, despite its seeming harshness, it left unimpaired much that was good in the Covenant. McNary told reporters: "The proponents of the treaty among the Democrats missed a great opportunity. The mild reservationists were forced to deal with the radical element on their own side. The result is the committee report on reservations, which to my mind must be adopted if the treaty is to be ratified."[20]

18. H. A. Yeomans, *Abbott Lawrence Lowell, 1856–1943*, 453.
19. Taft to McCumber, 22 October 1919, to Colt, 23 October 1919, Colt to Taft, 25 October 1919, McNary to Taft, 28 October 1919, McCumber to Taft, 24 October 1919, and Gus Karger to Taft, 6 November 1919, all in Taft Papers.
20. *St. Louis Post-Dispatch*, 24 October 1919.

McCumber took pains to explain to Taft that the reservation to Article 10 was the best one obtainable under the circumstances, considering the intense feeling among Republican senators on the subject of coercive obligations. Above all, the boycott had been preserved, by stripping from the committee's original reservation its reference to coercive measures and by inserting the words *under the provisions of Article Ten*. Later, when Taft wrote a newspaper column in which he noted this accomplishment, McCumber, in an uncharacteristic show of timidity, berated him for poor timing. "We have been month after month working on some kind of reservation that would retain to some extent, at least the obligation of Article Ten, and which would leave the boycott provision of other articles untouched," he wrote Taft. "There are a number of those nine mentioned by you, like Senator Hale for instance, who declare that they want it clear that the United States shall not be obliged to bring to bear any kind of force, either military or economic, to protect the political independence and territorial integrity of any other nation." McCumber and others had mollified the doubters by pointing out that tariffs and laws relating to exports, which would be involved in boycott activity, could not be changed except by Congress. Now, however, McCumber feared that Taft's claim that the boycott was safe would evoke amendments on Article 10. He added: "I feel quite certain that Senator Hale and some others would still vote for such an amendment to the reservation to No. 10."[21]

In the Senate, without going into detail, McCumber said that he would support the first four or five reservations "because I feel confident that we can not get the sixty-four votes for the treaty unless we have them, and that is the only reason that guides me in supporting them." Like McNary, then, he thought that enough good remained in the Covenant to warrant concessions to expediency. Going further than any of his mild reservationist colleagues, he said that if the initial resolution of ratification, embodying the committee reservations, failed, he would move for reconsideration, with the hope that the Senate would adopt enough modifications to gain the support of two-thirds. But, referring to reconsideration, he said, "I recognize the fact that a majority can vote that down, and I do not know of any way to escape it."[22] Thus, McCumber felt that the best hope for ratification lay with at least the main committee reservations.

Colt too put the best face on the reservations. They would not cut

21. McCumber to Taft, 24 October 1919, Taft Papers.
22. *CR* 66:1, p. 7886 (3 November 1919).

the heart out of the Covenant, he told a home-state reporter. Obligatory conferences, compulsory arbitration, the economic boycott, and arms reduction remained unchanged. And the League could create a judicial tribunal to deal with problems of international law. He was confident too that the reservations, which largely concerned policies of the American government, would be accepted by Britain, France, and Italy. Nor did he think that the Democrats would reject the treaty because of the committee reservations.[23]

Defensive or not, the mild reservationists generally agreed that, given the earlier failure of the Democrats to negotiate, the committee program was the best they could get, that it left much of worth in the Covenant, and that it alone could command a majority in the Senate. The problem was to win the Democrats to ultimate acceptance of the reservations, in the resolution of ratification. For Kellogg, as for others, that task required a show of unity behind the program, not only from supporters within the Senate but also from friends of the Covenant outside. With that in mind, following Lowell's visit to Washington, Kellogg promptly wrote him to urge that the LEP back the reservations. He complained that various members of the LEP were fighting one reservation or another, without any concert among themselves. As noted, McCumber, McNary, and Colt tried to win Taft to support of the committee's program, in whole or part, and Kellogg did too. As Wilson's incapacitating illness persisted, Taft was more and more the leader of pro-Leaguers around the country, especially in the Protestant churches, and the mild reservationists recognized this fact.[24]

The mild reservationists did come to favor one change, suggested to them by Lowell during his visit to Washington. This was a modification of the preamble so that the assent to the reservations by three Great Powers might come through an exchange of notes. As the preamble was worded in committee, it vaguely referred to acceptance by three of the Allied powers. Some senators and others feared that renewed negotiation at the peace conference might be required or that France would have to go to its legislature for approval. But Lowell, in contact with Europeans through the LEP, thought that acceptance would be no trouble if it could be accomplished in the way he suggested. Avoiding prolonged delay had been and remained a major consideration for mild reservationists, so the group had

23. *Providence Sunday Tribune,* 26 October 1919.
24. Lowell to William Howard Taft, 1 November 1919, Taft Papers; James L. Lancaster, "The Protestant Churches and the Fight for Ratification of the Versailles Treaty," 613–19.

every reason to support the change, if it could be effected. Furthermore Kellogg, Hale, and Lenroot worried that France or Italy, for selfish commercial reasons, might refuse the reservations in order to keep the United States in a technical state of war with Germany. Lowell's suggestion, if adopted, would lessen the danger. And the proposed change seemed feasible, since the revised form would still meet the demands of those strong reservationists who insisted on explicit acceptance.[25]

Before minds were made up, Lowell had returned to Boston, and by chance Lodge had gone there too. Presuming that Lowell, from his LEP connections and association with Massachusetts Republicans, would have influence with Lodge, Kellogg telegraphed and wrote him, urging that he see Lodge and argue for the change. Lowell did, and Lodge acquiesced. Lodge surely welcomed the chance to solidify mild reservationist support on the first item of his program. He was not himself happy with the original wording and was probably one of the unnamed Republican leaders who had been defending the preamble with the argument that acceptance might take the form of an exchange of notes. As in Denmark's purchase of the Virgin Islands in 1917, this would entail no great delay. He could hardly object to making the point explicit in the preamble.[26]

Despite its improvement, the preamble remained unpopular with the mild reservationists, who may have been influenced by discreet warnings from League of Nations officials.[27] Silent acquiescence in the reservations seemed safer and more expeditious than an exchange of notes. If the matter could be arranged, and at the appropriate time, the preamble was the one part of the committee program that the mild reservationists were prepared to bargain away. But Hitchcock was not close to contemplating such a deal.

During the two weeks between the completion of committee action and the start of Senate consideration of reservations, Hitchcock, acting on his own and after consultation with Democratic col-

25. Gus Karger to William Howard Taft, 3 and 6 November 1919, Taft Papers; Chandler P. Anderson Diary, entry for 31 October 1919, Anderson Papers; Lowell to William Short, 1 November 1919, Lowell Papers.

26. Lowell to Taft, 1 November 1919, Taft Papers; *New York Tribune*, 6 November 1919; Lodge to Root, 3 December 1919, Root Papers; *Providence Evening Tribune*, 31 October 1919.

27. Memorandum prepared by Arthur Sweetser, Manley Hudson, and R.B.F. (Raymond B. Fosdick), 1 November 1919, "The Senate Reservations From the European Standpoint," Fosdick to Eric Drummond, 14 November 1919, in Fosdick, *Letters on the League*, 46–54, 61–63. McCumber was most alarmed, and he memorialized his mild reservationist colleagues on the subject (McCumber to A. Lawrence Lowell, 1 November 1919, Lowell Papers).

leagues, attacked the reservations, predicted the defeat of the resolution of ratification embodying them, and planned for compromise with the mild reservationists after that defeat.[28] He said that most of the reservations were disguised amendments and criticized especially the preamble and the reservation to Article 10.[29] From Vice-president Marshall he received assurances of favorable rulings to permit continued consideration of the treaty after the Lodge resolution was rejected, though he knew Lodge would appeal such rulings.[30] But he hoped that mild reservationists would vote with the Democrats on the parliamentary status of the treaty and that, having fulfilled their obligations to Lodge, they would then treat with the Democrats on a set of truly mild reservations.[31]

Hitchcock and his colleagues Swanson, Simmons, Underwood, and others considered the situation in the Senate to be very delicate, and they were uncertain of the outcome. They could count on the mild reservationists to support reconsideration if the Lodge resolution failed, and they presumed that in the event of reconsideration, the floor would be open for a new, compromise program of reservations.[32] But they had to wonder whether, if the treaty was rejected at that session of Congress, it would have any better prospects in the next. They held off intruding on the president through October, but when the reservations came before the Senate, they could wait no longer to inform him of the situation and to see if he would modify his position. Hitchcock got an appointment for 7 November, a day after the Senate began debate on the preamble.

Hitchcock's interview with the president was not wholly satisfactory. An emaciated figure, propped up in bed, Wilson was guarded by his wife and doctor against anything too distressful.

Hitchcock risked the suggestion of meaningful compromise, but Wilson rebuffed him. During the thirty-minute interview, Hitchcock told Wilson that the "Lodge reservations" would get majority support but could be turned down in the ratification vote. Wilson, though now willing to accept reservations in the resolution of ratification, objected especially to the Article 10 reservation as "destructive" and to the preamble as "very embarrassing." He approved Hitchcock's strategy of seeking compromise only after a deadlock.

28. *Providence Evening Tribune*, 31 October 1919; *New York World*, 25 October 1919; *St. Louis Post-Dispatch*, 24 October 1919.
29. *New York Times*, 23 October 1919; *New York World*, 23 October 1919.
30. *New York World*, 7 November 1919; *New York Journal*, 4 November 1919.
31. *New York World*, 3 November 1919.
32. Talcott Williams to A. Lawrence Lowell, 4 November 1919, Lowell Papers.

As Hitchcock later reported it, Wilson would "leave the matter of compromise to the friends of the treaty here, [but] any time a serious doubt arose in our minds about any procedure he would be glad to have the suggestions submitted to him." Hitchcock left with Wilson a copy of the seven McCumber reservations.[33] In substance, Hitchcock found himself still on a short leash. And his master, though insisting on control, remained neither fully aware of the situation in the Senate nor emotionally prepared to adapt to it.

On his return to the Capitol from the White House, Hitchcock put out feelers for future compromise from the mild reservationists. They discouraged him. After another attempt the following day, a "leading mild reservationist," probably McNary, told the *Portland Oregonian's* correspondent that the Democrats would have to accept Republican reservations or lose the treaty.[34]

The preamble battle, already on in the Senate, foreshadowed what was to come and was important for its own sake, considering the attention focused on it by both sides. McCumber put forth the main alternative, as an amendment, and led in debate. He moved to strike the requirement of written acceptance by three of the principal Allied and Associated powers, leaving only the sentence making the reservations "a part and a condition of the resolution of ratification." Arguing strongly for his amendment on 6 and 7 November, McCumber said that tacit acceptance was the ordinary and effective procedure. But the Senate rejected McCumber's amendment by 48–40. No Republican joined him in support of it.[35] The preamble was part of the program to which middle grounders felt committed, at least for the time being.

They were not committed to an amendment offered by Borah. He wanted acceptance not by three of the Great Powers but by all four. The amendment, if adopted, could seriously jeopardize the chances for the United States to join the League, for as McCumber had noted, it would be hard for Japan to accept the Shantung reservation. The Senate rejected Borah's amendment, 63–25. Of the middle grounders, only Cummins supported it. The amendment disposed of, Republicans reunited to approve the preamble, 48–40, with McCumber alone breaking ranks.[36]

33. Gilbert Hitchcock, "Events Leading to the World War," 13 January 1925, Hitchcock Papers.

34. *Des Moines Register,* 8 November 1919; *Portland Oregonian,* 9 November 1919.

35. *CR* 66:1, pp. 8024–26 (6 November 1919), p. 8068 (7 November 1919).

36. Ibid., 8069, 8074 (7 November 1919).

Next came the withdrawal reservation. A number of senators spoke, focusing on the question of whether withdrawal should be by joint or concurrent resolution. Before the issue was decided, Hitchcock reportedly offered to back the reservation if the Senate would approve an amendment, offered by Nelson, to switch from concurrent to joint resolution. Nelson's initiative, supported by McCumber, evidently gave Hitchcock hope that he could yet divide the Republicans and make an overall deal with the mild reservationists. The hope proved groundless. Nelson invoked patriotism against partisanship and in emotional tones decried what he saw as an insult to the president. But only he and McCumber of the Republicans supported the amendment, and it lost, 39–45.[37]

Soon the Senate acted on the reservation itself, approving it 50–35. All the Republicans, including Nelson and McCumber, voted for it, and Kellogg, paired with an administration Democrat, announced that if free to vote he would support it. Five Democrats—Gore, Reed, Hoke Smith, David Walsh, and George Chamberlain of Oregon—voted for it. Shields was paired for the reservation. Chamberlain's vote, his first break with the administration on the treaty, surprised many.[38]

The Senate action on the withdrawal reservation ended all doubt about the rest of the committee's program, exclusive still of the Reed and Shields reservations. That night, Lodge predicted that all the reservations would go through. Hitchcock said that there was no point in seeking compromise yet. The Republicans were bound together by pledges, and he would have to await a deadlock, by which he meant the defeat of both Republican and Democratic resolutions of ratification. McCumber drew closer to his party. He thought that the issue of withdrawal would come up soon after the United States ratified the treaty. Now that the Senate had voted to Congress exclusive power over withdrawal, by simple majority vote, he deemed the reservations essential to weaken the irreconcilables in their prospective campaign for withdrawal.[39]

Taft lent further support to the committee program. At Carnegie Hall in New York on the night of 8 November, following the vote on withdrawal, he said that only the Reed reservation menaced American entry into the League; the rest of the reservations would proba-

---

37. Ibid., 8135–37 (8 November 1919); *Portland Oregonian*, 9 November 1919.
38. *New York Times*, 9 November 1919; *St. Louis Post-Dispatch*, 8 November 1919.
39. *New York World*, 9 November 1919; *St. Louis Post-Dispatch*, 9 November 1919; *CR* 66:1, p. 8074 (7 November 1919); *New York Tribune*, 15 November 1919.

bly be accepted by Great Britain, France, and Italy. The speech was a follow-up on a syndicated column published earlier that day. He hoped to "back up McCumber and his group." Taft's backing related not to the character of the reservations but to the relationship between the mild reservationists and the Democrats. The Democrats were playing with fire, he thought, and should quickly compromise.[40]

When the Senate turned to the third reservation, on Article 10, no one thought it would be weakened, despite Wilson's strong objections to it. A much livelier possibility was that the reservation would be strengthened. Debate began even before Lodge formally submitted the reservation. Borah had introduced an amendment to the treaty to strike out Article 10, and on 4 November he and Lenroot, with interjected comments by a few others, took up the meaning of the article and of the committee reservation. Borah took the position that the reservation left untouched the obligation, affirmed in the first sentence of the article, for members to "respect and preserve as against external aggression the territorial integrity and existing political independence of all Members of the League" and simply shifted, from the executive to Congress, the job of implementing it. He argued that by sending a representative to Geneva and by participating in Council decisions, which had to be unanimous, the United States would commit itself morally. Lenroot disagreed. "Mr. President, it certainly is a most novel proposition that if a principal sends an agent, and the agent is given authority only to make recommendations back to the principal as to a given course of action to be pursued, the principal feels himself obligated to carry out the recommendations of the agent." Borah argued the point, but Lenroot reaffirmed his position. He did agree with Borah that the first sentence of the article involved an obligation, but he thought that the reservation adequately disavowed it. Lenroot also agreed that a clause to which Borah objected—"which, under the Constitution, has the power to declare war or authorize the employing of the military or naval forces of the United States"—was unwise, but he did not feel that it lessened the disavowal of obligation. Borah disagreed and thought that the clause suggested that the reservation was merely reciting American constitutional requirements. Borah ended the debate by withdrawing his amendment, "in view of the construction which has been placed upon this reservation by one of those who, I presume, helped to frame it." He wanted to consult on the reserva-

40. Ruhl J. Bartlett, *The League to Enforce Peace,* 149; Taft to Talcott Williams, 7 November 1919, Taft Papers.

tion "and see if we can not change the language to make it speak the construction of the Senator."[41]

In the course of the debate, Cummins and Jones supported Borah in the demand for a stronger reservation. Jones agreed that participation by an American in a unanimous Council decision involving the use of force implied a moral commitment. He would require that Congress authorize the American vote. The next day a reporter wrote that Lodge had agreed to strengthen the reservation. His purpose was not to satisfy Borah so much as Jones, Cummins, and others.[42] If such was Lodge's purpose, he did not adhere to it. The reservation, so painstakingly developed, was the principal basis of understanding with the mild reservationists and was not easily put aside.

Borah persisted, on his own. Early in the Senate consideration of the reservation, on 10 November, he offered a substitute: "The United States assumes no obligation, legal or moral, under article 10 and shall not be bound by any of the terms or conditions of said article." If adopted, the reservation would have scuttled the negative guarantee to respect the territorial integrity and political independence of members, as well as the obligation to consult in the Council and consider Council advice. And to middle grounders it seemed unnecessary. Kellogg and Lenroot had earlier defended the committee reservation as disavowing obligation respecting the armed forces. Without further debate, the Senate rejected the motion, 18–68. Cummins and McLean voted for it; other middle grounders, along with Lodge, voted "nay."[43]

The adoption of the reservation as submitted was now almost certain. Nevertheless, individual Democrats, realizing the reservation's importance to the prospect of ratification, to the party's political hopes, and perhaps to the cause of world peace, submitted a number of amendments and substitutes and argued strongly for them. The Democrats seemed almost desperate to produce something different from the reservation that Wilson had so strongly repudiated. The middle grounders proved virtually united against them.

41. *CR* 66:1, pp. 7942–50 (4 November 1919). For the "Lodge reservations" of 19 November, see *CR* 66:1, pp. 8777–8888. These reservations, together with those of 19 March, may also be found in Thomas A. Bailey, *Woodrow Wilson and the Great Betrayal*, 387–94.

42. *CR* 66:1, pp. 7946, 7950 (4 November 1919); *New York Tribune*, 6 November 1919.

43. *CR* 66:1, pp. 8212, 8203–4 (10 November 1919).

At the start of the Senate consideration of the reservations, Charles Thomas had offered a substitute that McCumber had presented in September. To the dismay of some Democrats, McCumber now opposed it.[44] Reviewing recent history, he said that his reservation "had the indorsement of a number of Senators on this side of the Chamber." But they got no encouragement from the Democrats. A number of those who agreed with him "were very desirous that we should come to some kind of an arrangement, fearing that unless there should be an agreement there would be adopted a reservation which would be far more radical than the one we now have before us. We attempted during a period, I think, of about two months, to secure a reservation that would be more in harmony with my views and with the views of one or two other Senators." Failing in that, they had agreed to the committee's reservation. Now, the senator said, he was "honor bound to support the committee reservation." The Senate rejected Thomas's substitute, 36–48. No Republican supported it.[45]

Townsend alone of the middle grounders voted for a Democratic amendment. He backed Tom Walsh's motion to strike from the reservation the words *or authorize the employment of the military or naval forces of the United States*, a minor weakening of the reservation. The Senate rejected the amendment, 38–45.[46] Walsh then tried a different tactic. He offered an amendment to add at the end of the reservation: "And the United States hereby releases all members of the league from any obligation to it under Article 10 and declines to participate in any proceedings by the council authorized thereby." The amendment appealed to irreconcilables and, if attached, might split the Republicans and cause the defeat of the reservation, opening the way for a softer alternative. For a time, some thought it might pass.[47]

Townsend took the lead in opposition. He spoke seriously and soberly, as one who had not participated much in debate or in behind-the-scenes negotiation. Townsend could conceive that Article 10 would do some good, for the world and the United States. The Walsh amendment, he thought, made a farce of the article. The committee reservation, on the other hand, simply made explicit what Wilson had told the country: that the Council could only advise, subject to action by Congress. Disagreeing with Hitchcock,

44. *New York Tribune*, 11 November 1919.
45. *CR* 66:1, p. 8207, 8282 (10 November 1919).
46. Ibid., 8312–13 (10 November 1919).
47. *Minneapolis Tribune*, 12 November 1919.

Townsend denied that through the reservation the United States would renounce responsibility to Poland or others. Those peoples knew that America would do her duty.[48]

Walsh's amendment was a ploy, and when it failed to lure reservationists, Democrats and irreconcilables abandoned it too. Following a three-day delay occasioned by an irreconcilable near-filibuster, the Senate voted it down, 4–68. Swiftly, senators rejected other reservations to Article 10. One of them, offered by Hitchcock, was inspired by suggestions submitted earlier by Wilson. As before, Hitchcock did not reveal the source of the reservation, or of four others that he read. Finally, the Senate approved the committee reservation, 43–33. No Republican voted against it, and Gore, Reed, Hoke Smith, and David Walsh supported it. Shields was announced in favor; Chamberlain did not vote, and his position was not announced.[49]

The defeat of the Democrats was almost complete. The Senate, albeit still in Committee of the Whole, had approved a reservation that Wilson said cut the heart out of the treaty, and the Republicans had staked out a tough negotiating position for the future. McCumber did indicate that he supported the reservation only to keep his word and that he did not really approve it. When his obligation ended, he might prove more tractable. But Townsend, who showed some independence, supported the reservation on its merits. So did Lenroot, the emerging floor leader for the mild reservationists, and Colt, one of the mildest of the lot.

Compromise efforts lay ahead. Meanwhile, the Senate had to complete action on the reservations. To expedite that, the Senate adopted cloture, to limit debate. "Cloture was unavoidable," Lodge explained to Beveridge, "because an overwhelming majority of the senate had got so weary of the thing that they wanted to bring it to an end."[50] Since neither party wanted to be seen as abetting delay, the leaders of both parties supported cloture. They differed, however, as to its extent. Their differences reflected rival scenarios for the post-reservation stage of the contest.

Mild reservationists gave cloture its most ardent and active support. They shared the general fatigue, but beyond that, they wanted to hasten ratification. They therefore favored a thoroughgoing form of cloture. That form, in turn, fitted well with the tactic of offering Democrats little hope for compromise and pressuring them to accept the "Lodge reservations."

48. *CR* 66:1, pp. 8213, 8215–17 (10 November 1919).
49. Bailey, *Great Betrayal*, 393–94; *CR* 66:1, pp. 8433–37 (13 November 1919).
50. Lodge to Albert J. Beveridge, 15 November 1919, Lodge Papers.

First Hitchcock presented his petition, signed by twenty-two Democrats. It would limit debate during the further consideration of reservations but said nothing about the situation after that. Kellogg was the first to condemn the deficiency, and in short order, on a parliamentary point, the petition was set aside. Meanwhile Hale and Kellogg for several days had been circulating among Republicans a cloture petition of their own. By the time the Senate was done with the third reservation, thirty had signed, including all the middle grounders. More sweeping than Hitchcock's, the Republican petition would limit each senator to an aggregate of one hour on all matters relating to the treaty until it was disposed of and would block additional amendments and reservations introduced after the adoption of cloture.[51]

Presented at the end of the day by Lodge, despite objection from irreconcilables, the petition was not voted on until 15 November, after a recess of a day to permit senators to attend the funeral of Democratic Leader Thomas Martin. Before the vote, Vice-President Marshall indicated that he would entertain further motions if the Lodge resolution of ratification was later defeated. Democrats, still hopeful that mild reservationists would back that approach, and in any case reluctant to seem the party of delay, supported the cloture motion, which carried 78–16. It was the first time the Senate had used the cloture rule since its adoption in 1917.[52]

Just before the Senate approved cloture, Hitchcock presented, as part of the instrument of ratification, the five mild reservations that he had submitted earlier. They would be in order later under the cloture rule. The executive committee of the LEP was to meet the next day to consider endorsement of the "Lodge reservations," and Hitchcock was deeply worried. He wrote Taft, arguing that his reservations would constitute a basis for future compromise with twenty-five or thirty Republicans, once those men were freed from present promises. Also, his reservations would stand a better chance than the committee's of being assented to abroad. British and French authorities had led him to think that their governments would probably not feel that they could accept the "Lodge reservations" without going to their legislative bodies for approval, which would start far-reaching disturbances. The Nebraskan urged that the LEP take no backward step.[53]

51. *CR* 66:1, pp. 8413–17, 8437 (13 November 1919); *Minneapolis Tribune*, 13 November 1919; *New York World*, 14 November 1919.

52. *CR* 66:1, pp. 8555–56 (15 November 1919).

53. Ibid., 8546–47 (15 November 1919); Hitchcock to Taft, 12 November 1919,

Hitchcock was far from sure his strategy would work. After presenting his five very mild reservations in the Senate, he prepared for another contingency by making known a much stronger reservation, on Article 10, with the option of bringing it up for action later. He passed on information in brief form to the president, through Mrs. Wilson, as she had suggested. Telling of the reservation to Article 10 approved in Committee of the Whole, he said that it was "not quite as obnoxious as it was when the President denounced it at Salt Lake, a slight change in phraseology having been made in order to secure the support of four or five 'mild reservation' senators." As an afterthought, he penned: "Still it is bad." Then he outlined his plan of action—to offer a resolution of ratification, without reservations, that would lose and then to offer interpretive reservations that would also lose but that would "make the democratic record clear." Then the Democrats could defeat the Lodge resolution. "This plan is subject to modification," he went on, "in case when the time arrives we shall determine, or the President shall advise us to vote for the Lodge resolution." Some Democrats wanted the president's advice in advance of that vote, he added. One infers that Hitchcock hoped Wilson would modify his stand and that he was uncertain of his strategy of deadlock and future compromise but was not ready to act independently of the president. Indeed, after Marshall made it clear that the first vote would be on the Lodge resolution, Hitchcock asked for an early interview with Wilson, to get definite instructions that he could pass on to his party colleagues to make the Democratic vote "as nearly solid as possible."[54]

Lodge also prepared for the final stages of the contest. Disputing Marshall, he asserted that under the cloture rule, if his resolution was defeated, the treaty would be dead. At his home on Sunday, the sixteenth, he conferred with Brandegee, Borah, Knox, Watson, and Lenroot on parliamentary procedure in view of Marshall's ruling. Other senators dropped in during the day. None of them publicly disagreed with Lodge, on that day at least.[55]

It remained for the Senate to complete action on the reservations. With the aid of cloture, the senators acted swiftly. Republican lines held quite firm, but twelve Democrats broke ranks on one reservation or another. In a matter of six hours, on Saturday, 15 November, the Senate, still in Committee of the Whole, adopted ten reserva-

Taft Papers.

54. *CR* 66:1, p. 8547 (15 November 1919); Hitchcock to Mrs. Wilson, 13, 15 November 1919, Wilson Papers.

55. *New York Tribune*, 16, 17 November 1919.

tions. Except for the domestic questions reservation, in which a minor change was inserted at the behest of Hale and was later deleted, the committee program passed unchanged.[56]

Only Shantung provoked any significant controversy. McCumber pressed for his substitute, whereas Lenroot defended the committee reservation that he had written. McCumber argued that the committee reservation, by which the United States would withhold its assent to the Shantung articles of the treaty, could not be accepted by the Allies because of their obligations to Japan. He preferred his own reservation, by which the United States would refrain "from entering into any agreement" relating to the Shantung provisions. Lenroot said that Britain, France, and Italy would not have to go back on Japan respecting Shantung but could merely recognize America's unwillingness to assent. The United States, he thought, should make its position clear on what was generally acknowledged to be an evil. The Senate rejected McCumber's substitute, 42–50. Only Nelson of the Republicans voted with McCumber and the Democrats. On the committee reservation, McCumber alone defected from the Republicans.[57]

The Senate took no action the following day, but the LEP did. It issued a statement calling for the rejection of the treaty if the Reed reservation was adopted and, by implication, for the acceptance of the other committee reservations. The announcement, coming on the eve of Senate consideration of the Reed reservation, had been authorized by the executive committee three days earlier. The Republicans on the committee, following the advice of the Washington bureau people and led by Taft and Lowell, overrode McAdoo and other Democrats after a hot debate. The vote was 10–5.[58]

Undoubtedly, politics played a part. Beyond that, though, the decision reflected the fact that for Taft, Lowell, and others, Article 10 was but an appendage, which they had belatedly accepted, to an earlier internationalist program that remained largely represented in the Covenant notwithstanding the reservations. The negative guarantee, Council consultation, and Senate consideration remained under Article 10. Disarmament remained, though impaired, and

56. *New York Times*, 16 November 1919; *Portland Oregonian*, 16 November 1919; *CR* 66:1, pp. 8437–71 (15 November 1919).

57. *CR* 66:1, pp. 8561–64 (15 November 1919).

58. Bartlett, *League to Enforce Peace*, 151–54; Raymond B. Fosdick to Arthur Sweetser, 14 November 1919, in Fosdick, *Letters on the League*, 60–61; H. N. Rickey to William Short, 5 February 1920, LEP Papers; A. Lawrence Lowell to Talcott Williams, 22 October 1919 and 7 November 1919, Williams to Lowell, 4 November 1919, Lowell Papers.

above all, pacific settlement remained, with the boycott to back it.[59]

The LEP's action, which Kellogg had urged on Lowell, strengthened the Republican supporters of ratification against the Democrats just before final Senate action. More immediately, it weakened the prospects for the Reed reservation, for now that the LEP had become tractable, Republicans had some grounds for accommodating to it, thus isolating the Democrats before the country. Taft pitched in on his own, with a syndicated editorial against the Reed reservation. McCumber had prompted him, but Taft needed no prompting, for he felt that on the fate of that reservation "hangs the fate of the treaty."[60]

First the Senate had to deal with the fourteenth reservation, which had been accepted by the committee to please John Shields but which was understood to be something Republicans might reject with no loss of honor. The reservation, it will be recalled, declined trusteeship or other responsibility for the United States over the German overseas possessions. Townsend and Sterling spoke against tying the country's hands for the future, and in short order the Senate rejected the reservation, 29–64.[61] As they debated the Shields reservation, senators looked forward to the fifteenth reservation, Reed's. Townsend, in opposing the fourteenth reservation, also announced his opposition to Reed's and argued against it.

Under the Reed reservation, the United States might determine for itself what was a matter of national honor or interest and might withhold such an issue from pacific settlement procedures. Townsend said that he wanted the United States to assume some responsibility and was willing that the country take some chances. Under the Reed reservation, the United States could prevent world consideration of any question, and that went too far.[62]

When the Reed reservation became the order of business, Lodge defended it. He noted that the United States had adopted similar provisions as recently as 1908, and he said that contrary to the views of many senators, "vital interests" meant just that and not every conceivable subject of dispute. Colt disagreed. The terms *national*

59. Yeomans, *Lowell*, 453; Taft to Frank Irving Cobb, 10 November 1919, and to Caspar Yost, 13 November 1919, Taft Papers; Taft, in *Minneapolis Tribune*, 10 November 1919; Lowell to Samuel Clarke, 17 and 19 December 1919, and to E. A. Kirkpatrick, 12 January 1920, Lowell Papers.

60. *Minneapolis Tribune*, 17 November 1919; McCumber to Taft, 15 November 1919, Taft to McCumber, 16 November 1919, Taft Papers.

61. *CR* 66:1, pp. 8619–34 (17 November 1919).

62. Ibid., 8618 (17 November 1919).

honor and *vital interests* could not be defined and had no definition in international law. The main mechanisms of the Covenant for preventing war—obligatory conferences, compulsory arbitration or compulsory submission to inquiry and report, and the reduction of armaments—had survived the other reservations but were jeopardized by Reed's. "The fact is, Mr. President, the incorporation of a reservation of this kind spells death to the league." Sterling, McCumber, and Edge joined in opposition, arguing mainly that other reservations gave ample protection.[63]

After a few more speeches, the senators voted. By a tally of 36–56 they rejected the reservation. Middle grounders could claim credit for the outcome. Just four of them—Capper, Spencer, Jones, and McLean—voted for the reservation; the other fourteen opposed it, as did another Republican, Francis E. Warren of Wyoming.[64]

With the committee reservations disposed of, the Senate next turned to reservations submitted by individuals. Many reservations had been submitted, but adoption was assured on just two subjects. McCumber's reservation to the labor provisions of the treaty had been approved in committee but was not presented by Lodge because the North Dakotan wanted to modify the language slightly. His party, though, insisted on a reservation on the subject, as did some Democrats. In addition, senators were determined to adopt a reservation on equal voting with the United Kingdom. Viscount Grey of Fallodon, ambassador on special mission to the United States, had been on the scene since late September. For himself and for Hitchcock, Lansing, and Lowell, he persistently urged his government to mollify Americans in several ways, especially by promising that in the event of a dispute involving a member of the Empire, the other members would not vote in the Assembly. But Lord Curzon, the foreign secretary, delayed so that he could consult the others. He finally demurred altogether because of objections from Jan C. Smuts of South Africa and William H. Hughes of Australia.[65] Without such a statement, the issue was emotionally hot and politically sensitive.

McCumber's reservation on labor came first. The United States would withhold assent to the treaty's labor provisions unless Con-

63. Ibid., 8634–39 (17 November 1919).

64. Ibid., 8640 (17 November 1919). Spencer may have been reluctant to oppose his fellow Missourian, Reed.

65. Grey to Curzon, 24, 26, 29 October, 1, 6, 14 November 1919, Curzon to Grey, 24, 31 October, 13, 18 November 1919, in E. L. Woodward and Rohan Butler, eds., *Documents on British Foreign Policy, 1919–1939,* 5:1008–23.

gress provided for representation in the organization established under Part 13, the International Labor Organization, "and in such event the participation of the United States will be governed and conditioned by the provisions of such act or joint resolution." McCumber called Part 13 "the only feature of the treaty that is obnoxious and abhorrent." A labor organization like the radical Industrial Workers of the World could complain to the international labor office and cause a sovereign state to defend itself before that organization. Earlier, McCumber said, he had been willing to swallow the labor provisions, knowing they would fail, but now that reservations had come into vogue he felt justified in offering one on the subject.[66]

Democrats William H. King of Utah and Charles Thomas of Colorado argued for a substitute, to cut the United States off altogether from the I.L.O. If not adopted, Thomas warned, he would join the irreconcilables. McCumber declared the substitute too drastic, and in the voting that followed the mild reservationists and three moderates accomplished its defeat, 43–49. Swiftly, the Senate approved McCumber's reservation.[67]

The Senate then took up the equal-voting issue. First, McCumber offered his reservation, which stated that the United States construed the Covenant to mean that when a case before the Assembly or Council involved a member of the British Empire, no part of the Empire could vote. Hitchcock approved the reservation as consistent with the Covenant. Hiram Johnson offered a substitute: the United States would have as many votes as the British Empire; when the United States was in dispute with a member of the Empire, neither the United States nor any part of the Empire would vote; when the United States was in a dispute with a nation not a member of the Empire, the Empire would cast but one vote.[68]

Three middle grounders quickly joined the debate. Townsend faulted Johnson's wording; Colt said that twenty-seven nations would have to assent and that voting in the League would be changed from membership voting to "some other kind of voting"; Lenroot argued that the reservation was really an amendment, and he read his own reservation as an alternative, which he would offer if the Johnson substitute was defeated. Lenroot's reservation remained virtually unchanged from what he had proposed at the time of the

---

66. *CR* 66:1, pp. 8640–41 (17 November 1919).
67. Ibid., 8641 (17 November 1919), pp. 8699–702, 8729–30 (18 November 1919).
68. Ibid., 8731 (18 November 1919).

debate on the Johnson amendment: the United States would disavow obligations in matters in which the British Empire cast more
than one vote; and the United States would not be bound when, in a
dispute with a part of the Empire, any part of the Empire voted.[69]

After some further debate, including a barbed exchange between
Johnson and Lenroot, the Senate voted on the Johnson substitute.
Presented as a reservation, albeit a most drastic one, Johnson's six-
vote proposal came close to passing, but it fell by a tally of 43–46.
Five Democrats supported it, but they were outweighed by nine
mild reservationists. Edge did not vote and was not paired. Lenroot
then offered his reservation as a substitute for McCumber's. McCumber tried to soften the Lenroot substitute by amendment but failed,
and the Senate adopted it, 55–38. Of the Republicans, only McCumber opposed it.[70]

The Senate turned aside all other reservations, and in some cases
middle grounders were responsible for the result. Most middle
grounders viewed the committee program, plus reservations on
labor and equal voting, as the sum of the party's reservation program. It seemed sufficient to protect the national interest, was
defensible politically should the Democrats reject it on the final
vote, and, partly for that reason, might in fact be accepted by the
Democrats and the president and thus bring treaty ratification.
These middle grounders were reluctant to add reservations that had
not been developed in intraparty negotiation and that might jeopardize what had been accomplished.

One noncommittee reservation had been rejected the previous
day. Offered by Democrat Robert Owen of Oklahoma, a supporter of
the League, it would construe the British protectorate in Egypt as
not depriving the Egyptians of any of their rights to self-government.
Senators paid Owen little attention, and he twice asked for order.
Despite his arguments, and those of Norris and Lodge, the Senate
rejected the reservation, 37–45. Capper, Cummins, Jones, Kenyon,
Lenroot, McLean, and Smoot supported it, more middle grounders
than usual on reservations not part of the Republican program. However, the other eleven middle grounders, along with two strong reservationists, opposed it. Most Democrats opposed the reservation,
and the thirteen Republicans gave them the victory margin.[71]

Following the adoption of Lenroot's equal-voting reservation, the

69. Ibid., 8732–33, 8735–36 (18 November 1919).
70. Ibid., 8736–37, 8739, 8741 (18 November 1919).
71. Ibid., 8642–44 (17 November 1919).

Senate acted swiftly on the other reservations offered by individual senators. Knox proposed a reservation giving the United States complete liberty of action in relations with the League and asserting that American ratification would depend on affirmative action by the four Great Powers within sixty days. By a vote of 30–61, the Senate rejected it. Capper voted for it, and McLean was paired with a pro-League Democrat, but the other middle grounders, along with four strong reservationists, voted "nay."[72]

The Senate turned next to Wesley Jones's reservation requiring that the American representative on the League Council not approve anything, without prior approval by Congress, that might entail the use of the military or naval forces of the United States. Kellogg argued that the matter was covered in the eighth reservation, which stated that the powers and duties of a representative on the Council should be fixed by law. Furthermore, the reservation to Article 10 preserved the power of Congress. Jones replied that he wanted the present Congress to make it clear that it did not want its representative to approve force on his own authority. In the voting, middle grounders divided. Except for Edge, all mild reservationists voted "nay." Of the moderates, all but Spencer supported the reservation. Four strong reservationists helped defeat the motion, 34–50.[73]

Next came a reservation, offered by Thomas Gore, reaffirming America's traditional policy of no foreign entanglements. The Senate rejected it, 28–50. The mild reservationists, abetted by three moderates and three strong reservationists, caused its defeat. After the Senate rejected two other reservations by voice vote or overwhelmingly on roll call, it turned down a series, offered by La Follette, on tallies ranging from 24–49 to 10–60. The proposals would have affirmed the right of revolution for non–self-governing peoples and would have required American withdrawal from the League under a series of circumstances. They got some backing from moderates but none from mild reservationists.[74]

The last reservation considered in Committee of the Whole was proposed by the administration Democrat Tom Walsh. Relevant to the touchy Irish situation, it specified that the provisions of Article Eleven should not abridge the right of free speech, liberty of the press, "and advocacy of the principles of national independence and self-determination." It was defeated by the comparatively close mar-

72. Ibid., 8742, 8744 (18 November 1919).
73. Ibid., 8744–45 (18 November 1919).
74. Ibid., 8746, 8748–53 (18 November 1919).

gin of 36–42. The mild reservationists voted against it, the only Republicans to do so.[75]

The treaty was now before the Senate but was still subject to perfecting amendments. The Senate quickly adopted the reservations approved in Committee of the Whole, then rejected new ones. Hitchcock moved to strike out most of the preamble, leaving only that the reservations be part of the resolution of ratification. He lost, 36–45, with McCumber alone breaking ranks. Reed again raised his national honor or interest reservation and lost, 33–50. As before, moderates divided, but mild reservationists were solidly opposed.[76]

Owen offered an Egyptian independence reservation, which lost, 31–46. Vice-President Marshall then declared the treaty closed to amendments or further reservations, and at 10:15 in the evening, the Senate adjourned, to reconvene at noon the following day to deal at last with at least one resolution of ratification.[77] Unknown to most senators, the outcome had already been determined outside the Senate chamber.

Senators and those who would influence them did much conferring in the days immediately preceding final action, and on that day itself. But the cause was hopeless. On the morning of 17 November, Wilson made it clear to Hitchcock that he would not compromise substantially. The mild reservationists would compromise on the preamble, to which Wilson strongly objected, but they would not or could not yield more, and what they offered did not meet Wilson's conditions. Hitchcock played at negotiation but gave more serious attention to keeping his Democratic colleagues in line behind the president. Aided by a letter from Wilson, he succeeded, and in the Senate an ill-tempered deadlock resulted.

When Hitchcock saw the president on the seventeenth, he was looking better than he had ten days before and was conversant with the "Lodge reservations." The senator described the situation in the Senate and suggested compromise. Otherwise, he said, adjournment might occur with the treaty pending. "There is merit in that suggestion," Wilson replied. "I would like to have some of the Senators go home to their constituents while the treaty is still pending." Certainly, he would not accept the whole of the "Lodge reservations." If the Senate approved the treaty with them, he would pocket it, he said. The reservations amounted to nullification, he thought.

75. Ibid., 8753–54 (18 November 1919).
76. Ibid., 8754–55, 8756 (18 November 1919).
77. Ibid., 8756–60 (18 November 1919).

In particular, Wilson criticized the preamble and the reservation to Article 10.[78]

Hitchcock hoped that Wilson might yet yield a little, but he had to prepare for deadlock. So he asked the president for a letter that he might present to the Democratic caucus, which would meet just before the final voting. Wilson agreed, and Hitchcock volunteered to submit a draft embodying the president's views. Afterward, Hitchcock told the press of Wilson's objections and purposes but said that the president did not oppose all the "Lodge reservations." Hitchcock added that, once the Lodge resolution had been disposed of, "we will get together with the Republicans who really want the treaty ratified. All pledges of the Republicans to vote for the Lodge reservation program will be off after that has been rejected. The Republicans will then be released and can treat with us." Hitchcock knew, however, that negotiations, whenever they came, would require substantially greater concessions than Wilson had shown himself ready to make. Either on the seventeenth or one of the following two days, Hitchcock asked Mrs. Wilson to see if she could persuade her husband. McAdoo had already tried in vain, but Mrs. Wilson nevertheless agreed. "For my sake," she later remembered as having said to Wilson, "won't you accept these reservations and get this awful thing settled?" He would not; it was a matter of personal and national honor.[79]

Wilson was unrealistic in his intransigence. The mild reservationists, essential to ratification, could not accommodate to it and hope to achieve ratification. Several Republican senators took polls of their colleagues and found that thirty-eight would vote against ratification should the mild reservationists compromise with the Democrats.[80]

What the mild reservationists could do, they did. They agreed to a change in the preamble but insisted that a compromise based on that concession be proposed by Hitchcock through Lodge. In other

---

78. *Providence Evening Tribune*, 17 November 1919; Robert Lansing to Frank Polk, 17 November 1919, Frank Polk Papers, Yale University, in Daniel M. Smith, *The Great Departure: The United States and World War I, 1914–1920*, 194; *Minneapolis Tribune*, 18 November 1919. Hitchcock's own hope was to defeat the Lodge resolution and then compromise on the basis of the elimination of the preamble and "possibly a moderate change in the reservation to Article Ten" (Hitchcock to A. Lawrence Lowell, 15 November 1919, Lowell Papers).

79. Hitchcock to Mrs. Wilson, 17 November 1919, Wilson Papers; *Minneapolis Tribune*, 18 November 1919; Arthur Walworth, *Woodrow Wilson*, 2:386; Edith Bolling Wilson, *My Memoir*, 297.

80. *New York Tribune*, 17 November 1919.

words, they would not break with their party. Lodge's involvement, mentioned by a few mild reservationists in interviews on 17 November, won group approval the following day. The main topic among mild reservationists in the wake of Hitchcock's visit to the White House was the preamble, partly because Hitchcock, in summarizing Wilson's views, stressed the president's objection that the preamble was tantamount to an amendment, since it required renegotiation.[81]

Even before Hitchcock announced Wilson's position, McNary, Kellogg, Lenroot, and Colt were talking with Oscar Straus of the LEP. Straus proposed a preamble modification that would eliminate the requirement for an exchange of notes and would allow for silent acquiescence by the Great Powers. Afterward, McNary said that Straus's suggestion had been well received and would probably be agreed to. In separate statements to reporters, Lenroot and Kellogg spoke guardedly of such a change.[82]

The mild reservationists had good reason to want to change the preamble. They had to consider the pleas of Straus and three other LEP representatives who appeared at the Capitol on the seventeenth.[83] LEP backing, so recently gained, needed to be held, for purposes of intra- and interparty bargaining. And the mild reservationists had not themselves favored formal Allied assent but had acquiesced reluctantly. For the British, Lord Balfour had spoken in Parliament on 11 November against reservations that would relieve the United States of responsibilities that others would still bear. There was little the mild reservationists could do about that. But, following Anglo-French discussions in London on 14 November, a Paris paper published an officially inspired statement noting that the Allies would find it hard to accept any reservations requiring their assent. The mild reservationists took notice. It was understood that the Allies did not want to give formal assent to the Shantung reservation, or to interfere between branches of the American government, which so many reservations entailed, or to open the door to new demands from their own countries, even though they had already ratified the treaty.[84]

81. Ibid., 18 November 1919; *New York World*, 18 November 1919.

82. *Portland Oregonian*, 18 November 1919; *New York Tribune*, 18 November 1919.

83. *New York World*, 18 November 1919; *Minneapolis Tribune*, 18 November 1919.

84. George W. Egerton, *Great Britain and the Creation of the League of Nations: Strategy, Politics, and International Organization*, 185–88; David Lawrence, in *St. Louis Post-Dispatch*, 28 October 1919.

Furthermore, Elihu Root opposed specific assent. In a November letter to Kellogg, Root argued that a failure to win assent would discredit the Senate and vindicate the president. The Senate, then, ought to make it as easy as possible for the Great Powers to assent, instead of making it difficult. And Lodge, at least in his subsequent correspondence with Root, claimed not to like the form of the preamble. He wanted prior assent to American reservations by all League members but was agreeable to silent acquiescence. He had told mild reservationists that the form of the preamble was insisted on by several strong reservationists, yet at the suggestion of Lowell, he had changed it to require simply an exchange of notes. Perhaps, if ratification hung in the balance, along with the welfare of the party, he could persuade the strong reservationists to drop their demand for written assent.[85]

The mild reservationists charted their course more fully and definitely on the morning of 18 November. They met in the Appropriations Committee room at the invitation of Reed Smoot, who was considered a "regular." Smoot may have acted at the suggestion of Lodge, but that is not clear. Nor is it entirely clear who came. McCumber, McNary, Spencer, Edge, Colt, Hale, Kellogg, and Lenroot came, and perhaps Nelson and Capper also. Certainly, this was mostly a gathering of mild reservationists.[86]

The group agreed to a four-part program. They would support a motion to reconsider the Lodge resolution if it was defeated on the first vote. This action, opposed by party leaders, would guarantee the Democrats a second chance. Second, though, they would not vote to sustain the chair in a ruling that would open the way for a Democratic resolution of ratification. Third, as a basis for compromise, they would support modification in the preamble. Fourth, further compromise negotiations on the part of the Democrats would have to be conducted through Lodge, the party leader. And any Democratic proposal would have to be submitted by the end of that day, to give time for consideration by Republicans.[87]

Hitchcock was not offered much time, but little seemed needed for what the mild reservationists had in mind. The Democratic "proposal" would have to be, in fact, a commitment to accept the

85. Root to Kellogg, 12 November 1919, and Lodge to Root, 3 December 1919, Root Papers.
86. *New York Times*, 19 November 1919; *New York World*, 19 November 1919.
87. *New York World*, 19 November 1919; *New York Times*, 19 November 1919; *Minneapolis Tribune*, 19 November 1919; *Providence Evening Tribune*, 18 November 1919; Henry Cabot Lodge to F. H. Gillett, 26 July 1920, Lodge Papers.

"Lodge reservations" with the preamble modified to permit silent acquiescence by the Great Powers.[88] What Hitchcock could not do was to proceed with his long-held plan of trying to separate the middle grounders from the rest of the Republicans after the defeat of the Lodge resolution. That was made clear in the insistence that future negotiations be directed through Lodge and that the deal be struck before voting began, not afterward, when Republicans would be free of pledges to the "Lodge reservations." Under the circumstances, there could be no thought of modifying the reservation to Article 10.

The mild reservationist program bore the marks of Lenroot's thinking, in particular. On the previous day, McCumber had led Democrat Atlee Pomerene to think that after the defeat of resolutions by Lodge and Hitchcock, he would offer a compromise resolution. Meanwhile Lenroot, though ardent in his opposition to the assumption of obligations under Article 10, had told Hitchcock through the LEP's Talcott Williams that he was willing to modify the preamble and that he thought ratification would occur on that basis. But he insisted that Hitchcock "submit any proposition he has to Senator Lodge, and then we would decide what we are going to do." It was natural that Lenroot should have been deputized to tell Hitchcock and Lodge of the group's decisions.[89]

Republican senators hailed the action of the mild reservationists as paving the way for party unity in the climactic battle ahead. McCumber and Nelson might desert, some thought, but they would be counterbalanced by four Democrats.[90] Presumably, some of those Republicans who rejoiced at the prospect of party unity on the nineteenth had no great regard for the Covenant. Yet the mild reservationists were seeking not just party unity but ratification, and Lodge proved cooperative. Informed by Lenroot of the mild reservationist stand, he revised his resolution of ratification to permit silent acceptance by three of the four Great Powers. The matter came to light at the start of the session on the nineteenth when, to Lodge's red-faced embarrassment, he inadvertently submitted that resolution, obviously designed for use in the event of compromise, in place of the

88. Lenroot, quoted in *Milwaukee Sentinel*, 2 December 1919; Kellogg, quoted in *Minneapolis Tribune*, 23 November 1919.

89. Gus Karger to William Howard Taft, 17 November 1919, Taft Papers; Talcott Williams to A. Lawrence Lowell, 21 November 1919, Lowell Papers; *New York Tribune*, 18 November 1919; *New York World*, 19 November 1919.

90. *New York Tribune*, 19 November 1919.

unmodified resolution. He rectified the error but not before creating a small sensation. Soon after, Stimson and Taft learned that compromise had been within reach.[91]

Since the mild reservationists' offer to the Democrats was rejected, destroying all chance for ratification, at least in that session of Congress, one must ask whether the mild reservationists were unwise, or unduly timorous, in limiting their concessions to the preamble and in refusing to deal directly with the Democrats. The two issues were really one—working through Lodge, on the basis of a relatively united Republican party, implied that there could be concessions only on the preamble.

The mild reservationist position, though surely based in part on emotion, was reasonable. For months, the Democrats had spurned all opportunities to deal with them. Under these circumstances the mild reservationists, with some difficulty, had come to an agreement within their own party on the basis of a reservationist program that, if it was not ideal, was at least acceptable. The party stood on strong ground before the country on the strength of that program. Now, at the last moment, Hitchcock expected them to splinter their party and join with an almost united Democracy behind an as yet undetermined program that, if ever agreed to, might be no closer to their ideal than was the Lodge program. Though the move would be unfair, exasperating, and politically hurtful, for the sake of ratification the cost might be worth paying. But would ratification result from a breakaway to the Democrats? It seemed most unlikely. Even if all the mild reservationists played Hitchcock's game, the new coalition would fall well short of two-thirds without the support of the moderates and a few strong reservationists. These men could hardly be expected to sacrifice conviction and party in such a quixotic move.

That was especially so because the strength of the Republican position, combined with a major concession on one of the two issues Wilson had stressed, the preamble, made it reasonable for moderates and strong reservationists to expect that the Democrats would acquiesce. Understanding the thinking of their colleagues, and to a large degree sharing it, the mild reservationists felt that their proposal to change the preamble and to vote for a motion to reconsider and thus permit a second vote on the Lodge resolution was as much

91. *New York World*, 20 November 1919; Stimson Diaries, entry for 3 December 1919, Stimson Papers; Taft to Horace Taft, 26 November 1919, Taft Papers.

as they could safely concede, not just for party unity but for ratification itself.

The argument turns, in large part, on the strength of the Republican position. Inadvertently, the party found itself able to make a strong appeal to proponents of the League in the electorate, as well as to opponents. Contrary to the wishes of most Republican senators, amendments had been rejected, as had highly destructive reservations, headed by Reed's. Even with the "Lodge reservations," much of the Covenant remained intact, including the widely popular pacific settlement provisions, the stipulation for conference when war threatened, under Article 11, and the possibility of disarmament. The LEP Executive Committee, long identified with the cause of the League, had come around to support the reservations, with the exception of the preamble, and on the evening of the eighteenth, the Washington bureau of the organization issued a statement to that effect.[92]

In addition Taft and Lowell, well known as champions of the League, might be expected to lend their continuing support should Wilson reject the compromise that the Republicans offered. In the country, bankers and other commercial people, Protestant church leaders, and women remained strong for the League, but by mid-November many of these were following the lead of Taft and Lowell and the LEP, not the stricken Wilson. Far less vocal than the Irish-Americans, British-Americans had to be reckoned with, and they generally favored the League. But they tended also to be Republicans and to accept the "Lodge reservations." These aspects of public opinion were understood by senators and close observers. Of course, through the "Lodge reservations" the GOP had met the widespread appeal, promoted most strongly by irreconcilables, to "Americanize" the treaty.[93]

Republicans had some hard evidence that their League position satisfied voters. The party did well in normally Democratic areas in nationwide elections on 4 November, and in Oklahoma City four days later in a special congressional election that turned on the League issue. And some Democrats, in votes for Republican reservations and in comments on the floor and in the lobbies, evidenced a

92. *CR* 66:1, pp. 8773–74 (19 November 1919).
93. *New York World*, 20 October 1919; Lancaster, "Protestant Churches," 613–14; John Bernard Duff, "The Politics of Revenge: The Ethnic Opposition to the Peace Policies of Woodrow Wilson," 199; *Portland Oregonian*, 18 November 1919; Charles DeBenedetti, *Origins of the Modern American Peace Movement, 1915-1929*, 11.

drift toward acceptance of the "Lodge reservations," encouraging pro-League Republicans.[94]

Soon after Lenroot told them of the mild reservationist stand, Hitchcock and Lodge met. The Democrat suggested that after the Lodge resolution had been beaten, as was conceded to be probable, Lodge should support a resolution to reconsider. When that was carried, Hitchcock would propose a resolution of ratification without reservations, "whereupon the Senate would recess for the day to give an opportunity for conference to see whether a compromise could be effected." After some discussion, Lodge said that he would confer with colleagues and report back. He soon returned and rejected the proposal. But he added that he would reconsider if Hitchcock could state, in advance of the vote on his resolution or at least in advance of the vote on the motion to reconsider, what compromise the Democrats could offer. Hitchcock replied that he could not be quickly definite because he would have to consult not only the president but also the Democratic senators in caucus or conference.[95]

Though Hitchcock had put Lodge off instead of coming to terms, he clung to old hopes, for want of anything better. He viewed the Republican approach to him as a favorable sign and hoped that, even without a prior agreement, "enough republicans will support my motion to keep the matter before the Senate in some form, pending a possible compromise." Indeed he was willing, "when our proposition is before the Senate to have the Senate adjourn until the first Monday in December." Lodge, however, did not favor that. Later Hitchcock and Lodge differed on what had been agreed to. Hitchcock claimed that Lodge had promised to go along with a recess of a day or two after the initial voting. The claim, however, is not supported by Hitchcock's 18 November letter to Mrs. Wilson.[96]

In the course of the day, Hitchcock let it be known that he had a letter from Wilson, in a sealed envelope, that he would open at the Democratic conference the next day. He professed not to know its contents, though in fact he had prepared the first draft, but in re-

94. *Providence Evening Tribune*, 10 November 1919; Duff, "Politics of Revenge," 207; *New York World*, 15 November 1919; *New York Tribune*, 21 November, 28 December 1919, cited in Denna Frank Fleming, *The United States and the League of Nations, 1918–1920*, 395–96.

95. Hitchcock to Mrs. Wilson, 18 November 1919, Wilson Papers.

96. *CR* 66:2, pp. 534–35 (13 December 1919); William Short, "Report on the Treaty Situation," enclosed in Short to Taft, 18 December 1919, Taft Papers; Hitchcock to Mrs. Wilson, 18 November 1919, Wilson Papers.

sponse to reporters' questions he intimated that the letter expressed a hard line. Speaking for himself, he insisted that the obligation remain under Article 10; no small verbal changes in the reservation would do. In effect, Hitchcock prepared for deadlock and sought to put a good face on it. Still, he hoped that Wilson would yet backtrack. Hitchcock enclosed with his letter to Mrs. Wilson a letter from the astute and well-respected Tom Walsh urging ratification on Lodge's terms. Walsh argued that even without Article 10, much that was good remained, in the pacific settlement provisions. Hitchcock commented that many Democrats held the same view.[97]

Meanwhile, Lodge reported back to the mild reservationists, through Lenroot, on his unsatisfactory interview with Hitchcock. Some of them, disgusted, said in the lobbies that they would abandon their efforts and " 'let Hitchcock shift for himself.' " Republicans generally agreed that there was nothing to do but "go straight on," as Lodge put it.[98] But the matter could not really end so precipitously. In practice, mild reservationists awaited the results of the Democratic conference.

The Democrats in conference on the morning of the nineteenth rejected ratification with the "Lodge reservations." Hitchcock read the president's letter, which Wilson had revised from Hitchcock's draft. It dealt the coup de grâce to all hope of immediate ratification. Eschewing detail, Wilson wrote simply that the resolution with the "Lodge reservations" "does not provide for ratification but, rather, for the nullification of the treaty. I sincerely hope that the friends and supporters of the treaty will vote against the Lodge resolution of ratification. I understand that the door will probably then be open for a genuine resolution of ratification."[99]

Some Democrats, sympathetic to Wilson's position, said that they could not accept the preamble, the reservations on Shantung and equal voting, and one or two other reservations. Others were made acutely unhappy by Wilson's letter. Oscar Straus later claimed to have added, to an original group of seventeen, enough additional Democrats ready to vote for the Lodge resolution to make two-thirds.[100] Most of these were not prepared to oppose the president's wishes, however, especially since, under the circumstances, he

97. *New York World*, 19 November 1919; *New York Tribune*, 19 November 1919; Hitchcock to Mrs. Wilson, 18 November 1919, Wilson Papers.

98. *New York Times*, 19 November 1919; Lodge to F. H. Gillett, 26 July 1920, Lodge Papers.

99. *CR* 66:1, p. 8768 (19 November 1919).

100. Fleming, *League of Nations*, 395–96.

would probably pigeonhole the treaty if the Senate approved it, thus taking all the blame for himself and his party. Several senators nevertheless said that they would vote for the Lodge resolution if the preamble was modified. These dissidents could not carry the conference with them, however, and the Democrats emerged more or less committed to opposition to the Lodge resolution and committed also to Hitchcock's vague hopes for subsequent compromise.[101]

The Senate convened at noon, and ten minutes later newspapers containing Wilson's letter were brought into the chamber. Lodge, who did not seem to like what he saw, promptly read it into the *Record*. The letter embarrassed and dismayed Democrats. It enraged mild reservationists, according to Senator Ashurst, who heard two or three of them "let off oaths in an undertone."[102]

The mild reservationists showed some resentment in debate that day—at Wilson, Hitchcock, and all the Democrats who acquiesced against their better judgment. But their own intransigence resulted less from pique than from perseverance in the tactic they had decided on the previous morning. Lacking a firm deal with the Democrats, they defended the Lodge resolution, appealing desperately to the Democrats while also excoriating and threatening them. The politics of the situation was clear, but the political threat implicit in the development of a superior case dovetailed with exhortations to the Democrats. The mild reservationists would not separate themselves from the program that had united their party, and in their speeches they disparaged the idea of further compromise. But to the last, according to the later testimony of Lenroot and McCumber, they were ready to entertain a concrete offer from Hitchcock based on the modification of the preamble.[103]

Little suspense surrounded the vote on the Lodge resolution. To no one's surprise, the Senate rejected it, 39–55, with a coalition of administration Democrats and irreconcilables making up the majority. Four Democrats—Shields, Gore, Hoke Smith, and David Walsh— voted with thirty-five Republicans for the resolution. Reed, hoping to be done with the treaty from a parliamentary standpoint, immediately moved for reconsideration. Lodge led his forces in opposition, but the motion carried, 63–30. Eighteen Republicans—William Dillingham of Vermont and seventeen middle grounders—

101. *St. Louis Post-Dispatch*, 19 November 1919; *New York World*, 20 November 1919.

102. *New York World*, 20 November 1919; George F. Sparks, ed., *A Many Colored Toga: The Diary of Henry Fountain Ashurst*, entry for 19 November 1919, p. 115.

103. *CR* 66:2, p. 401 (11 December 1919); *New York Tribune*, 21 November 1919.

joined the Democrats in supporting the motion. Of the middle grounders, Cummins alone opposed the motion.[104]

The real battle began only after the adoption of the motion to reconsider. Hitchcock and others would reopen the whole question of reservations. If successful, they might win enough mild reservationists to make up a majority and thus shift the weight of political pressure in their own favor. With the exception of McCumber, the mild reservationists rejected the gambit. Placing a narrow construction on what constituted "reconsideration," a difficult parliamentary point that the senators had been discussing for several weeks, they held that only a second vote on the Lodge resolution was in order. To the last, mild reservationist leaders were open to a definite offer from Hitchcock based on the modification of the preamble as the sole price for Democratic acceptance of the "Lodge reservations." Without such an offer, they would not give the Democrats any parliamentary opening to divide the Republicans.[105]

Democrats whose motives were less suspect than Hitchcock's crossed the aisle through the day and into the evening, to plead with the mild reservationists and with Republican leaders. Claude Swanson was notably active. But in addition to delay, Swanson asked for some face-saving modification in the reservation to Article 10, for Wilson's benefit. Even mild reservationists were not disposed to grant that.[106]

The reasons for this intransigence, and the wisdom of it, are subjects for speculation. Human weakness—pique at Wilson, in the wake of his latest condemnation of the reservations as "nullification," and impatience born of fatigue—surely played some part. But a comment by a *Portland Oregonian* correspondent is also relevant. After noting that through the day Democrats had sought out mild reservationists, he added, "But the situation had reached the stage where the reservationists found it no longer possible to control their own group." The following day, some "middle of the road" senators said that the reservations should be strengthened and that the economic boycott should be limited under the third reservation. Hale, in particular, had taken that view earlier, and McCumber had for some time been wary of it. Under those circumstances, quite apart

104. *CR* 66:1, pp. 8786–87 (19 November 1919).
105. *Milwaukee Sentinel*, 4 November 1919; Gus Karger to William Howard Taft, 20 November 1919, Taft Papers; *Washington Evening Star*, 20 November 1919; *New York Tribune*, 20, 21 November 1919.
106. *Portland Oregonian*, 20 November 1919; Gus Karger to William Howard Taft, 20 November 1919, Taft Papers.

from other considerations, Kellogg, Lenroot, and McNary, singled out as the mild reservationist leaders by the *Portland Oregonian*'s reporter, had to adhere to their group's decision of the eighteenth and insist on the "Lodge reservations," unchanged.[107]

Following the vote to reconsider, the Democrats sought a vote on alternative reservations, or adjournment, to allow time for negotiation. The Republicans successfully resisted, overturning several rulings by Vice-President Marshall. They insisted that only the Lodge resolution could be considered, and finally the Senate voted again on that. Seven Democrats—Gore, Shields, Hoke Smith, David Walsh, Robert Owen, Atlee Pomerene, and Henry Myers—voted for it, but it lost, 41–51. Had its chances been better, as many as fourteen other Democrats might have supported it, according to the reliable *New York Tribune*.[108]

Then, surprising many, Lodge agreed to a vote on the approval of the treaty as Wilson had presented it, without reservations. The motion, Underwood's, lost by 38–53. McCumber voted in favor, and Nelson was absent and not paired, but seven Democrats voted with the other Republicans in opposition. For months, each party had jockeyed to make the other one seem the party of negation. Lodge's willingness to allow a vote in which his own side would be cast in opposition to the League showed his confidence in the Americanizing stand that the Republicans had developed. At the end of the evening, Lodge offered a concurrent resolution, which would not require the president's signature, declaring the war with Germany to be over. The resolution was referred to the Foreign Relations Committee. When the Senate adjourned, *sine die* to convene in regular session on 1 December, the adoption of the resolution loomed as a possible course of action.[109]

Despite the threat that Congress would end the war by resolution, few senators believed that they had seen the last of the Treaty of Versailles and the League of Nations. Certainly, the mild reservationists did not think so. Furthermore, they would continue to occupy center stage and to shape events. The role the mild reservationists would play in the next act of the drama closely related to

107. *Portland Oregonian*, 20 November 1919; *New York Tribune*, 20 November 1919.
108. *CR* 66:1, p. 8802 (19 November 1919); *New York Tribune*, 20 November 1919.
109. *CR* 66:1, pp. 8802–4 (19 November 1919); *Minneapolis Tribune*, 20 November 1919.

what had gone before, to the parts that they had developed in the act just ended.

During the period between 22 October, when the Foreign Relations Committee began to update the reservations, and 19 November, the mild reservationists revealed themselves more clearly than before. Conscious of common purposes and recognized by others as distinctive, the group continued intact from the battle on amendments.[110] More than other Republicans, including fellow middle grounders, they voted to limit both the severity and the number of reservations. Then, on 18 November, most of them laid down compromise terms that, if hard by earlier standards, were realistic for the time and were more generous than most Republicans thought desirable.

The anti-amendment group consisted of Colt, Edge, Hale, Kellogg, Keyes, Lenroot, McCumber, McNary, Nelson, and Sterling. Newspaper accounts listed all but Keyes and Sterling as present at the meeting on the eighteenth, though Nelson was omitted from one report. Their votes cast on amendments to the reservations, on the Reed reservation and certain others, and on reconsideration show that all ten remained relatively milder than others and readier to facilitate ratification.[111] On ten key votes, cast between 7 and 19 November, Colt, Hale, Kellogg, Keyes, McCumber, McNary, Nelson, and Sterling had perfect pro-ratification records. Lenroot and Edge deviated on one vote each, and in another instance Edge did not vote.

By contrast, moderates Cummins and McLean voted "wrong" eight times, Jones and Capper six times, Kenyon and Smoot five times. Two moderates, Spencer and Townsend, lurked at the fringe of the group, in their voting and in other ways. Spencer voted "wrong" three times and Townsend twice. Townsend, more than Spencer, held aloof from the mild reservationists, contributing less than he might have to the task of pressuring Lodge and Hitchcock. The moderates, though not part of the mild reservationist faction, remained nevertheless distinguishable from strong reservationists and irreconcilables. Most notably, all of them but Cummins voted with the mild reservationists for reconsideration on 19 November, and only one other Republican, William Dillingham, did that.

The meaning of mild reservationism for the months of September

110. Hiram Johnson to Arch Johnson and Hiram Johnson, Jr., 21 November 1919, Johnson Papers; *Providence Evening Tribune*, 10 November 1919; Warren Harding, in *CR* 66:1, p. 8792 (19 November 1919).

111. See Appendix 2.

through November, partially suggested already, warrants direct attention. The mild reservationists were far from homogeneous, in action, thought, or motive, and their internal differences should not be overlooked. There were, however, common threads. Warren Harding, a strong reservationist, addressed the Senate on 19 November and defined the mild reservationists as "those who are anxious to ratify, who are anxious to safeguard the interests of the Republic, but at the same time desire to make the reservations as little offensive as possible to those who assumed to negotiate the Treaty in contempt of the Senate."[112] Harding's view, if incomplete and unkindly put, is not far from the mark. The mild reservationists did indeed want to ratify, and as soon as possible. To that end, they wanted to make the reservations as palatable to Wilson as was expedient, as Harding suggested. Similarly, they hoped to make them acceptable to the Allies. In the interest of expedition, they had earlier opposed amendment. They were sincere internationalists, though differing among themselves on the extent of their internationalism and the degree to which the United States required protection.

All of them had come a long way from the time when they had supported reservations that were purely interpretive. By November, although they construed some of the reservations as interpretive, they could not easily deny Wilson's charge that the Article 10 reservation and some others changed the treaty. Their concern was that the changes not affect the relations of the other signatories to one another. Whereas some form of acceptance of reservations on American obligations was needed, they hoped to avoid general renegotiation. Others, even strong reservationists, shared their internationalism, to a degree. But they would not go so far, as the widespread support for the Reed reservation demonstrated. Nor were most Republicans so concerned for a speedy ratification and the avoidance of renegotiation. Their irreconcilable opponents liked to call them weak-kneed straddlers who tried to keep a foot in both camps and who were driven toward the pro-League side by the pressure of the LEP.[113] Such judgment was necessarily subjective, and must remain so.

The politics of the League fight seem to have mattered little to McCumber, Nelson, and Colt. The emotions of wartime remained strong in them, and the transcendent importance of the issues

112. *CR* 66:1, p. 8792 (19 November 1919).
113. An example is Hiram Johnson to Arch Johnson and Hiram Johnson, Jr., 21 November 1919, Johnson Papers.

impressed them. Unlike some, they felt no strong political pressure, so they could freely indulge their sentiments and convictions. During the late summer and fall, rural North Dakotans gave more attention to the fight over the Nonpartisan League than to that over the League of Nations. Those who did follow the battle in Washington tended to support McCumber's position. Minnesota opinion was divided, but Nelson's personal strength in the state gave him wide leeway.[114] Colt enjoyed not only the support of Rhode Island's leading newspaper but also personal prestige as a judicious elder statesman. Had he been more politically minded, he might have tried to exploit the large Irish-American contingent's discontent with the Democrats, but he did not.

Political considerations weighed more heavily with other mild reservationists. Since the inception of the League issue, in late 1918 and early 1919, Hale, Kellogg, Lenroot, and later Edge made every effort to be done with it, through speedy ratification and in a form that Wilson and the Allies could accept. Republican voters were deeply divided on the issue, so for a time it was a dangerous one to bring into the campaign of 1920. Reservationism developed not only as a devise for timely and acceptable ratification but also as a convenient way station between the extreme elements in the electorate and among party leaders in the states. By mid-November, while the politics of straddle still held appeal, the need to end the matter before 1920 had materially lessened. Republicans could comfortably go into the campaign on the issue of Americanizing the treaty. But when the LEP accommodated to the Republicans, it became politically expedient to reciprocate, as the mild reservationists did with the preamble and réconsideration.

Yet it is hard to believe that, at each stage, most of the mild reservationists were moved mainly by politics, be it personal interest or party considerations. Purely personal political concerns would have dictated a less obtrusive role than that played by Kellogg and Lenroot, in particular, but also by McNary, Hale, Sterling, and Edge. And the silence of Keyes is attributable to his freshman status in the Senate. The activism of the mild reservationists stands in contrast to the inaction of many strong reservationists. Political considerations were not lost sight of, one may conclude, but they did not predominate over conviction, as mild reservationists recognized the

114. Paul Willard Morrison, "The Position of the Senators from North Dakota on Isolation, 1889–1920," 309; *Des Moines Register*, 10 September 1919.

importance of the issue and grew progressively more engaged emotionally.

Since politics was a consideration for mild reservationists, the adjustment that it dictated was toward a tougher stance, and the mid-November accommodation to the LEP stands as a fine-tuning correction in the larger context. Though he remained one of the mildest of the reservationists, the shift is most apparent in McNary, who steadily drifted away from McCumber during September through November. McNary's shift from McCumber, evident in his solid support for the "Lodge reservations," coincided with pressure from Oregon Republicans but met tactical needs as well, so the senator did not have to choose between motives. What was true of McNary was true also of the other mild reservationists. Indeed even McCumber, Nelson, and Colt adjusted to the drift of opinion.

As national opinion hardened in favor of "Americanizing" the treaty, Kellogg and Lenroot in November confirmed the mild reservationist leadership positions that they had gained in late September and October. Instrumental in developing reservations that would serve as alternatives to amendments, and more sympathetic than McCumber to reservations that would limit American obligations or assert congressional authority, they naturally took the lead when reservations reached the Senate floor. McCumber took no subordinate place, but the positions he put forth so strongly, as on withdrawal, Shantung, and equal voting, separated him from most of the other mild reservationists. Only Nelson gave McCumber occasional support, and he was more than outweighed by the other mild reservationists and the moderates. The latter, lacking internal cohesion or leadership, either acted independently or supported Kellogg and Lenroot. These two men of unusual ability were easy to follow.

However able their leadership, although the mild reservationists had seemed to hold the balance of power, they had not been able to achieve treaty approval. Gleeful, Hiram Johnson thought they shared the responsibility. They had played a prolonged game of bluff and counter-bluff with the Democrats "until finally both got into a bitter snarl and so deeply mired, that within the brief time the cloture admitted, they could not extricate themselves." The mild reservationists of course rejected that view. McNary, Colt, and Lenroot blamed Wilson, for his letter, and the Democratic leadership, for not acting on their own and counting on the president, once restored to health, to complete the ratification. Taft agreed that the blame was

Wilson's.[115] There would be another chance, but historians have focused on the prolonged battle that ended in failure in November. Were the mild reservationists at fault? Hiram Johnson commented on the events of 19 November, but one may question also the mild reservationists' decision of the previous day, as well as the longer-range strategy of working within the Republican party.

Repeatedly, Lenroot and Kellogg made the point that the reservations had been drawn by friends of the treaty. They were correct in a literal sense, but they passed over the fact that the mild reservationists were not able to dictate terms but had to accommodate to the whole Republican party, through Lodge. Furthermore, the mild reservationists were not the sole authors of the reservations. To be sure, the Democrats had excluded themselves from timely negotiations, but the mild reservationists, in coming to terms within their own party, had committed themselves to reservations that were more difficult for Wilson and the Senate Democrats to accept than was the Kellogg program of July and August. Would the cause of ratification have been better served had the mild reservationists adhered to their original program of reservations and in.the November voting made their compromises not with the Republicans but the Democrats, producing a majority for a resolution that Wilson could accept? The purpose of entering such a coalition would have been to put pressure on other Republicans by making them, not the Democrats, choose between ratification and rejection and by making them accept the political consequences if they chose rejection. This, essentially, was what Hitchcock for a long time had thought would happen when the Senate reached the stage of adopting reservations.

Before considering the wisdom of such a course, one must ask whether it was possible. The initiative lay with the mild reservationist leaders—McCumber, McNary, Colt, Kellogg, Lenroot, and Nelson—men who in September began to negotiate with Lodge. Could they realistically envision the creation of a Democrat-based majority? The prospect was in doubt from the first and grew progressively cloudier as Wilson's tour proceeded. Mild reservationist colleagues—Edge, Hale, and Sterling in particular—supported the kind of reservations adopted by the committee, more than the interpretive reservations the Democrats privately favored. The same was

115. Johnson to John Francis Neylan, 24 November 1919, Johnson Papers; *Portland Oregonian*, 23 November 1919; *Providence Evening Tribune*, 21 November 1919; *Milwaukee Sentinel*, 6 December 1919; *Minneapolis Tribune*, 21 November 1919.

true of the moderates. Under those circumstances, it seemed hardly likely that they would break with their party, in advance of a major election, and bale out a president who first ignored them and then denounced them. If a coalition with the Democrats was to be formed, the mild reservationist leaders could count on none but themselves.

The six faction leaders, as a small minority of Republicans joining with Wilson and the Democrats, would have paid a tremendous cost, politically and psychologically, in Washington and at home. Further, Lenroot rejected all obligation under Article 10, and Colt and Kellogg agreed with him. On this most difficult of issues, they could foresee no easy compromise with the Democrats and had little reason to stand aloof from the Republicans. If the Democrats lost Gore, Reed, Shields, and David Walsh, as seemed probable in September, at least five Republicans were needed to create a tie that the vice-president might break. But on some matters, Charles Thomas and Hoke Smith figured to defect also, and still other Democrats were not wholly reliable in early September. The six leaders, then, might not all act in unison with the Democrats, even if some of them wanted that, and if they did act together, they might still fail to create a majority coalition.

The mild reservationist leaders had to wonder too whether a majority created in tandem with the Democrats would be worth the price to themselves and their party. Early on, Lodge had secured more than a third pledged to reject unreserved ratification. Even without the help of any of the eighteen middle grounders, he could still command more than a third, drawn from irreconcilable Republicans, strong reservationists, totaling thirty-one, and four Democrats. And, as noted, he could count on most of the middle grounders too. As the public grew tougher and battle lines became clearer, Lodge's one-third stood against not just unreserved ratification but also ratification with merely interpretive reservations. Thus, the mild reservationist leaders might cause the Republicans to take the blame for treaty rejection, but they could not force ratification.

However unlikely their chances of success by isolating themselves from their party, the mild reservationist leaders may still be faulted for not taking the chance, if the course of coalition had seemed most likely to bring success. That was not the case, however. Even McCumber, who found the most fault with the "Lodge reservations," thought them acceptable on the whole. Certainly, from his standpoint and that of the others, the best features of the Covenant remained unimpaired. By any rational standard, the Democrats, having forced the Republicans to unite, should have acquiesced in the results of that situation, to save the treaty and the League.

Unhappily, rational standards did not prevail. Democrats in the Senate had good reason to follow the president's lead, since he had the power to pigeonhole the treaty and assume for himself and his party the blame. And Wilson refused to acquiesce, or even to compromise on the basis of a modified preamble. Wilson's physical condition was not fully understood in the Senate, but even had it been, mild reservationist leaders could hardly have expected many of their Republican colleagues to sacrifice, for irrational objections, what they conceived to be in the national interest.

Once committed to the tactic of securing ratification through a Republican program of reservations, the mild reservationists played their cards reasonably well. If they are to be faulted at all, it is not for yielding too little to the Democrats but for giving them false hopes. McCumber, ardent for ratification in any way possible and opposed to parts of the committee program, contributed most to these false hopes by his opposition to several reservations and his guarded talk of the possibility of compromise later. But McCumber was cautious in what he said and openly warned the Democrats not to risk total defeat by rejecting the "Lodge reservations." Other mild reservationists were emphatic and clear in reinforcing that warning. If Hitchcock, in particular, indulged in false hopes, it was due less to the mistakes of the mild reservationists than to the fact that, despite his own efforts, Wilson left him nothing else.

The mild reservationists did offer the Democrats the best terms that they could manage. After encompassing the defeat of amendments at the price of the toughened program of reservations, they successfully beat back efforts to harshen the reservations by amendment or to add destructive ones, such as Reed's. Then, on 18 November, they offered a major concession, in the preamble, which met one of Wilson's principal objections and which went to the vital issue of renegotiation and the prospects of Allied acceptance. The deadline accompanying the offer, though hardly conciliatory, served to put the situation to the Democrats in an accurate and forceful way.

But were the mild reservationists too stubborn on the following day, when they refused to broadly construe reconsideration? Were they trying to show their toughness in the face of irreconcilable criticism, as Johnson believed, and were they moved by petty irritation with Wilson and the Democratic senators? They shared the failings of the species. Kellogg, in particular, was given to nervousness and irritability, and Lenroot, co-leader with Kellogg, was a cautious man who felt most comfortable working within his party.

Yet there was some point to the position they took. Although some Democrats felt that a few verbal changes were enough, Hitchcock, the leader, did not. Only meaningful compromise by the Democrats warranted hope, and that compromise seemed doubtful. If this was the last opportunity, the mild reservationists would have had good reason to break ranks. But they knew it was not. The factors that had impelled them to work within their party still argued for sticking with the party. It would not do to show weakness to no purpose when, in future dealings, the best prospect for ratification remained the acceptance of the "Lodge reservations" as at least the basis for negotiation.

Tactics aside, the question remains: Did the mild reservationists acquiesce in reservations so offensive that Wilson was right in rejecting them? The distinguished diplomatic historian Thomas Bailey judged not. In his view, the reservations were inconsequential or useless or repetitious of the Covenant and the Constitution, as well as tasteless and offensively worded, but "a few ill chosen words, one way or another, were not going to make or break this great treaty." Others, however, though not necessarily condemning the reservations, have seen them as transforming the League in important ways. It would have become a non-coercive body, according to William Widenor. Cecil Hurst, a British official prominent in drafting the Covenant, judged some of the changes seriously harmful. He objected particularly to the Article 10 reservation that would let the United States enter the League on a special footing, thereby placing an undue burden on Britain and undermining faith in the League among small powers. But George Egerton has suggested that a more modestly constructed League might have caused nations and peoples to place fewer false hopes in international organization and to rely more than they did, in the twenties and thirties, on traditional methods of peace keeping. The reservations, if put into effect, would have conduced to that end.[116]

Other historians have regarded the design of the League as of secondary importance. "What the country needed was a turning of attention to Europe's political problems—where the danger of war lay," Robert Ferrell has observed. "A League with or without reservations might have done just that, which was all that mattered." In the same vein, Alfred Zimmern, the great British authority on the

116. Bailey, *Great Betrayal*, 339; Egerton, *Creation of the League*, 191–92, 204–5.

League, commented, "What the League is, at any given moment, is determined in fact by the degree of willingness on the part of the powers to cooperate with one another." Structure could not be dismissed, and though the reservations seriously weakened the prospects for collective security and disarmament through the agency of the Covenant, much remained unimpaired, notably international conference, the possibility of joint action under Article 11, the pacific settlement tools backed by sanctions, and the unglamorous but important special agency functions under the secretariat. Ultimately, however, one must agree with Zimmern on the critical importance of public opinion. In that connection, the words of Viscount Grey about the United States and the American reservations are germane. "If they enter the League as willing partners with limited obligations, it may well be that American opinion and American action . . . will be much more fruitful than if they enter as a reluctant partner, who felt that her hand had been forced."[117]

117. Robert H. Ferrell, *Woodrow Wilson and World War I, 1917–1921*, 156; Alfred Zimmern, *The League of Nations and the Rule of Law, 1918–1935*, 282; Grey quoted in *New York Times*, 1 February 1920. See also Lloyd E. Ambrosius, *Woodrow Wilson and the American Diplomatic Tradition: The Treaty Fight in Perspective*, for criticism of the Wilsonian view.

5 A SECOND TRY,
20 November 1919–30 January 1920

Wilson and Lodge, each with loyal supporters in the Senate, emerged from the November battle unwilling to compromise. Wilson remained so through January 1920, when an informal bipartisan conference abandoned compromise efforts. Lodge was less consistent, but for a time he refused to consider changes in the reservations, while promoting a separate peace with Germany.

In the nation a powerful demand developed for a settlement, as much to restore peace as to approve entry into the League. Senators of both parties responded. A number of Democrats threatened independent action and to some extent engaged in it, causing their leader, Hitchcock, to accommodate cautiously to their insistence on compromise efforts. Irreconcilables were unmoved, but among Republicans, mild reservationists and moderates negotiated with Democrats and pressured Lodge toward a more conciliatory posture.

In mid-January Hitchcock and Lodge headed the delegations in the bipartisan conference. For a time, agreement seemed near. Ultimately, however, the conference faltered over Article 10. Senators disagreed then, as observers do now, on whether the failure sprang mainly from differences over principle or from politics.

McNary and Colt reemerged as prominent mild reservationist leaders, particularly in the early stages, when negotiation with Democrats flourished. Because the mild reservationists depended on an alliance with Lodge, Lenroot and Kellogg, proponents of that approach and closest to Lodge, represented their faction in the bipartisan conference. Several moderates, especially Kenyon and Cummins, showed fresh zeal for ratification and took active roles. In contrast, McCumber and Nelson played only minor parts. The North Dakotan was absent from Washington much of the time, while Nelson was dispirited and ill.

Wilson remained in delicate health. Not until Christmas was he able to sit up for a few hours a day. His wife screened out potentially disturbing news or visitors. Twice in late November Colonel House wrote Wilson advising compromise, but he got no response. Hitchcock failed to win an audience until 5 December, nor was Underwood admitted.[1]

Hitchcock hoped to accomplish ratification, or at least to put his party in a favorable light, by detaching Republican middle grounders from their party. To do that, he wanted to make concessions, but he required authorization. On 24 November he wrote Wilson that he had found enough reservationist Republicans desirous of compromise to "give good promise that we can control the Senate to start with when we reassemble." To get these promises, he hoped the president would agree to substantial concessions. He had in mind, in particular, a sweeping concession on Article 10. As he confided to William Jennings Bryan, he would "limit our guarantee of independence and territorial integrity to Poland, Bohemia, the Hugo Slavs, France & Belgium & to them only for ten years." When they met, however, Wilson told Hitchcock that it was up to the Republicans to extend the olive branch. Afterward, Colonel House urged Hitchcock to assert leadership and seek compromise, but the senator declined; success, he felt, would require Wilson's backing.[2]

Wilson, convinced that the people were overwhelmingly with him, devised two alternatives to compromise. Both were unrealistic, and one of them he abandoned. But he acted on the second. He hoped to convert the presidential election of 1920 into a "solemn referendum" on the League, with himself as his party's nominee. Pursuing this idea, he even drafted a party platform and an acceptance speech. On 8 January, without referring to his own candidacy, Wilson presented his referendum plan to the luminaries of his party, who were gathered in Washington for a meeting of the national com-

1. Edith Bolling Wilson, *My Memoir*, 299, 272–74; David Lawrence, *The True Story of Woodrow Wilson*, 288–90; Charles Seymour, ed., *The Intimate Papers of Colonel House*, 509–11; Arthur Walworth, *Woodrow Wilson*, 2:387; Kurt Wimer, "Senator Hitchcock and the League of Nations," 197–98; Joseph Tumulty to Mrs. Wilson, 1 December 1919, Tumulty Papers.
2. Hitchcock to Wilson, 24 November 1919, Wilson Papers; Hitchcock to William Jennings Bryan, 30 November 1919, Bryan Papers; Joseph Tumulty to Mrs. Wilson, 18 December 1919, Tumulty Papers; H. N. Rickey to W. H. Short, 8 December 1919, enclosed in Short to William Howard Taft, 12 December 1919, Taft Papers; Diary entry, 11 December 1919, Edward House Papers, Yale University, cited in James E. Hewes, Jr., "William E. Borah and the Image of Isolationism," 264.

mittee and a Jackson Day dinner. Party chairman Homer Cummings read Wilson's letter.[3]

On the same occasion, William Jennings Bryan countered Wilson's appeal with one of his own, for compromise, ratification, and the removal of the League issue from the upcoming campaign. But though many Democrats publicly and privately agreed with Bryan, Wilson could count on a hard core of loyalists who agreed with him, including most of his Cabinet and, in the Senate, the fiery Mississippian John Sharp Williams. More important, he was able to marshal those who, despite private reservations, were reluctant to oppose him. Prominent among these were Hitchcock and Underwood, who were vying for presidential support in the contest for party leadership.[4] A week after the Jackson Day letter, the more pliable of the two, Hitchcock, triumphed. Because of the absence of some senators and the insistence of Underwood, Hitchcock had postponed the 20 December caucus. But on 15 January, as the result of a 19–19 tie vote, Hitchcock was continued as acting minority leader, on a temporary basis. In April he lost to Underwood, but it was too late to make a difference.

If the mild reservationists received little encouragement from the Democratic leadership, Lodge pleased them only marginally better. With no great faith in the League, he did not care whether the United States joined, with proper safeguards, or stayed out. The Republican party must remain united, to achieve control in 1920 and restore sound foreign policy management.

The outcome in November pleased him. His party had united behind acceptable reservations, and the Democrats had voted down the most serious resolution of ratification. Immediately afterward, Lodge let his enthusiasm get the better of him and opened himself to criticism from advocates of ratification in some form. The treaty was dead so far as the Senate was concerned, he said. It would be up to Wilson to withdraw and then resubmit it, if he wished. Further-

3. Warren F. Kuehl, *Seeking World Order: The United States and International Organization to 1920*, 331; Arthur S. Link, *Woodrow Wilson: Revolution, War, and Peace*, 124–25. To the last, despite overwhelming indications to the contrary, Wilson thought his party would win in the election of 1920 (David F. Houston, *Eight Years With Wilson's Cabinet, 1913–1920*, 92; Josephus Daniels, *The Wilson Era: Years of War and After, 1917–1923* [Chapel Hill: University of North Carolina Press, 1946], 2:481).

4. Paolo E. Coletta, *William Jennings Bryan*, Vol. 3, *Political Puritan, 1915–1925*, 98; Williams to Hitchcock, 9 January 1920, Hitchcock Papers; Evans C. Johnson, *Oscar W. Underwood: A Political Biography*, 295.

more, there could be no compromise on the reservations of 19 November. Elihu Root remained important to Lodge, but even he could not budge the majority leader when he suggested three "face-saving modifications."[5] Although other Republicans actively discussed compromise, Lodge declared that he was "standing pat." Then, when Underwood proposed a conciliation committee, which might act over the Christmas recess, Lodge prevented the consideration of the resolution. At the same time, without consulting mild reservationists, he pushed through the Foreign Relations Committee the Knox resolution for a separate peace.[6]

Irreconcilables were pleased with Lodge's attitude but were not entirely trustful. They closely watched him, pressured him, and made preparations to project the issue of the League into the 1920 campaign. Borah even threatened a third party, if not satisfied.[7]

Despite the irreconcilables' threats and pressures, Wilson's uncompromising stance, Lodge's temporary intransigence, and Hitchcock's uncertainty, in mid-January serious bipartisan negotiations occurred. On the Republican side, the push came from the middle grounders, chiefly mild reservationist leaders. They, in turn, responded to pressures from large segments of the public and from influential Republicans outside the Senate.

Economic considerations took on new urgency. Europe proved slow to recover from the devastating war, and her economic dislocations were reflected in a severe deterioration of currencies. At its monthly meeting on 4 December, the chamber of commerce of New York City urged immediate ratification. "The prosperity of America's export trade is largely dependent upon the extension of credits to our customers abroad," its resolution stated.

[But] pending the ratification of the treaty, thus establishing a known basis for the continuance of international trade, no adequate credit plans can possibly be established. The alarm of the whole world of business over this protracted delay is evidenced by the continued and wholly unprecedented fall in the rates of exchange—a fall almost as detrimental for us as expor-

5. *Providence Evening Tribune*, 22 November 1919; Root to Lodge, 1 December 1919, and Lodge to Root, 3 December 1919, Root Papers.
6. *New York Times*, 19, 21 December 1919; *CR* 66:2, pp. 956, 958 (20 December 1919); Thomas A. Bailey, *Woodrow Wilson and the Great Betrayal*, 403; *Proceedings of the Committee on Foreign Relations, United States Senate, from the Sixty-Third Congress to the Sixty-Seventh Congress*, 211–12.
7. William Borah to Hiram Johnson, 23 December 1919, Borah Papers; *New York World*, 27 December 1919; Ralph Stone, *The Irreconcilables: The Fight Against the League of Nations*, 147–52.

ters, as it is for the unfortunate peoples of Europe who are unable to buy from us the food and materials which they so sorely need.[8]

Chambers of commerce in Cleveland and Syracuse and the Chicago Board of Trade also resolved for treaty compromise. When Oscar Underwood revived the treaty issue in the Senate a week later, it was on the basis of the decline in exchange rates and the cancellation of export orders.[9]

Herbert Hoover sounded the alarm among senators. A self-made multimillionaire, the head of a Belgium relief effort, the food administrator during the war, and more recently the director of European relief efforts, Hoover commanded great prestige. Now he was back in Washington, as vice-chairman of the Second Industrial Conference, and was in a position to meet informally with senators.[10] A consultant to the executive committee of the LEP, on 19 November Hoover wrote Wilson, appealing for treaty compromise. His letter went unacknowledged, and probably unread; however, the letter indicates what Hoover was telling senators.[11] The economic recovery of Europe had already been greatly impaired by America's delay, and a dangerous situation loomed. The League, once in motion, could be of great help. "We must recognize," Hoover wrote, "that if Europe is to survive it must import an enormous quantity of supplies from the United States, that these supplies can only be found on credit, that already the existing supplies show exhaustion in many parts of Europe, that no credit facilities or commercial machinery for meeting this situation can be erected until ratification is over." The United States would suffer from her surpluses, with hardship especially to farmers, he warned.[12]

Economic considerations aside, leaders of internationalist opinion were not content to see the United States remain outside the League when eighty senators had voted for treaty approval. They directed much of their pressure toward Wilson and the Democrats, but they also called on Republicans to compromise. The call came from liberals and conservatives, Democrats and Republicans. Culminating the liberal, Democratic effort, though with other support

8. *New York World*, 5 December 1919.

9. *New York Times*, 18, 22 December 1919; *CR* 66:2, p. 532 (13 December 1919).

10. Herbert C. Hoover, *The Ordeal of Woodrow Wilson*, 290–91; Clara Lenroot to Nellie Nichols, 15 December 1919, Lenroot Papers.

11. Hoover, *Woodrow Wilson*, 282.

12. Hoover to Wilson, 19 November 1919, Wilson Papers. For the description and explanation of Europe's financial and monetary plight, with special reference to Britain and France, see Dan P. Silverman, *Reconstructing Europe After the Great War*.

too, on 13 January twenty-six organizations, claiming in excess of twenty million members, met in Washington. They sent deputations to the White House and to meetings with Lodge and Hitchcock. They asked for ratification in a form that would not require renegotiation.[13]

The LEP declined dramatically between November and April. Earlier, at the local level, many Republican members, following Lodge, had drawn apart, and Democrats had gained prominence. But the executive committee's 18 November appeal for ratification with the "Lodge reservations" alienated Democratic members and diminished financial support.[14] The extent of decline was not immediately noted, however, and in any case, neither the LEP nor such well-known leaders as Taft and Lowell could be ignored by Republican politicians.

The LEP leaders applied pressure that was cautious but intensive. The executive committee called for compromise and orchestrated a campaign of letter writing and publicity. Initially, the executive secretary, William Short, asked only for the concession that Lodge had been ready for earlier, a change in the preamble. Lowell wrote widely, delivered one speech, and lobbied senators for compromise. He expressed the view that the preservation of Article 10 was not so important as to warrant treaty defeat. Given that conservative posture, his call for "slight amendments" to the reservations seemed reasonable. Taft went further, publicly calling for softer language and later submitting to McNary a list of proposed changes.[15]

Henry L. Stimson kept in touch with his close friend and associate Elihu Root, supporting Root's inclination toward compromise. Root, in turn, chose to work through party chairman Will Hays. Root pressed especially for the modification of the preamble. Stim-

13. Wolfgang J. Helbrich, "American Liberals in the League of Nations Controversy," 591–92; James G. McDonald, Chairman, League of Free Nations Association, to Members, 20 December 1919, Jordan Papers; Walworth, *Wilson*, 2:389; James L. Lancaster, "The Protestant Churches and the Fight for Ratification of the Versailles Treaty," 615; *New York World*, 14 January 1920; *Minneapolis Tribune*, 14 January 1920; Bailey, *Great Betrayal*, 225–26.

14. Ruhl J. Bartlett, *The League to Enforce Peace*, 155–56; Charles DeBenedetti, *Origins of the Modern American Peace Movement, 1915–1929*, 24; W. H. Short to A. Lawrence Lowell, 29 December 1919, Taft Papers.

15. William H. Short to William Howard Taft, 22 November 1919, Taft Papers; *New York World*, 25, 27 November, 20 December 1919, 9, 10 January 1920; H. A. Yeomans, *Abbott Lawrence Lowell, 1856–1943*, 454–57; *CR* 66:2, p. 1251 (9 January 1920); Lowell to J. W. Holcombe, 15 December 1919, Lowell Papers; Stephen Bonsal, *Unfinished Business*, 280; *Minneapolis Tribune*, 21 November 1919; Taft to Raymond B. Fosdick, 24 December 1919, in Raymond B. Fosdick, *Letters on the League of Nations*, 89.

son too urged compromise on Hays, who was more than ever concerned about party unity prior to the 1920 campaign. After Lodge
said that there would be no concessions and that the issue of the
League would enter the campaign, Hays phoned Taft to deplore the
statement. He thought that the GOP's greatest strength lay with
domestic issues. In January one of Hays's subordinates deduced that
Republicans in the states had reached a near-consensus against making the League a campaign issue and for speedy ratification. He, in
turn, disseminated this news widely. Members of the national committee had advised senators to compromise early in December.[16]

After the Christmas recess, Warren Harding found that most senators were disposed to wrapping up the League issue and that Republicans were willing to make minor changes in the reservations. As a
former LEP lobbyist explained, the senators had returned from
home aware that constituents wanted ratification in some form.[17]

The mild reservationists and some other middle grounders had to
convert possibilities into actuality. Initially, they moved with caution. Porter McCumber, the one Republican to vote for the treaty
without reservations, was especially cautious. Aware that some
middle grounders were calling for stronger reservations, and fearful
about the inclusion of the boycott in the reservation directed at Article 10, he could do little more than stand pat, he felt. "There can be
no compromise so far as the pending reservations to the peace treaty
are concerned," he said on 22 November. Only the preamble might
be modified. "If any [other] substantial change is made, it will be to
make the reservations more drastic." McCumber left Washington
and did not return until the end of December, traveling first to
Arizona to be with his wife and sick daughter, then to the West
Coast, North Dakota, and Minnesota. While away, he restated his
position.[18]

16. Stimson to William Calder, 28 November 1919, to James Wadsworth, 1 December 1919, and to Will Hays, 1 December 1919, S. R. Bertron to Stimson, 1 and 5
December 1919, Stimson Papers; Frank Brandegee to Albert J. Beveridge, 28 December 1919, Beveridge Papers; Hays to Henry Cabot Lodge, 22 November 1919, Lodge
Papers; Taft to Casper Yost, 27 November 1919, Taft Papers; H. N. Rickey to William
Short, n.d. [11 December 1919], Lowell Papers; Henry W. Rose to "My Dear Sir,"
23 January 1920, Stimson Papers; *New York Times*, 26 December 1919.

17. Harding to C. A. Hudson-Pillar, 29 November 1919, and to Myron H. Bent,
3 January 1920, Harding Papers; Charles D. Warner to William Short, 5 January 1920,
in Short to William Howard Taft, 6 January 1920, Taft Papers.

18. *New York Tribune*, 21, 23 November 1919; *New York World*, 23 November
1919; McCumber to William Jennings Bryan, 30 November 1919, Bryan Papers; *Portland Oregonian*, 16, 20 December 1919.

During the last days of November, preceding the 1 December start of the second session, other middle grounders spoke in a similar vein. When the new session began, the middle grounders continued to insist that the Democrats make them an offer and said that the "Lodge reservations" could not be substantially changed. Behind the scenes, however, several of them negotiated directly with Democrats. Indeed a Republican, LeBaron Colt, initiated compromise efforts.

Colt and William Kenyon, both former judges and neither vigorous partisans, bemoaned the 19 November failure as the product of petty politics. So did Nelson, but he took no part in early negotiations. Colt, however, sought out a close friend on the Democratic side, Kenneth McKellar of Tennessee, and soon enlisted Kenyon in the talks. On his side, McKellar brought in John Kendrick of Wyoming. Soon Lenroot and then Kellogg joined the conferences, as did Democrats Furnifold Simmons and Tom Walsh. Kenyon's involvement may seem surprising, but though he was strong for certain reservations and even some amendments, he had always favored entering the League.[19]

From the first, a certain ambiguity marked the bipartisan efforts. According to the recollections of one of the Democratic participants, the original four conferees proposed to unite pro-Leaguers of both parties and to exclude Lodge from the discussions.[20] But the mild reservationists could not ignore the need for Lodge's help, nor could the Democrats act without an awareness of what Wilson would ultimately accept. Lenroot pointed the way toward involving Lodge after Underwood reopened the League issue on 13 December. In the course of an arid floor debate over which side had been to blame in November and which side currently blocked compromise, Hitchcock pointed to Lodge's anticompromise statements of late November. Lenroot replied, "Does the Senator from Nebraska believe that is the position of the Senators on this side of the aisle?" A moment later, reconciling his position with Lenroot's, Lodge said that he was always ready to listen.[21]

Although Hitchcock, tethered by Wilson, remained hypercautious in December, other Democrats were more accommodating.

19. Bailey, *Great Betrayal*, 195–96; Nelson to Scott Bone, 2 December 1919, and to Lee Willcuts, 29 January 1920, Nelson Papers; H. Maurice Darling, "Who Kept the United States Out of the League of Nations?" 199–200, 210; *New York World*, 8 January 1920.
20. Darling, "Who Kept the United States?" 211.
21. *CR* 66:2, p. 539 (13 December 1919).

During the week preceding the holiday recess, which began on 20 December, middle grounders became encouraged about compromise prospects. Dissatisfied with the 14 December White House statement that the president "has no compromise or concession in mind," Hoke Smith and Henry Myers spoke in the Senate for Democratic concessions, and Smith called for a nonpartisan conference. Informally, Democrats joined in a flurry of conferences with Republicans, and two unidentified senators, a Democrat and a Republican—perhaps McKellar and Colt—took soundings on specific reservation possibilities. Under the circumstances, Lenroot announced that he would not at that time support a resolution for a separate peace, and mild reservationist leaders predicted that from nine to twelve Republicans would oppose such a resolution.[22]

As the holiday recess approached, Lodge jolted the mild reservationists. First, despite hopeful signs of compromise, he caused the favorable reporting of the Knox resolution. Then he blocked Underwood's resolution for a conciliation committee to meet during the recess. The mild reservationists responded quickly and forcefully. If they could not act effectively without Lodge, then they had to pressure him.

On 20 December Kellogg said that the mild reservationists had not been consulted about the Knox resolution and would not support it until shown that ratification with reservations was impossible. He spoke for Lenroot, McNary, and unnamed others "of the mild reservation Republicans."[23] The mild reservationists held a whirl of conferences, culminating the next morning in a meeting instigated by McNary and attended by Colt, Kellogg, Hale, Edge, and Cummins. The six agreed to notify Lodge of their strong opposition to the Knox resolution and their belief in the need for compromise and prompt ratification.[24] That evening, in a lengthy meeting at Lodge's home, the group impressed their views on him, insisting that he treat with the Democratic leadership and suggesting specific concessions. Theodore Roosevelt's daughter, Alice Longworth, a spirited irreconcilable, dropped in unexpectedly and afterward quizzed Lodge about his session with the mild reservationists. The

22. Ibid., 738 (17 December 1919); *New York Times*, 16–20 December 1929; *New York World*, 16–21 December 1919; *Milwaukee Sentinel*, 18 December 1919. Lenroot is quoted in *New York Times*, 16 December 1919; the mild reservationist prediction is in *New York World*, 21 December 1919.

23. *New York Times*, 21 December 1919.

24. *Portland Oregonian*, 23 December 1919; McNary to William Howard Taft, 22 December 1919, Taft Papers.

senator told her that he wanted to pass the treaty with reservations, and he went into detail about changes in the preamble and other reservations. He added that he did not want the issue in the campaign. Mrs. Longworth later remembered, "He was very high-handed over the whole matter."[25]

The mild reservationists, assisted now by men like Kenyon and Cummins, were not pacified by Lodge when, the day after their meeting with him, he held a long conference with Underwood. Evidently, Lodge's stance at the conference gave no basis for any follow-up. And some thought that by meeting with Underwood, instead of Hitchcock, Lodge was simply trying to widen the breach among the Democrats. On top of that, Lodge speculated with reporters about a disruption among the Democrats and boasted that they would come around to the "Lodge reservations." A few mild reservationists proved sufficiently irritated to talk of contesting his leadership position.[26]

Meanwhile Hitchcock, ever-ready to lure Republicans from Lodge, had sought out mild reservationists for a series of conferences. These proved unsatisfactory, however. Hitchcock asked the mild reservationists for something that was very difficult politically: he asked that any compromise offer come from them. He was afraid to have the Democrats make an offer that Wilson might repudiate. At the same time, he could give no assurances about Democratic support. And he created the impression that he did not really want an agreement until after the Democratic leadership contest had been decided on 15 January, since he stood to gain votes so long as he continued to direct the Democrats on the treaty issue.[27]

Though Colt was of a like mind, so long as direct negotiations between mild reservationists and Democrats were occurring or in contemplation, the younger and more vigorous McNary took the lead in organizing his faction. When the group, including Hale, Kellogg, and Lenroot, held an important conference on 26 December, it was, as had become usual, in McNary's office, perhaps at his instigation. The meeting culminated a series of informal gatherings attended by a dozen or more, a sizable number considering that some senators were away for the holidays. Indeed, in the view of Demo-

25. Charles McNary to William Howard Taft, 22 December 1919, Taft Papers; Alice Roosevelt Longworth, *Crowded Hours*, 294–95.

26. *New York Times*, 25 December 1919; *New York World*, 24, 25 December 1919; *New York Tribune*, 24 December 1919.

27. *New York Tribune*, 24, 25, 27, 30 December 1919; *New York Times*, 30 December 1919; Gus Karger to William Howard Taft, 31 December 1919, Taft Papers.

cratic leaders, some eighteen or nineteen Republicans were ready to coalesce with a near-solid Democracy for ratification.[28]

Even so large a number, however, would not be enough to produce a two-thirds majority. Furthermore, some among the group would insist on reservations not too different from those of November. Under the circumstances, the help of Lodge remained important. It seemed attainable too. Lodge would not have to abandon the main principles of the "Lodge reservations," and by accomplishing ratification, he could avoid an embarrassing and divisive defeat on the Knox resolution, to which he had committed himself. To the mild reservationists, friendly persuasion seemed in order, and Lenroot seemed the suitable emissary. After conferring with Lodge four days earlier, Lenroot had said that he would make no independent offer to the Democrats but would support Lodge.[29]

The group adhered to Lenroot's view and rejected the idea of submitting a plan to Hitchcock. At the same time, though, they authorized Lenroot to warn Lodge of independent action unless he treated with the Democrats and achieved noticeable progress before the end of the recess on 5 January. More specifically, reflecting the results of the Colt-McKellar initiative and other conferences, they wanted Lodge to make concessions on the preamble, the Shantung reservation, and, most important, on at least the wording of the Article 10 reservation.[30] Unfortunately, the group had not yet achieved agreement on that most critical reservation, either with the Democrats or among themselves, so they had no specific wording to suggest. That left Lodge with leeway to act on their urging, but it also left room for later intransigence.

Lenroot may or may not have seen Lodge on the afternoon of 26 December; accounts differ.[31] The two did meet at Lodge's home on 28 December. Before that, McNary elaborated somewhat on the purposes of the mild reservationists generally and on his own outlook in particular. The mild reservationists wanted to persuade Lodge to take active steps toward compromise, McNary told reporters, before the irreconcilables could influence him in the opposite

28. *New York Tribune,* 27 December 1919; *New York Times,* 27 December 1919; *New York World,* 24, 27 December 1919.

29. Frederick Hale to Raymond Calkins, 2 December 1919, Lowell Papers; *New York Times,* 27 December 1919; *New York Tribune,* 24 December 1919.

30. *New York Tribune,* 27 December 1919; *New York Times,* 27 December 1919; *New York World,* 27 December 1919.

31. Major newspapers reported the meeting, but the *New York Times* corrected itself on 28 December.

direction. Escalating the pressure somewhat, McNary made public the threat of "independent action" by the mild reservationists should the irreconcilables succeed with Lodge. Habitually optimistic, McNary foresaw agreement with the Democrats, based on the modification of the preamble and of the reservations relating to Shantung and Article 10, and he discounted the chances that the Democrats would again defeat ratification on orders from Wilson. Conditions had changed, he explained. In November, the reservations had born Lodge's name; now they would result from bipartisan compromise. Most important, McNary thought that Article 10 posed no insuperable obstacle. Wilson simply needed to save face, he thought. And he saw little difference between the Lodge reservation's outright repudiation of any obligation and what Democratic senators had told him they would accept: an assumption of obligation on the condition that "Congress in the future shall so determine."[32]

Whatever Lodge may have thought of McNary's view, in his meeting with Lenroot he was cooperative. Specifically—perhaps on his own initiative or perhaps at Lenroot's suggestion—Lodge agreed to discuss compromise with Atlee Pomerene, a Democratic member of the Foreign Relations Committee. To achieve ratification, Pomerene had reluctantly voted for the Lodge resolution in November and had been active for compromise thereafter. For his part, Lenroot afterward told reporters that he differed little from Lodge and that ratification would occur when the Democrats accepted the main features of the Lodge program.

As more and more senators drifted back to Washington, the pace of informal negotiation and private drafting of reservations increased, and friends of ratification waxed optimistic.[33] Mild reservationists, McNary in particular, continued to pressure Lodge and to negotiate directly with Democrats, but for the most part they adhered to the line that Lenroot consistently took: ratification would come with the cooperation of Lodge; and the Democrats would have to offer terms, albeit after consultation with mild reservationists.

The day after Lenroot's meeting with Lodge, Democrat William King offered proposals. McNary, for his group, turned them down as unsatisfactory respecting Article 10. Already, he possessed more

32. *New York Tribune*, 28 December 1919.
33. George F. Sparks, ed., *A Many Colored Toga: The Diary of Henry Fountain Ashurst*, entry for 4 January 1920, p. 120; Raymond Fosdick to Sir Eric Drummond, 30 December 1919, in Fosdick, *Letters on the League*, 90–92; Charles E. Warner to W. H. Short, 5 January 1920, in Short to William Howard Taft, 6 January 1920, Taft Papers; *New York World*, 31 December 1919; *New York Times*, 3 January 1920.

promising, though tentative, Democratic suggestions. These sprang from the McKellar-Colt initiative. Those mild reservationists on hand in Washington were prepared, as they had been through December, to give these close study and, if acceptable, to tell that to Lodge. First, though, they needed to know that the proposals were authoritative. Anxiously, they waited for Hitchcock to recover from a minor illness. When he did, McNary sought him out, on 30 December. McNary found Hitchcock reluctant to risk repudiation by Wilson before the Democratic caucus of 15 January. But McNary pointed out that the Underwood resolution for a conciliation committee would come up before then, and its adoption would strengthen Underwood's leadership candidacy. McNary thought that it was this argument that persuaded Hitchcock to call a meeting of Democratic members of the Foreign Relations Committee for the following evening.[34]

Only three Foreign Relations Committee Democrats could meet with Hitchcock on New Year's Eve. The gathering produced no definite proposals and served only to close out the possibility of Pomerene's serving as intermediary between Lodge and Democrats other than Hitchcock. Even so, anticipating acceptable and authoritative proposals from the Democrats, McNary thought it advisable to renew pressure on Lodge. He called on the majority leader on 2 January and warned him that unless Lodge continued to be receptive to forthcoming Democratic proposals, the Underwood resolution, which Lodge opposed, might pass, with the help of some Republicans. At the same time, though, McNary reiterated his understanding that the "Lodge reservations" must be the starting point for any compromise. The very fact of his effort indicated his continuing intention to work through Lodge, if he could.[35]

Lodge seemed tractable. Before the new session, he spent a good deal of time with middle grounders. In addition to McNary, he conferred with Lenroot, Kellogg, Capper, and probably others. He talked also with Claude Swanson, who came, Republicans thought, as Hitchcock's emissary. Afterward Lodge said, "It looks as though we will get together." Lenroot, who saw Lodge the same day, 2 January, predicted interesting developments within days.[36]

34. *New York Tribune*, 30 December 1919; *Milwaukee Sentinel*, 30 December 1919; *New York Times*, 30, 31 December 1919; Gus Karger to William Howard Taft, 31 December 1919, and McNary to Taft, 8 January 1920, Taft Papers.

35. *New York Tribune*, 1, 5 January 1920; *New York Times*, 3 January 1920; *New York World*, 3 January 1920.

36. Hitchcock to Mrs. Woodrow Wilson, 5 January 1920, Hitchcock Papers; *New*

Developments on the Democratic side suggested to mild reservationists that Lodge and his followers could be satisfied—that the Democrats would make an authoritative offer and that they would accept the principles of the "Lodge reservations" in return for concessions, which Lodge was ready to yield, on the preamble and on some verbal changes in the reservations. Hoke Smith proposed to host a conference of independent Democrats to formulate a specific program to offer the Republicans. Smith later called it off, ostensibly because too few senators had returned to Washington by 4 January, when the gathering was scheduled. Nevertheless, many Democrats, including influential ones such as Tom Walsh, had made clear their willingness to yield a good deal and to take action without presidential authorization. An LEP insider detected "unmistakable indications that a considerable number of Democrats will join with the mild reservationists and that ratification of the Treaty with slight modification of the 'Lodge reservations' will result eventually."[37]

Apparently, Colt had been away for the holidays. McKellar and Kendrick presented their proposals to him on 6 January, a copy was passed on to Lodge, and the mild reservationists intensified discussions among themselves. The following day McNary saw the Democrats and told them that the changes in the "Lodge reservations" were too drastic but that "if they could not be taken as a finality, I would attempt to arrange a conference favorable to the ratification of the Treaty." The Democrats agreed to negotiate but suggested a short delay pending the Jackson Day dinner of 8 January. McNary emerged confident that a bipartisan conference would take place and sent news of this to Taft, continuing the collaboration that was developing between the two. Through Taft, McNary could intensify pressure on Lodge and, if forced, could attempt to promote mild reservationist action independent of Lodge.[38]

Wilson's Jackson Day call for a solemn referendum, though tem-

---

York Times, 3 January 1920; Minneapolis Tribune, 1 January 1920; Lodge quoted in New York Journal, 3 January 1920; New York World, 3 January 1920.

37. New York World, 4, 5 January 1920; Miles William Dunnington, "Senator Thomas J. Walsh: Independent Democrat in the Wilson Years," 208; Charles D. Warner to W. H. Short, 5 January 1920, in Short to William Howard Taft, 6 January 1920, Taft Papers.

38. McNary to William Howard Taft, 8 January 1920, Taft Papers. The McNary-Taft collaboration was reflected in some confidential correspondence, in Taft's presentation to McNary of his own reservation proposals, and in McNary's signature on an LEP call for Taft to speak for compromise before a bipartisan meeting in Washington (McNary to Taft, 22 December 1919, Taft Papers; New York Times, 30 December 1919; Minneapolis Tribune, 30 December 1919; New York World, 5 January 1920).

pered by his willingness to accept "interpretive reservations," seemed a body blow to compromise hopes. But Democratic newspapers and politicians reacted so adversely to the referendum idea that in fact the pace of compromise discussion intensified. However, Democratic politicians took care not to repudiate Wilson or to associate themselves too closely with William Jennings Bryan. McNary and Lenroot spoke hopefully, but in private conversation with the LEP's William Short, they, along with Kellogg, conceded that Wilson's letter would make the Democrats timid about yielding essential points. Short, who had talked with Hitchcock and a few others, thought that this would be the case.[39]

In his report on his conversations, Short did not distinguish between the views of the three mild reservationist leaders, but it was probably Kellogg and Lenroot, more than McNary, who convincingly pointed out that the "Lodge reservations" themselves were "the result of compromise and that large additional concessions should not be expected." Pressure would have to be brought on the Democrats to make large concessions. In that vein, Lenroot told reporters: "All talk of interpretive reservations is idle. They must be vital." At the same time, the three mild reservationists understood that they were prepared to make concessions that would divide their party, in sharp contrast to the situation in November when Republicans of all stripes had united behind the "Lodge reservations." As they outlined the plan to Short, a successful compromise would require the support of forty or more Democrats, implying that they hoped to rally no more than twenty-four Republicans. To do that, they explained that they would have to pressure certain middle grounders to yield more to the Democrats. They had in mind Hale, Edge, Sterling, Keyes, Spencer, Jones, Townsend, Kenyon, and Cummins. But even with this help, they would need others, including followers of Lodge. The mild reservationists were prepared to treat directly with the Democrats to secure agreement, but Short inferred, correctly, that the three would not "put themselves in the position of ignoring him [Lodge] during the conferences and dictating to him at their end."[40]

39. *New York Times*, 10 January 1920; Charles McNary to William Howard Taft, 13 January 1920, Taft Papers; *New York Tribune*, 10 January 1920; *New York World*, 9, 10 January 1920; "Report of W. H. Short on Treaty Situation in Washington . . . January 8th and 9th," enclosed in Short to William Howard Taft, 10 January 1920, Taft Papers.

40. "Report of W. H. Short on Treaty Situation," in Short to William Howard Taft, 10 January 1920, Taft Papers; *New York Times*, 10 January 1920.

An important meeting took place on 10 January. McNary reported to Taft three days later. He wrote:

Saturday, Senator Colt and I, in a spirit of desperation, took the first step looking towards the setting of the stage for compromise. We insisted that Senator Lodge consider the Democratic proposals that had been placed with us. After a long conference we went to the Democrats stating that we could satisfy them on the Preamble, on Article 13, which deals with the labor provisions of the Treaty, and Article 14, which refers to the voting strength of the Members of the League in the Assembly. We reported that we would hold fast to Reservation 2, which qualifies Article 10, and that we would insist upon the retention of Articles 7, 8, and 9, which in my opinion are largely legislative in character. Indeed this report did not reflect the opinion of either Judge Colt or myself, but it was the best at that time that could be gotten out of Mr. Lodge, supported by Mr. Lenroot.

The controversy, he wrote, hinged on Article 10. The Democrats insisted on some change in wording, and he thought that they were entitled to that much. "The trouble in the situation is that the President treats the covenant as sacred, and Mr. Lodge treats the reservations as sacred." Nevertheless, McNary remained optimistic.[41]

McNary and Colt, in agreeing to offer the Democrats less than what they were privately willing to concede, yielded to Lenroot quite as much as to Lodge. Strength among moderates and conservative mild reservationists was essential, and for that the help of Lenroot was indispensable. Also, McNary and Colt had reason to believe that Lenroot was prepared to go further, once formal bargaining began. Short, summarizing his talks with Lenroot, McNary, and Kellogg a day or two before, understood that all three were willing to change the language, if not the substance, of the critical second reservation. They also all seemed willing to modify reservations on the Monroe Doctrine, on domestic questions, and on the division of power between the executive and legislative branches and to tone down the language of other reservations.[42] Some of these issues, though not referred to by McNary in his letter to Taft, were later raised by the Democrats at the bipartisan conference and were surely part of the McKellar-Kendrick proposal.

There was something else that McNary did not mention to Taft but that the conferees made known to reporters. Lodge remained preoccupied with numbers and asked how many votes the Demo-

---

41. McNary to Taft, 13 January 1920, Taft Papers.
42. "Report of W. H. Short on Treaty Situation," in Short to William Howard Taft, 10 January 1920, Taft Papers.

crats could deliver. When told that they did not know, he charged the mild reservationists with finding out. He was reluctant to enter negotiations or make concessions without good prospects of success. Lodge did not insist on full Democratic support. To the contrary, he preferred that Republicans be chiefly responsible for ratification. But he could hope for no more than thirty-five Republican votes at most, so he needed at least twenty-nine votes from the Democrats.[43] This approach, consonant with the relatively tough stand that Lodge took on Article 10 in particular, varied importantly from the other major alternative—forty-four Democrats joining twenty Republicans. Since even that would probably require Lodge's help, however, McNary had reason to be glad about the limited encouragement given by Lodge.

The usually sedate Senator Colt served as emissary to McKellar and Kendrick. Emerging from the meeting with Lodge, he said: "It is just as sure as anything in the world that we are going to get together. It may be three days from now, it may be three weeks, but to talk of delaying things for fourteen months or until November is pure idiocy." McKellar and Kendrick responded encouragingly to Colt. Meanwhile Lodge talked with Underwood and sent Kellogg to see Hitchcock, a man Lodge disliked and avoided when possible.[44]

Robert Owen, a Bryanite who was willing to accept substantial reservations in exchange for ratification, invited all Democratic senators to his home on the night of 11 January, to seek agreement on a program and on fuller negotiations with the Republicans. Approximately twenty senators came. Afterward Hitchcock said that the possibility had been raised that Wilson "might be willing to accept as the final action of the Senate something that he would not accept beforehand. We therefore have to take chances. We don't know just what he will accept." The reservations, he added, should be interpretive. In sum, Hitchcock would not resist his colleagues' pressure for negotiation, but he hoped to avert open rebellion and to steer Democratic policy with an eye toward Wilson.[45]

Only a little more pressure on the party leaders was needed. Colt and McNary brought Lodge the word from McKellar and Kendrick: though no Democrat was formally pledged, thirty-five votes were

43. *New York Times,* 11 January 1920.

44. Colt quoted in *Minneapolis Tribune,* 11 January 1920; *New York Times,* 13 January 1920; *New York Tribune,* 11 January 1920; Gus Karger to William Howard Taft, 31 December 1919, Taft Papers.

45. Hitchcock quoted in *New York Times,* 13 January 1920; *New York Tribune,* 12 January 1920.

certain and others were sympathetic to the compromise program. If further pressure on Lodge was needed, Kenyon supplied it when he agreed with Owen that they should secure seven signatures from each party, calling for a bipartisan conference.[46]

With the implicit threat of a conference from which the party leaders would be excluded, both Lodge and Hitchcock fell into line. Owen and Kenyon went to Lodge, told him of the restlessness among senators and the general demand for ratification, and urged him to approve a modification of the reservation to Article 10. Lodge agreed to meet again the following day with Owen, Lenroot, and some others; only the irreconcilables would not be represented.[47] Owen then persuaded Hitchcock to lead a delegation into conference with Lodge and associates.[48] Following the party caucus, the Democrat appeared on 15 January accompanied by Owen, McKellar, Simmons, and Tom Walsh. He found Lodge ready with his own delegation—Lenroot, Kellogg, and Harry New of Indiana, a member of the Foreign Relations Committee and a strong reservationist. The meeting marked the start of a full-scale, albeit unofficial, bipartisan conference. When it began, Owen and his friends, and their middle-grounder counterparts, put aside, at least for a time, the project of a conference that would include friends of the treaty and that would exclude the party leaders.

Lenroot may have had something to do with both arranging the conference and channeling the negotiation through the leadership. According to the later recollection of one of the Democratic participants, either Walsh or Simmons, "Lenroot made it a condition of his participation [in the McKellar-Colt talks] that Lodge should be a member."[49] Further, Lenroot later spoke knowledgeably of the origins of the conference and the initiative of "a Republican Senator" who suggested "that certain Democrats see the Republican leader . . . and ascertain if an agreement could not be made for an informal bipartisan conference." He himself saw Lodge on 14 January. The *New York World*, a day before the first meeting, was able to name him and Owen, but not others, as ones who would participate,

46. *New York Times*, 13, 15 January 1920; *Minneapolis Tribune*, 15 January 1920.
47. *New York Times*, 19 January 1920; *New York Journal*, 15 January 1920; *New York World*, 15 January 1920.
48. Hitchcock to Joseph Tumulty, 16 January 1920, Wilson Papers; *New York Times*, 16 January 1920.
49. Letter to H. Maurice Darling, n.d. [1926], in Darling, "Who Kept the United States?" 211.

which also suggests his initiative.[50] But Lenroot was far from alone among the mild reservationists in feeling the need for Lodge's help; indeed, NcNary and Colt had pressed for it.

The outcome of the conference was forecast on its first day. The Democrats presented a slate of modifications to the "Lodge reservations," including several alternatives on Article 10, and in the two hours available the conferees discussed most of the proposals. The Republicans reacted favorably to suggestions for the preamble, the withdrawal reservation, and some others. However, when Simmons offered his compromise on Article 10, Lodge and New said that Republicans probably would not accept it. Similarly, Lodge rejected Article 10 suggestions offered by McKellar.[51]

Hitchcock was not displeased. Privately, he thought that both the Simmons and the McKellar proposals went too far. He intended to suggest later that any reservations be put in the form of "interpretations and understandings," as Wilson wanted but Republicans did not. On the sixteenth, the same day that the Republican members of the conference discussed the Democratic proposals and prepared their reply, Hitchcock presented to the Senate the results of a poll of college students, who mainly supported his side. "Lodge and some of his colleagues seemed to be rather indignant that I brought the subject up as I did in the Senate," he explained to Tumulty, "but I think it is just as well to emphasize the weakness of the Lodge reservations in public opinion."[52] From the start, then, Hitchcock negotiated with an eye on the White House. He was not really prepared to take chances. If the Republicans would make the major concessions, fine. Otherwise, however, he wanted his party to be well prepared to argue the League issue in the campaign.

Hitchcock would have welcomed a conciliatory signal from Wilson, of course, but none came. Tumulty, aided by Lansing and others, drafted a letter for the president to send to Hitchcock. It proposed to modify the "Lodge reservations" to appeal to the mild reservationists and to accept the core of the reservations while safeguarding the rights of the executive. But Mrs. Wilson, to whom these appeals were directed, made no reply. And when asked by Tumulty to read

---

50. *CR* 66:2, pp. 3179, 3178 (20 February 1920); *Milwaukee Sentinel*, 15 January 1920; *New York World*, 15 January 1920.
51. Gilbert Hitchcock to Joseph Tumulty, 16 January 1920, Wilson Papers.
52. Ibid.

her husband a pro-compromise editorial from the Democratic *Oregon Journal*, she refused.[53]

Tortuously, the conference progressed, on the basis that all agreements would be tentative. They would require the support of non-participants in the conference, and even the conferees would not be bound until agreement was complete on all reservations. In five hours on Saturday, 17 January, the Republicans made concessions on most of the reservations up to the tenth but passed over the preamble and Article 10 and disagreed on the Monroe Doctrine. Two days later the conferees wrangled fruitlessly over the Lenroot equal-voting reservation. Lodge himself wanted a change in that, and Lenroot had prepared one that Lodge considered excellent. Lodge told the conferees that Viscount Grey had assured him that Great Britain would accept the reservations, of which the fourteenth was the most difficult, but the Democrats were not so sure.[54]

The next day the senators talked some more of equal voting and, as Lenroot understood it, found themselves close enough to agreement to warrant going on to Article 10. Immediately, according to a participant, "just as soon as Article 10 was mentioned the fur began to fly." Only the diplomacy of Simmons kept the conference going, but both sides foresaw a swift end to the negotiation and began to prepare statements to be delivered in the Senate. At the same time, they prepared to consider new proposals on Article 10.[55]

Restive and discouraged, several mild reservationists who were not members of the conference, McNary among them, talked of joining the Democrats to make up a majority to bring the treaty to the floor of the Senate. Lodge and New tried to dissuade McNary but failed. Taft endorsed the idea, in a letter to McCumber, and proposed to discuss it with him, Colt, McNary, and Kellogg on 23 January. "The only way that Lodge can be brought around is to put him in the minority in the Senate," Taft wrote Gus Karger, "and if enough mild reservationists could unite with the Democrats and do that, even though it does not mean two thirds, it will put him where he belongs and where he does not like to appear." When Taft met with the four mild reservationists, McNary told him that twelve Republicans

53. John M. Blum, *Joe Tumulty and the Wilson Era*, 234–36; Walworth, *Wilson*, 2:390.

54. *New York Times*, 18 January 1920; Gilbert Hitchcock to Joseph Tumulty, 17 January 1920, Wilson Papers; Lodge to James T. Williams, Jr., 20 December 1919, 2 February 1920, and to F. H. Gillett, 26 July 1920, Lodge Papers; Darling, "Who Kept the United States?" 209.

55. *CR* 66:2, p. 3179 (20 February 1920); *Minneapolis Tribune*, 22 January 1920; *New York Times*, 22 January 1920.

would vote with the Democrats to bring up the treaty, if need be. They were ready to "put the burden on the objecting Republicans for the defeat of the Treaty."[56]

The effect of the threat conveyed by McNary cannot be determined. But in its wake, on 22 January, the conferees had some success. Lodge afterward declared that great progress had been made, and Owen and Simmons predicted full agreement within days. A new reservation to Article 10 had been proposed. Hitchcock, though not openly supportive of it, thought that the conferees were close enough to agreement to warrant presenting the reservation to Wilson.[57] Based on the original Lodge reservation, the new proposal included two additions and a significant deletion. In a memorandum that Hitchcock prepared for himself, he used capital letters to indicate the additions and used parentheses for the deletion. The proposal stated:

> The United States assumes no obligation to EMPLOY ITS MILITARY OR NAVAL FORCES OR THE ECONOMIC BOYCOTT to preserve the territorial integrity or political independence of any other country (or to interfere in controversies between nations whether members of the league or not) under the provisions of Article Ten, or to employ the military or naval forces of the United States under any article of the treaty for any purpose, unless in any particular case the Congress, which, under the Constitution, has the sole power to declare war or authorize the employment of the military or naval forces of the United States, shall by act or joint resolution so provide. NOTHING HEREIN SHALL BE DEEMED TO IMPAIR THE OBLIGATION IN ARTICLE XVI CONCERNING THE ECONOMIC BOYCOTT.[58]

Hitchcock erred on the side of caution. In fact, the conferees were not so close to agreement as he and his Democratic colleagues thought. Lodge, in particular, objected during the conference to the removal of the phrase "or to interfere in controversies between nations whether members of the league or not." Walsh, who had proposed the deletion, argued that the phrase added nothing. Simmons, however, appreciated its importance, to Wilson, as a complete renunciation of responsibility. The two Democrats inferred

56. *New York Times*, 21, 23 January 1920; *Minneapolis Tribune*, 21 January 1920; *Portland Oregonian*, 21 January 1920; Taft to McCumber, 21 January 1920, to Karger, 21 January 1920, and to Mabel Boardman, 28 January 1920, Taft Papers.

57. *New York World*, 23 January 1920; *New York Times*, 23 January 1920; *CR* 66:2, p. 3179 (20 February 1920); Hitchcock to Wilson, 22 January 1920, Wilson Papers.

58. Memo, n.d., Hitchcock Papers; *New York Times*, 28 January 1920.

that Lenroot and Kellogg differed with Lodge, but in fact they were merely noncommittal and soon showed themselves hostile to the change.[59]

The conferees differed too on the use of the word *employ* rather than *preserve*. Again, the basic issue of obligation was involved. A reservation denying obligation to *employ* the armed forces, without congressional authorization, was merely interpretive, stating the constitutional situation; but Lenroot and Kellogg wanted a rejection of the obligation to, as Lenroot later phrased it, "preserve by the use of the means set forth." This, to him and Kellogg, suggested a much broader renunciation of obligation. Simmons was aware of the difference in meaning. There was another difficulty. Lenroot, in particular, thought the Democratic proposal retained a financial obligation.[60] These issues were still unresolved when Lenroot suggested that the group take a break to allow the Republicans to caucus. Perhaps to give Hitchcock a chance to report to the president, the Democrats soon suggested that the conference not reconvene until the following day.[61]

Marked-up committee prints in Lodge's handwriting, located in the McNary manuscripts, may date to the caucus of the four Republican conferees on the afternoon of 22 January. The prints indicate a rejection of the proposal to delete the phrase "or to interfere in controversies between nations whether members of the League or not" and a rejection too of the use of the word *employ*, as the Democrats wanted. Alternative formulations had been discussed in the bipartisan conference, and on the Senate floor some time later, Kellogg presented one of these, which avoided the two objectionable features and which he and Lenroot considered a better basis for negotiation.[62]

Though the conferees were not so close to agreement as the Democrats thought, neither were they on the verge of complete failure. Yet, following a well-publicized meeting with irreconcilables the next day, Lodge first postponed the next conference until the twenty-sixth and then announced that there could be no change in the second reservation, to Article 10. Seemingly, Lodge had succumbed to the threats of the irreconcilables.

59. *CR* 66:2, p. 3232 (21 February 1920), p. 4323 (15 March 1920), p. 4533 (18 March 1920).

60. Ibid., 4323 (15 March 1920); *New York Times*, 28 January 1920.

61. *CR* 66:2, p. 3179 (20 February 1920).

62. Hewes, "William E. Borah," 267–68; Bailey, *Great Betrayal*, 231; *CR* 66:2, p. 4323 (15 March 1920).

Irreconcilables significantly influenced Lodge, but others also influenced him, as well as Lenroot and Kellogg. Amid rumors of progress in the bipartisan conference, on the morning of 22 January Joseph Frelinghuysen of New Jersey, a strong reservationist, issued a statement warning that "a considerable number" would join him against any substantial changes and that "there can be no compromise upon Article 10." The next day, before Lodge's encounter with the irreconcilables, another strong reservationist, Howard Sutherland of West Virginia, cornered Lodge and talked emphatically against compromise on Article 10, then issued a statement to the same effect. After the irreconcilable intervention, Lodge told Kellogg, perhaps self-servingly, that it was Frelinghuysen and even some middle grounders such as Hale—not the irreconcilables—who had influenced him.[63]

If the irreconcilables did not cause the failure of the bipartisan conference, they certainly contributed to it. And they, principally, caused the conference to break up in the way that it did. Hiram Johnson gave a first-hand account of their meeting with Lodge. Writing to his sons on 24 January, the Californian reported that on the previous day "came suddenly like a clap of thunder the news that Lodge had broken under the pressure and that he was engaged in compromising on his reservations. Nobody seemed to want to take the initiative, and so, on my return [from political campaigning] I took it." Johnson called a meeting of eight irreconcilables, then sent for Lodge. "We had three corking hours. There was bitterness and indignation on our side and apologies on his. We tried to make him see that a great victory had been won in the Lodge reservations, and that a compromise now meant not only to give that victory away, but the destruction of the proud position the Republican party had assumed."[64]

The irreconcilables offered other arguments, as well as threats. Thirty-eight senators, including some Democrats, would oppose ratification if the reservations were changed. Further, the erratic Lawrence Sherman of Illinois threatened a party bolt and, with others, made it clear that Republican control of the Senate was at stake. Johnson and Borah warned that they would not recognize Lodge's party leadership and would carry their fight into the campaign and

63. *Milwaukee Sentinel*, 23 January 1920; *New York Times*, 24 January 1920; *New York Journal*, 24 January 1920; William Howard Taft to Gus Karger, 2 February 1920, Taft Papers.

64. Johnson to Arch M. Johnson and H. W. Johnson, Jr., 24 January 1920, Johnson Papers.

the Republican national convention, at which Lodge was slated to be temporary and permanent chairman. For the record, Borah put his threat into writing in a formal letter to Lodge, written the following day.[65]

Seventeen years later, Borah told historian Thomas Bailey of the confrontation with Lodge. One may doubt that his recollection was precise, but the gist of it rings true. Lodge, evidently shaken, said, "Can't I discuss this matter with my friends?" "No, Cabot," Borah replied, "not without telling your other friends." Lodge offered to resign as majority leader, but Borah said: "You won't have a chance to resign! On Monday, I'll move for the election of a new majority leader and give the reasons for my action." In reiterating his warnings the following day in his letter to Lodge, Borah stated: "Not one of these reservations was written by the so-called irreconcilables. They were all the handiwork of the friends of the League. . . . The standard, the test of protection is one that the friends of the League set up and which you as spokesman of the party announced."[66]

The party in October had arrived at a position on reservations, and the irreconcilables had acquiesced in that. Now, without consulting them or most other senators, the party leader was trying to go back on the agreement. Quite apart from the irreconcilables' threats, one can appreciate the discomfiture that the group caused Lodge. He had entered the bipartisan conference seeking a basis for ratification. Since the irreconcilables would not vote for the treaty in any case, it had seemed reasonable to exclude them from the formulation of the new set of reservations. But when they asserted their right to be consulted by their party leader, they put Lodge in the position of having exceeded his authority and of having acted highhandedly. The irreconcilable offensive jolted Lodge to the extent that he postponed the session of the bipartisan conference set for Saturday, 24 January, and launched a series of meetings with Republicans of all factions. Among others, he met with his three Republican partners to prepare a joint position to present to the Democrats at the next meeting on 26 January.[67]

By Monday the Republicans were ready. When the conference

65. *New York Times*, 24 January 1920; *New York Journal*, 24 January 1920; *Minneapolis Tribune*, 28 January 1920; Borah to Lodge, 24 January 1920, Borah Papers. On 22 January Borah had voted with the Democrats against a resolution, sponsored by Hale, that related to the navy. Earlier, he had warned Lodge of such independent action (*Milwaukee Sentinel*, 23 January 1920).

66. Bailey, *Great Betrayal*, 230–231; Borah to Lodge, 24 January 1920, Borah Papers.

67. *Minneapolis Tribune*, 25 January 1920; *Portland Oregonian*, 25 January 1920.

resumed, Lodge, with the acquiescence of Kellogg, Lenroot, and New, told the Democrats not only that there could be no deviation from the principles of the "Lodge reservations" but also that the reservations to Article 10 and the Monroe Doctrine must stand unchanged. Sentiment was such among Republicans, he said, that otherwise ratification would be impossible. To lessen the impression that he was yielding to irreconcilable pressure, he told reporters that he had intended to make such a statement from the beginning. And indeed, he privately wrote along these lines not only afterward but also two days before his encounter with the irreconcilables.[68] However, these statements referred to the principles of the main reservations, not the exact wording. His insistence on the precise words of the Article 10 and Monroe Doctrine reservations reflects the influence of the irreconcilables.

Later, after the breakup of the bipartisan conference, Kellogg and Lenroot urged verbal changes in the two key reservations. The support the two mild reservationists gave Lodge in his 26 January declaration to the Democrats needs clarification. Lodge had explained his difficulty to them, stressing the roles of Frelinghuysen and Hale.[69] Whatever they may have thought, it was apparent that Lodge remained sympathetic to a settlement but found his battle lines overextended. The bipartisan conference format, with participation by party leaders, simply would not work. Even if Kellogg and Lenroot were at some point to break with Lodge, this hardly seemed the time. Their own positions were weak in that they, with no official authorization from a caucus, purported to represent a party that was in the process of repudiating that representation. Was it not wiser to cut their losses and fight another day? Once freed from the now anomalous position of being party representatives, they might yet reach an agreement with the Democrats. And Lodge, if not isolated and alienated by their hostile action, might be very useful in that effort.

Additionally, Kellogg and Lenroot were both party men. To break with Lodge on the issue that might dominate the campaign of 1920 would have severely hurt the party. As dark-horse presidential prospects or, alternatively in Lenroot's case, as a candidate for reelection, both men would personally suffer from such a breach. Even so, it might have seemed to them justified, had they felt themselves

68. *New York Times*, 27 January 1920; Lodge to F. H. Gillett, 26 July 1920, and to J.D.H. Luce, 21 January 1920, Lodge Papers.
69. William Howard Taft to Gus Karger, 2 February 1920, Taft Papers.

close to an agreement with the Democrats on Article 10 and able to command a two-thirds majority for such an agreement. But neither of those conditions obtained. They were not close to an agreement, and they figured to win few followers by leaving their party's leader alone on a limb with a national election fast approaching.[70]

Whatever their motives, by their support for Lodge, Lenroot and Kellogg further politicized the treaty question. During the heady days of the Colt-McKellar talks, the informal exchanges across party lines, and the Owen-Kenyon initiative, some talked of restoring the tradition that partisanship stops at the water's edge. But Wilson's talk of a "solemn referendum," followed a week later by the inclusion of party leaders Hitchcock and Lodge in the bipartisan conference, set negotiations in a political mode. Lodge's response to the pressure from irreconcilables and others accentuated the tendency.

Hitchcock responded in kind. The Nebraskan had good reason to try to make political capital of the situation. Wilson's negative response to the Simmons reservation that Hitchcock had submitted to him probably did not reach the senator at this time, though it was dated 26 January, but the very absence of a response, let alone encouragement, signaled danger.[71] If Wilson was to discourage compromise, and if the issue was to enter the campaign, then it behooved Hitchcock to provide ammunition.

To show that the Republicans were to blame for the situation, Hitchcock issued a flurry of statements over a period of five days. He revealed the Simmons reservation proposal and said that the conferees had been practically in agreement on it when the irreconcilables had intervened; he claimed that the conferees had tentatively agreed to everything except reservations to Article 10 and the Monroe Doctrine; and he took the initiative in announcing that he would move to call up the treaty in the Senate. In the bipartisan conference, after first proposing on 27 January that the conference be abandoned in light of Lodge's attitude, Hitchcock two days later baited Lodge by proposing an Article 10 reservation

70. On Lenroot as a presidential prospect, see Herbert F. Margulies, *Senator Lenroot of Wisconsin: A Political Biography, 1900–1929*, 322–24; on Kellogg, see Millard L. Gieske, "The Politics of Knute Nelson, 1912–1920" 653–55, and Knute Nelson to L. M. Willcuts, 29 January 1920, Nelson Papers.

71. On the delay in the sending of the Wilson letter, see Wimer, "Hitchcock and the League," 200 n. 37. Further, a letter from Mrs. Wilson to Hitchcock, said by the Library of Congress to have accompanied the Wilson to Hitchcock letter of 26 January, was probably written early in February, since it refers to "Senator Glass" and since Glass became a senator on 2 February.

submitted by Taft. Lodge, as Hitchcock had surely foreseen, rejected it.[72]

The Republican conferees, including Kellogg and Lenroot, responded to Hitchcock in a partisan way during the last week of January as the clearly doomed conference dragged to a close. Lenroot and Kellogg prepared a statement, which Lodge and New approved, saying that, contrary to Hitchcock, there had been no agreement on Article 10. From outside, Colt pitched in to help, commenting to reporters that a two-thirds vote could be obtained for nothing short of the "Lodge reservations" and that Hitchcock stood in the way because he did not want to compromise but rather to blame the Republicans for failure. After the conference broke up following the 30 January session, Lodge denied Hitchcock's claim that the conferees had agreed on everything except Article 10 and the Monroe Doctrine. He maintained that four other reservations remained in dispute—those on withdrawal, League expenses, the economic boycott, and equal voting. And he explained the difficulty about the Monroe Doctrine reservation. The Democrats had proposed to strike from the reservation the words *said doctrine to be interpreted by the United States alone.* But, Lodge noted, at Paris the British had said that the doctrine would be interpreted by the League. The United States had always interpreted it alone, and to omit the assertion of that would imply that she was abandoning the right.[73]

At the last, Lodge positioned himself to regain lost ground. He accepted the agreements tentatively reached, causing the Democrats to refuse to do so. And, reversing field, he intimated that instead of allowing the Democrats to seize the initiative, he himself would call up the treaty in the Senate. Hitchcock's threat to bring up the treaty and Lodge's decision to beat the Democrats to it sprang from the failure of the bipartisan conference and from the politicization of the conference in its last week, 26–30 January. The political origins of the new effort in the Senate portended difficulties. "The fundamental trouble is that we are in the midst of a presidential campaign and party politics seem to cut too much of a figure," Nelson judged.[74]

72. *Milwaukee Sentinel,* 26 January 1920; *New York Times,* 28, 31 January 1920; *Minneapolis Tribune,* 29, 31 January 1920. Lenroot later tried to show that the Taft reservation contained an obligation (*CR* 66:2, p. 2951 [16 February 1920]).

73. *New York Times,* 28 January 1920; *New York Tribune,* 27 January 1920; *Minneapolis Tribune,* 31 January 1920.

74. *New York World,* 31 January 1920; *Milwaukee Sentinel,* 31 January 1920; *Minneapolis Tribune,* 1 February 1920; Nelson to S. Listoe, 29 January 1920, Nelson Papers.

On the other hand, that political considerations dictated a further effort suggested that there was some hope. Most senators and much of the nation still wanted a settlement.[75] Furthermore, the situation was not completely politicized. Before Lodge committed himself, some mild reservationists had decided to vote with the Democrats, if needed to bring up the treaty. By McNary's vague estimate, there were "from five to seven . . . possibly twelve." McNary implied to Gus Karger that McCumber was one and that Colt would go along if Taft would reassure the Rhode Islander that he supported the plan. The vote could be politically risky to the Republican party, should reservations get majority support but fall short of the two-thirds because of Republican votes, but McNary thought the risk worth taking. "It now becomes the turn of the mild reservationists to show a truculent spirit," Karger said, expressing his own view and McNary's. Their hope was that "enough Republicans will see the light to accept any compromise reservations that may now be approved by a majority."[76]

Within the bipartisan conference, Kellogg and Lenroot had to stay with Lodge, and at one point they joined him in disparaging the idea of action on the Senate floor.[77] But following the irreconcilable initiative, those middle grounders outside the conference for whom McNary temporarily served as organizer and spokesman made it clear to Hitchcock and to reporters that they would act independently, if need be. Indeed for a time McNary and his colleagues contemplated initiating the motion to take up the treaty and then putting forth their own program of reservations. By the time the bipartisan conference had ended, however, McNary had accepted Hitchcock's version of events. He thought that the tentative agreements covered everything except Article 10 and the Monroe Doctrine and that there thus was no need for a new program, except on those two issues.[78] McNary tended toward vagueness and overoptimism. But the promise that he offered Hitchcock and the threat that he presented to Lodge were credible enough to allow Hitchcock to talk of winning a majority to call up the treaty, and to contribute to Lodge's decision to himself bring the treaty to the floor.

75. *New York World*, 26, 30 January 1920; Warren Harding to H. M. Rose, 24 January 1920, Harding Papers; Charles Warner to William Short, 5 January 1920, in Short to A. Lawrence Lowell, 5 January 1920, Lowell Papers.

76. Gus Karger to William Howard Taft, 31 January 1920, Taft Papers.

77. *New York Times*, 31 January 1920.

78. *Portland Oregonian*, 25 January 1920; *New York Times*, 27, 31 January 1920; *New York World*, 27 January 1920; *Providence Sunday Tribune*, 25 January 1920; Gus Karger to William Howard Taft, 31 January 1920, Taft Papers.

The mild reservationists remained a force to be reckoned with, as they had shown themselves since the ratification failure in November. Jarred by that event, and by Lodge's intransigence afterward, some of them had rejected the Knox resolution and had negotiated directly with Democrats, while others had lent tacit support to that negotiation. Their efforts proved serious enough, and successful enough in narrowing differences between the parties, to cause Lodge to back down and lead a group, which included Kellogg and Lenroot, into semiofficial negotiations with the Democrats.

The format was ill conceived, and the mild reservationists must share the blame. Lodge and his colleagues lacked official standing, yet they had to answer to the whole party. The bipartisan conference revealed a further and perhaps greater problem—the reconciliation of differences over Article 10. The issue had a life of its own, but it also symbolized party division and reflected the deep partisanship that provided much of the context for the treaty's consideration.

Occasionally, a few mild reservationists, notably McNary and Colt, showed a willingness to yield substantially on Article 10. Paralleling that, they showed some willingness to deal directly with the Democrats on a nonpartisan basis, excluding the leadership of both parties. But the Democrats were not prepared to fully ignore Wilson and Hitchcock, and McNary and Colt ultimately chose to work through Lodge and on the basis of the "Lodge reservations," including the no-obligation stand on Article 10. The approach taken by these most independent-minded of mild reservationists may or may not have been realistic; certainly it seemed so. However one judges it in the abstract, it comported with the character of the middle grounders, on whom success would depend. Before the bipartisan conference, mild reservationist leaders had doubted how far their colleagues would go toward concessions.[79] Some middle grounders, such as Hale and Cummins, had long shown themselves to be firmly against obligations under Article 10. And Lenroot and Kellogg, though willing to yield a good deal on the preamble, Shantung, and a number of other reservations, stood against major concessions on Article 10 and were strongly inclined toward working with Lodge.

Yet all of the mild reservationists and some of the moderates remained strongly favorable toward ratification and thus retained some bargaining power in Republican councils. The shock of the failure in November reinforced their enthusiasm for treaty approval,

79. "Report of W. H. Short on Treaty Situation," in Short to William H. Taft, 10 January 1920, Taft Papers.

and they soon felt too the force of public opinion generally and business opinion in particular. From the political standpoint, although they and their party could probably cope with the League issue in the 1920 campaign if need be, it seemed better to decide the divisive question, as Will Hays and state party leaders urged. Feeling that way, they could credibly pressure Lodge, as the majority leader tacitly acknowledged when he intimated that he would call up the treaty in the Senate.

As the treaty battle moved into its final phase, the mild reservationists faced the perennial question: Should they stick with Lodge and a relatively hard line on reservations to win as many as thirty-five Republicans, counting on the Democrats to provide the rest of the two-thirds? Or should they break away and make common cause with the Democrats to constitute a majority, in the hope that enough other Republicans would fall in line to make up the two-thirds? The problem was particularly acute for men like McNary and Colt and McCumber and Nelson, men who were relatively indifferent to the character of the reservations and who were, on the League issue at least, less partisan than others. Much would depend on the actions of Lodge and Wilson and Hitchcock and on the influence of external events, as yet unknown and unforeseen.

6 THE LAST CHANCE, 1 February–19 March 1920

Senator Lodge brought the treaty before the Senate on 10 February. For a time, action was spasmodic, but by the end of the month the senators were systematically at work debating and adopting reservations. When this work was finally done, on 19 March, the Senate voted on a new resolution of ratification, embodying the reservations recently adopted. This time the treaty won a majority, but it fell seven votes short of two-thirds. The Versailles Treaty was not again considered by the Senate.

With the national party conventions just months ahead, politics shaped the deliberations of February and March. In part, the effect was constructive. Irreconcilables aside, neither party wanted to take the blame for the treaty's defeat, and many senators wanted to be done with the League issue before the conventions and campaign. On the other hand, when specific reservation formulations became identified with one party or the other, political considerations and politically based bitterness worked against accommodation. This was especially true for Article 10, but party division also prevented a greater softening of the other reservations.

Constitutional problems remained—senatorial resentment over prolonged executive high-handedness. As before, this issue of high principle mingled intimately with very personal resentment against Wilson. The president, by his continuing intransigence on reservations and by some other actions not directly related to the treaty, refreshed the feeling. Whereas Hitchcock followed Wilson and closed, to the mild reservationists, the front door to the Democracy, Lodge tacked in their direction. But what he would concede was not enough to meet the demands of Wilson, Hitchcock, and their followers.

Though occasionally rebellious, the mild reservationists for the most part judged it feasible and advantageous to work through

215

Lodge. Their main hope, as it evolved, was to detach from Hitch-cock enough Democrats to make up two-thirds. Many did come over, but not enough. Twenty-one Wilson Democrats, chiefly from the South, joined with fourteen irreconcilables to defeat the treaty. Though the mild reservationists failed, it is not clear if they would have been more successful using other tactics.

Lenroot, Kellogg, and McNary led the mild reservationists in this period. McCumber had to leave Washington in mid-February, and Colt and Nelson played supporting roles. McNary's work was exclusively behind the scenes. Of the mild reservationist leaders currently active, he was the most conciliatory toward the Democrats. Lenroot and Kellogg worked assiduously on the floor as well as in the lobbies. They established a close liaison with Lodge and his Republican followers, while occasionally, with McNary, they also pressured Lodge. Their mild reservationist colleagues supported them with speeches and occasional votes.

Following the breakup of the bipartisan conference, Republican and Democratic leaders competed to seem reasonable and constructive. Lodge made himself agreeable to the mild reservationists, and they welcomed his cooperation, which he offered for a number of reasons. Pro-League organizations, though not so strong as before, remained active, and their representatives came together on 9 February in Washington. Whatever their original sentiments, by now they were content with any reservationist compromise that could secure ratification.[1] Party leaders in the states and the national organization, led by Will Hays, continued to urge a settlement before the campaign, and such strong reservationists as Harry New and James Watson of Indiana agreed. Some talked of getting on with legislation that could help in the campaign. And Lodge was mindful too of the risk of "having the treaty ratified over our heads with much weaker reservations."[2] This might occur as mild reservationists joined forces with the Democrats. Taft urged that course, and McCumber, though admittedly unfamiliar with the situation because of his absences from Washington, openly accepted it. Earlier, Lodge knew, McNary had threatened such a step. Another factor was personal:

1. James L. Lancaster, "The Protestant Churches and the Fight for Ratification of the Versailles Treaty," 616–17; *New York World*, 10 February 1920.
2. Gus Karger to William Howard Taft, 5 February 1920, and Taft to Karger, 7 February 1920, Taft Papers; Albert J. Beveridge to Louis Coolidge, 6 February 1920, and Coolidge to Beveridge, 11 February 1920, Beveridge Papers; *New York World*, 11 February 1920; Lodge to Louis A. Coolidge, 28 January 1920, Lodge Papers.

the irreconcilables had humiliated Lodge, and he wanted to show his independence.[3]

Lodge did not want to yield too much. But he did not have to. As matters developed early in February, he could come to terms with the mild reservationists without sacrificing principle. Anti-British feeling remained high among segments of the population. Discreetly, Lodge helped Hiram Johnson fan the flames.[4] But Lodge's major fortification came from a British source. Sir Edward Grey, recently special ambassador to the United States, on 31 January published a letter in the *Times of London* explaining America to Britain and saying, in effect, that it would be wise to accept America's reservations. He objected only to the equal voting one, which could be adjusted. Although Grey's statement was widely assumed to have been inspired by British authorities, in fact it was not. However, both the British and the French governments had come to feel that the reservations were far less consequential than the possible abstention of the United States from the League.[5] And in the United States, the letter was a bombshell. Linked with similar statements from less authoritative sources, it attacked one of Wilson's principal arguments against the "Lodge reservations." Republicans made full capital of it, and contradicting Hitchcock, many Democrats acknowledged its importance.[6]

By then, John Maynard Keynes's *The Economic Consequences of the Peace* was in wide circulation. A member of the British peace delegation who had resigned in protest, Keynes damned the treaty, feeling that its territorial and reparations provisions were too harsh

3. William Howard Taft to Gus Karger, 2 February 1920, and Karger to Taft, 6 February 1920, Taft Papers,; *New York World*, 6 February 1920; *New York Tribune*, 7 February 1920; Ralph Stone, *The Irreconcilables: The Fight Against the League of Nations*, 160.

4. Raymond B. Fosdick to Huntington Gilchrist, 28 January 1920, in Raymond B. Fosdick, *Letters on the League of Nations*, 115; Charles C. Tansill, *America and the Fight for Irish Freedom*, 371; John Richards Edwards Correspondence, Johnson Papers. Lodge passed on to Johnson material giving historical precedent for the equal-voting idea.

5. Thomas A. Bailey, *Woodrow Wilson and the Great Betrayal*, 236–37; George W. Egerton, *Great Britain and the Creation of the League of Nations: Strategy, Politics, and International Organization, 1914–1919*, 194–99; John A. Garraty, *Henry Cabot Lodge: A Biography*, 387; Lloyd E. Ambrosius, *Woodrow Wilson and the American Diplomatic Tradition: The Treaty Fight in Perspective*, 214, 244–45; Arthur Walworth, *Wilson and the Peacemakers: American Diplomacy at the Paris Peace Conference, 1919*, 514.

6. Arthur Walworth, *Woodrow Wilson*, 2:381; *Minneapolis Tribune*, 2, 4, 6 February 1920; *New York World*, 3, 4 February 1920; *New York Tribune*, 3 February 1920.

on Germany. Keynes wrote that the treaty doomed the economy of Germany and, with it, that of Europe. Wilson got much of the blame, as the naive American outwitted by Old World diplomats. Publication began in serial form in *The New Republic* on 24 December. In January the book achieved large sales in America. Even before that, irreconcilables had used it effectively. Keynes had his greatest influence among liberals and Democrats around the country, and he fortified strong reservationism by lessening the zeal of treaty defenders. Senators were influenced by their own reading of the book. Reluctant earlier to hear condemnation of a Carthaginian peace, by February 1920 some senators were ready to consider Keynes's argument, especially since he saw the treaty as disastrous not only to Germany but to the world.[7]

Activity of various sorts on the Democratic side, just before renewed treaty consideration in the Senate, also contributed to cooperation between Lodge and the mild reservationists on a basis satisfactory to Lodge. Wilson further weakened his own cause by showing new signs of obstinacy.[8] A number of Democratic senators, both before and after these fresh signals from the president, were anxious to compromise with a coalition of mild reservationists and Lodge men. They were not dissuaded by a tough letter from Wilson that was presented to them at a 7 February party caucus.

The Grey letter encouraged mild reservationists and supported the Lodge connection as the practical course. To McNary, Kellogg, and Lenroot, Grey's letter made it plain that the British would accept the previously adopted reservations. As Lenroot said, "[that] should make it very much easier to reach an agreement when the treaty again comes up on the floor."[9] Meanwhile Lenroot, in consultation with Kellogg and others, including some Democrats, took the lead in drafting a new reservation to Article 10. His purpose, it

7. John Bernard Duff, "The Politics of Revenge: The Ethnic Opposition to the Peace Policies of Woodrow Wilson," 219; Seth P. Tillman, *Anglo-American Relations at the Paris Peace Conference of 1919*, 400–401; Lancaster, "Protestant Churches," 617; Thomas J. Walsh to Reinhard Ruhr, 26 February 1920, in Miles William Dunnington, "Senator Thomas J. Walsh: Independent Democrat in the Wilson Years," 209.

8. *Minneapolis Tribune*, 6, 7 February 1920; George F. Sparks, ed., *A Many Colored Toga: The Diary of Henry Fountain Ashurst*, entry for 7 February 1920, pp, 122–23; *New York World*, 8 February 1920; Wilson to Gilbert Hitchcock, 26 January 1920, Wilson Papers; *New York Tribune*, 8 February 1920; Baker notebooks, entry for 3 February 1920, Ray Stannard Baker Papers, Library of Congress; *Portland Oregonian*, 8 February 1920; Warren G. Harding to O. A. Bennett, 4 February 1920, Harding Papers.

9. *New York Times*, 2 February 1920; Lenroot quoted in *Milwaukee Sentinel*, 2 February 1920.

soon became clear, was to offer the Democrats a verbal change while keeping the renunciation of obligation that the vast majority of Republicans insisted on.[10]

On 6 February, a day before the Democratic caucus, McCumber tried to induce some mild reservationists to accept whatever the Democrats agreed to. He got no support. Colt, McNary, and others declared that they would back Lodge in the upcoming Senate battle, even though the Lodge program remained undetermined. Colt explained his thinking to Taft. He was willing to threaten a coalition with the Democrats, if needed to pressure Lodge, but he drew back from actually doing it. Mild reservations adopted by such a coalition could not command enough Republican support to win ratification, he was sure. Furthermore, Colt remained hopeful that changes in phraseology could be agreed on that would bring together the necessary two-thirds.[11]

On 7 February, while the Democrats were caucusing, mild reservationist leaders conferred in an adjoining room. They agreed to submit to Lodge three possible reservations to Article 10 and to assure him that they would work through him. Lenroot and Kellogg delivered the message. Lodge said that he would confer with middle grounders.[12] Two days later, with the treaty about to come up in the Senate, Lenroot, Nelson, McNary, Keyes, Colt, Kellogg, and probably Hale met with Lodge. McCumber was away and Sterling, with the group in spirit, was at another meeting. Lodge agreed to either of two possible changes in the second reservation. Neither yielded much, yet Colt saw in them the solution to the impasse. He understood that Democrats Josiah Wolcott, a first-termer from Delaware, and McKellar had suggested the verbiage. Lodge would seek an agreement among the Republicans, excluding the irreconcilables, and would then confer with Hitchcock and Underwood. Further, Lodge would introduce the bipartisan conference agreements and some minor changes from the 19 November resolution. To give the treaty its best chance, the conferees agreed to hold off on Senate consideration of the second reservation until the other reservations were disposed of. Colt emerged from the meeting optimistic. Lodge, he thought, had changed and was now really

10. *New York World*, 3, 7, 10 February 1920; *New York Times*, 3 February 1920; *Milwaukee Sentinel*, 7 February 1920.

11. *New York Tribune*, 7 February 1920; Gus Karger to Taft, 6 February 1920, Taft Papers.

12. *New York Times*, 8 February 1920; *Minneapolis Tribune*, 8 February 1920; *New York Tribune*, 8 February 1920.

working for the treaty. "Everything is working right," he told Gus Karger.[13]

The following day, the treaty was again before the Senate, reported by the Foreign Relations Committee with the "Lodge reservations" of November. Borah, invoking Keynes, talked of the bad economic conditions in Europe. He blamed the treaty, but Sterling replied that the United States could help ameliorate the situation in Europe by joining the League and exercising "a stabilizing and steadying effect upon conditions there." Benefit would accrue to the whole world, the United States included.[14]

Underlying Sterling's argument were political and economic considerations that had broad appeal among conservatives. That week a break in the price of the pound sterling occurred, resulting in a practical embargo for a time on British imports of cotton and other goods. The English blamed the slowness of reconversion to peace and foresaw a limitation on imports to strengthen the pound for some time to come. Disturbed economic conditions served as a breeding ground for communism, and in the United States the postwar red scare had not yet run its course. Sterling, one of those deeply concerned, had sponsored a rigorous antisedition bill.[15]

Because of the absence of senators, and the press of other business, Lodge put off Senate action on the reservations until the following Monday, 16 February. Meanwhile, however, he offered nine changes to the reservations and the preamble, based mainly on tentative agreements of the bipartisan conference. Lodge also permitted the mild reservationists to announce his acceptance of a modification of the second reservation, one of the two possible changes that the mild reservationists had discussed with him on 9 February.[16] The delay would permit critical negotiations among Republicans, and between Republicans and Democrats, on the new reservation to Article 10.

The events of the week 9–16 February worked against ratification, by polarizing pro-treaty elements. By the end of the week, instead of a speedy ratification, only the prospect of a long and fruitless wrangling lay ahead. The discussion began when the mild reser-

13. Karger to William Howard Taft, 11 February 1920, Taft Papers. Several papers listed Hale as among those at the meeting, though Karger did not (*New York Tribune*, 10 February 1920; *Minneapolis Tribune*, 10 February 1920).

14. *CR* 66:2, pp. 2696–99 (10 February 1920).

15. *New York World*, 5 February 1920; *New York Times*, 7 June, 14 November 1919, 8 January 1920.

16. *CR* 66:2, pp. 2736–37 (10 February 1920); *New York Times*, 10, 12 February 1920.

vationists put their new reservation to the Democrats on 11 February. Elaborating on the original Lodge reservation, the new proposal (with the new wording in parentheses) stated, in part, "The United States assumes no obligation to preserve (by its military or naval forces, or by the economic boycott or by any other means,) the territorial integrity or political independence of any other country."[17] The reference to military or naval forces and the boycott had been included in the Democratic bipartisan conference proposal that Hitchcock had submitted to Wilson, though it had been somewhat differently located. The words *by any other means* were new and became the focus of criticism.

"It is not a compromise, it is a surrender," said Hitchcock. Adding *by any other means* would eliminate every weapon under Article 10, he argued. Equally important, the influential Tom Walsh, a leading member of the bipartisan conference, agreed with Hitchcock and said that the Democrats would not accept just any verbal change in the second reservation, merely to save face.[18] Walsh's statement was ominous, for with but few exceptions the Republicans were not prepared to offer more than a mere verbal change. Compounding the difficulties for those seeking compromise, six strong reservationists immediately declared themselves against any change in the Lodge reservation. The six—Frelinghuysen, Wadsworth, Dillingham, Ball, Calder, and Sutherland—were soon joined by eight others, including the moderates Kenyon, Cummins, Capper, and Spencer.[19] Hitchcock secured twenty-eight signatures and promised others for a counterproposal. The Democrats would support either the bipartisan conference reservation or Taft's proposal, which the Democrats had also offered at the bipartisan conference. Since both had been publicly rejected before, there seemed little likelihood that these suggestions would provide a basis for agreement, as Hitchcock surely realized.[20]

17. Medill McCormick to Albert J. Beveridge, 17 February 1920, Beveridge Papers; *New York Tribune*, 12 February 1920.

18. *New York Times*, 12, 13 February 1920.

19. *New York World*, 13 February 1920; *New York Times*, 15 February 1920.

20. The Taft reservation stated: "The United States declines to assume any legal or binding obligation to preserve the territorial integrity or political independence of any other country under the provisions of article 10, or to employ the military or naval forces of the United States under any article of the treaty for any purpose; but the Congress, which under the Constitution has the sole power in the premises, will consider and decide what moral obligation, if any, under the circumstances of any particular case, when it arises, should move the United States, in the interest of world peace and justice, to take action therein, and will provide accordingly" (*CR* 66:2, p. 3176 [20 February 1920]); *New York Times*, 14 February 1920.

Briefly, the mild reservationists fell into disarray. McCumber, with some support from Colt, was ready to accept Hitchcock's proposal. McNary would consider it as a last resort, but only after all else failed. He said that the mild reservationists were pledged to the proposal they had drafted. Already, however, at the suggestion of Underwood, some of them were considering substituting *or its natural resources* for *by any other means*, to make the reservation slightly less offensive to Democrats but without suggesting an obligation. When the majority of the Republicans rejected Hitchcock's proposals at a party conference, they effectively restricted the area in which Lenroot and Kellogg, in particular, could operate. And the recalcitrance of the fourteen nonirreconcilable Republicans to any verbal changes meant that converts would have to be found on both sides of the aisle.[21]

President Wilson contributed to the polarizing tendency. On 13 February he fired Secretary of State Lansing, on the grounds that Lansing, without authorization, had convened meetings of the cabinet. To the public, as to senators, the action seemed petty and peevish.[22] The public might infer that these same qualities in Wilson were blocking the treaty ratification. Already on high ground politically, the Republicans could afford to stand firm. For the mild reservationist leaders, it would be that much harder to wring concessions from party colleagues.

Before the furor over Lansing subsided, newspapers carried the text of a note from Wilson to Italy, France, and Britain saying that the United States could not accept a proposed settlement of the Adriatic territorial dispute, since the settlement unduly advanced the interests of Italy at the expense of the new state of Yugoslavia. Wilson warned the Allies that if they proceeded on their course, the United States would no longer be able to concern itself with European affairs.[23] Wilson's position antagonized Italian-Americans and seemed to be yet another rash act. At the Capitol, amid fresh discussion of the president's condition, Republican congressmen offered legislation and a constitutional amendment on the subject of presidential disability. The Adriatic affair remained in the news for some time, a continuing drain on Democratic strength.[24]

---

21. *CR* 66:2, pp. 2950–53 (16 February 1920); *New York Tribune*, 15 February 1920; *New York Times*, 13 February 1920; *New York World*, 15 February 1920.

22. Bailey, *Great Betrayal*, 245–50; Raymond Clapper Diaries, entry for 14 February 1920, Clapper Papers.

23. *New York World*, 16 February 1920.

24. Duff, "Politics of Revenge," 226; *Portland Oregonian*, 19 February 1920; *New*

Wilson's actions, by weakening the Democrats, made it politically more feasible for the Republicans to stand on principle about Article 10. The mild reservationists, wanting the votes of the strong reservationists, had to take note. At the same time, the president gave the Democrats scant reason to make concessions. Hitchcock, in particular, drew away from mild reservationist proposals. The Lansing episode, he confided, had convinced him that he could not afford to yield much to the Republicans; Wilson was in no mood for concessions.[25] In rejecting the Republican proposal, and offering the Taft reservation or the Democratic bipartisan conference proposal, Hitchcock was subordinating ratification, which seemed hopeless, in favor of political advantage. That approach was reasonable under the circumstances, but it undermined those, in both parties, attempting compromise.

Between 16 February and 9 March, with some interruptions at the start but more steadily after 25 February, the Senate disposed of all the reservations except those on equal voting and Article 10. Given the dim prospects when senators began considering the reservations, politics loomed large in their deliberations. As a result, any opportunities for compromise on lesser reservations were lost, and behind-the-scenes negotiations on Article 10 became more difficult.

Hitchcock's motives were political, and his Wilsonian stance blocked compromise. Mild reservationists set out to pressure him or detach Democrats from him. But since they acted in concert with Lodge, who mainly remained cooperative, their own motives were suspect and they found it hard to build bridges across party lines. Yet many senators of both parties still wanted ratification. Periodically, as the Senate considered the reservations on the floor and in the cloakroom and corridors, they approached or reached agreements, and their hopes flared. Among the Republicans, mild reservationists led in pressuring Lodge for compromise and in seeking an agreement with the Democrats.

The events of 16 February foreshadowed a little of what lay ahead. McCumber, in what proved to be his last Senate speech on the

York World, 19, 20, 23, 27 February, 6 March 1920; Leon H. Canfield, *The Presidency of Woodrow Wilson: Prelude to a World in Crisis*, 258–59; Kellogg, in *CR* 66:2, pp. 3612–13 (28 February 1920).

25. Warren F. Kuehl, *Seeking World Order: The United States and International Organization to 1920*, 331. Kuehl cites Karger to Taft, 5, 20 February 1920, "Report of Conference with Senator Hitchcock," 29 February 1920, Hamilton Holt Papers, Mills Library, Rollins College; R. M. Boeckel, "Congress, the People, and the Presidency," *Independent* 101 (28 February 1920).

treaty, called for bipartisanship and declared himself willing to back either the Lodge reservation to Article 10 or one of the two offered by Hitchcock—the Democratic bipartisan conference proposal or the Taft reservation. He saw little difference in the three proposals. Colt agreed with him in his construction of the Taft reservation. But Lenroot opposed it as being subject to two interpretations and said that the Democrats, at the bipartisan conference, had refused to make clear that under the reservation there would be no obligation beyond congressional consideration of an act of aggression.[26]

Lenroot's was the more important viewpoint. Colt did not aggressively push his view thereafter, and McCumber left Washington the following day to be with his sick daughter, not returning until after the treaty battle was over.[27] Since McCumber was already somewhat isolated from his Republican colleagues on issues relating to the treaty, his continuing presence would not have mattered. Lenroot, on the other hand, was a recognized leader on the subject of the treaty, and he remained the most active of the mild reservationist leaders.

Lenroot was suspicious of Hitchcock's motives. The Democratic leader did nothing to lessen that suspicion when he presented the two Article 10 reservations, on behalf now of forty Democrats, and privately told Lodge that unless the Republicans accepted one of the two, or offered a new compromise of their own, it would be pointless to go on with the treaty. To the dismay of mild reservationists generally, he suggested to Lodge that the Senate take up the second reservation after finishing with the one on withdrawal, instead of moving the second reservation to the end of the list. The mild reservationists continued to hope that agreements on the other reservations, many of them softened since November, would pave the way for a settlement on Article 10.[28]

During the next few days, while the Senate put aside the treaty because of Lodge's minor illness, Hitchcock canvassed in vain among the mild reservationists for the votes that would produce a majority for one of his two Article 10 proposals. Prepared for failure in that attempt, he told reporters that the treaty would be a campaign issue

26. *CR* 66:2, pp. 2950–53 (16 February 1920).
27. McCumber announced that he would leave, and periodically thereafter McNary explained McCumber's absence and indicated how he would have voted (*CR* 66:2, p. 2950 [16 February 1920], p. 3242 [21 February 1920]).
28. *CR* 66:2, p. 2958 (16 February 1920); *New York Times*, 17 February 1920; *New York World*, 17 February 1920.

and that though the present Senate effort seemed doomed, ratification might occur afterward.[29] Then, on 20 February, he delivered a speech that blamed the Republicans for the likely ratification failure. In reply Lenroot, with the help of Kellogg, set out to show that Hitchcock had not been in the past and was not now a friend to ratification. Hitchcock's consistent purpose, Lenroot charged, had been "to pick off two or three or four Republicans in order to give that side a majority and put the onus on the Republican side for defeat of the treaty." Lenroot invited Democrats to break from Hitchcock and Wilson, to achieve ratification.[30]

That the remarks of Kellogg and, more fully, of Lenroot had political overtones of their own was obvious. Furthermore, they dovetailed with the developments at an informal Republican state convention in New York State. Elihu Root's speech, combined with a platform fashioned largely by Nicholas Murray Butler, laid down a line that most Republicans could comfortably adhere to in 1920. The platform called for ratification but with protective reservations, to Article 10 especially. Root urged a reform of the League charter after American entry, including a strengthening of the machinery for adjudication of disputes. Lodge, though differing with Root on some particulars, asserted that the New York party's position would be the national Republican position.[31]

Though Lenroot and Kellogg themselves served political ends, their positions and Hitchcock's differed. Hitchcock, constrained by Wilson, was seeking only a simple majority, as Lenroot charged. Kellogg and Lenroot, by contrast, were trying to bring together two-thirds of the senators. But whatever the motives of Lenroot, Kellogg, and their mild reservationist colleagues—and these were suspect among the Democrats—the possibility remained open for a successful coalition across party lines. Much would depend on patterns established in the Senate consideration of the first few reservations, on withdrawal, mandates, and domestic questions.

Action on the first of these proved unsatisfactory to mild reservationists and other friends of ratification and ultimately had serious

29. *New York World*, 18, 19 February 1920; *New York Times*, 19 February 1920. Hitchcock persisted in that view (*New York Tribune*, 27 February 1920; *New York Times*, 28 February 1920).

30. *CR* 66:2, pp. 3176–79 (20 February 1920).

31. *New York World*, 20, 21 February 1920; *New York Times*, 20, 21 February 1920; on Butler, a candidate for the Republican presidential nomination, see Butler to W. Murray Crane, 21 December 1919, and to James W. Wadsworth, Jr., 12 February 1920, Butler Papers, as well as Butler to Henry L. Stimson, 12 February 1920, Stimson Papers; *CR* 66:2, p. 3237 (21 February 1920).

consequences. One problem was that the bipartisan conference had reached no agreement on the subject. What Lodge offered was a change from the November reservation and was in some respects a concession, but not a wholly satisfactory one. It was one of three changes in the original reservations that Lodge himself had wanted. Whereas the old reservation had attempted to remove the president from the withdrawal process, the new one provided for two modes of withdrawal, by action of Congress or of the president. Though less offensive to Wilson than the original one, the new reservation was thought to make withdrawal easier, and for that reason McCumber objected to it before his departure.[32]

Hitchcock offered an amendment to require presidential assent to a congressional withdrawal resolution. It lost, 26–38. But Lodge, who had been attacked by his irreconcilable friend Brandegee for offering changes, foresaw defeat for his reservation at the hands of a coalition of irreconcilables and Democrats. Hoping to rally his forces later, he moved to adjourn. To Lodge's apparent consternation, the Senate voted him down and then rejected the main motion, 32–33. Quickly, with the irreconcilables making the difference, the Senate adopted the original Lodge reservation of November, 45–20.[33]

Just seven Democrats voted for Lodge's proposed compromise, and nine for his original reservation. None of them were major leaders. Most of the Democrats voted with Hitchcock. McCumber was announced as opposed to the modification, but no other middle grounders opposed it. They, with Lodge, suffered defeat in what was to have been the start of a process of compromise. If Lodge could not count on Democrats, he would have to rely again on irreconcilables to guarantee majorities for his reservations. Their price would be high, however, especially for the critical second reservation, and compromise with Democrats, to get the two-thirds for ratification, would be that much more difficult.

32. The original Lodge reservation provided for withdrawal by concurrent resolution, in theory avoiding the need for presidential assent. On second thought, however, Lodge and others came to feel that in a matter of foreign policy, a presidential signature would be needed, and Congress would need a two-thirds majority in both houses to override a veto. The new wording followed the language used in the Constitution in connection with constitutional amendments, which Congress alone proposed. McCumber objected to this feature of the new reservation, as well as to giving the president alone the power to give notice of withdrawal (*CR* 66:2, pp. 3257–59 [16 February 1920]; *New York Times*, 17 February 1920; *New York World*, 22 February 1920).

33. *CR* 66:2, pp. 3241–42 (21 February 1920); *New York World*, 22 February 1920.

Following the decision on withdrawal, the Senate had to put the treaty aside to consider the conference report on the railroad bill. In light of the outcome on withdrawal, especially the critical role of the irreconcilables in blocking change, some senators talked of delaying the treaty further, to take up other legislation, and pessimists saw no point in moving the second reservation from its normal order. Get on with it, they said.[34]

In actions that pleased the mild reservationists, on 24 February Lodge announced that he would call up the treaty in two days and would insist that it stay before the Senate until disposed of. And he persisted in the plan to move the Lenroot second reservation to the end of the list. Confiding to William Short a few days later, in words reminiscent of Colt's statement weeks earlier, Lenroot stated that Lodge had changed and now definitely wanted to ratify. Other mild reservationists shared the view, and the closest student of the matter judges that Lodge was sincere in seeking compromise and that he anticipated the possibility that Wilson would complete the ratification. Lodge would not, however, compromise away important national protections.[35]

Mild reservationists understood that they could not yield on principle on Article 10 and the Monroe Doctrine. Yet despite the unsatisfactory outcome on the withdrawal reservation, they saw some prospect of ratification. Some Democrats, led by the influential Furnifold Simmons, were calling for a party conference, to reconsider the party's course. Outside the Senate, the prestigious Herbert Hoover, who was rumored to be a possible presidential candidate for the Democrats, called for a prompt ratification with reservations. Hitchcock felt it necessary to warn Wilson, in a 24 February letter. He told of the "probability . . . that enough will surrender to send the treaty to you unless something can be done to regain some of them." He wanted Wilson to make it clear that he would not complete ratification on unsatisfactory terms. In an interview with Senator Glass, Wilson complied, briefly stemming the tide. At the same time, though, Wilson worsened his own situation, and gave fresh encouragement to Democratic dissidents, when he appointed Bainbridge Colby to succeed Lansing as secretary of state. Colby, a former Republican and former Bull Mooser, met widespread opposition

34. *New York Times*, 23 February 1920.

35. Ibid., 25, 27 February 1920; "Substance of an Interview with Senator Lenroot, 29 February 1920," in W. H. Short to A. Lawrence Lowell, 9 March 1920, Lowell Papers; *New York World*, 16 February 1920; William C. Widenor, *Henry Cabot Lodge and the Search for an American Foreign Policy*, 344–45.

among Democrats, who felt he had an uncertain temperament and limited international experience.[36]

On 26 February, having passed over the second reservation, the Senate adopted the third reservation by a vote of 68–4. The reservation, which was the same as in November and which had been agreed to by the Democrats at the bipartisan conference, said that the United States would accept no mandate except by act of Congress. One of the four to vote against the reservation was Tom Walsh. Walsh was surely correct in his contention that the reservation was unnecessary, that the United States could not become a mandatory except by act of Congress.[37] By the same token, though, the reservation was inoffensive in that it was merely interpretive. Walsh, whose influence was both recognized and enhanced by his earlier participation in the bipartisan conference, showed an ominous contentiousness in his vote and his explanation.

Discord among potential allies persisted as the Senate considered the domestic questions reservation. Debate ranged widely and extended from 26 February to 2 March. While the outcome was still in doubt, Hitchcock conferred at length with Borah. The Democrat wanted to know how much trouble the Republican irreconcilables would cause at the June party convention and in the campaign. A failure to ratify, and the projection of the League issue into the campaign, might not work wholly against the Democrats, he realized. The mild reservationists inferred an alliance between Hitchcock and Borah, and it complicated matters. They wanted to soften the domestic questions reservation but thought that they might be blocked by the Hitchcock-Borah coalition, as they had been on the withdrawal reservation. When they found Hitchcock uncooperative, instead of pushing for compromise they chose to, in the words of William Short summarizing Lenroot's position, "expose this relation between Hitchcock and Borah so fully as to make it impossible for Hitchcock to hold the Democratic Senators together in opposition to ratification of the amended Lodge reservations." They either would detach Democrats from Hitchcock or would bring sufficient pressure on him, through his party colleagues, to force him to compromise.[38]

36. *New York Times*, 24, 26, 29 February, 2, 7 March 1920; *New York World*, 18, 23, 24, 26 February 1920; *New York Tribune*, 24 February 1920; Hitchcock to Wilson, 24 February 1920, Tumulty Papers.

37. *CR* 66:2, pp. 3515, 3514 (26 February 1920).

38. *New York Times*, 29 February 1920; *New York World*, 29 February 1920; "Interview with Senator Lenroot," in W. H. Short to A. Lawrence Lowell, 9 March

On 26 February Lodge offered the first of two modifications to the domestic questions reservation, modifications that he understood the Democrats had favored at the bipartisan conference. It would insert the word *internal* before *commerce*, thus leaving the door open to international arbitration or Council consideration of disputes relating to foreign commerce. But when the Democrats, in the face of irreconcilable attacks, offered no defense for the modification, Lodge withdrew the proposal and a companion concession and reverted to the wording of November. Mild reservationists, aware that Hitchcock would offer an unacceptable substitute instead of supporting the modifications, made no protest.[39]

Hitchcock's substitute, the same as what he had offered in November, would apply not merely to the United States but to all members of the League. Without the preamble, which had accompanied it in November and which had made all reservations interpretive, the proposal seemed to be not a true reservation but an amendment. Kellogg attacked it as such and frankly impugned Hitchcock's motives. "I have believed for a long time that it was the intention of the Senator from Nebraska to defeat this treaty, to defeat it with Republican votes if he can, and with Democratic votes if he could not accomplish it in any other way." Bitterly, he congratulated Hitchcock and Borah on their new alliance.[40]

Before Hitchcock could formally offer his substitute, Democrat Duncan Fletcher of Florida, who was eager for ratification, offered an amendment to strike from the Lodge reservation the word *commerce*. When Hitchcock supported the proposal, Lenroot asked him whether he would support the reservation if it was amended in that way. Hitchcock admitted that he would not, though Hoke Smith, still a leader of Democratic dissidents, interjected, "Many of us will." Lenroot brushed that aside, saying he was asking Hitchcock. Hitchcock replied, "I decline at this time to publish a census of what the vote is going to be on this side." "Very well," said Lenroot. "I am only going to say a word. The Senate might as well understand that this is a part of a plan of the Senator from Nebraska to amend these reservations and then with the vote of the irreconcilables upon this side he expects to defeat the reservations entirely. For that reason I shall vote against the amendment proposed by the Senator from Florida." In the voting that followed, Republican lines held solidly

1920, Lowell Papers; Irvine Lenroot to William Kent, 6 March 1920, William Kent Papers, Sterling Library, Yale University.

39. *CR* 66:2, pp. 3515–17 (26 February 1920).

40. *Minneapolis Tribune*, 1 March 1920; *CR* 66:2, p. 3611 (28 February 1920).

against Fletcher's amendment, and it lost, 34–44. Under other circumstances, the mild reservationists would have been glad to have supported it. Hitchcock next improved on his original proposal, but too late. Following its defeat, by Republican votes, the Senate approved the original Lodge reservation, 56–25. Twelve Democrats broke from Hitchcock to vote for it, a number not sufficient to lend much encouragement to the mild reservationists, especially since none of the leaders were among the group.[41]

Prior to the voting on the domestic questions reservation, Borah and Brandegee met with Lodge and threatened to deny support for any modified reservations, especially on Article 10. They threatened also to prolong debate. Lodge conferred with Lenroot, Kellogg, and James Watson. Reportedly, they hoped to pacify the irreconcilables.[42] Though the character of subsequent proposals by Lodge showed that the irreconcilables did not get all that they wanted, evidently some deal was struck, probably on the Monroe Doctrine and Article 10, for the irreconcilables voted with Lodge not only on the domestic questions reservation but on all the reservations that followed. Although useful in some ways, this show of Republican unity also lessened the effect of mild reservationist attacks on Hitchcock and discouraged Democrats from breaking with him.

After adopting the domestic questions reservation, the Senate turned to the Monroe Doctrine and by a vote of 58–22 approved the original Lodge reservation, which said that the United States alone would interpret the doctrine. This time seventeen Democrats came over, and two absentees were counted as favorable. But none of the leaders did, and head-counters judged that at least twenty-seven Democrats would vote against ratification. Combined with Republican irreconcilables, this number was more than enough to encompass the treaty's defeat.[43]

The pattern of events varied somewhat as the Senate took up the sixth reservation, on Shantung, on 3 and 4 March. The Senate approved a bipartisan conference proposal, which eliminated specific reference to China and Japan. But Hitchcock opposed it and received fresh excoriation from Lenroot and Kellogg. As before, Lenroot challenged the Democrats to show the sincerity of their professed devotion to ratification, by supporting the modified reservation. Only ten did. Hitchcock foresaw considerable slippage on the final vote,

    41. *CR* 66:2, p. 3737 (2 March 1920).
    42. *New York World*, 1 March 1920; *New York Times*, 2 March 1920.
    43. *CR* 66:2, pp. 3731, 3748 (2 March 1920); *New York Times*, 3 March 1920; *New York Tribune*, 3 March 1920.

on ratification, but until then he hoped to hold his forces in line against even softened reservations. So far, he was succeeding.[44]

As of late February and early March, most senators saw little hope for ratification. The general conviction that the League was dead was supported by Wilson and Lodge's adamancy, reflecting in large part matters of high principle; by the politicization of the conflict; and by the destructive combination of the irreconcilables and Democrats, which contributed to disappointing results on the withdrawal reservation.[45] Yet among many senators, including the middle grounders, a strong desire for ratification remained, and a number of senators, Republican and Democrat, sought compromise. Capper and McNary remained cautiously optimistic, and Lenroot wrote a friend on 6 March: "There is . . . such a widespread revolt upon the part of a lot of good Democrats that Hitchcock at last has got badly scared. It may be we will still ratify the treaty."[46]

Though in general Lodge was able to maintain his position of leadership, when he strayed from the course of compromise, on the seventh reservation, eight middle grounders briefly broke with him. The reservation concerned U. S. representation on bodies created by the League, and initially, on 4 March, Lodge offered a short compromise version drawn by Tom Walsh and tentatively approved at the bipartisan conference. But when Hitchcock objected to it and noted that all the conference agreements were tentative, Lodge angrily withdrew the reservation and offered the longer and more explicit one of November. Walsh promptly moved his reservation as a substitute, and Lenroot defended Walsh's wording. Lodge said that he preferred the original, but Townsend praised the Walsh reservation and urged its adoption because of its origin in the bipartisan conference. Walsh, limiting his break with Hitchcock, limited also the extent of the middle grounders' rebellion when he said that he saw no need at all for a reservation on the subject. Lenroot rejoined that if Walsh would not support the modification that he himself had

44. *CR* 66:2, pp. 3793–802 (3 March 1920), pp. 3839–57 (4 March 1920); *New York World*, 26 February 1920; Kurt Wimer, "Senator Hitchcock and the League of Nations," 201.

45. On the general mood and the politicization of the issue, see *New York Times*, 2, 3 March 1920. On the view that the treaty had little chance, see the following: Henry Cabot Lodge to W. Cameron Forbes, 1 March 1920, and to Louis A. Coolidge, 3 March 1920, Lodge Papers; William Howard Taft to Horace Taft, 1 and 8 March 1920, Taft Papers; Frederick Hale to Nicholas Murray Butler, 6 March 1920, Hale Papers; Albert Cummins to Nicholas Murray Butler, 26 February 1920, Butler Papers.

46. *Kansas Farmer and Mail and Breeze*, 3 April 1920, in Homer E. Socolofsky, *Arthur Capper: Publisher, Politician, and Philanthropist*, 133; *New York World*, 4 March 1920; Lenroot to William Kent, 6 March 1920, Kent Papers.

drafted, then he, Lenroot, would support the original reservation of November. Walsh, explaining himself further, said that since no Republican had offered a reservation to Article 10 "expressing the views of the conference committee so far as they had reached an agreement," he felt no obligation to vote for any bipartisan conference agreements. Lodge then expressed dismay at the Democratic plan to oppose the bipartisan conference agreements and said angrily that he would offer no more of them, except for two that he himself favored. Kellogg quickly interjected that he might offer further changes in the November reservations, and Lenroot, to restore the *status quo ante* among Republicans, asked Lodge whether it was not true that each Republican member of the bipartisan conference stood ready to keep the tentative agreements. Lodge agreed that they were. But, given the statements of Hitchcock and Walsh, both Lenroot and Lodge voted against the Walsh substitute. It carried nevertheless, 37–32, as eight Republicans deserted Lodge—Cummins, Edge, Hale, Kellogg, Keyes, McNary, Townsend, and New. McCumber and Nelson were absent. The other middle grounders sided with Lodge, however, and the dissident middle grounders and Lodge very soon patched up their quarrel. The incident not only registered the pro-treaty feelings of middle grounders but also served notice on Lodge that he could not afford to concede too much to the irreconcilables.[47]

The minor rebellion was fueled, in part, by the fact of promising bipartisan negotiations on Article 10. Kellogg took the lead. He formulated a modification of the reservation and secured support for it from perhaps eight mild reservationists. He then presented it to Lodge, with the implicit threat of uniting with the Democrats if they would accept it and Lodge refused to. The new reservation omitted the open-ended phrase *by any means* and substituted more specific references, to *diplomatic pressures and financial resources* in clarifying the denial of obligation.[48]

Privately, Lodge expected no acceptance from Wilson or the Democratic leaders, but he found the reservation acceptable in principle and was willing to try to stir the restive Democrats to open rebellion. Without committing himself to the proposal he cooperated with Kellogg by authorizing Democratic soundings conducted by his trusted party whip James Watson, a skilled and amiable negotiator. Watson, in turn, passed it on to Furnifold Simmons, and

47. *CR* 66:2, pp. 3857–62 (4 March 1920); *New York World*, 6 March 1920.
48. *New York Times*, 7, 9 March 1920; *New York World*, 4 March 1920; *New York Tribune*, 2, 5 March 1920.

though negotiations were never completed, the proposal achieved some notoriety as the "Watson-Simmons proposal." Simmons, deeply involved earlier as part of the McKellar-Colt compromise group and then of the bipartisan conference, was to be a key figure on the Democratic side in the days that followed. A politician most of his life and a senator since 1901, the sixty-six-year-old North Carolinian was a Senate insider. Magnetic though quiet, he was respected for his intelligence and hard work. Long experience with tariff legislation had bred in him a pragmatic attitude toward issues, and he blended that with a spirit of optimism.[49]

To determine the president's attitude toward the Republican proposal, Hitchcock wrote Wilson asking that he see Simmons. He warned that Simmons might vote for the Lodge ratification resolution and that the Democrats could not afford to lose him. Offhandedly, Hitchcock added that Watson had talked with Simmons about a modification of the Article 10 reservation. "I doubt the good faith of the effort," Hitchcock added, "but I would like to have you discuss it with him."[50] Wilson was by then under strong pressure from party leaders and Democratic newspapers to compromise on Article 10 and settle the League question before the election. Nevertheless, he declined the gambit. Through a spokesman, he said that he had made his views known to Glass a few weeks earlier and that pressure should be brought on Lodge, not him. He would, however, complete the ratification if the bipartisan compromise reservation to Article 10 was adopted.[51]

Those senators most ardent for compromise and ratification persisted in their efforts, and on the Republican side, Lodge cooperated with the mild reservationists. Even before Wilson's rebuff to Simmons became known, Borah, Hitchcock and others had pressed for an immediate consideration of the second reservation. But Lodge adhered to the program, which the mild reservationists had favored, of acting on the lesser reservations first. After Wilson refused to invite Simmons, Lodge continued on that course.[52]

49. Lodge to Elihu Root, 6 March 1920, Root Papers; *New York Tribune*, 5 March 1920; *New York Times*, 5 March 1920; Richard L. Watson, Jr., "Furnifold M. Simmons: 'Jehovah of the Tar Heels,'" 166–87; *New York World*, 5 March 1920.

50. Hitchcock to Wilson, dated by the Library of Congress as 6 March 1920 but actually 5 March 1920 according to newspaper reports, Wilson Papers.

51. Bailey, *Great Betrayal*, 266; *New York World*, 3 March 1920; John M. Blum, *Joe Tumulty and the Wilson Era*, 238–39; Oscar Straus to Woodrow Wilson, 4 March 1920, Oscar S. Straus Papers, Library of Congress; *Milwaukee Sentinel*, 7 March 1920; *New York Tribune*, 7 March 1920.

52. *CR* 66:2, p. 3891 (5 March 1920), pp. 3952–53 (6 March 1920).

The action on reservations eight through thirteen, occurring between 5 and 8 March, evidenced the middle grounders' zeal for compromise and their willingness to pressure Lodge, or to act independently of him when necessary. Reservations eight, twelve, and thirteen were November carry-overs that had been agreed to at the bipartisan conference. Hitchcock, backed by most Democrats, refused to support them, but they carried nevertheless. They concerned the Reparations Commission, illegal acts in contravention of American rights, and the International Labor Organization. Townsend argued strongly for the first of these.[53]

On the ninth reservation, dealing with the expenses of the League and related agencies, Kellogg won the adoption of an amendment that had been approved at the bipartisan conference. And on the tenth reservation, relating to disarmament, Harry New, a member of the bipartisan conference, offered the reservation agreed to there. In an amended form, it won adoption. Only on the eleventh reservation, relating to the boycott, was there no effort to adhere to the bipartisan conference agreement.[54]

While the Senate acted on reservations eight through thirteen, offstage negotiations continued on Article 10. Although, in the wake of Wilson's refusal to see Simmons, no fresh discussions occurred across party lines, senators within each party talked earnestly. On the Democratic side Simmons, "vexed" at the rebuff from Wilson, worked on a counteroffer to the proposal that Watson had given him, in case one was necessary later. And Democrats, after conferring informally among themselves, implied that if they approved a reservation to Article 10, Wilson would also. On the Republican side, middle grounders led, as usual, in pushing for compromise. Lodge had not previously pledged himself to the Watson-Simmons proposal and had been erratic about the bipartisan compromise reservations. Feeling that it was time to brace him up once again, ten middle grounders met with him at his home on Sunday, 7 March, and secured a commitment to the reservation. McNary went so far as to say, afterward, that if that failed, the mild reservationists might join the Democrats and back the bipartisan conference reservation. For the moment, however, they planned to work not with Hitchcock but with other Democrats. Lenroot discounted the possibility that the mild reservationists would bolt to the Demo-

53. Ibid., 3885–93 (5 March 1920), pp. 4007–10 (8 March 1920).
54. Ibid., 3939–49 (6 March 1920), pp. 3955–57 (6 March 1920), pp. 4005–7 (8 March 1920).

crats. He was not sure what would be done but thought it certain that the Republicans would stick together. From the comments of McNary and Lenroot, it is clear that the mild reservationists were not in agreement on future contingencies. For the moment, however, in light of Lodge's willingness to test the Democrats, they could afford to await developments. McNary hoped to get the Democratic response by Tuesday, March 9.[55]

How the Democrats would have responded cannot be known, though senators later said that an agreement had been very near.[56] Alarmed at events, Wilson decisively intervened, sending to Hitchcock a letter that was quickly distributed among Democratic senators and reporters. Designed to prevent the Democrats from conceding too much on Article 10, the letter served to interrupt the negotiation then in progress and to inhibit Democrats in future negotiations. The letter reflected the effects of Wilson's continuing illness and isolation from affairs. He believed that a failure in March would be only temporary, that the 1920 election might become a referendum on the League, and that he could personally lead the crusade as a candidate for a third term. Baruch, Glass, and others, at a meeting in early March, agreed that Wilson was wrong, but none would confront him.[57]

Wilson's letter to Hitchcock was in preparation for some days. Conceived by some of Wilson's confidants as being helpful in securing an acceptable compromise on Article 10, it proved anything but. Focusing on Article 10, Wilson slapped at the Allies, especially the French, warning that any weakening of the article would open the door to imperialists, who remained ambitious, and to the old war-breeding game of the balance of power. The obligation under Article 10 was the heart of the League, was essential to a new world order, and was a debt owed the American soldiers and the people of the world. Wilson wrote that Watson's proposed reservation, disavowing obligation, would perpetuate the old order. Furthermore, he concluded, almost all of the proposed reservations constituted "a sweeping nullification of the terms of the treaty itself." In a gratuitous blow to the mild reservationists, Wilson attracted much attention when he wrote, "I hear of reservationists and mild reserva-

55. James E. Watson, *As I Knew Them: Memoirs of James E. Watson*, 196; *New York World*, 8 March 1920; *New York Tribune*, 8 March 1920.

56. *New York World*, 10 March 1920; *Portland Oregonian*, 9 March 1920.

57. *New York World*, 9 March 1920; Cary T. Grayson, *Woodrow Wilson: An Intimate Portrait*, 2d ed. (Washington: Potomac Books, 1977), 106, 114–17; Edward N. Hurley, *The Bridge to France*, 325–27.

tionists, but I cannot understand the difference between a nullifier and a mild nullifier."[58]

Wilson's stand, unchanged during the remaining days of the treaty fight, made ratification difficult. The high principle issue of a prior American commitment to repel aggression, blended with intense partisanship on both sides, as well as the constitutional problem of Congress's war-making power and the continuing resentment against Wilson for ignoring the Senate, proved to be unsurmountable obstacles for senators. Yet despite Wilson's words, a majority of Democrats and Republicans urgently wanted ratification, acknowledged the need for compromise, and ardently pursued it. Periodically, between 8 and 19 March, when the Senate took its last vote on the treaty, some senators and observers thought that ratification might yet succeed.

Despite Wilson's letter, on 9 March Democrat Robert Owen delivered a strong pro-compromise speech. He minimized the differences between the alternative reservations to Article 10, noted the strong public demand for ratification, disparaged the idea of a "solemn referendum," and complained that other issues, such as the cost of living, profiteering, and monopolies, would be neglected. The following day, Owen convened a meeting of about twenty like-minded Democrats, and they called in Hale to inform them of compromise prospects.[59]

Article 10 was more than ever the critical issue, but before the Senate could at last turn to that, it had to dispose of the fourteenth reservation, on equal voting. Though more important than any other reservation from the standpoint of international acceptance, and though still very ticklish politically, the equal-voting reservation was not of paramount importance to Wilson, so in the larger picture it appears as background to the Article 10 issue. Lodge offered a version of the November reservation, modified in accordance with his own ideas. The bipartisan conference participants had discussed and passed over the revised reservation, drawn by Lenroot, but had not returned to it before the conference broke up. Although the new wording embodied the principle of the Johnson six-vote amendment, it did not do so in a mandatory form. And a second modification softened the effect of the reservation, which

58. Albert Burleson to Joseph Tumulty, 5 March 1920, and [Tumulty] to Mrs. Wilson, 7 March 1920, Tumulty Papers; New York Times, 9 March 1920.
59. New York World, 11 March 1920.

Lodge had considered too drastic in its treatment of the British Empire. The new reservation still said that the United States would not be bound by decisions in which the British Empire cast more than one vote. But it qualified that with two stipulations: the refusal to be bound would not apply if the United States was granted six votes, an unlikely contingency; and it would not apply if Congress had previously given its consent.[60]

The concessions did not satisfy Hitchcock. Once more, the mild reservationists charged that Hitchcock was sabotaging ratification. In the vote that followed, seventeen Democrats made up part of the 57–20 majority for the reservation.[61] Considering the reservation's political attractiveness, and the fact that no leaders broke from Hitchcock, the vote marked neither a breakthrough nor an improvement in the atmosphere as the Senate at last took up the second reservation.

Much of the important action took place offstage during a turbulent week that culminated on 15 March with the adoption of a new Lodge reservation to Article 10. Lenroot and Kellogg took leading parts. They pressured Lodge, worked on reservation drafts, and in cooperation with Lodge, sought to secure the fullest Republican support for the new proposal. McNary too kept busy, principally in polling members and conducting some negotiations. And Elihu Root was drawn into the discussion on 9 March. He was in Washington to argue a case before the Supreme Court, and he served as a consultant after his return to New York. His influence was helpful to both the mild reservationists and Lodge. Root, in conference with Lodge, Watson, and Kellogg, approved the Watson-Simmons proposal on 9 March.[62]

In the face of strong pressure from irreconcilables, Lodge withdrew the offer the following day. Learning of it, Kellogg, Lenroot, and McNary confronted him, threatening a bolt of fourteen or fifteen Republicans to the Democrats on a mild Article 10 reservation. The mild reservationists, however, did not insist that Lodge continue to offer the Watson-Simmons proposal. At stake, they now realized, were the votes of several strong reservationists, notably Wadsworth, Frelinghuysen, Ball, Sutherland, and Dillingham, and

60. Lodge to James T. Williams, Jr., 20 December 1919, 2 February 1920, Lodge Papers; *CR* 66:2, p. 4010 (8 March 1920).

61. *CR* 66:2, pp. 4010–18 (8 March 1920), pp. 4055–65, 4067 (9 March 1920).

62. Stimson Diaries, entry for 13 March 1920, Stimson Papers; Kellogg to Root, 12 March 1920, and Root to Lodge, 11 March 1920, Root Papers; *New York World*, 10 March 1920; *New York Times*, 10 March 1920.

perhaps even a backsliding irreconcilable or two. They did insist that Lodge continue to offer verbal changes along lines calculated to have some appeal for Democrats. Lodge acquiesced and promised to introduce a new reservation.[63]

Lenroot and Kellogg may have been the principal authors of the new reservation.[64] Whatever the case, they and their colleagues approved it. As described by Kellogg to Root, it was the same reservation that Root had seen on the ninth but with the language of the first part transposed, thus restored in form to that of the original Lodge reservation instead of that advanced by the Democrats at the bipartisan conference and afterward.

On 12 March Lodge introduced the substitute.

The United States assumes no obligation to preserve the territorial integrity or political independence of any other country by the employment of its military or naval forces, its resources, or any form of economic discrimination, or to interfere in any way in controversies between nations, whether members of the league or not, under the provisions of article 10, or to employ the military or naval forces of the United States under any article of the treaty for any purpose unless in any particular case the Congress, which, under the Constitution, has the sole power to declare war or authorize the employment of the military or naval forces of the United States, shall, in the exercise of full liberty of action, by act or joint resolution so provide.[65]

Frelinghuysen leaped to the attack, followed soon by McCormick, Knox, Wadsworth, and Brandegee. Lenroot led in the defense of the new reservation, arguing that it did not leave any obligation but might nevertheless bring enough votes to achieve ratification. He appealed to the strong reservationists, who professed to support ratification, to approve the new reservation. Kellogg and Sterling supported him in debate.[66]

Afterward Kellogg conferred with Lodge, Lenroot, and others, then wrote and phoned Elihu Root. He painted an optimistic picture, claiming for the substitute reservation all the Republicans except the irreconcilables, Frelinghuysen, and possibly Wadsworth, and enough Democrats to win its approval. He foresaw thirty-four or

63. *New York World*, 11, 12 March 1920; *New York Times*, 11, 12 March 1920; Lodge to Elihu Root, 13 March 1920, Root Papers; Lodge to Louis A. Coolidge, 13 March 1920, Lodge Papers; *New York Tribune*, 12 March 1920; *Minneapolis Tribune*, 12 March 1920.

64. *Milwaukee Sentinel*, 10 March 1920; *Minneapolis Tribune*, 13 March 1920; Kellogg to Elihu Root, 12 March 1920, Root Papers.

65. *CR* 66:2, p. 4211 (12 March 1920).

66. Ibid., 4211–18 (12 March 1920).

thirty-five Republicans voting for ratification, "and we are assured that there are twenty-nine Democrats . . . and probably thirty." He wanted Root to write Wadsworth. He also wanted him to certify that the new reservation contained no obligation. Kellogg phoned Charles Evans Hughes with the same request.[67]

Root gave his approval to the reservation, since it was not unlike the original, but he declined to write Wadsworth. He did, however, permit Kellogg to quote him in conversation with Wadsworth and to show his letter to Lodge. In this letter written on 13 March, as in his phone conversation with Kellogg, Root stressed the point that the American people were accustomed to legislation being strangled by amendment in their legislatures. If ratification did not pass, he held, they would blame the reservationists. Kellogg chose not to use the various testimonials to the toughness of the substitute reservation, for the threat from the strong reservationists abated and there was great danger "of driving away Democratic votes." The change in the situation was due in part to events of 13 March.[68]

Wadsworth began a fresh attack on the Lodge substitute, with the argument that whereas the original Lodge reservation had left no doubt about obligation, the new one was subject to several constructions. The pro-League *New York Times* had that morning endorsed the reservation as acceptable, he noted, and the line of defense suggested by Lenroot and others on the previous day raised doubts. "I think it was intimated . . . that while this compromise reservation does not remove the obligation imposed by Article 10, it nevertheless withdraws all the means by which the obligation could be performed if it were assumed; in other words, that as this reservation provides that the United States does not promise or refuses to promise to use its Army or its Navy or its resources or a blockade in performance of its obligation, that in effect wipes out the obligation. But my questions is, does not the obligation still exist?" Some thought it did. The United States could still use the specified resources, despite the reservation, and in a crisis would be pressured to do so; the obligation would make it a matter of good faith. The reservation, Wadsworth argued, lacked candor. "It does not hit straight from the shoulder and deal with the obligation in the first instance and deal with it conclusively." It leaves, he said, an element of doubt.[69]

67. Kellogg to Root, 12, 18 March 1920, Root Papers.
68. Stimson Diaries, entry for 13 March 1920, Stimson Papers; Root to Kellogg, 13 March 1920, and Kellogg to Elihu Root, 18 March 1920, Root Papers.
69. *CR* 66:2, pp. 4233–34 (13 March 1920).

There was some merit in Wadsworth's criticism. The substitute reservation adhered to the formula proposed by the Democrats, at the bipartisan conference and before, of focusing principally on methods of implementation that would remain under the control of Congress, rather than directly and solely on the obligation itself. Lenroot saw the point but said that there was more to the reservation. Why, he asked, did Wadsworth omit reference to the phrase whereby the United States refused to interfere in controversies between nations? "Can the Senator imagine any case of external aggression that we would get into that did not involve a controversy between nations?" Wadsworth replied that the position of the phrase still left him in doubt as to its meaning.

Borah then proposed the addition of a clarifying phrase. Article 10, he explained, made no reference to controversies between nations; that phrase came from the original Lodge reservation. He proposed to use language showing "that it refers to the same kind of controversies which article 10 covers." Specifically, he would add, after *controversies between nations*, the explanatory phrase *including all controversies relating to territorial integrity or political independence*. Lenroot said, "I see no objection to it."[70] The concession, though seemingly made offhandedly, was important. It is not reasonable to believe that Lenroot acted solely on his own. That night Lodge, delighting in the turn of events, explained that Borah had asked for additional words, which Lodge construed as not changing the substance of the reservation. He added, "Lenroot and all the 'mild nullifiers,' as Wilson kindly calls them, agreed to it." They felt, as Lodge did, that the addition merely elaborated the clear meaning of the reservation.[71]

Borah, Wadsworth, Frelinghuysen, and one or two others quickly huddled outside the chamber, framed the amendment, and agreed to support the reservation as amended. Lodge promptly introduced the new wording. The modification paved the way for a full Republican reunion behind the second reservation and guaranteed its adoption. Although the danger of schism at the party convention and afterward was not eliminated, it was lessened. "All is now well," Lodge wrote four days later. "We are all reunited. . . . They must either take it with my reservations or reject it,—a situation which I managed to bring about before and have brought about again."[72]

70. Ibid., 4264–65 (13 March 1920).
71. Lodge to James T. Williams, Jr., 13 March 1920, Lodge Papers; *Portland Oregonian*, 14 March 1920.
72. *Milwaukee Sentinel*, 14 March 1920; *New York World*, 14 March 1920; *CR*

The mild reservationists, remembering the defeat of the withdrawal reservation through irreconcilable votes, were not unconcerned about getting the support of the irreconcilables for the reservation. But for them the principal gain was the recovery, for the cause of ratification, of from two to five senators whose votes had seemed in doubt—Wadsworth and Frelinghuysen, and perhaps Ball, Sutherland, and Dillingham. Their votes could hardly be spared, polls of senators showed. To be sure, as of 12 March Kellogg had judged that only the votes of Wadsworth and Frelinghuysen were questionable. But fresh doubts about the others had arisen since then, and in any event, even one of the two votes could prove decisive.[73]

But the price of the deal was high, probably too high. Simmons, the most important of the Democratic compromisers, either had not been consulted or, if he had been, had seen his advice ignored. He reacted with despair and some bitterness. "I have been studying the story of the treaty from the time it came to the Senate until the present moment," he told reporters the following day. "It looks now as if the Republican leaders were determined from the beginning to kill the treaty by indirect means." Simmons rehearsed the story of the bipartisan conference, when the Republicans had drawn back at the last moment from accepting a compromise on Article 10. Leaping ahead to the events of the thirteenth, Simmons said: "We were polling the Senate on the Lodge substitute for the original reservation on Article 10. But before we knew what could be done we were confronted with an amendment to it which made it worse than the first one."[74] Other Democrats, men who had been ready to compromise, denounced the change, some saying that it would destroy the whole force of the League and that the irreconcilables had proposed it for that purpose.[75]

An unstated but important feature of the problem was this: until the acceptance of the Borah proposal, the Republicans had sought Democratic support on the basis of compromise. Each side would make concessions to the other, and each would supply for the reser-

66:2, pp. 4265, 4273 (13 March 1920); Lodge to Louis A. Coolidge, 17 March 1920, Lodge Papers.

73. *New York Tribune*, 11 March 1920; *New York Times*, 12 March 1920; Kellogg to Elihu Root, 12 March 1920, Root Papers.

74. *New York World*, 15 March 1920; *New York Times*, 15 March 1920. Simmons had received a letter from Wilson explaining why he had declined to see him (Wilson to Simmons, 11 March 1920, Wilson Papers). The letter may have helped to deflect Simmons's ire to the Republicans.

75. *Providence Sunday Tribune*, 14 March 1920; *New York World*, 14 March 1920.

vation, and ultimately for ratification, about the same number of votes, ranging from thirty to thirty-five.[76] The irreconcilables, mainly Republicans, would not be counted on. The Republicans would have some partisan advantage, since their leader, Lodge, would be party to the agreement while Hitchcock would not, and the Democrats would risk a damaging rebuff from Wilson. Even so, the deal would have enough bipartisan flavor to let the Democrats claim a share of the credit. Mild reservationist accommodation to the irreconcilables drastically changed that situation. As Lodge boasted, the Republicans were reunited. But for the Democrats, it was a matter not of compromise but surrender.

Though the prospect of ratification seemed to lessen rather than improve after the concession to Borah as Democrats fell away, the mild reservationists' deal with Borah and his strong reservationist allies was not wholly responsible. Hitchcock continued to believe that following the rejection of the treaty in March, the Republicans, in four or five weeks, would make satisfactory concessions, to keep the issue out of the campaign. Consoled by that idea, he declined to join with those who would act on their own while counting on Wilson to approve afterward. Instead, Hitchcock continued to seek Wilson's prior approval for each significant proposal. And so he sent the president a copy of the Lodge substitute, not yet amended, with the comment, "I assume you would not accept it." Wilson returned the letter with the penned reply at the bottom: "You are quite right. W.W." Hitchcock, Swanson, and Underwood spread the word among Democrats before the vote on the reservation.[77]

Furthermore, even before the Borah amendment, Democratic support for the Lodge reservation was uncertain. Some of the Simmons men complained that they had not been involved in drafting it and that it was not as satisfactory as the Watson-Simmons proposal. Other Simmons men revealed to reporters that their support was not firm but was conditional on the likelihood of ratification. Some Democrats privately explained the situation. The Democratic national convention would endorse Wilson and his administration. It would be embarrassing to have voted for a resolution that Wilson did

76. In transmitting the Lodge reservation to Wilson, before the Borah amendment had been incorporated or Wilson had commented on it, Hitchcock predicted that twenty-nine Democrats and thirty Republicans would vote for it and that the vote on ratification would be the same (Hitchcock to Wilson, n.d. [12 March 1920], Hitchcock Papers).

77. Allan Nevins, *Henry White: Thirty Years of American Diplomacy*, 482; Hitchcock to Wilson, n.d. [12 March 1920], Hitchcock Papers; *New York Times*, 13–16 March 1920; *New York Tribune*, 13, 14 March 1920.

not want and would clearly repudiate. And it would be calamitous to have done so if Wilson was to be nominated for a third term, as they admitted was quite possible. This was an argument Hitchcock had been making for some time.[78]

Before adjourning on the thirteenth, a Saturday, the senators agreed to limit debate and also to vote on the second reservation on 15 March. The intervening Sunday was hardly enough time to patch up partisan wounds and fabricate a new compromise. Thus the Senate acted predictably that Monday. After the senators rejected an extreme formulation by Frelinghuysen, to renounce military or financial obligations under any article of the treaty, they rejected several proposals offered by Democrats, including Simmons, on the grounds that these recognized obligations under Article 10. Finally, they approved the Lodge reservation by a vote of 56–26. The Republicans maintained a solid front except on the Frelinghuysen motion, and on that the middle grounders voted solidly in opposition. Lenroot led in opposing all the alternatives to the Lodge reservation.[79] McCumber was still away, and Kellogg reported Nelson as ill. Neither Nelson nor McCumber participated in any of the debate or voting in the days that followed.

Among the motions that the Republicans defeated was one by Tom Walsh. To be added at the end of the Lodge reservation, this would have expressed the U. S. concern about aggression that menaces world peace and the country's willingness to cooperate with others to end that menace. It was drawn, Walsh said, on the basis of remarks made by Knox on 6 November. Lenroot, though not opposed to the substance of Walsh's motion, tried to draw from him some comment on whether its adoption would bring him and his associates to support the reservation as amended and then ratification. When Walsh declined to make any promises, Lenroot opposed the motion, and it failed. As events showed, however, Lenroot and other mild reservationists found in Walsh's idea a possible peace offering to the Democrats.

The Lodge reservation was supported by only fourteen Democrats, far fewer than would be needed for ratification. Simmons and Owen, as well as George Chamberlain, all apostles of compromise, voted against it. Afterward, most senators predicted the rejection of the treaty. Still, senators realized that some Democrats, although

78. *New York World*, 13 March 1920; *New York Times*, 14 March 1920; *New York Tribune*, 15 March 1920; William Short, "Conference with Senator Hitchcock, 29 February 1920," Lowell Papers.
79. *CR* 66:2, pp. 4317–33 (15 March 1920).

reluctant to oppose Wilson more than was necessary, would break to the Republicans on the final vote. McNary thought that the Democratic break would be decisive.[80]

Pessimism predominated, and with it came intensified partisanship. Thus in the days after the adoption of the new Lodge reservation, senators gave only limited and bored attention to the further discussion of Article 10. As they took up additional reservations, they saved their emotion for those that had the greatest political punch, especially the Irish independence reservation drawn by Democrat Peter Gerry of Rhode Island. On balance, the middle grounders led in resisting further encumbrances to the resolution of ratification.

First came a proposal by Owen for construing the treaty's reference to the British protectorate in Egypt as recognizing merely a war measure "to preserve the integrity and independence of Egypt during the war." Shields made the issue more political with an amendment in favor of Irish independence. Sterling, Kellogg, Townsend, and Kenyon spoke in opposition to the Owen motion, the Shields amendment, or both. The debate spilled over to a third day, 17 March, when Kellogg led the criticism. On his motion, the Owen reservation and two amendments to it were collectively tabled, 54–21. The middle grounders, except for Jones, voted with the majority or not at all. Swiftly, the Senate then defeated anticolonial proposals by Reed and Norris.[81]

The senators then turned, all too briefly, to a more serious and potentially much more important proposal. Several weeks earlier Lenroot had drawn a reservation declaring future American policy toward Europe, along the lines of several Knox proposals made in 1919. Kellogg and some other mild reservationists had given their approval. When Tom Walsh had proposed his similar amendment of the fifteenth, Lenroot had questioned Walsh's seriousness of purpose and had led in its rejection. But afterward he, McNary, and Kellogg had decided that to appease the Democrats and vitiate the isolationist tendency of the second reservation, Lenroot should offer the new reservation. Late on 16 March he presented it, to be considered the next day.[82]

80. Ibid., 4333 (15 March 1920); *New York World*, 16 March 1920; *Minneapolis Tribune*, 16 March 1920; *New York Times*, 16 March 1920; *Portland Oregonian*, 16 March 1920; *New York Tribune*, 15 March 1920.
81. *CR* 66:2, pp. 4334–36 (15 March 1920), pp. 4378–79, 4386, 4389 (16 March 1920), pp. 4442–48 (17 March 1920).
82. *New York World*, 16 March 1920; *Portland Oregonian*, 16 March 1920.

Lenroot's proposal stated, "It shall be the declared policy of this government that the freedom and peace of Europe being again threatened by any power or combination of powers, the United States will regard such a situation with grave concern and will consider what, if any, action it will take in the premises." The words *grave concern* conveyed deep significance in diplomatic usage, a Republican senator told the *Portland Oregonian*. The reservation, he thought, would deter aggression in Europe and would reassure France. Lenroot, also commenting to reporters on his proposal, said that it coincided with Tom Walsh's construction of the Taft reservation; that is, it asserted an internationalist policy, without stating a prior commitment to anything more than the consideration of matters arising under Article 10.[83]

On the floor the next day, Lenroot further explained his reservation, trying to win over Democrats. But John Sharp Williams ridiculed the reservation as contrary to the idea of collective security, and senators gave it only limited attention, some of them discussing procedure by which action on the treaty might be hastened.[84] Very soon the senators voted, rejecting the proposal, 25–39. Its defeat came at the hands of irreconcilables and Democrats. Under other circumstances, Lenroot's reservation might have proved useful. But coming so soon after the failure to achieve bipartisan agreement on Article 10, and with little or no prior discussion with Democrats, it did not appease them. For his part, Simmons's hopes rested with Article 10 amendments, to be considered the next day when the reservations moved from Committee of the Whole into the Senate.[85]

On 18 March a long day of Senate business began with Reed's reservation to exempt from pacific settlement procedures matters of national honor and interest. The reservation had been an issue of great contention in the November proceedings, when internationalists such as Taft had denounced it as crippling to the most useful parts of the Covenant. It now received cursory attention. Quickly voted down, 27–48, the reservation was supported by several moderates but by none of the mild reservationists. The latter also opposed another Reed reservation, which stated, "The United States as-

83. *CR* 66:2, p. 4458 (17 March 1920); *Portland Oregonian*, 17 March 1920; *New York Times*, 17 March 1920.

84. Lenroot, seeing the need for more time, objected to a waiver of the rule that the resolution of ratification move to the day following its presentation (*CR* 66:2, pp. 4458–63 [17 March 1920]).

85. *CR* 66:2, pp. 4464, 4462 (17 March 1920).

sumes no obligation to employ its military or naval forces or resources under any article of the treaty." It lost, 16–57.[86]

In contrast to the desultory action taken on the Lenroot and Reed reservations, the Senate engaged in four hours of spirited debate on the Gerry reservation. Introduced the previous day by the Rhode Island Democrat, it expressed adherence to the principle of self-determination, urging self-government for the Irish and then the prompt admission of Ireland to the League. Clearly political, the reservation reflected the dimness of ratification prospects and the resultant willingness of senators to play politics with the treaty. On balance, observers saw the reservation as destructive, and most middle grounders opposed it, with Kellogg, Sterling, and Townsend speaking strongly against it. Nevertheless, the Senate approved the reservation, 38–36. Of the middle grounders, only Capper, Colt, Jones, McLean, and McNary voted "yea." Kellogg gave notice that he would ask for a separate vote in the Senate.[87]

After the quick defeat of a Gore reservation, Cummins, the president *pro tempore*, declared that there were no further reservations or amendments and that the treaty was now in the Senate. One reservation had been reserved for a separate vote. At the suggestion of Underwood, the rest were to be voted on en bloc, by voice vote. But after the request of the absent and ill Simmons was conveyed by Hoke Smith, Lodge agreed to a reconsideration of the second reservation, to Article 10, and the fourth reservation, on domestic questions.[88]

The senators were determined to get the treaty into shape for final action the next day, and they pressed on through the evening. Quickly they disposed of the fourth reservation, tabling Smith's motion to strike the word *commerce*. No Republican broke ranks. With Simmons still absent, but said to be on the way, the senators turned to the fifteenth reservation, Gerry's. After opponents failed in several efforts to amend, the Senate adopted the reservation,

86. Ibid., 4497–98 (18 March 1920).

87. *CR* 66:2, pp. 4498, 4501, 4506, 4522 (18 March 1920). It is hard to explain the votes of Colt and McNary except in political terms. Colt would not be up for reelection until 1924, and at his age he might not have wanted it. But to oppose the pro-Irish reservation of his Democratic colleague from Rhode Island would have been a grave disservice to his party in the state, where Irish-Americans were numerous. McNary's problem was less severe, but he did, on more than one occasion, tell the strong reservationist Warren Harding that Harding's stand on the treaty met with approval in Oregon (Harding to C. M. Idleman, 2 March 1920, Harding Papers).

88. *CR* 66:2, pp. 4522–24 (18 March 1920).

45–38. The middle grounders voted as they had the day before.[89] Now the Senate took up the second reservation. It was the last chance to secure a compromise. Simmons, still ill but back in the Senate, passionately argued for amendments to the Lodge reservation. In a bored manner Republicans, including the middle grounders, held firm. They were fortified by a letter written by Lowell in support of the Lodge reservation and made public by David Walsh shortly before debate began on the reservation.[90]

Simmons offered a substitute reservation, the same one that had been defeated earlier, as a vehicle for discussing the Lodge reservation amendments that he would soon offer. The changes he called for seemed relatively modest, and as he viewed it, they promised to win the support of Wilson. Simmons thought that the president objected to "the broad proposition that the government shall not interfere in any way whatever with controversies between other nations unless Congress so provides." The Lodge reservation, in disavowing an obligation to preserve territorial integrity, referred to specific means—the use of the armed forces, resources, and boycott. But it was not similarly specific about interference in controversies between nations. Simmons would render the second disavowal specific, like the first, in effect leaving the door open to interference through diplomacy. Lenroot debated Simmons, inconclusively, but Lodge got to the nub of the matter when he said that the Senate was impatient to vote on the reservation. He added, "It is a reservation which, if reopened, would lead to endless debate, and unquestionably to defeat of the treaty." He went on to note a difference, which Simmons had not mentioned, between his reservation and Simmons's. He moved to table Simmons's reservation, and the Senate complied, 45–34.[91]

Simmons turned to the amendments that he hoped to secure in the Lodge reservation. With reference to the phrase *or to interfere in any way in controversies between nations*, he moved to strike *in any way* and substitute *by the employment of its military or naval forces, its resources, or any form of economic boycott*. He said that he wanted changes that would let him vote for the reservation. As it now stood, he could not "because I think the substitute of the Senator is nothing more than that we shall not interfere in any contro-

89. Ibid., 4528, 4531–32 (18 March 1920).
90. *New York Times*, 19 March 1920; *CR* 66:2, pp. 4513–14, 18 March 1920.
91. *CR* 66:2, pp. 4332–34 (18 March 1920).

versy whatever in any way whatsoever, even by the exercise of our good offices, unless the Congress shall first so provide." That went too far, he said. His amendment, if accepted, would do much toward removing his objection to the reservation. "I would then very seriously consider whether I would vote for the resolution of ratification," he promised.[92]

Torn, Simmons castigated but also cajoled. Bitterly, he said, "Of course, I know that my appeal to the Senator will fall upon deaf ears." Twice he had thought an agreement had been reached, and each time the irreconcilables had interfered and Lodge had "lost his courage." The Republicans, he asserted, were bound "by reasons of an iron-bound agreement of some sort, which they solemnly entered into at the very inception of this controversy." Yet he renewed his appeal to Republican reservationists to break loose from the irreconcilables and make it possible for him to vote for ratification. Lodge, standing on principle, rejected the appeal, and his motion to table carried, with the support of all Republicans present. Hoke Smith then moved to strike *or interfere in any way in controversies between nations, including all controversies relating to territorial integrity or political independence, whether member of the League or not.* He did not himself regard the words to be of great importance, Smith said, but some Democrats did. Lodge, however, thought that many Republican votes would be lost if the words were struck. Again he moved to table, and again he won with solid Republican support.[93]

At last the Senate voted on the reservation, unchanged in any way, and approved it, 54–26. The motion was not supported by Simmons, Tom Walsh, McKellar, Underwood, Swanson, or any other Democratic leader.[94] Simmons oversimplified to the point of distortion when he described the Republicans as bound from the first to the irreconcilables. But it was important that he believed this.

Action on reservations and amendments was completed. Noting that the resolution of ratification could not be acted upon until a subsequent day, Lodge said that the Senate must adjourn. Further, he asked for unanimous consent to set a vote on the resolution of ratification for three o'clock the next afternoon. Lenroot objected. Lodge urged that some time be set, since many senators had important engagements outside Washington. But Lenroot objected to fix-

92. Ibid., 4532–34 (18 March 1920).
93. Ibid., 4534–36 (18 March 1926).
94. Ibid., 4536 (18 March 1920).

ing any time. He agreed to limiting speeches to an hour, but though pressed by several irreconcilables, he would go no further. With that, the Senate adjourned, to meet again at eleven the following morning.[95]

On the surface, the unwillingness of mild reservationists to break party ranks in order to woo Simmons bespoke partisanship fanned by pessimism about ratification prospects. Lenroot's objection to fixing a time for a final vote contrasts with that impression, suggesting some lingering hope. Indeed, some reservationists remained cautiously hopeful, and their hopes related in a complementary way to their action, or inaction, on Article 10. The thought was that Democrats might record themselves as on the side of Wilson and Hitchcock in the initial vote on ratification, but that after a Democrat moved to reconsider, and after the motion won with the help of mild reservationists, enough Democrats to accomplish ratification would switch on a second vote.[96]

To be sure, such a second vote switch would have been facilitated, or even made unnecessary, by granting some concessions to Simmons. That course, though, was not then practical. Strong reservationists of the Frelinghuysen-Wadsworth type had already conceded more than they liked, in approving an Article 10 reservation that differed from the formulation of November. Others, including such staunchly anti–Article 10 moderates as Cummins, agreed with them. Furthermore, the party had united, with some difficulty, on the new Lodge reservation. Any change in it would have been politically disruptive. Finally, the party's program of reservations met with widespread public approval, as stated by Lodge in debate and as supported by Harding's recent soundings of the public while he was on the presidential stump.[97] Any last-minute attempt to deviate from the program would surely have caused aggravation among Republican senators, as well as repercussions in the voting. An earlier rapprochement with Simmons might have been wise, but as of 18 March, concessions entailed great risk. The mild reservationists' failure to make them bespoke neither an abandonment of hope nor a full politicization of the issue.

On 19 March, as the Senate, with some relief, came to what most

95. Ibid., 4536–38 (18 March 1920).
96. Frank Kellogg to Elihu Root, 18 March 1920, Root Papers; *New York Times*, 17 March 1920; *Portland Oregonian*, 17 March 1920; *Providence Evening Tribune*, 19 March 1920.
97. Harding to J. S. Aydelott, 17 March 1920, Harding Papers.

presumed to be the end of the prolonged struggle, ratification seemed unlikely but not impossible. Speeches rarely make a difference, but on occasion, when some votes are in doubt, they can. On this day a few of them almost did. Tom Walsh, in particular, gave powerful aid to the cause of ratification. The treaty met defeat nevertheless, and though the anticipated reconsideration ploy was tried, it failed. Not presuming the outcome, however, proponents and opponents of the Lodge resolution of ratification geared for battle. Bryan had been in Washington for a few days, but his intervention was ineffective. A pro-ratification statement by Herbert Hoover, together with fresh newspaper endorsements for the Lodge resolution, carried more weight. On the other side, Postmaster General Albert Burleson and Secretary of the Navy Josephus Daniels appeared at the Capitol early in the afternoon, representing the president in opposing the Lodge resolution.[98]

As though to underline the uncertainty and importance of the matter, spectators filled the galleries, and House members stood in the rear of the chamber. While the speakers held the floor, for almost seven hours, groups of senators conferred frequently, and rumors of Democratic defections kept bobbing up, only to be squashed and replaced by new rumors.[99] Irreconcilables and administration Democrats, anxious to get on with the vote, took little part in the speechmaking; the proponents of ratification, chiefly Democrats, talked the most.

The first order of business was the adoption of a new preamble or, more properly, resolving clause. Lodge had announced his proposal the day before, as the rules required. Though it was different and, on balance, was more satisfactory to the Democrats than the preamble of November, it occasioned no surprise, since the change had been anticipated since December.[100] The new proposal eliminated the requirement of acceptance by note from three of the four Great Powers. Instead, silent acquiescence was deemed acceptable, though needed from all the signatories. This was one of the changes that Lodge himself had wanted, and its advocacy by Root and Britain's Lloyd George gave him further reason to make it.[101]

98. *New York Times*, 19 March 1920; *New York World*, 19, 20 March 1920; Walworth, *Wilson*, 2:393.

99. *New York World*, 20 March 1920.

100. More recently, during debate on the fourteenth reservation, Lenroot had said that the preamble would be changed (*CR* 66:2, p. 4059 [9 March 1920]).

101. *CR* 66:2, p. 4567 (19 March 1920); Lodge to F. H. Gillett, 26 July 1920, Lodge Papers; Philip C. Jessup, *Elihu Root*, 408; Julius W. Pratt, *America and World Leadership, 1900–1921*, 210.

Brandegee offered an amendment that would require the instrument of ratification to be filed within sixty days of the adoption of the resolution of ratification; if not filed in that time, the ratification would be voided. In the face of a technical objection, he changed the period to ninety days. Nevertheless, his amendment failed, 41–42.[102]

Lenroot began the formal speechmaking with what was one of the more notable and noticed speeches of the day. Talking at some length, and with some passion, he updated his effort of 19 November. Lenroot reviewed and defended the reservations, pointed to the Covenant's good features that remained unimpaired, and deplored the prospect of a year's delay in consummating peace. Recognizing the charge that the reservations of November required the votes of irreconcilables for adoption, he noted that except for the reservation to Article 10, all the reservations were supported by majorities that favored ratification. He failed to note, however, that the votes of irreconcilables for the reservations made the support of dissident Democrats superfluous.[103] Throughout his speech, implicitly and explicitly, he warned the Democrats of the political consequences of attempting Wilson's solemn referendum. Lenroot's speech was chiefly significant as a powerful example for Democrats of what might be expected in the campaign if ratification failed through their votes.[104]

Soon it was Tom Walsh's turn. A leader among the Democrats, by force of mind, character, energy, and experience, Walsh had periodically sought compromise, as in the bipartisan conference, but had just as often drawn back, remaining an administration man. He had not been among those to vote with the Republicans for the new set of reservations. What he said could make a difference, and nearly the whole Democratic membership, including all those classified as wavering or doubtful, listened closely.[105] Most significant, he came out strongly for ratifying with the new "Lodge reservations" as the lesser evil. But in the study of the treaty's defeat in the Senate and of

102. Of the Republicans, only Cummins, Jones, and Townsend voted against Brandegee's amendments; McCumber and Nelson were still absent and not voting (*CR* 66:2, pp. 4569–74 [19 March 1920]).

103. See the table in W. Stull Holt, *Treaties Defeated by the Senate: A Study of the Struggle Between President and Senate Over the Conduct of Foreign Relations*, 295.

104. *New York Times*, 20 March 1920; *New York World*, 20 March 1920; *CR* 66:2, pp. 4574–78 [19 March 1920]. Lodge's secretary later recommended Lenroot's speech for campaign use (C. F. Redmond to Samuel McCune Lindsey, 30 July 1920, Lodge Papers).

105. *New York World*, 20 March 1920; *New York Times*, 20 March 1920.

the role of the mild reservationists, Walsh's comments on that faction are of special interest.

Early on, he jibed at Republicans generally and reservationists in particular. Republicans, in the main, had criticized the Covenant more than they had praised it, he said. Insofar as reservationist Republicans would take joy at ratification, it would be due mostly to "a supposed party victory." They had shown no disposition, he thought, to altering the form of reservations to make them less objectionable to Wilson. Walsh then turned to the solemn referendum idea and demonstrated its impracticability. His party would need to capture at least fourteen Republican seats; there would be many issues in the campaign, not just the League; and the Democrats, unjustly to be sure, were vulnerable on some of these, such as extravagance, incompetency, and presidential autocracy. And while the United States delayed, the League plan might fail in the face of world disorder.

Soon Walsh resumed his excoriation of the Republicans, including the mild reservationists. He rehearsed the past failures to compromise, showing that little could be hoped for in the way of concessions should ratification fail that day. Following the treaty's defeat in November, Walsh said, Democratic conciliation efforts had all met the demand that "Lodge should approve and participate." He reviewed the failure of the bipartisan conference, including the irreconcilables' ultimatum to Lodge, and said, "Apparently the so-called mild reservationists would not proceed without the concurrence of the Senator from Massachusetts, and the Senator from Massachusetts found himself obliged to conform to the counsel or advice of the irreconcilables." Afterward, Republican disappointment at the collapse of negotiations "was neither widespread nor poignant." On balance, public opinion after November had induced Democrats to accept the "Lodge reservations" but had not caused Republicans "to yield in any degree with respect to the same." This, he thought, was because the Democrats really favored the League, whereas only an "insignificant few" Republicans did, the remainder being hostile or indifferent. The situation would not change, he predicted.

Turning away from the partisan aspects of the issue, Walsh argued that although Article 10 was virtually destroyed by the reservation, there was much more to the Covenant than Article 10. He himself had in the past attributed too much importance to that article. In particular, he extolled the pacific settlement articles. He developed the point that any violation of Article 10 would also violate articles 12 and 15 and would bring into play the penalties of Article 16.

Explaining his consistent opposition to the "Lodge reservations," he said that his chief objection, and that of other Democratic senators, was that the reservations asked for special privileges for the United States. But he yielded his judgment to the majority on that and, having done so, found the path of duty clear.[106]

Walsh's attacks on the Republicans, including the mild reservationists, may be seen as compensatory partisanship to soften the political effect of his dramatic rebellion against Hitchcock and Wilson. But one detects conviction too, suggesting the possibility of an earlier failure on the part of the mild reservationists—a failure to overcome the partisan cast of the negotiations and to break through on a personal basis to men like Walsh and Simmons. Of more immediate importance, some senators saw in Walsh's passionate speech the possible start of a stampede. The impression was heightened when, much more briefly than Walsh but no less ardently, another administration loyalist, Joseph Ransdell of Louisiana, announced that he would vote for ratification. Ransdell, who had opposed all the reservations, said that much good remained in the Covenant and that if the state of war continued, "great unrest and disquietude in our own country and throughout the world will prevail."[107]

No overt break came, however, while Democratic reservationists Myers, Smith, and Owen held the floor. Despite their strong pleas, when the roll call began, at around six o'clock, the prospects for ratification seemed dim. Briefly, early in the roll call, some saw the chance of a breakaway. Of the first four Democrats to respond, three voted for the treaty. A "yea" from the next senator, the venerable and invalid Democratic loyalist Charles Culberson of Texas, might have triggered the stampede. Culberson looked perplexed, and he hesitated, but finally he said "nay." The senators who followed acted true to form, and the treaty failed, by seven votes short of two-thirds, 49–35. Including pairs, it stood 57–39.[108]

The treaty died at the hands of irreconcilables, mainly Republicans, and of administration Democrats. All but two of the latter were from the South, where loyalty to Wilson and the League remained strong. Other Democrats, on the other hand, especially those from the West, chafed at the persistent administration favoritism to the South, as seen in the cotton and wheat prices during the war, and at taunts of subservience to the White House and the

106. *CR* 66:2, pp. 4581–85 (19 March 1920).

107. *New York Times*, 20 March 1920; *New York Tribune*, 20 March 1920.

108. *CR* 66:2, pp. 4585–96 (19 March 1920); *New York Times*, 20 March 1920; Bailey, *Great Betrayal*, 267; *CR* 66:2, p. 4599 (19 March 1920).

South. Their regions suffered too from the loss of German trade. Coming from two-party states, moreover, they had reason to fear the political consequences of a failure to ratify.[109]

For the mild reservationists, some hope remained. Treaty approval might yet occur, in one of several ways. According to plans formulated that morning, Lodge moved to return the treaty to the president. Hitchcock preferred to keep it before the Senate, but Lenroot, reflecting a consensus among the mild reservationists, said rather dramatically over the general din that he would support the resolution. Ratification could not occur until Wilson gave his consent. The president could resubmit the treaty at any time. The Republicans united to carry Lodge's motion, 47–37.[110]

Joseph Robinson of Arkansas, one of the inner circle among administration Democrats, moved to reconsider the vote on ratification. Watson moved to table. On that important issue Republicans divided. Seven mild reservationists, evidently with torn feelings, broke with Lodge to reject Watson's motion to table, 34–43. These seven—Colt, Edge, Hale, Kellogg, Keyes, Lenroot, and McNary—had in mind the scenario in which Democrats, having made their record, would switch on reconsideration. The other middle grounders voted with Lodge, except for those not voting—McCumber, McLean, Nelson, and Townsend. Robinson then moved to adjourn, in order to delay reconsideration and to leave time for negotiation. The Republicans voted solidly against the motion, however, and it lost, 35–42.[111] The mild reservationists had made it clear that there could be no further negotiation across party lines. Democrats would have to switch on the Lodge resolution as it stood. The same reasoning that had prevented the approval of Simmons's amendments to the Article 10 reservation the day before still held.

Brandegee made the point of order that Robinson's motion to reconsider was out of order, since the Senate had voted to return the treaty to the president. In the course of discussion, Lodge said that he would not object to a second vote on his resolution, if done without debate. He wanted to finish that night, he said, because many senators had to leave. Hitchcock saw no point in an immediate vote—he wanted to delay for a day or two. Finally, Cummins ruled in

109. Dewey W. Grantham, Jr., "The Southern Senators and the League of Nations, 1918–1920," 200–201; J. Leonard Bates, "Senator Walsh of Montana, 1918–1924: A Liberal Under Pressure," 157–58; Dunnington, "Thomas J. Walsh," 210.

110. *New York World*, 20 May 1920; *CR* 66:2, pp. 4599–600 (19 March 1920); *Portland Oregonian*, 20 March 1920.

111. *New York Tribune*, 20 March 1920; *CR* 66:2, p. 4601 (19 March 1920).

favor of the point of order but admitted doubt, opening the door for a challenge to the ruling. None came.[112]

The mild reservationists had conferred hastily and had agreed with Lodge that there should be an immediate vote or none. They had so informed Robinson and had told him also that if he could not at that time deliver some Democratic votes, they could no longer support him. Robinson could make no satisfactory response. By one account Hitchcock, back from a cloakroom phone conversation with Wilson, held a whispered conversation with Robinson. Whether influenced by Hitchcock and other Democrats or simply impressed with the hopelessness of the situation, Robinson withdrew his motion for reconsideration.[113]

Knox then moved to consider his resolution to repeal the declaration of war. Republicans had talked of this as the next step, but Lenroot held it up for a time. He said that the resolution should be taken up in the near future but not that night. He would vote against it, he said, if it was pressed. Lodge then moved to adjourn until Monday. By then, reconsideration would no longer be in order. The motion carried.[114] Wilson could still resubmit the treaty, the effect of Lenroot's objection to immediate action on the Knox resolution, but few if any senators expected that. For the Sixty-sixth Congress at least, and probably forever, the prospect of American adherence to the League of Nations was dead.

The outcome was of course a disappointment to the mild reservationists, and a defeat. Arguably they were themselves, to a limited extent, responsible for it. But at least they had tried to achieve ratification, albeit with what they viewed as acceptable reservations. Having established a group identity in October and November, they had maintained it when the treaty had again come before the Senate in February. By working together, as in their conference with Lodge on 9 February, they had magnified their influence. In their votes too they had advanced their ends, especially by opposing the Reed reservation, supporting Robinson's motion to reconsider on 19 March, and supporting the bipartisan conference reservation on American representation in League bodies, in opposition to Lodge. Force of circumstance had limited the roles of McCumber and Nelson, but they had done what they could through speeches

112. *CR* 66:2, pp. 4602–3 (19 March 1920).
113. *New York Times*, 20 March 1920; *New York Tribune*, 20 March 1920; *Portland Oregonian*, 20 March 1920.
114. *CR* 66:2, pp. 4603–4 (19 March 1920); *New York World*, 20 March 1920.

and, in the case of Nelson, participation in the 9 February conference.[115]

Moderates too had contributed to the cause of treaty approval. Townsend was the closest to the mild reservationists, though still not affiliated with them. More definitely, in their votes and comments, the others had held apart, separate from both mild and strong reservationists. Thus the mild reservationists, led in this period by Lenroot and Kellogg, could count on themselves—ten Republicans—and, for some purposes, on others of their party. Though not a negligible force, it had proved insufficient. Had the mild reservationists misplayed their hand?

Though the mild reservationists were ardent for ratification, and were supported by a public that wanted an end to the legal state of war, to accomplish their purpose in February and March 1920 was a herculean task. With elections near, politics more than ever stood as a barrier, dividing Republican and Democratic proponents of ratification. Principle too stood in the way, closely intertwined with politics, as the issue of obligation under Article 10 predominated and symbolized victory or defeat for each party. The nagging constitutional question of the role of the Senate under the treaty-making power, a question tied closely to the still strong personal animosities between the president and senators, also persisted. Given reasonableness and goodwill on both sides, the differences, though serious, were far from insurmountable. However, the adamancy of Wilson and the reluctance of Democratic leaders, especially Hitchcock, to cross him made the barrier between the two sides extraordinarily strong. The mild reservationists, themselves party to and sympathetic with the original "Lodge reservations," could not hope to deviate greatly from them and still achieve ratification. The country wanted movement, but the Grey letter, Keynes's book, Wilson's periodic showing of erratic behavior and intransigence, and the defensibility of the Lodge positions all served to limit what seemed to be desirable and feasible in the way of concessions.

The mild reservationists did pressure Lodge periodically, as needed. And they were largely responsible for a softening of a number of reservations, including those on Shantung, equal voting, and the selection of American representatives, along with the preamble. But on Article 10 they acquiesced in a reservation that though verbally

115. Nelson, in brief Senate remarks, defended the treaty as fair (*CR* 66:2, p. 3613 [28 February 1920]). The records of Edge and Sterling were not perfect by the standards alluded to above but were good enough to distinguish them from other Republicans.

different from the one of November and in that sense a concession, was scarcely weaker. Moreover, they found themselves united with the irreconcilables behind all but the first of the reservations. The situation, unforeseen earlier, was in part a consequence of the Hitchcock-irreconcilable coalition in defeating Lodge's compromise effort on the first reservation, on withdrawal.

Realizing that Hitchcock, in loyalty to Wilson, stood against treaty approval on the only terms by which it could be accomplished, the mild reservationists set out to discredit the Democratic leader and detach Democrats from him. But the unity of their own party behind reservations, and behind the leadership of Lodge, made it difficult to transcend politics and bring about ratification on a bipartisan basis. The mild reservationists did not, of course, depend on the irreconcilables for ratification. But they did need the strong reservationists and made concessions on Article 10 in an effort to keep them. In so doing, they asked of Simmons and Walsh, in particular, perhaps more than the two senators could reasonably have been expected to give.

One must consider the possibility that the mild reservationists bet on the wrong horse. Arguably, concessions to Simmons on Article 10, though costing Republican votes, might have won enough Democratic support to ratify, and on a basis that Wilson could later accept. Were the mild reservationists oversensitive to any suggestion of obligation, reading too much into Simmons's amendments? Or, granted some obligation, did they make too much of it? Were they excessively nationalistic? Probably so. Yet the questions are themselves not entirely relevant. On the basis of all that had gone before, accepting Simmons's amendments on 18 March, or in negotiations a week earlier, would have cost the mild reservationists not just the votes of a few strong reservationists but those of the mass of reservationist Republicans. That is not to say, however, that the acceptance of the Borah amendment to the Article 10 reservation was essential.

Under the circumstances, the mild reservationists were probably wise in seeking to maximize the Republican vote on the resolution of ratification. But that course, which required an Article 10 position that was tough even without the Borah amendment, "including all controversies relating to territorial integrity or political independence," put a great strain on the Democrats they hoped to win over. Emerging from the background of a "bipartisan conference" that to the Democrats had seemingly run aground on the reef of partisanship, and acting thereafter through their party's leadership, the mild reservationists, Lenroot and Kellogg in particular, needed to establish some measure of mutual trust between themselves and leaders like Simmons and Walsh. This they failed to do.

Walsh and Simmons were strong party men. To break with Hitchcock and Wilson, they needed to feel that the terms offered them, though harsh, were just, in the sense of being the best the mild reservationists could do. They needed to be able to show this also to their own followers. Instead, they gained the impression that the mild reservationists were weak and insincere, that they were playing their party's game. Reluctantly, Walsh came over at the end. Had he done so earlier, the slippage among Democrats might have been so great as to cause even Hitchcock to act independently of Wilson, taking his chances on presidential acceptance later. Failing that, an earlier break by Walsh could easily have influenced enough Democrats to override Hitchcock's influence. Simmons never did make the break. Had he done so, southerners especially might have been influenced.

Lenroot and Kellogg may have been to blame, in part. The two were astute, able, hard-working, and dedicated. In some respects they were good at the art of compromise: they knew the need for it; they were keen draftsmen and assiduous negotiators. But they were partisans too, and beyond that, they appreciated the need for Republican votes and Lodge's assistance. Thus, they gave much of their behind-the-scenes time to negotiation among themselves and with Lodge, rather than with the Democrats. It was Lodge, or Watson, on whom they relied to deal with the Democrats. The strategy was not an oversight but was deliberate. It was consonant with their effort to disabuse Democrats of the idea, entertained by Hitchcock, that two or three or four of them could be "picked off" to yield to the Democrats a majority, without, however, producing two-thirds. So they did indeed say to the Democrats, as Simmons charged, that the Democrats should work through Lodge. But this strategy carried a price: the appearance of partisanship and the lack of personal relationships with the key Democrats to lessen the impression of partisanship. Further, Lenroot and Kellogg were not ideal senatorial types.[116] Nervous, intense men, they lacked the personal touch of the southern "good old boy." They were a little insensitive too and failed to cultivate the key Democrats. McNary had the easy congeniality that Lenroot and Kellogg lacked, but they did not deputize

116. William S. White, *Citadel: The Story of the United States Senate*.

him, and it is not clear that he could have accomplished much acting on his own.

But the point should not be overstated. The effect of an earlier break by Walsh, or a final break by Simmons, is purely conjectural. And though the two Democrats lacked trust in the mild reservationists, including the principal leaders, they might well have acted as they did in any case. Walsh did not want to make the division in his party any wider than necessary; and without any real concessions on Article 10, Simmons had good reason to feel that it was pointless to vote approval, only to have the president pocket the treaty and assume the blame.

On balance, then, the mild reservationists took a reasonable approach in the last stages of the battle. They pursued it steadfastly and capably. They permitted the battle to take on more of a partisan cast than was desirable or necessary, but a considerable degree of partisanship was inherent in the situation and in their strategy. Whether some fine tuning in their approach would have yielded dramatically different results one cannot say.

Did the failure in the Senate really matter? If the Senate had approved the treaty in March, with the new reservations, would Wilson have completed ratification? If so, would the Allies and the other signatories have accepted the American reservations? Senate approval could have come only through the help of prominent Democrats, some of them influential with the president. Had Simmons and a few others joined Walsh on the final vote, they would surely have pressured Wilson to accept the result rather than to assume for himself and his party full responsibility for the treaty's rejection. The president might have yielded, but in the light of his hopes for a solemn referendum, that seems unlikely. But Hitchcock later speculated that in November, after election results were known, Wilson might have reconsidered.[117] Perhaps he would have. Further, if the Senate had given its approval once, it might very well have done so again, in 1921, and if so, the new president, Harding, probably would have completed the ratification.

The Allies showed their unhappiness with the reservations prior to the 19 November voting. After that, they implied acquiescence in what seemed the lesser evil. On a major obstacle, the preamble,

---

117. Evidence that Wilson would have pocketed the treaty is adduced in Bailey, *Great Betrayal*, 397; Hitchcock's speculation is in Hitchcock, "Events Leading to the World War," Hitchcock Papers.

Lodge had been ready to compromise in November and did so in March, permitting tacit acceptance. Of the reservations, the one that caused the most concern for Allied acceptance was the one on equal voting, but the March version was considerably softer than that of November and Great Britain strongly desired American adherence to the League. Many of the reservations, as Grey had noted, concerned American internal affairs—relations between the legislative and executive branches—and were of no concern to other nations. The other reservations, though they lessened America's potential contribution to League efforts and were far from welcome, were preferable to outright rejection. Foreign acquiescence was probable.[118]

118. Bailey, *Great Betrayal*, 140, commented on the probability of Allied acceptance.

7 AFTERMATH

To most senators and observers, the events of 19 March ended all prospect of ratification during the Wilson administration. Thus, most mild reservationists joined in supporting a resolution to end the state of war, despite the certainty of a successful Wilson veto. They realized that if the Republicans won in the election of 1920, a similar resolution would take effect. It was something the mild reservationists had resisted for over a year but would resist no longer. But their new commitment to some form of the Knox resolution did not preclude a continuing effort to secure ratification with suitable reservations. Lenroot and Kellogg, in particular, continued the fight, with a last-stand battle at the Republican National Convention in Chicago for a pro-League platform plank. The battle proved intricate, intense, and unsuccessful.

Prominent reservationists outside the Senate, such as Hoover, Root, Taft, and Lowell, tried to influence the Republican presidential nominee during the campaign and set out to construe his views and statements as favorable to the League. Warren Harding hedged for a time. Once elected, however, he promptly condemned the League, thus keeping in step with the vocal and influential irreconcilables. The mild reservationists of the Senate did not contest his decision.

Wilson took the news of the Senate's 19 March action calmly, counting on vindication in the upcoming elections. From an opposite standpoint, Lenroot wrote a friend, "It will be fortunate indeed for the country when the next fourth of March comes and Wilson is no longer President." More concretely, Taft thought that in the campaign the Republicans would back the treaty with reservations, against Wilson's all-or-nothing position, and that the effect of Wilson's prospective defeat would be the release of enough Democrats to ratify the treaty.[1]

As the people concerned about the League and the treaty looked toward the campaign and beyond, weak compromise efforts came to nothing. In mid-May Congress repealed the declaration of war against Germany and Austria-Hungary while retaining for the United States all advantages gained under the Treaty of Versailles. Of the middle grounders, only McCumber and Nelson voted no. They thought that a simple restoration of trade would suffice, and they still hoped for treaty ratification. As expected, Wilson vetoed the resolution.[2]

The mild reservationists, in voting for the Knox resolution, by no means abandoned all hope for the treaty and the League. Lenroot and Kellogg hoped to pledge their party, at the Chicago convention, to ratification with the "Lodge reservations." The matter was of more than ordinary importance, for the Republicans had every reason to expect to win not only both houses of Congress but also the presidency. Platform pledges are not automatically translated into law, but on so prominent an issue as that of the League, the Republican pledge would mean much.

Will Hays, more fearful of Republican disunity than of Democratic campaigners, acted energetically and imaginatively in the months preceding the party's national convention. He created an advisory group of 171 members and divided it into twenty-four topical subcommittees, to make recommendations to the convention's resolutions committee. Aware of the power and sensitivity of representatives and senators, he saw that they were well represented on the advisory committee and that all congressional members of the advisory committee would serve on the executive committee, which screened the subcommittee reports.[3]

1. Edith Bolling Wilson, *My Memoir*, 303; Oscar Straus Diary, entries for 5 and 10 May 1920, Straus Papers; Lenroot to James Stone, 22 March 1920, James A. Stone Papers, State Historical Society of Wisconsin; Taft to Horace Taft, 21 March 1920, Taft Papers.

2. *Providence Sunday Tribune*, 21 March 1920; Lenroot to James Stone, 22 March 1920, Stone Papers; Gus Karger to William Howard Taft, 20 March 1920, Taft Papers; Oscar Straus to Bainbridge Colby, 5 April 1920, Straus Papers; Charles DeBenedetti, *Origins of the Modern American Peace Movement, 1915–1929*, 17; Evans C. Johnson, *Oscar W. Underwood: A Political Biography*, 296; *CR* 66:2. pp. 6852–57 (11 May 1920), pp. 7101–2 (15 May 1920). McCumber was paired with Cummins and announced as opposed to the resolution.

3. Marie Chatham, "The Role of the National Party Chairman from Hanna to Farley," 54; James Oliver Robertson, "The Progressives in National Republican Politics, 1916–1921," 261; J. C. O'Laughlin to A. D. Lasker, 2 February 1920, John C. O'Laughlin Papers, Library of Congress; Ogden Mills to Henry Cabot Lodge, 20 April 1920, Lodge Papers; Will H. Hays to James R. Garfield, 17 April 1920, James R. Garfield Papers, Library of Congress.

Lenroot and Kellogg were among the senators serving on the advisory committee and the executive committee. In addition Lenroot, with Root and three others, served on Lodge's subcommittee on international relations. Kellogg's involvement resulted from his position as national committeeman from Minnesota. Lenroot was one of three senators recommended to Hays by Lodge in mid-December.[4]

Lodge was glad enough to have Lenroot serve as a representative of the mild reservationists, but he was not prepared to yield to him and Kellogg on the treaty plank. During discussions in early May, Lenroot and Kellogg pressed for a strong endorsement of the "Lodge reservations." But Lodge, aware that the irreconcilables had not voted for the ratification resolution incorporating these reservations, prepared a draft that did not fully satisfy the mild reservationists. The matter remained tentative, and Lodge took care to warn Hays to tread lightly when he saw Lenroot and Kellogg in Chicago. "Do not say anything of draft I sent you." Lodge wired. "Do not mention authorship. Did not wish you to think I bound others to draft."[5]

Hearing rumors of compromise, Root wrote Lodge and urged an outright platform endorsement of the reservations. By 14 May, however, the Republicans of Indiana were in the process of adopting a plank fashioned by Lodge in cooperation with Cummins and Knox. Approved by Hays, it was taken to Indiana by Senators New and Watson, who secured its adoption. Lodge and his colleagues hoped that it would serve as a model for the national plank.[6]

The Indiana platform blamed Wilson for incorporating the League in the treaty and for bringing about the treaty's defeat in the Senate; it approved the actions of the Republican senators, by implication including the irreconcilables; it favored an association of nations, judicial settlement of international disputes, a World Court, and disarmament; but it disapproved foreign control of American armed forces, domestic affairs, or the Monroe Doctrine. Finally, it said that the United States would view with grave concern any threat to the peace in Europe and in such an event would consult with the powers affected and be prepared to help again, as in 1917.[7]

4. Robertson, "Progressives in National Republican Politics," 262; Hays to Lodge, 17 December 1919, and Lodge to Hays, 18 December 1919, Lodge Papers.

5. Lodge to Hays, 9 May 1920, Lodge Papers.

6. Root to Lodge, 14 May 1920, and Lodge to Root, 17 May 1920, Lodge Papers; *Minneapolis Tribune*, 20 May 1920. For a slightly different account, see Lloyd E. Ambrosius, *Woodrow Wilson and the American Diplomatic Tradition: The Treaty Fight in Perspective*, 261–62.

7. *Minneapolis Tribune*, 15 May 1920.

Lodge thought that the plank would serve both to draw a clear line between his party and the Democrats and to preserve Republican unity, as he explained at some length to Root. Very quickly, however, he learned that it would not do. From the first, irreconcilables had divided among themselves, and though Knox was satisfied, Borah, Johnson, and Judge Daniel Cohalan, claiming to represent Irish-American and German-American opinion, objected strongly. They did not like the commitment to Europe and much preferred a blanket condemnation of the League rather than an endorsement of the actions of the Republican senators, which to them implied approval of the League. Mild reservationists too remained unsatisfied and ready to press for an endorsement of the reservations. But Lodge, who would be in a key position as temporary and permanent chairman of the convention, was mainly impressed with the danger from the irreconcilables.[8]

With the convention set to begin on Tuesday, 8 June, in Washington in late May Lodge pressed for an agreement among his colleagues. One of them, Medill McCormick, soon claimed that an agreement had been reached, but at the convention neither Lenroot and Kellogg on the one side nor Borah and Johnson on the other felt bound to anything. Lodge's understanding was that the platform would approve the action of the Senate, as the Indiana platform had suggested. "Whether we stop there, as I hope we shall, or not, is the question to be decided," Lodge wrote, "because the next step would be to declare against any League and for that there is a powerful movement on foot."[9]

Lenroot and Kellogg found important allies at Chicago: McCumber, Hale, and, from outside the Senate, Ogden Mills, who headed the advisory committee. Also in Chicago was W. Murray Crane of Massachusetts, a former governor and senator who, though in his late sixties and terminally ill, was aggressively ardent for the League. A conservative strongly identified with the Taft wing of the party in earlier battles, Crane was described sympathetically by the *New York Times* as representing the views "of the men of affairs." While the fight was still on in the Senate, he had told senators that the welfare of the country and of international finance called for the

---

8. Lodge to Root, 17 May 1920, Lodge Papers; James C. Malin, *The United States After the World War* (Boston: Ginn and Company, 1930), 36; *Minneapolis Tribune*, 4, 5 June 1920; John Hannan to Robert La Follette, 20 May 1920, La Follette Papers; Lodge to Robert Winsor, 4 June 1920, Lodge Papers.

9. *Washington Evening Star*, 28, 30 May 1920; McCormick in *Chicago Daily News*, 10 June 1920; Lodge to Robert Winsor, 4 June 1920, Lodge Papers.

entry of the United States into the League. Afterward he busied himself preparing for the convention, chiefly by trying to influence Root, directly and indirectly, to promote a League plank. Now he was ready to use all his energy and influence in what he must have believed to be the final and decisive battle.[10]

While Crane lobbied delegates, the mild reservationist senators, in cooperation with Mills, took advantage of a technicality. The fifty-three-member Resolutions Committee and its thirteen-member subcommittee that would actually draft the platform were to hear the report of the advisory committee. But that group had come to no agreement on a League plank. It had, however, chosen a committee of three, consisting of Mills, Watson, and Lenroot, to present the committee's recommendations. This committee evidently had some discretionary powers. The status of Lenroot and Kellogg was fortified by their membership on the advisory committee's executive committee. Thus when the mild reservationist senators, with the complicity of Mills, met to frame a League plank for presentation to the Resolutions Committee, they had some show of authority.[11]

The proposal agreed on by the mild reservationists reflected both a concern for the sensibilities of the irreconcilables and a determination to override the objections of that group and to pledge the party to ratification.[12] The irreconcilables were headed by Johnson, a candidate for the presidential nomination, and by Borah. With strong support from Brandegee, Medill McCormick, spokesmen for German-Americans and Irish-Americans, and major Chicago newspapers, the irreconcilables threatened before and during the convention to stage a disruptive floor fight and, if defeated in the convention, to sit out the campaign or bolt the party altogether. Since Johnson had served as Theodore Roosevelt's Bull Moose running mate in 1912 and had done nothing for Hughes in California in 1916 after a fancied snub, his threat was credible. And the core of his support came from others who had bolted the ticket in 1912. Borah had not

10. James E. Watson, *As I Knew Them: Memoirs of James E. Watson*, 214; Thomas A. Bailey, *Woodrow Wilson and the Great Betrayal*, 301; *New York Times*, 8 June 1920; Crane to A. Lawrence Lowell, 21 May 1920, Lowell Papers; Stimson Diary, entry for 20 March 1920, Stimson Papers.

11. *Milwaukee Sentinel*, 7 June 1920; "The Memoirs of Irvine L. Lenroot," 156, Lenroot Papers; *New York Times*, 8 June 1920.

12. The proposal was variously attributed to Lenroot and, by Crane's later account, to Kellogg, Lenroot, Hale, McCumber, and others (Herbert Parsons to Annie S. Peck, 18 October 1920, Parsons Papers; W. Murray Crane to A. Lawrence Lowell, 17 June 1920, Lowell Papers).

been a Bull Mooser, but few doubted either the deepness of his conviction on the League or the sincerity of his threats.[13]

The concession that the mild reservationists offered the irreconcilables was purely verbal. Instead of explicitly endorsing the League,
their plank referred to "an association of nations." Such an association, however, sounded much like the League as the mild reservationists wanted it. The crux of the matter was that the plank,
though critical of Wilson's Covenant, called for treaty ratification
with "American reservations."[14] Since the League was part of the
treaty, the "association of nations" referred to would in fact be the
League.

While the Resolutions Committee heard testimony and the convention listened to speeches, including Lodge's denunciation of
Wilson and his praise for all Republican senators, the subcommittee
of thirteen dealt with other parts of the platform before getting to
the treaty plank. Meanwhile, though, senators and other party leaders conferred intermittently for two and a half days, before a small
group of men reached an agreement in the early-morning hours of
Thursday, 10 June. From first to last, Borah, backed by other irreconcilables, stood against any pledge to ratify, with or without reservations. He would not object to a reference to an association of nations, Borah said, so long as it was qualified by an endorsement of
the policies of Washington and Monroe.[15]

The mild reservationist senators and their allies argued their case
publicly and privately and canvassed for support in the Resolutions
Committee, should they fail with the subcommittee. They warned
against forfeiting the middle-ground reservationist position to the
Democrats. And Lenroot cited reports that delegates felt that an
endorsement of ratification reflected public opinion.[16] As a result
Watson, who headed the thirteen-member subcommittee as well as
the full Resolutions Committee, and Smoot, a member of both committees, initially agreed to support the proposal of the mild reservationists. But in the face of strong threats from Borah, Brandegee,
McCormick, and Johnson, they backed off. Nor would Lodge support the mild reservationists. They in turn rejected a compromise

13. Borah to Daniel H. Thomas, 11 May 1920, Borah Papers; *New York Times*,
8 June 1920; *Minneapolis Tribune*, 8 June 1920; *Sun and New York Herald*, 9 June
1920; *Chicago Daily News*, 10 June 1920.
14. *New York Times*, 9 June 1920.
15. Ibid., 10 June 1920.
16. *Sun and New York Herald*, 10 June 1920; *New York Tribune*, 9 June 1920;
Washington Evening Star, 7 June 1920; *New York Times*, 8 June 1920.

tentatively agreed to by Lodge, Watson, Johnson, Brandegee, and some others. And McCumber and Crane said that they were willing to have a floor fight.[17]

At last, after an angry and inconclusive session of the subcommittee had broken up, a group of leaders gathered at the Blackstone Hotel at about two A.M. on 10 June. No mild reservationist senator was present. The *New York Times* identified the participants as Lodge, Crane, Mills, the irreconcilable George Wharton Pepper, Henry L. Stimson, the publisher George Harvey, Borah, Brandegee, and Smoot. McCormick was also present.[18] Though the irreconcilables were more than adequately represented, the men were not gathered to vote, and in Crane, Mills, and Stimson the mild reservationists had reasonable representation. Furthermore, Smoot and Lodge had been reservationists.

Out of the conference came a compromise agreement, but one that was widely heralded as a defeat for the mild reservationists. Crane was the last to yield, but finally, isolated, he capitulated. Several factors account for the result. The irreconcilables persisted in their threats, augmented hours earlier with the warning that in the campaign they would denounce Crane as the tool of Wall Street bankers, some of whom were present at the convention. Crane discounted the threats of a bolt, or even a floor fight, but the others were not so sure. Lodge clinched the argument against the mild reservationist proposal. Determined to mollify the irreconcilables and win the election for his party, he announced that if need be he would leave the chair and take the floor to oppose the endorsement of ratification with the reservations that bore his name.[19]

At this point Mills deserted Crane, and Stimson went with him. Mills brought forth a proposal prepared three weeks earlier by Root. After a private conference involving Mills, Smoot, Borah, McCormick, and Lodge, the irreconcilables agreed to the compromise. Lodge had been shown the proposal a week earlier and had rejected it, but now he too accepted the plank, recognizing the prestige attached to Root's name. Root had been rebuffed by Lodge when he

17. W. Murray Crane to A. Lawrence Lowell, 17 June 1920, Lowell Papers; *New York Tribune*, 10 June 1920; *Washington Herald*, 10 June 1920.

18. *New York Times*, 11 June 1920; Milton R. Merrill, "Reed Smoot, Apostle in Politics," 335; *New York Tribune*, 11 June 1920.

19. *New York Times*, 10, 11 June 1920; *Washington Herald*, 11 June 1920; Crane to A. Lawrence Lowell, 17 June 1920, Lowell Papers; Medill McCormick to Arthur W. Page, 21 August 1921, Josept Medill McCormick Papers, Hanna-McCormick Family Papers, Library of Congress. See also Medill McCormick in *Chicago Daily News*, 11 June 1920.

had urged an endorsement of ratification with reservations, and he had been influenced by Lodge's arguments or his power. Ardent for party unity and the election of a Republican president and probably urged to the task by Hays, Root had produced a plank that reflected his own views and that could be interpreted by the different factions to suit their own lights. Then the elder statesman had left for Europe to help form the charter for the new World Court.[20]

Mills had been installed as the head of the advisory committee by Hays. Their common purpose was to secure party unity. After Lodge, in a telegram sent to Mills on 4 June, had dismissed Root's draft, Mills had thrown in with the mild reservationists and with what probably seemed to be the sentiment of the convention and the country. Unity remained his goal, however, and when he realized that this could not be secured on the basis of the mild reservationist plank and then discovered that Borah and McCormick had not seen the Root proposal, he had no second thoughts about offering it.[21] Stimson was a staunch pro-Leaguer. But he was also the friend, partner, and protégé of Elihu Root. His ready acceptance of Mills's compromise proposal is understandable on that basis.

In due course Watson received endorsement of the Root plank from the subcommittee and then from the full platform committee. Before taking it to the convention floor, he, Lodge, and William Allen White talked with Lenroot and Kellogg and won their acquiescence.[22] No doubt Lenroot and Kellogg realized that under the circumstances a floor fight would be hopeless, would weaken the party in the campaign, and would lessen the chances of later securing from the presidential nominee a favorable interpretation of what was essentially an ambiguous plank. Possibly, either or both men considered too their own chances for the presidential nomination in the event of a deadlock. In the platform committee, and then on the convention floor, only La Follette's man, Edwin J. Gross, raised strong objection, from an irreconcilable standpoint.[23] The impa-

20. Jack E. Kendrick, "The League of Nations and the Republican Senate, 1918–1921," 320–21; *New York Tribune*, 11 June 1920; Mills, quoted in *Salt Lake Tribune*, 20 June 1920, in Merrill, "Reed Smoot," 335; Lodge to Archibald Hopkins, 15 July 1920, and Lodge to Root, 17 May 1920, Lodge Papers; Root to A. Lawrence Lowell, 27 May 1920, Lowell Papers; Mark Sullivan in the *Portland Oregonian*, 17 June 1920.

21. Kendrick, "League of Nations," 320; *Salt Lake Tribune*, 20 June 1920, in Merrill, "Reed Smoot," 335.

22. *Sun and New York Herald*, 11 June 1920.

23. Edwin J. Gross, "A Political Grab Bag," n.p., Edwin J. Gross Papers, State Historical Society of Wisconsin, Madison.

tient delegates gave ready approval to the platform and turned, at last, to the presidential nomination.

The convention's decision would be fateful for the cause of the League because Root's plank was open to several constructions. It supported international agreement for world peace, referring to an "international association." Such an association, the plank said,

must be based upon international justice, and must provide methods which shall maintain the rule of public right by development of law and the decision of impartial courts, and which shall secure instant and general international conference whenever peace shall be threatened by political action, so that the nations pledged to do and insist upon what is just and fair may exercise their influence and power for the prevention of war.

But the plan, which to that point expressed the reservationists' view, did not go further to endorse reservations or entry into the League. Instead, it criticized Wilson's Covenant and Wilson himself for his uncompromising stand and praised Republican senators for resisting him. In this connection, the plank referred to "the time-honored policies of Washington, Jefferson, and Monroe." In conclusion, it pledged the coming Republican administration "to such agreements with the other nations of the world as shall meet the full duty of America to civilization and humanity . . . without surrendering the right of the American people to exercise its judgment and its power in favor of justice and peace."[24]

The ambiguous plank evoked mixed reactions from both sides. Johnson expressed doubts about it, and Borah admitted that it was not all that he had wanted. But Borah reassured his ally that at least it had sidetracked Crane's proposal and had permitted the irreconcilables to continue to oppose the League while remaining in the party. On the other side, the *New York Times* saw the plank as a victory for the irreconcilables. So did Herbert Parsons, the former New York Republican national committeeman and the chairman of the New York County Republican committee. Nor was Crane at all pleased, blaming the Chicago press for the outcome. But Herbert Hoover and William Howard Taft, as well as the *New York Tribune*, saw the plank as paving the way for ratification.[25]

24. Kirk H. Porter and Donald Bruce Johnson, comps., *National Party Platforms, 1840-1968*, 231.

25. Johnson to Borah, 22 June 1920, and Borah to Johnson, 24 June 1920, Borah Papers; *New York Times*, 11 June 1920; Herbert Parsons to Annie S. Peck, 18 October 1920, and Charles D. Hilles to Parsons, 17 June 1920, Parsons Papers; Kendrick, "League of Nations," 325; Taft to Casper S. Yost, 19 June 1920, Taft Papers; *New York*

The platform battle having ended in stalemate, the fate of the League rested now with Senator Warren G. Harding, the party's tenth-ballot compromise choice for the presidential nomination. A strong reservationist, Harding was not lacking in conviction, but neither was he impervious to pressures from within his own party, as those who nominated him understood. Harding, like Lodge, saw in party unification the key to victory. Very soon, it became apparent that he would win against the Democrats' forty-fourth ballot choice, Governor James Cox of Ohio. But Harding had to concern himself with the magnitude and character of the victory. He wanted a Republican Congress, and a harmonious one. The House posed little problem, but only a third of the Senate seats would be decided, and in that body the Republicans held just a two-vote margin, including the votes of the undependable La Follette and of Truman Newberry, who faced possible expulsion for election fraud.

Long-practiced at straddling, Harding met the challenge masterfully. By private flattery and public pronouncements, he satisfied Johnson, Borah, and their cohorts. He condemned Wilson's dictatorial rule, Article 10, and the sacrifice of American independence. And he avoided clear-cut support for ratification with the "Lodge reservations." On the other hand, he often spoke of an association of nations and of a World Court with teeth in it. Stalling, he said that details could not be determined in the heat of the campaign, but he pledged to consult with the "best minds" and with the Senate in formulating a program to implement his vague promises. Herbert Parsons and other Republicans were not satisfied, and, led by Hamilton Holt and Professor Irving Fisher, they bolted the ticket. For the most part, though, the party's internationalist luminaries supported Harding, most dramatically with the issuance in mid-October of the Appeal of Thirty One, composed by Root and subscribed to by Hoover, Lowell, Hughes, and seventeen college presidents or executives, among others.[26]

Harding won in a landslide and carried with him an overwhelmingly Republican Congress. The event presaged the death of the League, so far as the United States was concerned. The election was not a referendum on the League. If it was a referendum on anything,

---

Tribune, 11 June 1920.

26. Robert K. Murray, *The Harding Era: Warren G. Harding and His Administration*, 54–60; Randolph C. Downes, *The Rise of Warren Gamaliel Harding, 1865–1920* (Columbus: Ohio State University Press, 1970), 563–95; John Chalmers Vinson, *Referendum for Isolation: Defeat of Article Ten of the League of Nations Covenant*, 114–16.

it was on Wilsonianism. Harding and the Republicans drew together the discontented and joined them with the traditional Republicans. But since Wilson had proclaimed the election to be a referendum on the League, Harding was in a position to take it as such, and he did. Two days after the returns were in, he declared the League "deceased." Months later, in his first Message to Congress, he declared that the election had been a mandate against the League.[27]

Harding had never been strong for the League. And he did not wish to disrupt his administration by resuming the fight in the Senate. Further, in the latter part of 1920 and into 1921 the public saw in overseas events good reason for avoiding entanglements. The scholar Roland Stromberg has asserted: "The chief cause of the League's total collapse in 1920 and 1921 was almost certainly the general world situation. There was a spectacular deterioration of relations among the Allies and, so it seemed, between everybody and everybody else. The world presented a picture of violence and greed that mocked the recent lofty aspirations of the righteous war and the just peace." Stromberg pointed specifically to the Russo-Polish war, the Russian Civil War, the turmoil in China, the continued conflict in Ireland with its consequent bad publicity for Great Britain, and the Korean revolt against Japan.[28]

The matter of an association of nations, such as Harding had talked of during the campaign, remained to be dealt with. Eventually, under pressure from Lodge, Johnson, and Borah, Harding dropped that idea too. Instead he concerned himself with naval disarmament, at the Washington Conference in 1921–1922, and then, in 1923, with the issue of American adherence to the World Court. Progressively, through the 1920s and beyond, entry into the League fell ever farther beyond the bounds of the possible. Thus when Franklin Roosevelt ran for president in 1932, he found it expedient to abandon the position he had taken as James Cox's running mate in 1920. He reassured his countrymen that he would not attempt to bring the nation into the League.[29]

Authorities differ on whether American ratification would have

27. Ralph Stone, *The Irreconcilables: The Fight Against the League of Nations,* 177; Warren F. Kuehl, *Hamilton Holt: Journalist, Internationalist, Educator,* 155.

28. Roland N. Stromberg, *Collective Security and American Foreign Policy: From the League of Nations to NATO,* 40–41.

29. Johnson to Hiram Johnson, Jr., 7 December 1920, Johnson Papers; *New York Times,* 28, 30 November 1921; James MacGregor Burns, *Roosevelt: The Lion and the Fox,* 126.

materially changed the future. Inis Claude and Alfred Zimmern thought that the treaty's rejection did matter, since the League, without the United States, could not pursue collective security as originally conceived. However, the second reservation would have undermined collective security in any case. Thomas Bailey pointed out that, quite apart from the matter of collective security, the League could not now rely on the boycott or make disarmament agreements. He noted also that the United States, by refusing to ratify, stayed not only out of the League but out of other instruments of the treaty as well, including the Reparations Commission and the commission for the administration of the Saar. Bailey described a number of other unfortunate consequences flowing from the treaty rejection and concluded that the United States had to bear "a very considerable share of the blame" for what happened in Europe between 1919 and 1939.[30]

Robert Osgood, among others, made the telling point that though American entry into the League might have been marginally useful, the basic problem was something else: the people and the leaders, in 1919 and 1920, showed themselves unready for realism in foreign affairs. "The breakdown of international security culminating in World War II may properly be attributed to the failure of the United States to concert its power with the status quo nations in checking the expansion of Fascist power, and not, simply, to the failure of the United States to follow Wilson's leadership by joining the League of Nations." Arthur Link agreed that the key problem was immature public thinking. "The postwar version of collective security failed in the crucial tests of the 1930s," he wrote, "not because the Treaty of Versailles was defective or the peacekeeping machinery of the League of Nations was defective, but because the people of Great Britain, France, and the United States were unwilling to confront aggressors with the threat of war."[31]

If the fundamental flaw lay with public opinion, then America's

30. Inis L. Claude, Jr., *Power and International Relations*, 154; Alfred Zimmern, *The League of Nations and the Rule of Law, 1918–1935*, 302; Bailey, *Great Betrayal*, 356–60.

31. Robert E. Osgood, *Ideals and Self-Interest in America's Foreign Relations*, 295; idem, "Woodrow Wilson, Collective Security, and the Lessons of History," in *The Philosophy and Policies of Woodrow Wilson*, ed. Earl Latham, 193; Arthus S. Link, *Wilson: Revolution, War, and Peace*, 128. Other studies that focus on American opinion as a root cause of international trouble include Selig Adler, *The Isolationist Impulse, Its Twentieth Century Reaction* (New York: Free Press, 1961); idem, *The Uncertain Giant, 1921–1941: American Foreign Policy Between the Wars*; and Robert Dallek, *The American Style of Foreign Policy: Cultural Politics and Foreign Affairs* (New York: Alfred A. Knopf, 1983).

failure to enter the League made little difference—the country would not have played a constructive role even had it joined. But public opinion is a changeable thing, subject to many influences. Bailey noted that some of the isolationism of the thirties was due to disillusionment with the League's effectiveness and that American participation might have obviated that factor.[32] To that argument this writer would add another. If the Senate had voted to ratify, with the "Lodge reservations," and if Wilson had pigeonholed the treaty, the Republicans would have felt strong pressure to endorse the Senate's action in the 1920 platform, to defend it in the campaign, and to act in accordance with it in their administrations of the 1920s. Though still rejecting Wilsonianism, they would have been committed to their party's more limited, but traditional, internationalism. They would not have quieted the irreconcilables, but instead of accommodating to them the mainstream Republicans, commanding the presidency, would have exerted a powerful counterforce in the battle for public opinion. In short, had the Senate approved the treaty, the process by which Americans adjusted to twentieth-century international realities probably would have been significantly accelerated. Viewed from that standpoint, the outcome in the Senate did make a difference, and the role of the mild reservationists in seeking ratification likewise gains in historical importance.

32. Bailey, *Great Betrayal*, 361.

APPENDIX 1 Voting by Middle Grounders on Amendments

MIDDLE GROUNDERS	Fall amendment regarding German-Belgium boundary commission	Fall amendment regarding Luxemburg commission	Fall amendment regarding Saar Basin commission	Fall amendment regarding treaty with Czecho-slovakia	Fall amendments regarding Upper Silesia	Shantung amendment	Johnson amendment
Capper	No		No	No	No	Yes	Yes
Colt	No		No	No	No	No	No
Cummins	No		No	No	Yes	No	Yes
Edge	No		No	No	Not Voting	Announced Against	No
Hale	No		No	No	No	No	No
Jones	No		Yes	Yes	Yes	Yes	Yes
Kellogg	No		No	No	No	No	No
Kenyon	No		No	No	Yes	No	Yes
Keyes	No		No	No	No	No	No
Lenroot	No		No	No	No	No	Yes
McCumber	No		No	Not Voting	Not Voting	No	No
McLean	Yes		Yes	Yes	Yes	Yes	Yes
McNary	No		No	No	No	No	No
Nelson	No		No	No	No	No	No
Smoot	No		No	No	No	No	Yes
Spencer	No		No	No	No	No	Yes
Sterling	No	Announced In Favor	No	Announced In Favor	Yes	No	No
Townsend	No		No	No	Yes	No	Yes
CITATIONS	CR 66:1 6929 10/2/19	CR 66:1 6929 10/2/19	CR 66:1 6276 10/2/19	CR 66:1 6278 10/2/19	CR 66:1 6279,80 10/2/19	CR 66:1 6997 10/16/19	CR 66:1 7548 10/27/19

Continued on Next Page

MIDDLE GROUNDERS	Shields amendment regarding British vote in Council	Moses amendment regarding British vote in Assembly	To table Sherman amendment to name Deity in covenant	Second Johnson amendment	Lodge amendment to strike Shantung	La Follette amendment to strike labor section	Gore amendment for war referenda
Capper	Yes	Yes	No	Yes	Yes	Yes	Yes
Colt	No	No	Yes	No	No	No	No
Cummins	Yes	Yes	Yes	Yes	Yes	Yes	No
Edge	No	No	Yes	No	No	No	No
Hale	No	No	No, by Misunderstanding	No	No	No	No
Jones	Yes	Yes	No	Yes	Paired In Favor	Yes	Yes
Kellogg	No	No	Yes	No	No	No	No
Kenyon	No	Yes	Yes	Yes	Yes	Yes	No
Keyes	No	No	Yes	No	No	No	No
Lenroot	No	No	Yes	Yes	No	No	No
McCumber	No	Paired Against	Yes	No	No	No	No
McLean	Yes	Yes	No	Yes	Yes	Yes	Yes
McNary	No	No	Yes	No	No	No	No
Nelson	No	No	Yes	No	No	No	No
Smoot	No	Yes	Yes	Yes	No	No	No
Spencer	No	Yes	Yes	Yes	No	No	No
Sterling	No	No	Yes	No	No	No	No
Townsend	No	Not Voting	Yes	Yes	No	No	No
CITATIONS	CR 66:1 7679,80 10/29/19	CR 66:1 7680 10/29/19	CR 66:1 7683 10/29/19	CR 66:1 7685,86 10/29/19	CR 66:1 7942 11/4/19	CR 66:1 7669 11/5/19	CR 66:1 8013 11/6/19

APPENDIX 2   *Voting by Middle Grounders on Reservations*

MIDDLE GROUNDERS	Reconsideration after defeat of Lodge resolution	T. Walsh pro-Irish independence reservation	Gore reservation vs. foreign entanglements	Jones reservation vs. approval of force in Council before Congress acted	Owen reservation regarding Egyptian self-government	Johnson six-vote reservation	King substitute to exclude U.S. from ILO
Capper	Yes	Yes	Yes	Yes	Yes	Yes	No
Colt	Yes	No	No	No	No	No	No
Cummins	No	Not Voting	Yes	Yes	Yes	Yes	Yes
Edge	Yes	No	No	Yes	No	Not Voting	No
Hale	Yes	No	No	No	No	No	No
Jones	Yes	Yes	Yes	Yes	Yes	Yes	Yes
Kellogg	Yes	No	No	No	No	No	No
Kenyon	Yes	Yes	Not Voting	Yes	Yes	Yes	Yes
Keyes	Yes	No	No	No	No	No	No
Lenroot	Yes	No	No	No	Yes	No	No
McCumber	Yes	No	No	No	No	No	No
McLean	Yes	Yes	Yes	Yes	Yes	Yes	Yes
McNary	Yes	No	No	No	No	No	No
Nelson	Yes	Not Voting	No	No	No	No	No
Smoot	Yes	Yes	No	Yes	Yes	Yes	Yes
Spencer	Yes	Yes	No	No	No	Yes	No
Sterling	Yes	No	No	No	No	No	No
Townsend	Yes	Not Voting	No	Yes	No	Yes	No
CITATIONS	CR 66:1 8786-87 11/19/19	CR 66:1 8753-54 11/18/19	CR 66:1 8746 11/18/19	CR 66:1 8744-45 11/18/19	CR 66:1 8644 11/17/19	CR 66:1 8738 11/18/19	CR 66:1 8729-30 11/18/19

Continued on Next Page

MIDDLE GROUNDERS	Reed reservation to exclude matters of "national honor and interest" from pacific settlement	Borah substitute to strengthen reservation to Article 10	Borah amendment for acceptance by four allies
Capper	Yes	No	No
Colt	No	No	No
Cummins	No	Yes	Yes
Edge	No	No	No
Hale	No	No	No
Jones	Yes	No	No
Kellogg	No	No	No
Kenyon	No	No	No
Keyes	No	No	No
Lenroot	No	No	No
McCumber	No	No	No
McLean	Yes	Yes	No
McNary	No	No	No
Nelson	No	No	No
Smoot	No	No	No
Spencer	Yes	No	No
Sterling	No	No	No
Townsend	No	No	No
CITATIONS	CR 66:1 8640 11/17/19	CR 66:1 8203-4 11/10/19	CR 66:1 8069 11/7/19

SELECTED BIBLIOGRAPHY

MANUSCRIPT COLLECTIONS

Chandler P. Anderson Papers, Library of Congress.
Ray Stannard Baker Papers, Library of Congress.
Albert J. Beveridge Papers, Library of Congress.
William E. Borah Papers, Library of Congress.
William Jennings Bryan Papers, Library of Congress.
Nicholas Murray Butler Papers, Butler Library, Columbia University, New York City.
George Chamberlain Papers, Oregon Historical Society, Portland.
Raymond Clapper Papers, Library of Congress.
Council on Religion and International Affairs, Butler Library, Columbia University, New York City.
John J. Esch Papers, State Historical Society of Wisconsin, Madison.
James R. Garfield Papers, Library of Congress.
Frederick Hale Papers, Syracuse University, Syracuse, New York.
Warren G. Harding Papers, Ohio Historical Society, Columbus.
Gilbert M. Hitchcock Papers, Library of Congress.
Hamilton Holt Papers, Mills Library, Rollins College, Sarasota, Florida.
Hiram Johnson Papers, Bancroft Library, University of California, Berkeley.
David Starr Jordan Papers, Hoover Institution on War, Revolution, and Peace, Stanford University, Stanford, California.
Frank B. Kellogg Papers, Minnesota Historical Society, St. Paul.
William Kent Papers, Sterling Library, Yale University, New Haven, Connecticut.
Robert M. La Follette Papers, La Follette Family Collection, Library of Congress.
Robert Lansing Papers, Library of Congress.
League to Enforce Peace Papers, Houghton Library, Harvard University, Cambridge, Massachusetts.
Irvine L. Lenroot Papers, Library of Congress.
Henry Cabot Lodge Papers, Massachusetts Historical Society, Boston.
Breckinridge Long Papers, Library of Congress.
A. Lawrence Lowell Papers, Pusey Library, Harvard University, Cambridge, Massachusetts.
William Gibbs McAdoo Papers, Library of Congress.
Joseph Medill McCormick Papers, Hanna-McCormick Family Papers, Library of Congress.

Vance C. McCormick Diary, Hoover Institution on War, Revolution, and Peace, Stanford University, Stanford, California.
Charles L. McNary Papers, Library of Congress.
Knute Nelson Papers, Minnesota Historical Society, St. Paul.
Thomas B. Neuhausen Papers, Special Collections Division, University of Oregon, Eugene.
John C. O'Laughlin Papers, Library of Congress.
Herbert Parsons Papers, Butler Library, Columbia University, New York City.
Gifford Pinchot Papers, Library of Congress.
Key Pittman Papers, Library of Congress.
Doane Robinson Papers, South Dakota Historical Resource Center, Pierre.
Elihu Root Papers, Library of Congress.
Edward A. Ross Papers, State Historical Society of Wisconsin, Madison.
Henry L. Stimson Papers, Sterling Library, Yale University, New Haven, Connecticut.
James A. Stone Papers, State Historical Society of Wisconsin, Madison.
Oscar S. Straus Papers, Library of Congress.
William Howard Taft Papers, Library of Congress.
Joseph P. Tumulty Papers, Library of Congress.
Thomas J. Walsh Papers, Library of Congress.
Henry White Papers, Butler Library, Columbia University, New York City.
William Allen White Papers, Library of Congress.
Woodrow Wilson Papers, Library of Congress.
Sir William Wiseman Papers, Sterling Library, Yale University, New Haven, Connecticut.

PUBLISHED DOCUMENTS

Documents on British Foreign Policy. Edited by E. L. Woodward and Rohan Butler. London, 1947–.
U.S. Congressional Record. Washington, D.C., 1919–1920.
U.S. Department of State. *Papers Relating to the Foreign Relations of the United States: The Paris Peace Conference, 1919.* 4 vols. Washington, D.C., 1943.
U.S. Congress, Senate. *Proceedings of the Committee on Foreign Relations, United States Senate, from the Sixty-Third Congress to the Sixty-Seventh Congress.* Washington, D.C., 1923.
U.S. Congress, Senate. *Treaty of Peace With Germany: Hearings Before the Committee on Foreign Relations, United States Senate.* 66th Cong., 1st sess., 1919, S.Doc. 106.
U.S. Congress, Senate. *Treaty of Peace With Germany: Report of the Conference Between Members of the Senate Committee on Foreign Relations and the President of the United States. At the White House, Tuesday, August 19, 1919.* 66th Cong., 1st sess., 1919, S.Doc. 76.
U.S. Senate. *Treaty of Peace With Germany, Reservations Reported by the Committee on Foreign Relations to Accompany the Treaty of Peace With Germany Done at Versailles on June 28, 1919.* 66th Cong., 1st sess., 1919. S. Doc. 87.

AUTOBIOGRAPHIES, MEMOIRS, AND PUBLISHED LETTERS

Atkinson, Henry A. *Theodore Marburg: The Man and His Work.* New York: N.p., 1951.

Bacon, Robert, and Scott, James Brown, eds. *Men and Policies: Addresses by Elihu Root.* Cambridge, Mass.: Harvard University Press, 1925.

Baker, Ray S., and Dodd, William E., eds. *The Public Papers of Woodrow Wilson: War and Peace, Presidential Messages, Addresses and Public Papers (1917–1924).* Vols. 5 and 6. New York: Harper and Brothers, 1927.

Baker, Ray Stannard. *American Chronicle: The Autobiography of Ray Stannard Baker.* New York: Charles Scribner's Sons, 1945.

Baruch, Bernard M. *Baruch: The Public Years.* New York: Holt, Rinehart, and Winston, 1960.

Bonsal, Stephen. *Unfinished Business.* Garden City, New York: Doubleday, Doran, and Company, 1944.

Butler, Nicholas Murray. *Across the Busy Years: Recollections and Reflections.* 2 vols. New York: Charles Scribner's Sons, 1939, 1940.

Danelski, David J., and Tulchin, Joseph S., eds. *The Autobiographical Notes of Charles Evans Hughes.* Cambridge, Mass.: Harvard University Press, 1973.

Edge, Walter Evans. *A Jerseyman's Journal: Fifty Years of American Business and Politics.* Princeton, N.J.: Princeton University Press, 1948, 1972.

Fosdick, Raymond B. *Letters on the League of Nations.* Princeton, N.J.: Princeton University Press, 1966.

Hays, Will H. *The Memoirs of Will H. Hays.* Garden City, New York: Doubleday, 1955.

Houston, David F. *Eight Years With Wilson's Cabinet, 1913–1920.* Vol. 2. New York: Doubleday, Page, 1926.

Hurley, Edward N. *The Bridge to France.* Philadelphia: J. B. Lippincott Company, 1927.

Jordan, David Starr. *The Days of a Man.* 2 vols. New York: World Book Company, 1922.

Keyes, Frances Parkinson. *All Flags Flying: Reminiscences of Frances Parkinson Keyes.* New York: McGraw-Hill, 1972.

Lamont, Thomas W. *Across World Frontiers.* New York: Harcourt, Brace and Company, 1951.

Lansing, Robert. *The Peace Negotiations: A Personal Narrative.* Boston: Houghton Mifflin Company, 1921.

Latane, John H., ed. *Development of the League of Nations Idea: Documents and Correspondence of Theodore Marburg.* 2 vols. New York: Macmillan Company, 1932.

Longworth, Alice Roosevelt. *Crowded Hours.* New York: Charles Scribner's Sons, 1933.

McAdoo, William G. *Crowded Years: The Reminiscences of William G. McAdoo.* Boston: Houghton Mifflin, 1931.

O'Brien, Francis William. *Two Peacemakers in Paris: The Hoover-Wilson Post-Armistice Letters, 1918–1920.* College Station: Texas A&M University Press, 1978.

Pepper, George Wharton. *Philadelphia Lawyer: An Autobiography.* Philadelphia: J. B. Lippincott Company, 1944.

Schlup, Leonard. "Selected Letters of Senator McCumber to Former President Taft Concerning the League of Nations." *North Dakota History* 46 (Summer 1979): 15–23.

———. "A Senator of Principle: Some Correspondence Between LeBaron Bradford Colt and William Howard Taft." *Rhode Island History* 42 (February 1983): 2–16.

Seymour, Charles, ed. *The Intimate Papers of Colonel House.* Vol. 4, *The Ending of the War.* Cambridge, Mass.: Houghton Mifflin Company, 1928.

Sparks, George F., ed. *A Many Colored Toga: The Diary of Henry Fountain Ashurst.* Tucson: University of Arizona Press, 1962.

Straus, Oscar S. *Under Four Administrations: From Cleveland to Taft.* Boston: Houghton Mifflin, 1922.

Villard, Oswald Garrison. *Fighting Years: Memoirs of a Liberal Editor.* New York: Harcourt, Brace and Company, 1939.

Watson, James E. *As I Knew Them: Memoirs of James E. Watson.* Indianapolis: Bobbs-Merrill, 1936.

Wilson, Edith Bolling. *My Memoir.* Indianapolis: Bobbs-Merrill, 1938.

NEWSPAPERS

Argus Leader (Sioux Falls), 1919–1920.
Boston Herald, 1919–1920.
Chicago Daily News, 1920.
Des Moines Register, 1919–1920.
Manchester Union, 1919–1920.
Milwaukee Sentinel, 1919–1920.
Minneapolis Tribune, 1919–1920.
Newark Star-Eagle, 1919–1920.
New York Herald, 1919.
New York Times, 1919–1921.
New York Tribune, 1919–1920.
New York World, 1919–1920.
Oregon Journal (Portland), 1919–1920.
Portland Oregonian, 1919–1920.
Providence Evening Tribune, 1919–1920.
St. Louis Post-Dispatch, 1919–1920.
Sun and New York Herald, 1920.
Superior Telegram, 1919–1920.
Washington Evening Star, 1919–1920.

PERIODICALS

Current History, April 1919–July 1920.
Independent, February 1919–June 1920.

DISSERTATIONS, THESES, AND UNPUBLISHED LETTERS TO THE AUTHOR

Bates, J. Leonard. "Senator Walsh of Montana, 1918–1924: A Liberal Under Pressure." Ph.D. diss., University of North Carolina, 1952.

Best, Gary Dean. "Herbert Clark Hoover in Transition, 1919–1921." Ph.D. diss., University of Hawaii, 1973.

Boothe, Leon E. "Wilson's Cold War: The President, the Public, and the League Fight, 1919–1920." Ph.D. diss., University of Illinois, 1966.

Chatham, Marie. "The Role of the National Party Chairman from Hanna to Farley." Ph.D. diss., University of Maryland, 1953.

Cleaver, Charles G. "Frank B. Kellogg: Attitudes and Assumptions Influencing His Foreign Policy Decisions." Ph.D. diss., University of Minnesota, 1956.

Daughan, George Christopher. "From Lodge to Fulbright: The Chairman of the Senate Foreign Relations Committee." Ph.D. diss., Harvard University, 1967.

Dodds, Archibald John. "The Public Services of Philander Chase Knox." Ph.D. diss., University of Pittsburgh, 1950.

Dubin, Martin David. "The Development of the Concept of Collective Security in the American Peace Movement, 1899-1917." Ph.D. diss., University of Indiana, 1960.

Duff, John Bernard. "The Politics of Revenge: The Ethnic Opposition to the Peace Policies of Woodrow Wilson." Ph.D. diss., Columbia University, 1964.

Dunnington, Miles William. "Senator Thomas J. Walsh: Independent Democrat in the Wilson Years." Ph.D. diss., University of Chicago, 1940.

Eagleton, Thomas F. "James A. Reed and the League of Nations." B.A. thesis, Amherst College, 1950.

Ferrell, Henry Clifton. "Claude A. Swanson of Virginia." Ph.D. diss., University of Virginia, 1964.

Fischer, Robert James. "Henry Cabot Lodge's Concept of Foreign Policy and the League of Nations." Ph.D. diss., University of Georgia, 1971.

Forth, William Stuart. "Wesley L. Jones: A Political Biography." Ph.D. diss., University of Washington, 1962.

Gieske, Millard L. "The Politics of Knute Nelson, 1912-1920." Ph.D. diss., University of Minnesota, 1965.

Hewes, James E., Jr. "William E. Borah and the Image of Isolationism." Ph.D. diss., Yale University, 1959.

Hoffmann, George Charles, Jr. "The Early Political Career of Charles McNary, 1917-1924." Ph.D. diss., University of Southern California, 1951.

Jewell, Jesse Paul. "The Senatorial Career of Arthur Capper From 1919 Through 1946." M.A. thesis, Kansas State Teachers College, 1947.

Johnson, Roger T. "Charles L. McNary and the Republican Party During Prosperity and Depression." Ph.D. diss., University of Wisconsin, 1967.

Kendrick, Jack E. "The League of Nations and the Republican Senate, 1918-1921." Ph.D. diss., University of North Carolina, 1952.

Keso, Edward Elmer. "The Senatorial Career of Robert Latham Owen." Ph.D. diss., George Peabody College, 1937.

Knock, Thomas J. "Woodrow Wilson and the Origins of the League of Nations." Ph.D. diss., Princeton University, 1982.

Lenroot, Katharine F. "Memorandum to Dr. Herbert F. Margulies from Katharine F. Lenroot," 10 December 1968, in the possession of the author.

Liljekvist, Clifford B. "Senator Hiram Johnson." Ph.D. diss., University of Southern California, 1953.

Merrill, Milton R. "Reed Smoot, Apostle in Politics." Ph.D. diss., Columbia University, 1950.

Morrison, Paul Willard. "The Position of the Senators from North Dakota on Isolation, 1889-1920." Ph.D. diss., University of Colorado, 1954.

Patterson, Robert Foster. "Gilbert M. Hitchcock: A Story of Two Careers." Ph.D. diss., University of Colorado, 1940.

Pogue, Forrest Carlisle, Jr. "The Monroe Doctrine and the League of Nations." Ph.D. diss., Clark University, 1939.

Robertson, James Oliver. "The Progressives in National Republican Politics, 1916–1921." Ph.D. diss., Harvard University, 1964.

Roots, John McCook. "The Treaty of Versailles in the United States Senate." Honors thesis, Harvard University, 1925.

Sayre, Ralph Mills. "Albert Baird Cummins and the Progressive Movement in Iowa." Ph.D. diss., Columbia University, 1958.

Schmickle, Edgar William. "For the Proper Use of Victory: Diplomacy and the Imperatives of Vision in the Foreign Policy of Woodrow Wilson, 1916–1919." Ph.D. diss., Duke University, 1979.

ARTICLES

Ambrosius, Lloyd E. "Wilson's League of Nations." *Military History Magazine* 65 (Winter 1970).

Boothe, Leon E. "Anglo-American Pro-League Groups Lead Wilson, 1915–1918." *Mid-America* 51 (April 1969).

———. "Lord Grey, the United States, and the Political Effort for a League of Nations, 1914–1920." *Maryland Historical Magazine* 65 (Spring 1970).

Current, Richard N. "The United States and Collective Security." In *Isolation and Security: Ideas and Interests in Twentieth Century American Foreign Policy*, edited by Alexander DeConde (Durham, N.C.: Duke University Press, 1957).

Curry, George. "Woodrow Wilson, Jan Smuts, and the Versailles Settlement." *American Historical Review* 56 (July 1961).

Darling, H. Maurice. "Who Kept the United States Out of the League of Nations?" *Canadian Historical Review* 10 (September 1929).

Dubin, Martin David. "The Carnegie Endowment for International Peace and the Advocacy of a League of Nations, 1914–1918." *Proceedings of the American Philosophical Society* 123 (December 1979).

———. "Elihu Root and the Advocacy of a League of Nations, 1914–1917." *Western Political Quarterly* 19 (September 1966).

Egerton, George W. "The Lloyd George Government and the Creation of the League of Nations." *American Historical Review* 79 (April 1974).

Finch, George A. "The Treaty of Peace with Germany in the United States Senate." *American Journal of International Law* 14 (1920).

Ferrell, Robert H. "Woodrow Wilson and Open Diplomacy." In *Issues and Conflicts: Studies in Twentieth Century American Diplomacy*, edited by George L. Anderson (Lawrence: University of Kansas Press, 1959).

George, Alexander, and George, Juliette. "Woodrow Wilson and Colonel House: A Reply to Weinstein, Anderson, and Link." *Political Science Quarterly* 96 (Winter 1981–1982).

Grantham, Dewey W., Jr. "The Southern Senators and the League of Nations, 1918–1920." *North Carolina Historical Review* 33 (April 1949).

Helbrich, Wolfgang J. "American Liberals in the League of Nations Controversy." *Public Opinion Quarterly* 31 (Winter 1967–1968).

Hewes, James E., Jr. "Henry Cabot Lodge and the League of Nations." *Proceedings of the American Philosophical Society* 114 (August 1970).

Lancaster, James L. "The Protestant Churches and the Fight for Ratification of the Versailles Treaty." *Public Opinion Quarterly* 31 (Winter 1967–1968).

Langer, William L. "Woodrow Wilson: His Education in World Affairs." In *The*

Philosophy and Policies of Woodrow Wilson, edited by Earl Latham (Chicago: University of Chicago Press, 1958).

Learned, H. B. "The Attitude of the United States Senate Towards the Versailles Treaty, 1918-1920." In *A History of the Peace Conference of Paris*, edited by H.W.V. Temperley, vol. 6 (London: H. Frowde, and Hodden and Stoughton, 1924).

Link, Arthur S. "Wilson the Diplomatist." In *The Philosophy and Policies of Woodrow Wilson*, edited by Earl Latham (Chicago: University of Chicago Press, 1958).

Marmor, Michael F. "Wilson, Strokes, and Zebras." *New England Journal of Medicine* 307 (26 August 1982).

Maxwell, Kenneth R. "Irish-Americans and the Fight for Treaty Ratification." *Public Opinion Quarterly* 31 (Winter 1967-1968).

Mervin, David. "Henry Cabot Lodge and the League of Nations." *Journal of American Studies* 4 (February 1971).

Nicholas, Herbert G. "Woodrow Wilson and Collective Security." In *Woodrow Wilson and a Revolutionary World, 1913-1921*, edited by Arthur S. Link (Chapel Hill: University of North Carolina Press, 1982).

Osgood, Robert E. "Woodrow Wilson, Collective Security, and the Lessons of History." In *The Philosophy and Policies of Woodrow Wilson*, edited by Earl Latham (Chicago: University of Chicago Press, 1958).

Redmond, Kent G. "Henry L. Stimson and the Question of League Membership." *Historian* 25 (February 1963).

Schlup, Leonard. "Wilsonian Republican: Porter James McCumber and the League of Nations." *International Review of History and Political Science* 19 (November 1982).

Startt, James D. "Early Press Reaction to Wilson's League Proposal." *Journalism Quarterly* 39 (Summer 1962).

Stromberg, Roland. "The Riddle of Collective Security." In *Issues and Conflicts: Studies in Twentieth Century Diplomacy*, edited by George L. Anderson (Lawrence: University of Kansas Press, 1959).

———. "Uncertainties and Obscurities about the League of Nations." *Journal of the History of Ideas* 33 (January–March 1972).

Trow, Clifford W. "Something Desperate In His Face: Woodrow Wilson in Portland at the 'Very Crisis of His Career.'" *Oregon Historical Quarterly* 82 (Spring 1981).

Vinson, J. Chalmers. "Military Force and American Foreign Policy, 1919-1939." In *Isolation and Security: Ideas and Interests in Twentieth Century American Foreign Policy*, edited by Alexander DeConde (Durham, N.C.: Duke University Press, 1957).

Watson, Richard L., Jr. "Furnifold M. Simmons: 'Jehovah of the Tar Heels.'" *North Carolina Historical Review* 44 (Spring 1967).

Weinstein, Edwin A.; Anderson, James W.; and Link, Arthur S. "Woodrow Wilson's Political Personality: A Reappraisal." *Political Science Quarterly* 93 (Winter 1978-1979).

Wimer, Kurt. "The League of Nations: A Victim of Executive-Legislative Rivalry." *Lock Haven Bulletin* 2 (February 1960).

———. "Senator Hitchcock and the League of Nations." *Nebraska History* 45 (September 1963).

———. "Woodrow Wilson and World Order." In *Woodrow Wilson and A Revolu-*

tionary World, 1913–1921, edited by Arthur S. Link (Chapel Hill: University of North Carolina Press, 1982).

———. "Woodrow Wilson's Plan to Enter the League of Nations through an Executive Agreement." *Western Political Quarterly* 11 (December 1958).

———. "Woodrow Wilson Tries Conciliation: An Effort That Failed." *Historian* 25 (August 1963).

Wright, Esmond. "The Foreign Policy of Woodrow Wilson: A Reassessment; Part II, Wilson and the Dream of Reason." *History Today* 10 (1960).

Wright, Quincy. "Woodrow Wilson and the League of Nations." *Social Research* 24 (Spring 1957).

OTHER BOOKS

Adler, Selig. *The Uncertain Giant, 1921–1941: American Foreign Policy Between the Wars.* 1965. Reprint, New York: Collier Books, 1971.

Ambrosius, Lloyd E. *Woodrow Wilson and the American Diplomatic Tradition: The Treaty Fight in Perspective.* Cambridge: Cambridge University Press, 1987.

Bailey, Thomas A. *Woodrow Wilson and the Great Betrayal.* New York: Macmillan Company, 1945.

———. *Woodrow Wilson and the Lost Peace.* New York: Macmillan Company, 1944.

Baker, Ray Stannard. *Woodrow Wilson and World Settlement.* Vol. 3. Garden City, N.Y.: Doubleday, Page, 1923.

Bartlett, Ruhl J. *The League to Enforce Peace.* Chapel Hill: University of North Carolina Press, 1944.

Blum, John M. *Joe Tumulty and the Wilson Era.* Boston: Houghton Mifflin, 1951.

———. *Woodrow Wilson and the Politics of Morality.* Boston: Little, Brown, 1956.

Bryn-Jones, David. *Frank B. Kellogg: A Biography.* New York: G. P. Putnam's Sons, 1937.

Buehrig, Edward H. *Woodrow Wilson and the Balance of Power.* Bloomington: Indiana University Press, 1955.

Burns, James MacGregor. *Roosevelt: The Lion and the Fox.* New York: Harcourt, Brace, and World, 1956.

Canfield, Leon H. *The Presidency of Woodrow Wilson: Prelude to a World in Crisis.* Madison, N.J.: Fairleigh Dickinson University Press, 1966.

Carroll, Francis M. *American Opinion and the Irish Question, 1910–1923: A Study in Opinion and Policy.* New York: St. Martin's Press, 1978.

Cecil, Robert. *A Great Experiment.* London: Oxford University Press, 1941.

Chrislock, Carl H. *Ethnicity Challenged: The Upper Midwest Norwegian-American Experience in World War I.* Northfield, Minn.: Norwegian-American Historical Association, 1981.

———. *The Progressive Era in Minnesota, 1899–1918.* St. Paul: Minnesota Historical Society, 1971.

Claude, Inis L., Jr. *Power and International Relations.* New York: Random House, 1962.

———. *Swords Into Plowshares: The Problems and Progress of International Organization.* 4th ed. New York: Random House, 1971.

Coit, Margaret L. *Mr. Baruch.* Boston: Houghton Mifflin Company, 1957.

Coletta, Paolo E. *William Jennings Bryan.* Vol. 3, *Political Puritan, 1915–1925.* Lincoln: University of Nebraska Press, 1969.

Cooper, John Milton, Jr. *The Warrior and the Priest: Woodrow Wilson and Theodore Roosevelt.* Cambridge, Mass.: Harvard University Press, 1983.

Cranston, Alan. *The Killing of the Peace.* 1945. Reprint, New York: Viking Press, 1960.

Curti, Merle. *Peace or War: The American Struggle, 1636–1936.* New York: W. W. Norton and Company, 1936.

Daniels, Jonathan. *The End of Innocence.* Philadelphia: J. B. Lippincott Company, 1954.

DeBenedetti, Charles. *Origins of the Modern American Peace Movement, 1915–1929.* Millwood, N.Y.: KTO Press, 1978.

———. *The Peace Reform in American History.* Bloomington: University of Indiana Press, 1980.

Egerton, George W. *Great Britain and the Creation of the League of Nations: Strategy, Politics, and International Organization, 1914–1919.* Chapel Hill: University of North Carolina Press, 1978.

Ferrell, Henry C., Jr. *Claude A. Swanson of Virginia: A Political Biography.* Lexington: University of Kentucky Press, 1985.

Ferrell, Robert H. *Woodrow Wilson and World War I, 1917–1921.* New York: Harper and Row, 1985.

Field, Carter. *Bernard Baruch.* New York: McGraw Hill Book Company, 1944.

Fite, Gilbert C. *Peter Norbeck: Prairie Statesman.* Columbia: University of Missouri Press, 1978.

Fleming, Denna Frank. *The United States and the League of Nations, 1918–1920.* New York: G. P. Putnam's Sons, 1932.

Floto, Inga. *Colonel House in Paris: A Study of American Policy at the Paris Peace Conference, 1919.* Princeton, N.J.: Princeton University Press, 1980.

Garraty, John A. *Henry Cabot Lodge: A Biography.* New York: Alfred A. Knopf, 1953.

———. *Woodrow Wilson: A Great Life in Brief.* New York: Alfred A. Knopf, 1956.

Gerson, Louis L. *The Hyphenate in Recent American Politics and Diplomacy.* Lawrence: University of Kansas Press, 1964.

Gilbert, Felix. *The End of the European Era, 1890 to the Present.* 2d ed. New York: W. W. Norton and Company, 1979.

Glad, Betty. *Charles Evans Hughes and the Illusion of Innocence.* Urbana: University of Illinois Press, 1966.

Guinsburg, Thomas N. *The Pursuit of Isolationism in the United States Senate from Versailles to Pearl Harbor.* New York: Garland, 1982.

Herman, Sondra R. *Eleven Against War: Studies in American Internationalist Thought, 1898–1921.* Stanford: Stanford University Press, 1969.

Hinsley, F. H. *Power and the Pursuit of Peace.* Cambridge: Cambridge University Press, 1963.

Holt, W. Stull. *Treaties Defeated by the Senate: A Study of the Struggle Between President and Senate Over the Conduct of Foreign Relations.* Baltimore: Johns Hopkins University Press, 1933.

Hoover, Herbert C. *The Ordeal of Woodrow Wilson.* New York: McGraw Hill Book Company, 1958.

Howe, M. A. DeWolfe. *Portrait of an Independent: Moorfield Storey, 1845–1929.* Boston: Houghton Mifflin Company, 1932.

Hughes, H. Stuart. *Contemporary Europe: A History.* Englewood Cliffs, N.J.: Prentice-Hall, 1961.

Israel, Fred L. *Nevada's Key Pittman.* Lincoln: University of Nebraska Press, 1963.

Jessup, Philip C. *Elihu Root.* Vol. 2. New York: Dodd, Mead, 1938.

Johnson, Allen, and Malone, Dumas, eds., *Dictionary of American Biography.* New York: Charles Scribner's Sons, 1928–1973.

Johnson, Evans C. *Oscar W. Underwood: A Political Biography.* Baton Rouge: Louisiana State University Press, 1980.

Juergens, George. *News From the White House: The Presidential-Press Relationship in the Progressive Era.* Chicago: University of Chicago Press, 1981.

Kennedy, David M. *Over Here: The First World War and American Society.* New York: Oxford University Press, 1980.

Kuehl, Warren F. *Hamilton Holt: Journalist, Internationalist, Educator.* Gainesville: University of Florida Press, 1960.

———. *Seeking World Order: The United States and International Organization to 1920.* Nashville: Vanderbilt University Press, 1969.

La Follette, Belle Case, and La Follette, Fola. *Robert M. La Follette, 1855–1925.* Vol. 2. New York: Macmillan Company, 1953.

Lawrence, David. *The True Story of Woodrow Wilson.* New York: George H. Doran Company, 1924.

Leffler, Melvyn P. *The Elusive Quest: America's Pursuit of European Stability and French Security, 1919–1933.* Chapel Hill: University of North Carolina Press, 1979.

Leopold, Richard W. *Elihu Root and the Conservative Tradition.* Boston: Little, Brown and Company, 1954.

Levering, Ralph B. *The Public and American Foreign Policy, 1918–1978.* New York: Morrow, 1978.

Levin, N. Gordon. *Woodrow Wilson and World Politics: America's Response to War and Revolution.* New York: Oxford University Press, 1968.

Levine, Lawrence W. *Defender of the Faith, William Jennings Bryan: The Last Decade, 1915–1925.* New York: Oxford University Press, 1965.

Link, Arthur S. *Wilson: Campaigns for Progressivism and Peace, 1916–1917.* Princeton, N.J.: Princeton University Press, 1965.

———. *Wilson: Confusions and Crises, 1915–1916.* Princeton, N.J.: Princeton University Press, 1964.

———. *Wilson: The New Freedom.* Princeton, N.J.: Princeton University Press, 1956.

———. *Wilson: The Struggle for Neutrality, 1914–1915.* Princeton, N.J.: Princeton University Press, 1960.

———. *Woodrow Wilson: A Brief Biography.* Chicago: Quadrangle Books, 1963.

———. *Woodrow Wilson: Revolution, War, and Peace.* Arlington Heights, Ill.: Harlan, Davidson, 1979.

Livermore, Seward W. *Politics Is Adjourned: Woodrow Wilson and the War Congress, 1916–1918.* Middleton, Conn.: Wesleyan University Press, 1966.

Lodge, Henry Cabot. *The Senate and the League of Nations.* New York: Charles Scribner's Sons, 1925.

Lowitt, Richard. *George W. Norris: The Persistence of a Progressive.* Urbana: University of Illinois Press, 1971.

Maddox, Robert James. *William E. Borah and American Foreign Policy.* Baton Rouge: Louisiana State University Press, 1969.

Marchand, C. Roland. *The American Peace Movement and Social Reform, 1898-1918.* Princeton, N.J.: Princeton University Press, 1972.

Margulies, Herbert F. *Senator Lenroot of Wisconsin: A Political Biography, 1900-1929.* Columbia: University of Missouri Press, 1977.

Marrin, Albert. *Nicholas Murray Butler.* Boston: Twayne Publishers, 1976.

Mayer, Arno J. *Politics and Diplomacy of Peacemaking: Containment and Counter-Revolution at Versailles, 1918-1919.* New York: Alfred Knopf and Company, 1967.

Miller, David Hunter. *The Drafting of the Covenant.* 2 vols. New York: G. P. Putnam's Sons, 1928.

Murray, Robert K. *The Harding Era: Warren G. Harding and His Administration.* Minneapolis: University of Minnesota Press, 1969.

Nevins, Allan. *Henry White: Thirty Years of American Diplomacy.* New York: Harper and Brothers, 1930.

Noggle, Burl. *Into the Twenties: The United States from Armistice to Normalcy.* Urbana: University of Illinois Press, 1974.

Notter, Harley. *The Origins of the Foreign Policy of Woodrow Wilson.* 1937. Reprint, New York: Russell and Russell, 1965.

Odland, Martin W. *The Life of Knute Nelson.* Minneapolis: Lund Press, 1926.

Osgood, Robert E. *Ideals and Self-Interest in America's Foreign Relations.* Chicago: University of Chicago Press, 1953.

Palmer, Frederick. *Bliss, Peacemaker: The Life and Letters of General Taskar Howard Bliss.* 1934. Reprint, Freeport, N.Y.: Books for Libraries Press, 1970.

Park, Bert Edward. *The Impact of Illness on World Leaders.* Philadelphia: University of Pennsylvania Press, 1986.

Perkins, Dexter. *Charles Evans Hughes and American Democratic Statesmanship.* Boston: Little, Brown, 1956.

Porter, Kirk H., and Johnson, Donald Bruce, comps. *National Party Platforms, 1840-1968.* Urbana: University of Illinois Press, 1970.

Pratt, Julius W. *America and World Leadership, 1900-1921.* London: Collier Books, 1970.

Rappard, William E. *The Quest for Peace.* Cambridge, Mass.: Harvard University Press, 1940.

Robbins, Keith. *Sir Edward Grey: A Biography of Lord Grey of Fallodon.* London: Cassell, 1971.

Schwarz, Jordan A. *The Speculator: Bernard M. Baruch in Washington, 1917-1965.* Chapel Hill: University of North Carolina Press, 1981.

Silverman, Dan P. *Reconstructing Europe After the Great War.* Cambridge, Mass.: Harvard University Press, 1982.

Smith, Daniel M. *The Great Departure: The United States and World War I, 1914-1920.* New York: John Wiley and Sons, 1965.

Smith, Gene. *When the Cheering Stopped: The Last Years of Woodrow Wilson.* New York: Morrow, 1964.

Smith, Rixey, and Beasley, Norman. *Carter Glass: A Biography.* 1939. Reprint, Freeport, N.Y.: Books for Libraries Press, 1970.

Socolofsky, Homer E. *Arthur Capper: Publisher, Politician, and Philanthropist.* Lawrence: University of Kansas Press, 1962.

Stone, Ralph. *The Irreconcilables: The Fight Against the League of Nations.* Lexington: University of Kentucky Press, 1970.

Stromberg, Roland N. *Collective Security and American Foreign Policy: From the League of Nations to NATO.* New York: Frederick A. Praeger, 1963.

Tansill, Charles C. *America and the Fight for Irish Freedom.* New York: Devin-Adair, 1957.

Tillman, Seth P. *Anglo-American Relations at the Paris Peace Conference of 1919.* Princeton, N.J.: Princeton University Press, 1961.

Vinson, John Chalmers. *Referendum for Isolation: Defeat of Article Ten of the League of Nations Covenant.* Athens: University of Georgia Press, 1961.

Walworth, Arthur. *Wilson and the Peacemakers: American Diplomacy at the Paris Peace Conference, 1919.* New York: W. W. Norton and Company, 1986.

———. *Woodrow Wilson.* 3d ed. 2 vols. New York: W. W. Norton and Company, 1978.

Ward, Alan J. *Ireland and Anglo-American Relations, 1899–1921.* London: Weidenfeld and Nicholson, 1969.

Weinstein, Edwin A. *Woodrow Wilson: A Medical and Psychological Biography.* Princeton, N.J.: Princeton University Press, 1981.

White, William S. *Citadel: The Story of the United States Senate.* New York: Harper and Brothers, 1956.

Widenor, William C. *Henry Cabot Lodge and the Search for an American Foreign Policy.* Berkeley: University of California Press, 1980.

Yates, Louis A. R. *United States and French Security, 1917–1921.* New York: Twayne Publishers, 1957.

Yeomans, H. A. *Abbott Lawrence Lowell, 1856–1943.* Cambridge, Mass.: Harvard University Press, 1948.

Zimmern, Alfred. *The League of Nations and the Rule of Law, 1918–1935.* London: Macmillan and Company, 1936.

INDEX

Allies, x, 33, 53, 58, 91, 120, 131, 132, 143, 147, 150, 158, 166, 177, 178, 182, 222, 259, 260, 271. *See also* Belgium; France; Great Britain; Italy; Japan

Ambrosius, Lloyd E., xiii

Anderson, Chandler P., 35, 36, 60n48, 114, 116, 130, 131

Article Ten: wording of, 2; interpretations of, 2, 75, 76, 101, 106, 106n37, 108; opinions on, 7, 10, 57, 59, 60, 91, 92, 105, 154, 158, 168, 172, 181, 190, 270; comments on, 16, 21, 24, 26, 30, 34, 37, 52, 57, 65, 74, 75, 107, 109, 122; proposed changes in, 24; proposed reservations to, 36, 39, 43, 47, 54, 58, 63, 85, 89, 103, 104, 105, 139, 141, 157, 174, 186, 191, 203, 205, 210–11, 218, 220, 221n20, 222, 225, 238, 240, 247; response to reservation proposals, 40, 44, 47, 54, 63, 85, 86, 96, 107–8, 134, 149, 152, 153, 163, 165n78, 168, 172, 177, 183, 203, 204, 205–6, 209, 211, 224, 236, 239, 241, 242, 247–48, 249, 252, 254, 256–57; negotiations about reservations, 73, 103–5, 133, 196, 200, 205–6, 209, 211, 223, 232, 233, 234, 237, 245; votes on proposals and amendments, 86, 155, 243, 248; proposals analyzed, 105–6, 240; mentioned passim

Ashurst, Henry F., 48, 89, 97, 173

Austria-Hungary, 262

Bailey, Thomas A., xiii, 88n151, 183, 208, 260n118, 272, 273

Balfour, Arthur, 166

Ball, Lewis H., 121, 221, 237, 241

Bankhead, John H., 66

Baruch, Bernard M., 78, 235

Belgium, 17, 186, 189

Beveridge, Albert J., 102, 155

Bipartisan conference, 185, 198, 200, 202, 203–13 passim, 216, 219–41 passim, 251, 252, 255, 257

Bliss, Tasker H., 99

Bohemia, 186

Bolshevism, 1, 5, 29, 76, 100, 105

Borah, William E., 11, 12, 14, 23, 27, 31, 32, 36, 46, 60, 66, 70, 78, 99, 121, 122, 132, 150, 152, 153, 157, 188, 207, 208, 208n65, 220, 228, 229, 230, 233, 240, 241, 242n76, 257, 264–71 passim

Borden, Robert, 111

Brandegee, Frank B., 18, 31, 32, 36, 66, 116, 157, 226, 230, 238, 251, 254, 265, 266, 267

British-Americans, 170

British Empire, xi, 25, 73, 75, 79, 83, 116, 117, 124, 125, 160, 161, 162, 237. *See also* Great Britain

Bryan, William J., 186, 187, 199, 201, 250

Bryce, James, 44, 69

Bullitt, William C., 79, 98

Burleson, Albert S., 101, 250

Butler, Nicholas Murray, 35, 35n111, 36, 37, 120, 225, 225n31

Calder, William M., 44n144, 221

Canada, 111, 125

Capper, Arthur, xii, 18, 22, 35, 38, 40, 48, 55, 63, 86, 112, 114, 115, 116, 117n71, 124, 129, 136, 160, 162, 163, 167, 197, 221, 231, 246, 274, 275, 276, 277

Cecil, Robert, 2, 2n5, 45

Chamber of Commerce of New York City, 188

Chamberlain, George E., 151, 155, 243

Chicago Board of Trade, 189

Chicago Tribune, 32, 80, 81

China, 31, 41, 62, 73, 78, 80, 121, 122, 123, 141, 230, 271

Claide, Inis L., 272

Clemenceau, Georges, 111

144; confers, 167, 193. *See also* Edge
Act
Edge Act, 37
Egerton, George W., 183
Egypt, 79, 162, 244
Equal voting: as a reservation issue,
129, 131, 135, 137, 138, 140, 145,
161, 162, 172, 179, 204, 211, 217,
217n4, 223, 236, 256, 260

Fall, Albert B., 32, 75, 79, 81, 144. *See
also* Fall amendments
Fall amendments, 79, 82, 113, 114,
116, 118, 123, 129, 143, 274
Ferrell, Robert H., xiii, 183
Field, Carter, 125
Fisher, Irving, 270
Fleming, Denna F., xiii, 16
Fletcher, Duncan U., 229, 230
Foreign Relations Committee, Senate,
xii, 6, 14, 20, 22, 31, 37, 39, 44, 47,
48, 50, 57, 58, 66, 67, 70, 71, 72, 74,
78, 79, 83, 84, 87, 88, 91, 94, 98,
100, 101, 114, 119, 124, 126, 129n10,
130, 131, 133–34, 134, 137, 138,
139, 175, 176, 196, 197, 202, 220
Fourteen Points, 5
France, 1, 2, 3, 4, 11, 17, 26, 29, 45, 68,
69, 80, 117, 121, 135, 140, 147, 148,
152, 158, 186, 189n12, 217, 222,
235, 245, 272
Frelinghuysen, Joseph S., 35, 98, 207,
209, 221, 237, 238, 240, 241, 243, 249
French security treaty, 4, 67
Friends of Irish Freedom, 99

Gardner, Augustus P., 13, 130
German-Americans, 13, 20, 31, 82, 99,
100, 111, 264, 265
Germany, xi, 4, 5, 10, 11, 13, 15, 17,
18, 29, 31, 31n99, 32, 33, 34, 38, 53,
65, 73, 74, 75, 78–79, 85, 88, 91, 97,
98, 99, 100, 101, 106, 107, 112, 117,
121, 122, 125, 141, 143, 148, 185,
218, 254, 262
Gerry, Peter G., 52, 244. *See also*
Gerry reservation
Gerry reservation, 244, 246, 247
Glass, Carter, 210n71, 227, 233, 235
Gore, Thomas P., 42, 53, 80, 90, 102,
115, 124, 151, 155, 163, 173, 175,
181, 246
Grant, Heber J., 123
Grantham, Dewey W., Jr., xiii
Great Britain, 1, 2n5, 3, 11, 20, 29, 44,
68, 69, 75, 79, 80, 97, 99, 106, 111,
117, 120, 121, 125, 135, 140, 147,
152, 158, 166, 189n12, 204, 211,
217, 220, 222, 250, 260, 271, 272.
See also British Empire

Grey, Edward, 4, 160, 180, 217, 218,
256, 260
Gronna, Asle J., 17
Gross, Edwin J., 268

Hale, Frederick, 59, 112, 123, 199,
208n65, 209; as mild reservationist,
xii, 95, 134, 176, 220n13; signs
Round Robin, 18; and Knox resolution, 34, 37, 38; described and characterized, 34–35, 178–79; background, 34–35; opinions, 35, 36, 95,
108, 144, 146, 148, 156, 158, 174,
180, 213; and Butler, 35, 35n111,
120; and Anderson, 35–36, 60n48;
role of, 46, 60, 236; LEP view of, 50;
opposes amendments, 95, 115, 119;
comments and speeches, 109, 112,
119–20, 123; and Keyes, 120; votes
of, 124, 126, 176, 232, 254, 274–77;
friend of, 130; and Roosevelt, 130,
130n111; and Lowell, 145; confers,
167, 193, 194; and Lodge, 207, 219;
tactics and strategies, 254; at convention, 264, 265n12

Harding, Warren G., x, 29, 32, 35,
35n111, 66n67, 97n9, 98, 112, 142,
177, 191, 246, 259, 270, 271
Harrison, Byron Patton (Pat), 66
Harvey, George, 69, 267
Hay, John, 6
Hays, Will H., 9–10, 13, 21, 22, 23, 24,
33, 40, 58, 69, 113, 123, 190, 191,
214, 216, 262, 263, 268
Hitchcock, Gilbert M.: actions evalu-
ated, xii, 41, 127, 223; comments
and speeches, 22, 40–41, 49, 63–64,
71, 87, 88, 128, 148, 149, 151, 156,
157, 161, 165, 166, 171–72, 192,
201, 203, 210, 212, 217, 221, 224,
224–25, 225, 242n76, 243, 259; and
Covenant revision, 25, 26, 80; and
party leadership, 40, 115, 187, 194,
197; tactics and strategies, 40–41,
44, 87–88, 94, 100–101, 110, 127,
128, 139, 148, 149, 151, 157, 164,
165n78, 171, 174, 180, 185, 186,
192, 194, 201, 210, 215, 221, 223,
225, 228, 230–31, 241, 254, 255,
258; and Wilson, 40, 49, 50, 63, 66,
71, 87, 88, 90, 94, 101, 107, 110,
128, 139, 149–50, 157, 165, 171,
182, 186, 187, 192, 197, 203, 205,
210, 225, 227, 233, 241, 255, 256;
described and characterized, 49,
128; opinions, 63, 70–71, 128, 223,
225n29, 237; negotiates, 71, 150,
171; files minority report, 100; and
Taft, 115, 118; actions in Senate,
126, 151, 156, 164, 203, 224, 226,